KU-325-462

THE CHIEF CONSTABLES OF ENGLAND AND WALES

Driving one morning with him to Shiply Lane End, a favourite 'meet', he said: "How would the Chief Constableship of the county suit you?" He had held the appointment himself before succeeding to a fortune. "Nothing in the world", I replied, "would suit me better". "Well", he continued, "I think that may be arranged. Allgood has completely broken down and can't last long now" (Sir Henry Smith, KCB., 1910: 82).

The Chief Constables of England and Wales

The socio-legal history of a criminal justice elite

DAVID S. WALL
Centre for Criminal Justice Studies
University of Leeds

Ashgate

DARTMOUTH

Aldershot • Brookfield USA • Singapore • Sydney

Published by
Dartmouth Publishing Company Limited
Ashgate Publishing Limited
Gower House
Croft Road
Aldershot
Hants GU11 3HR
England

Ashgate Publishing Company
Old Post Road
Brookfield
Vermont 05036
USA

British Library Cataloguing in Publication Data
Wall, David, 1956-
The chief constables of England and Wales : the socio-legal history of a criminal justice elite - (Socio-legal Studies)
1.Police chiefs - England 2.Police chiefs - Wales 3.Police chiefs - England - History 4.Police chiefs - Wales - History 5.Police chiefs - England - Social conditions 6.Police chiefs - Wales - Social conditions
I.Title
363.2'0922'42

Library of Congress Cataloging-in-Publication Data
Wall, David, 1956-
The chief constables of England and Wales: the socio-legal history of a criminal justice elite / David S. Wall.
p. cm. – (Socio-legal studies series)
Includes bibliographical references and index.
ISBN 1-85521-714-7 (hc.)
1. Police chiefs–England–History. 2. Police chiefs–Wales–History. 3. Police administration–England–History. 4. Police administration–Wales–History. I. Title.
HV8196.W35 1998
363.2'092'242–dc21

98-18562
CIP

ISBN 1 85521 714 7

Printed and bound by Athenaeum Press, Ltd., Gateshead, Tyne & Wear.

Contents

List of Figures and Tables

Statutes and Cases

1722 - Criminal Law Act (9 George 1, c. 22)
1829 - Metropolitan Police Act (10 George IV, c.44)
1830 - Lighting and Watching Act (11 George IV and 1 William IV, c.27)
1831 - Special Constables Act (1 & 2 William IV, c.39, 41)
1835 - Municipal Corporations Act (5 & 6 William IV, c.76)
1839 - Metropolitan Police Act (2 & 3 Vict. c.47)
1839 - Manchester Police Act (2 & 3 Vict. c.87)
1839 - County Police Act (2 & 3 Vict. c.93)
1840 - County Police Act (3 & 4 Vict. c.88)
1856 - County and Borough Police Act (19 & 20 Victoria c. 69)
1882 - Municipal Corporations Act (45 & 46 Vict. c. 50)
1888 - Local Government Act (51 & 52 Vict. c. 41)
1890 - Police Act (53 & 54 Vict. c. 45)
1919 - Police Act (9 & 10 Geo. V, c. 46)
1946 - Police Act (11 &12 Geo. 5 c. 31)
1964 - Police Act (c.48)
1972 - Local Government Act (c.70)
1984 - Police and Criminal Evidence Act (c.60)
1985 - Prosecution of Offences Act (c.23)
1986 - Public Order Act (c.64)
1991 - Criminal Justice Act (c.53)
1992 - Criminal Justice Act (c.36)
1994 - Criminal Justice and Public Order Act (c.33)
1994 - Intelligence Services Act (c. 13)
1994 - Police and Magistrates Courts Act (c.29)
1996 - Police Act (c.16)
1996 - Security Service Act (c.35)
1997 - Police Act (c.50)

Fisher v Oldham Corporation [1930] 2 K.B. 364
Ridge v Baldwin [1964] A.C. 40
R v Chief Constable of the Devon and Cornwall Constabulary, ex parte Central Electricity Generating Board [1981] 3 All ER 826
R v Secretary of State for the Home Department, ex parte Northumbria Police Authority [1987] 2 All ER 282
R v Chief Constable of Sussex, ex parte International Trader's Ferry Ltd [1995] 4 All ER 364

Preface

Gustave Flaubert once said that books are not made the same way that babies are, rather, they are made like pyramids. He went on to say that after some long pondered plan, great blocks of stone are placed upon each other through back-breaking, sweaty and time-consuming work. But to what purpose! it just stands there in the desert, yet towers over it prodigiously with the jackals urinating on the base and the bourgeois clambering up to the top (Barnes, 1984: 35-36).

This book is certainly the product of "some long pondered plan". It brings together "great blocks of stone" (data) from two studies that were carried out almost a decade apart. The first study was carried out under an ESRC research training award and the second was funded by the Nuffield Foundation. To both organisations, I am grateful as the first project enabled me to collect the bulk of the quantitative data and the second enabled me to collect the qualitative data and also more of the quantitative. I am also indebted to my colleagues in the Department of Law at the University of Leeds for giving me study leave during the first semester of 1997.

Along the way I have incurred many debts and here I acknowledge my creditors, or so to speak. *The Police Staff College at Bramshill*: former Commandant Barry Pain and former librarian Dennis Brett gave me access to the collections within the library. John Jones, Sue Adler and Joanne Ogilvy-Wright along with the current library staff also gave me extremely valuable assistance; *Staff at the University of York*: Tony Fowles (now Thames Valley University), Kathleen Jones, Jonathan Bradshaw, Doug Moncur and Rob Fletcher; *Various former and serving Chief Constables*: John Alderson, Sir Geoffrey Dear, Keith Hellawell, Lord Philip Knights, Richard Wells, Sir John Woodcock, plus a number whom I have not mentioned by name; *Staff of the Public Records Office at Kew*; *Staff at City of York Archives and City of York Reference Library*; *Personnel and Training Unit of the Police Policy Directorate of the Home Office*: Mel Hodgston.

My special thanks go to Gary Mason, editor, and Sean Howe, deputy editor, at the *Police Review* for giving me permission to reproduce the pictures that adorn the pages of this book.

I am also very grateful to my colleagues in the Centre for Criminal Justice Studies, especially Clive Walker and Adam Crawford, and also to Steve Savage and Sarah Charman at the University of Portsmouth, Tim Newburn at Goldsmith's College, Les Johnston at the University of Teeside and Ken Russell, formerly of de Montfort University.

I also owe some intellectual debts which might not be immediately apparent from the text, but are nevertheless felt (in alphabetical order): Thomas Critchley, Clive Emsley, Peter Manning, the late Jane Morgan, Robert Reiner. At a personal level I must thank Helen, Harrison and Sophie for their support.

In the current spirit of quality assurance the manuscript was read by John Alderson, John Jones, Tim Newburn, Robert Reiner, Steve Savage, Martin Stallion, and Clive Walker. I am grateful to them for giving me their time and also the benefit of their collective wisdom which they expressed through their immensely constructive comments. Needless to say, any errors in this book are mine alone.

It is perhaps, appropriate to finish this preface by returning to Flaubert. Ignoring his comments about the jackals and the bourgeois, I hope that my interpretation of Flaubert's analogy about sums up this book, although that is really for the reader to assess. My hope is that the reader will find this pyramid to be appropriately constructed and most importantly, that I've discovered the royal burial chamber. Mind you, I am quite sure that there is a bit more treasure, plus a few old skeletons, hidden away in some undetected secret passages still waiting to be discovered.

David S. Wall
Centre for Criminal Justice Studies
University of Leeds

May 1998

Abbreviations

ACPO	Association of Chief Police Officers
HM	Her /His Majesty
HMIC	Her /His Majesty's Inspector of Constabulary
BCU	Basic Command Unit
HO	Home Office
HOC	Home Office Circular
KPM	King's Police Medal
QPM	Queen's Police Medal
N/A	Not Applicable
NCIS	National Crime Intelligence Service
NCS	National Crime Squad
PACE	Police and Criminal Evidence Act 1984
PMCA	Police and Magistrates' Courts Act 1994
PRO	Public Records Office
RIC	Royal Irish Constabulary
RUC	Royal Ulster Constabulary
SJC	Standing Joint Committee
WC	Watch Committee

1 Introduction

Introduction

There are two fundamental views on the value of historical understanding. The first is the rather ahistorical view that "history is just one damn thing after another",[1] which implies that our understanding of the present is more important than our understanding of a past that we have either broken away from or is not deemed to be important. The second viewpoint is very much the converse. It understands there to have been no break or rupture with the past, just accelerations (and decelerations) in the rate at which modernity changes. Whilst respecting the many debates that have taken place over the nature of historicism, this viewpoint suggests that it is important to understand the many historical processes which have shaped the present on the basis that they will continue to shape our future. The latter approach is adopted here. This book is a social history of the chief constables who were in charge of the independent police forces of England and Wales between 1836 and 1996 and will demonstrate that this social history is more than just one damn thing after another. Furthermore, it will demonstrate that the history of the police does tend to repeat itself, so, debates which have been rehearsed in the past can be revisited to inform the present; plus there are also interesting stories about some colourful characters thrown in. The first part of this chapter will introduce the rationale behind this book, the second part will introduce some of the main issues and the third part will look at the methods used to conduct the study. The fourth, and final, part will outline the book's structure.

Rationale and objectives

Since their inception in the early nineteenth century the efforts of the police have been concentrated upon two main problems. The first has been the effective maintenance of order and the control of crime, the second has been to establish control over its own personnel (Manning, 1979); the discussion in this book relates more to the second problem than to the first.

---

[1] Henry Ford paraphrasing Mark Twain.

The book therefore seeks to fill a gap in our knowledge about the police themselves, an area which is largely overlooked by the considerable body of literature upon the sociology, history, psychology and politics of policing. Even where the literature does address the police, it tends to emphasise the lowly constable rather than chief officers. This is on the basis that those lower down the organisation possess the greater discretion and are therefore less easy to govern. By and large, the chief police officer is fairly absent from existing literature on the police. When they are featured, it tends to either be in terms of their powers or constitutional position, or they are consigned to a role that is little more than that of a glorified public relations executive. The literature neither tells us who they are, nor how they got to that position. Whilst a number of authors, for example, Hart (1955), Critchley (1978), Emsley (1996), Phillips (1977) and others, have all commented on the military origins of the early chief constables, none, with the exception of Steedman (1984) and later Reiner (1991), have made a systematic or analytical study of them. As part of her study on the Victorian police officer, Steedman looked at the first county chief constables and provided an interesting insight into this hitherto unknown world, but it was Reiner's 1991 study which started to bridge the gap in the literature and provides an excellent overview of the office of chief constable and a contemporary sociology of the chief officers holding office in September 1986. What it did not do is place the chief constable into a historical perspective and that is the function of this book.

The need to fill the gap in the literature by increasing our understanding of the chief constable has been highlighted by various changes during the past two decades which have increased the overall level of (central) influence over the management of the police and fostered a series of debates over the qualities and qualifications of chief police officers. At the root of these developments was the increasing politicisation of the role of chief constable during the 1970s and 1980s, as outspoken chief constables came into conflict with their police authorities. This was followed by the further politicisation of the role as the chief constables responded to new demands placed upon them by new public management philosophies which sought to make the police service more effective, economic and efficient. Encouraged by the incumbent Conservative government, these philosophies became important engines of change in police management, and indeed the police service in general, especially as they effectively blamed police managers for the increasing inefficiency and ineffectiveness of the police service which had resulted in rising crime rates.

The publication of both the Sheehy report (1993) and the White Paper on policing (1993) encouraged a debate over reducing the number of independent police forces and, importantly, putting experienced managers from elsewhere in the public or private sectors in charge of them. This debate struck at the heart of one of the fundamental ideological principles upon which modern police management is based, namely that police managers are drawn from within the police service. This ideology of internal recruitment has appeared to make natural the view that only police officers can become chief officers of police (Wall, 1994b). A few years on, these debates have subsided, but since police history has the uncanny knack of repeating itself, they will undoubtedly arise again. The following chapters will demonstrate exactly this point because these debates ironically took place in the centenary year, 1993, of the start of the main campaign to ensure that all chief constables were internally appointed from within the police. Indeed, it was as recent as the late 1960s that the last externally recruited chief constables retired from office.

As the title suggests, the following text is a genealogy of the chief constable. It is a historical study of the recruitment, selection and appointment of the chief constables in England and Wales who were, and still are, individually vested with the overall responsibility for the management and operation of their independent local forces of police. It will inform debates that are taking place in the areas of police history, the sociology of élites, local governance, policy networks and administrative law. It is important at this point to mention that the book does not look in any detail at the other UK police chiefs, although the Commissioners of the Metropolitan and City of London forces are mentioned by way of comparison at various points.[2] The discussion in this book focuses mainly upon the policies and processes of selecting and appointing chief constables, so whilst discussion may include law, the role of police cultures, community controls etc., they are not the focus of the work.

---

[2] A study of the other chief constables for example, in the Scottish, British Transport, Channel Islands, Isle of Man, War Department /M.o.D., Atomic Energy Authority and Royal Ulster Constabularies would make a very interesting and complementary research project.

An outline of the main issues

From their introduction in the early nineteenth century, the provincial police forces were locally controlled, and this principle of local governance remained unchallenged until after the turn of the century. During this period, the management of the police was a very amateur affair; chief constables themselves were little more than 'gifted amateurs' and in some cases not so gifted. County chiefs tended to be ex-military officers while borough chiefs tended to be serving police officers, however this latter group were chosen more for their trustworthiness than for their policing abilities. The local nature of policing, before the turn of the century, was compounded by the relative lack of interest within the Home Office about the police.

Labour unrest during the late 19th century, the police strikes of 1916-18, the fear of Bolshevism, combined with the bureaucratic inconvenience of dealing with over 180 different organisations encouraged the Home Office to reconsider its position over the local control of the police. It sought to gain greater control over the police, and from the end of the First World War, the Home Office sought to weaken the link between local government and the police and to strengthen the link with central government. Importantly, in the absence of formal statutory authority to control the police, the Home Office sought to increase its influence over police management, and therefore the police, firstly, by utilising its ability to frame rules and regulations for the police and, secondly, by continuing to direct the police with circulars that offered centrally determined guidance or ideas about best practice. Next, the Home Office encouraged the development of 'professional' relationships both within and also between police forces. The idea of policing as a profession was promoted, and was combined with, the development of the idea of constabulary independence through the interpretation of case law so as to encourage the police to see themselves individually both as part of a wider policing function and also as operationally independent of their police authority. It was further supported by the establishment of an ideology, later to be supported by a policy of internal recruitment which made the appointment of chief police officers from within the police appear to be the most natural or logical course of action. The policy of internal recruitment was a device which influenced the type of people who were appointed to manage police forces and further sustained the ideology of internal recruitment. Thirdly, was the non-discouragement of chief officers to form associations at which they would meet and later, through the Association of Chief Police Officers, become involved in the police policy making process.

These legal and ideological devices strengthened both the formal and informal links between the police and the Home Office and thus weakened the domination of the police by their police authorities, especially in the boroughs. Their impact has been to change substantively police management from a local activity to being one which is centrally influenced but locally responsive, but in an account-giving rather than account-taking way (see Reiner, 1995a). It changed policing from being essentially an amateur activity which relied upon local models of management and practice, to a professional activity which was informed by a shared knowledge and underpinned by centrally determined core values.

Recent police organisational history can be divided into four periods which are each defined by a particular process. First, there was the *standardisation* of various basic aspects of police, its organisation and practice between the mid-nineteenth century and the First World War. Second, was the *centralisation* of police policy which gained impetus just after the First World War. Third, after the Police Act 1964 and Local Government Act 1973 came the *unification* of the separate borough and county traditions of police in the provinces and also the amalgamation of local police forces into regions or police areas. Fourth, during the period since the 1979 Conservative government first took office there has been a notable increase in police *corporatisation* through the increased influence of ACPO and more specifically the structuring of the ACPO ranks and their relationships with the Home Office. This corporacy has emerged against the background of the simultaneous rationalisation and fragmentation of the traditional police function which has replaced the traditional public policing model with a multi-tiered and pluralistic model of public and private policing. Each of these processes has continued so that the police organisation is currently experiencing pressures which are simultaneously standardising, centralising, unifying, corporatising it, and yet, also fragmenting it through increasing pluralism. Such pressures result not from a coherent strategy, but from a number of different sources.

Moreover, their diverse origins reduce the degree to which the pressures are controllable.

In a society which values the independence of its police from overt party political control, the most practical way to exercise control over the police has been to govern the selection of the police managers. This book examines the thesis that in the absence of explicit legal control, groups wishing to exercise control over the police have sought to appoint managers whose personal characteristics and values were in accord with their own view of the world and that any changes in the qualifications of the office of chief constable reflected wider changes in the distribution of power within society, particularly between central and local government.

Research Methods

This book is based upon a study of all chief officers that are known to have held office in the provincial forces in England and Wales between 1836 and 1996. For a number reasons, the study ends in 1996. Practically, 1996 was a convenient date, being 160 years since the first Municipal Corporations Act came into force and because most data for that year would be at hand when writing took place in 1997. Perhaps more important was the historical significance of 1996, as it symbolised the end of one era of the British police and the start of another. Late in the previous year, for example, the traditional and symbolic male dominance of the office of chief constable had been broken when Pauline Clare became the first woman chief constable, at Lancashire. She was followed in April 1997 by Elizabeth Neville, who became chief constable of the Wiltshire Constabulary. Not only did it symbolise the end of the patriarchy, but it also symbolised the beginning of an era of police corporatisation. It was the year during which the Association of Chief Police Officers (ACPO) increased its (corporate) profile by disaggregating its representative function from that of being a forum for the determination of police policy. Furthermore, it was a time when there was considerable discussion which led to the development of the first statutory national police organisation, the National Crime Squad. Finally, it was a time when the impact of the Police and Magistrates' Courts Act 1994 started to become apparent.

Six main sources of data were used in the study, they were contemporary records, autobiographical accounts, biographical accounts, contemporary historical accounts (inc. records), analytical narrative and interviews with past and present chief constables. The data obtained from these difference sources provided the basis for a triangulation of three studies. The first study was a qualitative picture that was obtained from the chief constables' various autobiographical accounts of the recruitment, selection and appointment processes. In some instances these were taken from published autobiographies and in more recent instances they were derived from interviews with serving and former chief constables. The second study was of contemporary key policies and processes that were active in the recruitment, selection and appointments process. This study was based upon records, typically from HO45 and HO158 lodged in the Public Records Office, the autobiographical accounts and from the various biographical and historical literature.[3] The third study was a quantitative study of individual appointments to police forces, derived from the various published sources mentioned above; this database enabled appointments, individuals and force types to be mapped. Most of the information about the chief constables' careers was collected from various collections of police journals and force histories in the library of the Police Staff College at Bramshill. Together, the three main methods provided the basis for the study of the careers and backgrounds of chief constables. The quantitative data enabled issues of proportionality in outcomes to be identified, whereas the qualitative data identified the processes which created those outcomes.

A total of 1835 appointments to chief officer were identified and these posts were filled by 1485 individuals: 1053 held the 1241 borough chief constable posts, 320 held the 443 county chief constable posts and 112 held the 154 posts appointed since the force reorganisations in 1974. These data are outlined below in Table 1.

---

[3] For further information about the PRO classifications see Gale (1996).

Table 1: Numbers of appointments as chief police officer

	Appointments		Individuals	
Borough	1241	68%	1053	71%
County	443	24%	320	22%
Post-1973	151	8%	112	8%
All	1835	100%	1485	101%

When this project was planned, it was originally thought, in fact assumed, that the main source of data would be *Who's Who*, but it was subsequently found that only a minor percentage of all chief constables had entries. It was further discovered that a comprehensive list of all chief constables since 1836 did not exist and that the borough chief constables were treated as a separate entity to their county colleagues. So, a major problem from the outset was a lack of information about the organisation of police forces and about the people who commanded them. Therefore, one of the first tasks carried out for the quantitative study was to construct a list of all of the police forces that existed in England and Wales. A major help here was Hallett's (1974) list of British police forces which, although not entirely complete, provided an initial reference point. The list provided a starting point for the collection of information about the chief officers and the next task was to identify the names of the individuals who served as chief officer in those forces. The basic list of who commanded which force, and for what period, was derived from the *Police and Constabulary Almanac,* published annually since 1857, and *Whittaker's Almanac*. Also used were the annual reports of HM Inspectorate of Constabulary which, since 1857, have documented the changes in post holders. The details of incumbents before 1857 came from individual force histories. Finally, a valuable source of information relating to the early chief constables was a solitary edition of the *Police and Constabulary List* for 1844 that was reproduced by the Police History Society.

The compilation of the list of chief constables was not wholly straightforward and was complicated by a number of lacunae, for example, by the fact that a number of forces had only one chief officer between them. These arrangements ranged from the permanent linking of Cumberland and Westmoreland to the ephemeral connection of East and

West Suffolk. In other similar circumstances forces such as Herefordshire and Hereford, a county and a borough force, were also commanded by the same chief officer, whereas a number of forces, were under joint command, for example, Birkenhead, between 1841 and 1843.[4] This problem was compounded by the non-statutory nature of the early borough chief constable. Further complications were the fact that during the Second World War many of the south coast borough forces, typically in Kent and Sussex, combined with their county forces because of the threat of invasion. The chief constables of these forces became assistant chief constables of the combined forces. To complicate matters further they returned to their prior posts upon dis-amalgamation at the end of hostilities.[5]

These idiosyncrasies do not cause a problem for the data analysis as they were largely temporary arrangements. They do, however, provide an explanation for any differences between the numbers of forces given in this book and those given in any one year by other commentators who have derived their figures from Parliamentary returns, many of which were incomplete. One of the Home Office's earliest bugbears was that independent police forces did not regularly make their statistical returns (see chapter 2).

A number of methodological problems were anticipated in the collection of the data. Firstly, a number of practical problems arose from the accuracy of the data and competing versions of events. The sources used were subsequently found to lack precise accuracy particularly with regard to dates of appointment and leaving. Aside from human error, there was a genuine problem in identifying the precise date an appointment actually took effect and when it ceased. More specifically, it was often the case that different sources would give different dates for appointment to, or departure from, office. Some represented the date that the individual was appointed, whilst others represented the date upon which they took up office. There was a similar confusion over the date of resignation and the individual's departure from office. Collectively, this meant that there would sometimes appear to be an overlap where a chief constable left one

[4] Under the joint command of Supt. Boughey (1839-1844) and Supt. Porter (1841-1843).

[5] Only to be recombined later as the result of the various amalgamation programmes that took place after the Police Acts of 1946 and 1964 and the Local Government Act 1972.

force and started another. In the majority of cases the dates given are believed to be correct within a year.

Secondly, of particular concern were problems of continuity and reliability arising from the fact that the data set was derived from published sources. The data was second, and sometimes third, hand, and some of the qualitative data was occasionally derived from chief constables' own published accounts of their careers. These anticipated problems did not materialise in practice because the basic biographical details were usually derived from more than one source and, wherever possible, most of the data were cross-checked to ensure a greater degree of reliability. Two important sources of information about chief constables' backgrounds were *Who's Who* and until the 1930s *Kelly's Handbook of the Official and Titled Classes*. Initially, it was feared that these directories would only contain a select group of chief constables and this fear was borne out in practice because it was quite clear that until quite recently chief constables were included because of their personal social standing. Today chief constables are included because of their standing as senior police officers. However, these biases, in fact, provide an important part of the analysis in chapter 9. A number of other sources of information were identified which augmented the élite directories, but in practice, continuity was not found to be a problem. However, where concerns about the reliability of any of the data did arise, they are voiced in the relevant sections. In addition to directories of élites, the many force histories gave details of their early chief constables and, furthermore, the *Police Review*, after its introduction in 1893, regularly featured biographical details of newly appointed and retiring, chief constables, and thus spanned a considerable period of time. For example, a chief constable retiring in the mid-1890s might have been appointed as early as the 1850s. Other sources also provided some data, for example, *The Police Chronicle* and the annual reports of the *Inspectorate of Constabulary*. Other sources were the many painstakingly descriptive biographical accounts that have appeared in the *Journal of the Police History Society* since 1986. Next, a number of the orthodox, and not so orthodox, histories of the police, which, whilst limited in analysis, were also a good source of information and data. An advertisement appealing for information was also placed in the newsletter of the Police History Society, and relatives of a few past chief constables sent information. Together, these sources provided a broad range of information about the many chief constables. The relevant information, where it could be found, was transcribed onto a pre-coded pro-forma for computer analysis using SPSS.

The third problem encountered during data collection was missing data, however, while the level of information about each chief constable varied, the missing information appears to be randomly distributed and not the result of any specific factor. In the eyes of the *Police Review*, a chief constable was a chief constable regardless of background, type or size of force or career. This is important in the analysis as it means that for most variables the missing information can be excluded to leave a representative sample for analysis.

It is estimated that the data set represents between 98 and 99 per cent of all appointments as chief officer. However, the information is weakest during the 1840s, but this is hardly surprising given the aforementioned non-statutory status of the borough chief and also the fact that almost two thirds of borough forces in 1865 had an establishment of less that 15 officers (many had between one and five, including the chief officer). Part of the problem here was that some of the watch committees assumed most, if not all, of the functions of a chief officer and therefore did not declare a chief officer when providing information to the Home Office.

Chapter Outline

The structure of this book follows three main premises. The first is the historical premise that in order to be able to understand any changes in the recruitment, selection and appointment of chief constables, an historical understanding of the organisational context within which they took place is necessary. Chapter 2 looks at the origins of both the idea of police and also the police organisation. Chapter 3 illustrates how the role of the chief constable has been shaped by wider changes that have taken place in the organisation of the police since the early nineteenth century and also demands made upon the police.

The second premise is that changes in policy do not just happen and they also do not have to be the result of primary legislation. In this case, they were the result of policy initiatives, or devices, which sought to influence the formal and informal processes that governed the recruitment, selection and appointment of chief constables. Prior to the Desborough Committee's recommendations in 1919, there were no centrally determined policies for selecting chief constables, especially with regard to the qualities and competencies required of the individuals. Selection and appointment were mainly a local matter. That date therefore marks a chapter break in the analysis. Chapter 4 focuses upon the period before the Desborough Committee sat in 1919 and examines the composition of the appointing bodies, the selection process and other related issues. Chapter 5 explores some of the debates that dominated the recruitment, selection and appointment processes during the nineteenth and early twentieth centuries. Chapter 6 discusses the various centralised attempts to impose policies to govern the internal selection of chief constables after 1919.

The third, and final, premise is that the policy initiative will have a sociological impact upon the profile of the individuals it sought to affect. Analysis of this profile will illustrate the various processes which shaped its implementation, thus demonstrating the effectiveness of this type of policy initiative. Consequently, chapters 7 and 8 seek to establish the precise nature of the changes in the recruitment, selection and appointment processes and their effect upon the characteristics of the chief constables themselves. Drawing upon the study of chief constables, chapter 8 examines the careers of chief constables and chapter 9 their occupational and social backgrounds.

Chapter 10 draws together the findings of the earlier chapters to explore the development of the ideology of internal recruitment and the governance of police management.

2 The Origins of the Provincial Police in England and Wales

Introduction

In order to understand the nature of the office of chief constable,[1] it is important first to understand the organisation of the provincial police forces of England and Wales and the role of the chief constable within them. The following two chapters document these organisational developments and highlight key factors which influence the office and role of chief constable. This chapter focuses upon the origins of the provincial police from the early legislation until the introduction of compulsory police forces in 1856. The next chapter explores the various developments that have taken place between that date and today.

The more traditional or orthodox versions of police history imply that the so-called 'new police' in England and Wales quickly developed along fairly uniform lines to become a coherent police service. A more realistic account of this history reveals an entirely different picture. Yes, the police reforms of the 1830s did supplant the existing hotchpotch of watching and quasi-policing functions that were being performed in the parishes, but those same reforms created three separate traditions of policing in their respective areas[2] whose differences, in time, became more marked than cohesive. This chapter will outline the origins of the provincial police in England and Wales. The first part will, therefore, explore the origins of the police idea and the need for reform. The second part will look at the introduction of the Metropolitan Police and will show how it provided a model for the subsequent reorganisation of the provincial police. Part three discusses the provincial police reforms and illustrates the two quite separate traditions of policing which emerged in the provinces.

---

[1] See Lustgarten (1996) and Reiner (1991a), for further discussion on the legal and constitutional position of the chief constable.

[2] Metropolitan, County and Borough Police. The City of London Police bore characteristics of both the provincial and Metropolitan models.

The origins of the police idea[3]

Despite the tendency of 'orthodox' historians of the police to show a linear progression from the Anglo-Saxon Tythingman to the bobby of today, few comparisons can realistically be made between the systems of governance before and after the early nineteenth century police reforms. Yet, this 'ontological glorification' (Bourdieu, 1987: 846) continually serves to underpin existing conceptualisations of police professionalism. Since mediaeval times local governance was based upon the fundamental principles of deterring crime through severity of sentence and community self-regulation. This system had three components (Clay, 1974: 4). The first was the Assize of Arms, introduced in 1181, which required every male aged between 15 and 60 to retain arms in his house in accordance to his rank and property and ready for use in preserving the peace. The second, was "hue and cry" under which the Sheriff was ordered to raise the hue and cry and with others to "follow a thief until he was caught". Failure to catch the thief could lead to fines being imposed. Third, was "watch and ward" introduced by a writ of Henry III in 1252, but legally established by the Statute of Winchester in 1285. Watch and ward was to be kept in towns where the gates were to be closed between sunset and day break with six men to guard each gate. Every large borough was supposed to have a watch of 12 persons and small boroughs, according to their size. All male inhabitants were liable to serve their turn on the watch without payment (Clay, 1974: 4). Underlying these three functions was the Anglo-Saxon principle of Frankpledge which established a system of mutual responsibility, partly based upon land tenure, for maintaining the peace. In each town and village a constable[4] was appointed, and within each Hundred a head constable was appointed to be responsible for keeping the peace. Importantly, from the fourteenth century onwards, this communal responsibility existed alongside the Justices of the Peace Act 1361, which entrusted the justices with the power to investigate into the circumstances

---

[3] For more complete accounts of the history of the police see Emsley (1983; 1996), Critchley (1978), Rawlings (1995), Radzinowicz (1956), Reiner (1992).

[4] Constable is derived from *Comes Stabuli* or Count of the Stable. "Persons to be considered for the office must be honest, able and understanding men; to be men of substance and not of the meaner sort, and not to be elected if not fit to execute the office" (Clay, 1974).

surrounding an offence, prosecute a defendant if necessary and then make a judgement as to their guilt.

Between the thirteenth and sixteenth centuries the increase in trade and the expansion of populations caused the role of the justices of the peace to expand. With only a few minor developments, the system remained largely unchanged until the early nineteenth century. However, by the 18th century the existing system of governance was perceived to be ineffective, largely because of the social and demographic changes brought about by the industrial revolution (Webb and Webb, 1906): particularly increasing urbanisation and the crimes and disorder that became associated with it. Moreover, the demands placed upon the offices of petty and high constable far outweighed the effort and commitment given to them by their incumbents.[5] The unpaid and part-time nature of these offices, particularly the latter, encouraged corrupt, but widely accepted, practices, often to a point where posts were highly sought after because of their lucrative prospects and the possibility of further enterprise. The common practice of constables employing deputies and deputies employing deputies often meant that the persons who were actually performing the role of constable were the very people whom the system was intended to work against. This point was confirmed by the Royal Commission on the County Rates in 1836, when it reflected upon the appointment and qualifications of the old parish constables:

> the manner of appointing constables ... might be advantageously altered ... for the court leet jury and steward being irresponsible parties, and the jurymen not liking the burden themselves, often appoint persons of bad character, and sometimes for the purpose of keeping them off the parish. If respectable persons are sometimes chosen at the leet, they find substitutes for a small sum and these deputies blunder through the year, and when they are most wanted are never found (*Royal Commission on the County Rate*, 1836: xxvii, Young and Haydock, 1956: 630).

Furthermore the Royal Commission found that "no inquiry took place into the constables' qualifications or fitness for the office, and 'is said to be often the person in the parish the most likely to break the peace'" (*idem*: 629).

---

[5] The petty or parish constables were responsible for their parish whereas the High constables were responsible for all of the parishes within a Hundred.

The evidence placed before the Royal Commission gives a rare glimpse of the practicalities of the old policing system, especially its drawbacks. It found, for example, that even if appointees took their responsibilities seriously, the annual practice of appointing parish constables meant that they were entirely ignorant of their duties when first appointed and were just starting to become aware of the requirements of the job when replaced the following year (*idem*: 630).[6] On top of the lack of training was the problem of motivating them to act, because:

> belonging entirely to his class, and brought into constant contact with them by his ordinary occupations, he is embarrassed in the discharge of his duty by considerations of personal safety, interest, or feeling, and by an anxiety to retain the good will of his neighbours (*idem*).

The Treasurer of the West Riding of Yorkshire argued that the problem was more than "embarrassment" and referred to the "disposition shown by the lower orders to retaliate by committing destruction on their property". He added that parish constables dared not act, they had no encouragement to act and if they did act they were incompetent (*idem*). Another witness summed up the frustration of the times by stating that: "the great end of police is to prevent crime, who ever heard of this being the object of the present force? They are worse than useless" (*idem*).

During the eighteenth century, the term 'police' began to be used (Radzinowicz, 1956) and traditional understandings of governance began to change from "the regulation and government of a city or country, so far as regards the inhabitants",[7] to the more narrower, crime and order related, policing function that we understand today. Initially, the increasing severity of sentence served to focus attention upon the individual rather than the community. The Waltham Black Act, or Criminal Law Act of 1722 (9 George 1, c. 22), for example, criminalised many previously legal activities, such as stealing apples (Cale, 1996: 83), and made them punishable by death. It reflected the increasing commercialisation of the landed estates and sought to protect the newly developed property rights of estate holders. The unjust nature of the sentences, combined with the

[6] These debates are rather reminiscent of the debates of tenure and rotation that are currently going on in some modern police forces.

[7] Dr Johnson quoted by Rawlings (1995: 138).

reluctance of juries to convict in cases carrying the death penalty (Cale, 1996: 84) encouraged the more sophisticated idea of crime prevention through certainty of apprehension. Important here was the development of a 'police mentality' which found a voice in the various works of John and Henry Fielding, who built upon and articulated ideas and techniques imported from France which had been developed by their contemporaries. "What was new", states Rawlings, "was their systematic publicizing of the notion that social control was attainable - and worth attaining through an organised institutional effort" (1995: 143). The Fieldings believed that social control could be achieved by introducing a pro-active system of crime detection that would be directed by a state bureaucracy working under the justices of the peace and also by the rigorous regulation of the poor "by means of the criminal law, poor law, administrative regulation, institutions and philanthropy" (*idem*). This dual strategy was later to emerge in Peel's reform of the criminal law during the early nineteenth century.

Rawlings illustrates how the moral panics which arose from the increase in crime during the mid-eighteenth century were instrumental in creating further demands for a reformed policing system. But, he observes that the idea of permanent, paid law enforcement officers was not new, as customs officers, to give one example, had been using officers to suppress the illegal exportation of wool and a number of parishes in London had already established a regular, paid, watch (1995: 138). Moreover, these initiatives, which included the fabled Bow Street Runners, remained local and tended to be financed through bounties for the capture of felons. Critchley argues that they "offered no major departure from the past ... and Fielding seems to have intended none" (1978: 33).

In the 1820s, a new policing system replaced the inefficient and out-moded part-time voluntary 'old' system with local, independent, bureaucratically organised police forces of full-time paid constables (Rawlings, 1995: 138).[8] Although a number of characteristics of the old constables came to be embodied in the 'new' police, such as the local nature of the organisation, the constable as the basic unit and the subordination of constables to justices, the 'new' police were both

[8] Rawling's detailed account of the history of the idea of police illustrates that the development of the 'new' police was in practice less radical and much more incremental than many historical accounts have suggested.

organisationally and conceptually different from their predecessors (Jefferson and Grimshaw, 1984). The meaning and interpretation of those characteristics within the criminal justice system have changed considerably, so much so that Lustgarten has rightly argued that the present day police bear the same relation to the 18th century constable as does the titled president of the National Farmers' Union to the followers of Wat Tyler (1986: 25). More importantly, the new police and other reforms of the time symbolised the beginning of a new era of bureaucratic public governance by excluding individuals and communities who were hitherto centrally involved in policing (Rawlings, 1995: 138; Shearing, 1996: 83). And yet, whilst these ideas of police were revolutionary, the contemporary evidence offered below suggests that the transition from one system to the other was far more incremental than radical.

The origins of the modern police are to be found in the police reforms of the late 1820s and 1830s, and in subsequent legislation, however, the first major policy initiative for a full-time police organisation began in the aftermath of the Gordon riots of 1785 when Pitt introduced his Police Bill. Important here is the fact that the Bill was primarily driven by concerns about disorder rather than crime. The Bill failed to gain assent because of considerable opposition arising through fear of the police developing into a repressive system of policing similar to that operating in France after the revolution of 1789. A decade or so after the failure of Pitt's Police Bill, Patrick Colquhoun, a London Magistrate, sought to persuade those opposed to the idea of a police force by conducting an evaluation of the potential effectiveness of a preventative police. Colquhoun's *Treatise on the Police of the Metropolis* (1796) estimated that a full-time, salaried force of police operating in the docklands of London would pay for itself by reducing theft from cargoes. It resulted in the creation of the Thames River Police in 1798, a private police force which was the first accredited full-time body of police. Colquhoun's 'experiment' was given further force when in the early 1800s a number of local authorities successfully experimented with employing full-time watchmen under their city or borough improvement acts.

The main idea behind the moves to reform the police was the principle articulated by John Fielding fifty years previously, of crime prevention through "the certainty of ... speedy detection" (Fielding, 1768; Rawlings, 1995: 140). In 1811 over 200 offences carried the death penalty, yet the enforcement of the law was minimal in comparison to the incidence of crime and the severe sentences had little effect upon the level of crimes committed. Under the proposed system, a force of full-time police officers would perform the three-fold task of bringing law breakers to justice, suppressing disorder and deterring people from breaking the law. The idea of police reform gained further popularity shortly after the financial success of the Thames River police, and enabled the pro-police reformers to gain ground over their opposition. Nevertheless, subsequent attempts to reform the police during the first two decades of the nineteenth century failed. A Select Committee considered whether a full-time centrally organised police would be practicable in London[9] and decided against the proposal to introduce a full-time police force on the grounds that it would be a threat to personal liberty.

Yet, despite the opposition to the idea of police there were nine bodies in London which employed about four hundred people, in various ways, to perform watch and police type functions (Gash, 1961: 489). The main employers were the Bow Street Police Office and the Thames River Police. By today's standards, however, it would be wrong to call them police, they were more of a cross between security guards and bounty hunters. The detection of crime was over and above their ordinary duties (Gash, 1961: 490). Gash argues that even before Peel went to the Home Office in 1822, it was beginning to assert itself over these police bodies. So, Peel's proposals for a full-time police force were not wholly radical, especially as he had already tried out many of his ideas in Ireland (Walker, 1990). It was only the locus of control over the police that was controversial.

In 1828, a Select Committee considered the possibility of introducing a full-time police force for the capital and accepted the idea. Within twenty months, the Metropolitan Police Bill passed through Parliament with remarkably little debate (Critchley, 1978: 50) and became the Metropolitan Police Act 1829. Shortly afterwards, on September 29, the first 'new' police officers stepped onto the streets.

---

[9] Set up in the wake of the Queen Caroline affair of 1821, but also within recent memory of the Peterloo massacre of 1817.

The (Metropolitan) Public Policing Model[10]

The Metropolitan Police Act 1829 resulted from the effective parliamentary management and political entrepreneurship of Sir Robert Peel, the Home Secretary. It was the culmination of a humanitarian legislative programme by which Peel[11] reformed the criminal law, reduced the overall number of capital offences from 221 to 10, and introduced a full-time police force to ensure that the new laws were impartially and effectively enforced. Peel shrewdly managed the debate over police reform by placating any opposition from the City of London by excluding it from the jurisdiction of the proposed police force.[12] He also reduced opposition from the magistrature by placing magistrates in managerial control of the force. Finally, Peel persuaded Parliament to place the Metropolitan Police bill before the same Select Committee that had recommended its creation, thus ensuring that the bill received a sympathetic hearing (Gash, 1961: 497; Emsley, 1983: 60; 1996). The Metropolitan police provided a working model for an operational police force.

The Metropolitan Police were to be led by two individuals. Peel wished one to possess the skills of a "practical and efficient lawyer" and the other to be a soldier who was: "accustomed to discipline and capable of enforcing it". They would be supported by a third person, with legal training and business experience, who would take charge of the finances and collect the police rates from each of the London parishes (Gash, 1961: 498). Peel duly appointed Richard Mayne, an Irish Barrister aged 32, and Col. Charles Rowan aged 47, a veteran of the Light Brigade to the former posts and he chose a solicitor named Wray, who was active in the legal and commercial world, as Receiver.

Mayne and Rowan were magistrates, not police officers, but were forbidden to act as such at general, quarter or any other sessions[13] on any matter except the preservation of the peace, the prevention of crime, the

---

[10] The historical circumstances surrounding the build up to the police reforms of the 19th century are well documented elsewhere; see for example, Critchley (1978) and Emsley, (1996).

[11] And Romily before him.

[12] The City of London Police were formed in 1839, see Rumbelow's (1989) account of their formation.

[13] The Commissioner of the Metropolitan Police remained a magistrate until the 1970s. See Mark (1976).

detention or commitment of offenders and the general execution of the statute under which they were appointed (Gash, 1961: 498). They were given the power to recruit, train and discipline the officers under their command. Although the Commissioners, as they quickly came to be known, were in overall charge of the Metropolitan Police, it was Peel, the Home Secretary, who designed the framework of the organisation and determined its personnel structure. For this he drew upon his experiences of reforming the Irish police (Gash, 1961: 497-502). The principle underlying the personnel structure of the early police was that the working classes would police themselves and it was a principle that has underlined the personnel structure of the police until recently.[14] By employing constables from the working classes, Peel hoped to ensure that the relationship between the police and the public remained close and that control over what were seen as 'the dangerous classes' was maximised whilst the potential for disorder was minimised. Another equally important motivation for this strategy was the fact that the cost of running a police force of working class people would be much cheaper, hence the resistance to encouraging the employment of officers and gentlemen, even when their circumstances had been reduced (see later).

Peel imagined a police force in which "there was to be no caste system as in the Navy or Army; the Metropolitan Police was to be professional and homogenous", and ranks up to that of Superintendent were to be drawn typically, from ex-warrant officers and non-commissioned officers (Critchley, 1978: 52). Future promotions would be made from within the existing body of police (Davies, 1973). Peel believed that the fact that the commissioners were magistrates, and not police officers, would help to ensure that the police would not develop into a class ridden institution and would remain a socially homogenous body. This strategy of distancing the classes was important if the police were to fulfil the distasteful function of keeping the 'dangerous classes' off the streets for it was important to maintain the close link between the police and the community (*Report of the Select Committee on the Police of the Metropolis*, 1834). It is therefore not surprising that Peel had some very

[14] Since the Edmund Davies agreement in 1978, which increased police pay, improved conditions of service and also co-incided with broader changes in the job market, the social and educational profiles of entrants into the police have broadened considerably. This point is discussed in later chapters.

strong views on the type of person he saw as being a police officer: "a three shillings a day man is better than a five shillings a day man" for the work the constables would have to do (Gash, 1961: 502). Peel desired a disciplined working force and the police pay of 15 shillings per week, one twelfth that of a commissioner's salary, ensured that constables were drawn from the working classes and "would not become a sanctuary for the genteel" (Gash, 1961: 502). When challenged in Parliament over the low level of police pay, Peel replied: "I have refused to employ gentlemen - commissioned officers, for instance - as superintendents and inspectors, because I am certain they would be above their work" (Croker Papers, 1885: 19).

Peel's ideas about the type of person required to be constable were firmly supported by Commissioner Mayne who said, in his evidence to the Select Committee on Metropolitan Police and Crime in 1834, that "a man from the ranks is not disinclined to do what men of superior acquirements in point of education and higher station in life would think beneath them. It was therefore considered best to select persons of that class for Superintendents" (*Report of the Select Committee on the Police of the Metropolis*, 1834: q. 138). In keeping with Peel's philosophy about who should become police officers, three quarters of the men appointed as the first superintendents in the Metropolitan Police were ex-sergeant majors.

If Peel intended the first police officers to be a cross section of the population of London, it was an ambition that was never realised, as contemporary research reveals that they included a higher percentage of ex-servicemen and persons of Scots and Irish origin than the normal population (Emsley and Clapson, 1994). Moreover, the brutal experiences of the first police officers illustrated by Emsley (1983; 1996), Steedman and Phillips (1977) contrast sharply with the "historical sentimentality" (Hart, 1951: *v*) found in the benign descriptions of early policing given by the more orthodox (Reiner, 1992: 9-13) interpretations which tended to rely upon Parliamentary rather than contemporary local records (see later). So, the life of a constable in the new force was hard. The architects of British policing sought to control rigidly the constable's private life so as to neutralise the widespread suspicion and hostility which accompanied the creation of the new police (Reiner, 1995: 123). Moreover, the new police officers were expected to be "exemplary citizens" (De Lint, 1997: 247). This high level of control was to dominate the relationship between chief officer and constable until the next century. Police officers were expected to be highly disciplined, very principled, and be able to work alone for low wages. In 1829, the *Weekly Dispatch* published the views of some ex-constables on what was expected of them:

> what man of sober industrious habits would or could consent to take up his abode in a barrack for the pay of a bricklayer, labourer (sic) and work or watch 7 days and nights a week, it's absurd to expect it (*Weekly Dispatch*, 1829: 63).

In giving evidence to the 1834 Select Committee, Rowan and Mayne revealed that out of the 2,800 ordinary constables who had been employed since May 1830, 2,238 had left the force within four years. Of that number 40 per cent (897) were dismissed and 60 per cent (1341) left the police to better themselves. One of the main reasons for such a high rate of dismissal arises from the constables' motivations for joining the police, many joined to avoid the "stress of weather" rather than because they particularly wanted to be police officers. Furthermore, it was only after the introduction of a comparatively generous pension scheme and improvements in working conditions later in the century, that the job became more tolerable.

Peel's theories about the personnel structure of the police did not fully work out in practice because of the social, cultural and educational gap between the commissioners and the first superintendents. This personnel policy created problems for the management of the Metropolitan police from the start, and prompted the 1834 Select Committee to consider the possibility of employing "reduced gentlemen"[15] as superintendents. In reply to the suggestion, one of the committee members expressed the following reservations: "would it not be a painful thing for the reduced gentleman to mix with the other police?" When asked for his opinion on the matter, Mayne replied: "I think it must be naturally so" (*Report of the Select Committee on the Police of the Metropolis*, 1834: q. 138).

A working compromise had to be reached and an intermediary rank was introduced to act as a mediator between the constables and the commissioners and bridge the class divide. Introduced in 1840, at twice the pay of a superintendent, the 'visiting superintendent' was intended to act as

---

[15] Gentlemen without income.

an intermediary between the commissioners and the superintendents. In appointing the first visiting superintendent, preference was given to ex-army officers (*Departmental Committee on Metropolitan Police Personnel*, 1868). The first visiting superintendent died in 1869 and his successors became known as district superintendents (*The Administration and Organisation of the Metropolitan Police Force*, 1886: 4). In 1886, this intermediary role again became the focus of discussion following the failure of the Metropolitan Police in 1886 to deal with disturbances in the capital. One of the findings of the Disturbances Committee was an "insufficient number of officers of superior rank and education" and "a defective chain of responsibility among superior officers of the force" (*idem*: 3, Points 1 and 4). The Disturbances Committee proposed to take up the recommendation of the Committee on the State, Discipline and Organisation of the Metropolitan Police 1879, to strengthen the role of the district superintendent and improve the chain of command. Known by the title chief constable, because they were the highest rank of constable in the Metropolitan Police (Moylan, 1934), the 1886 Committee discussed the social position and qualifications for appointment. They agreed with the 1879 Committee who argued that "they should be gentlemen of good social standing, and as a general rule, be officers who have seen service in the Army or Navy" (*Committee on the State, Discipline and Organisation of the Metropolitan Police*, 1879). The reason for this choice, the 1886 Committee added, was that: "we believe that such men would be treated with respect and regarded with confidence by the force" (*The Administration and Organisation of the Metropolitan Police Force*, 1886: 4). This recruitment policy continued until the 1930s (see chapter 6). In the 1950s the title chief constable (Met) was changed to the, now defunct, rank of deputy commander.[16]

The organisation of the Metropolitan Police was not original, it merely brought together many tried and tested organisational and personnel practices that had existed in various institutions during the past century, for example the army and the Irish police:

> [Peel] made it, an imperial force, its chief officer appointed by the [sovereign], and the regulations under which it acts, made or approved by the Home Secretary ... while performing all the duties of a local force ... it is

[16] I am very grateful to Martin Stallion for this information.

> under complete Government control and is responsible for the safety and independence of Parliament and of the executive. (Troup, 1928: 10).

But at a time when the idea of bureaucratic policing was new, it provided a reference point, if not a full operational model, for future police organisations and their personnel and management. Regarding the latter point, it established the principle of excluding police officers from the executive management of the police by placing it in the hands of magistrates. Generally speaking, the underlying philosophy and relatively low cost of the Metropolitan Police model made it a very attractive proposition for the many local authorities, who had to install quickly a police force during the coming decade. In addition to cost, it was a politically advantageous alternative to the army for dealing with disorder, as had been demonstrated on a number of occasions since 1829. While the army were able to put down disorder they were, because of their training, not very proficient at arresting rioters (*Hansard* 3rd Series, 1839, vol. 49: cols. 727-731; Smith, 1990: 5). Additionally, the government were spared the political backlash and internal discipline within the army was not affected, as so often was the case when they were called to police disorder.

The provincial police in England and Wales

Before the County and Borough Police Act 1856 made the introduction of police forces compulsory in every borough and county, provincial police reforms were piecemeal, numerous and unfocused. On the one hand were the reforms promoted by central government which took place within the general atmosphere of reform that existed during the 1830s "when the flood tide of democracy, which followed the passing of the Reform Act, 1832, was still running strong" (*Police Review*, 1942: 173). Centred around the two main units of local government, the boroughs and the counties, the Municipal Corporations Act 1835 created the borough police, and the County Police Acts of 1839 and 1840 provided for the voluntary installation of county police. On the other hand there were also attempts to revive, and improve the efficiency of, the old police system through the Lighting and Watching Acts of 1830 and 1833, the Special Constables Act 1831 and later through the Parish Constables Acts of 1842 and 1850. In addition, a number of cities and boroughs had passed individual improvement acts under which commissioners created separate night and day patrols of watchmen.

Borough police reforms

The lack of any co-ordinated structure in the policing of the provinces led to it being both confusing and inefficient, as the findings of the Royal Commission on the County Rate demonstrated. The following examination of the old policing arrangements in York, an old and medium sized borough, further illustrate this point. In 1835, immediately before the Municipal Corporations Act came into force, three separate authorities were policing York's population of 30,000. First, were the city corporation who employed a peace officer and two constables from nine in the morning until midnight to execute warrants, serve summonses, apprehend vagrants, prevent disorders and breaches of the peace (1st Rep. York WC, 11/5/1836: 5).[17] The second group were the city commissioners who, under the 1825 York Improvement Act, employed a city patrol of nine constables to provide a night watch from ten at night until four in the morning. The final group were the magistrates who appointed a parish constable to each of the city's fifty or sixty parishes to provide a day watch.[18] The powers of these constables were restricted to their own parish and as a group were "almost entirely inefficient" (Swift, 1988: 6). When the peace of the city was threatened by large scale disorder, such as during the Reform Riots in 1832, the magistrates could appoint special constables or even summon military assistance (Swift, 1988: 6/fn 34). Swift observes that these arrangements were further weakened by the fact that "there was little co-ordination between the Corporation, the City Commissioners, and the parish vestries" (*idem*). The lack of an effective system of police within the city encouraged the formation of a number of self-help and private law enforcement initiatives, for example, the City of York Association for the Prosecution of Felons and Cheats which provided rewards for information leading to the arrest and conviction of offenders.

---

[17] Minutes of York City Watch Committee.

[18] Because of its age and religious significance, York tended to have more parishes than many other boroughs of a similar size.

It was precisely this chaos and inefficiency which led Lord Russell, the Home Secretary, when introducing the Municipal Corporations Bill to Parliament, to argue that the maintenance of order should be placed in the hands of a single, democratically elected, body. He believed that the keeping of the peace, or 'the quietening of the town', as it used to be known, should be placed under the control of people who have legitimate government of that town. The idea of extending the policing principles of the newly formed Metropolitan Police to the counties and boroughs was voiced by Peel as early as April 1829 when he told Parliament that he was considering the possibility. In May the following year he stated that he wished that all provincial towns would form their own police (Gash, 1961: 505). However, whilst the idea may have been Peel's, the initiative was taken by Russell.

The Municipal Corporations Act 1835 required each new chartered borough council to form a watch committee and, within three weeks of their first election, to employ a sufficient number of constables to preserve the peace within the borough (s. lxxvi.). Not all of the boroughs had completed charters; legal difficulties with the charters of Manchester, Birmingham and Preston, three rapidly growing industrial towns, led to their police being placed under the temporary control of Home Office commissioners (Young and Haydock, 1956: 613). By 1842, all three had come under the provisions of the Municipal Corporations Act 1835.

On finding themselves with an obligation to set up a police force at fairly short notice, many watch committees looked to see what was happening in other boroughs, many also approached the Commissioners of the Metropolitan Police for advice and help. The Commissioners responded to requests by sending advisers to the boroughs for a fee of 10 shillings per day, plus travel and accommodation (Mins. York WC, 25/8/1836). York Watch Committee, for example, fearful of the potential cost of introducing a full-time force of police, continued with the existing arrangements by placing the night patrol under the watch committee. Furthermore it "resolved to engage a London police man, experienced in the application of the Metropolitan Police Act of 1829, to reorganise and superintend the York police and to place it upon the most economical footing" (Mins. York WC, 18/8/1836). The committee employed an Inspector Stuart who "arrived from London bearing a letter of introduction from Richard Mayne, Metropolitan Commissioner" (Swift, 1988: 8). Stuart drew up a report on the state of policing in York. He recommended a force of at least twenty four men and the adoption of the Metropolitan police uniform. The Watch Committee agreed the latter and provided its constables "with lantern, rattle, staff and handcuffs" (Extracts Mins. York WC, Oct. 1836), but requested Stuart to revise his estimates in regard to the size of the force (Mins. York WC, 3/11/1836; Swift 1988: 8). Stuart then presented plans for a force of twenty one men which was approved by the committee, but later rejected by the council on the grounds of expense. Twelve constables were eventually appointed to police York and Stuart commented upon his return to London, that the number was too few to provide the city with adequate police cover. More importantly, Swift observes that after six months of debate and political in-fighting the new police remained relatively unchanged from the old. There were no major differences in personnel, even the new superintendent had previously been in charge of the old day watch, the only observable differences were that they now wore a uniform similar to that of the Metropolitan Police[19] and that they were now responsible to the city watch committee. This example of local politics was quite common in the development of the borough police forces throughout England and Wales. The Municipal Corporations Act's lack of clarity regarding the manner in which the "sufficient number of constables" was to be organised, left much room for interpretation by local councils.

The actual number of Metropolitan police that were sent to the provinces is open to debate. Reith (1943: 198, 213) found that 111 watch committees were lent men by the Metropolitan Police, but Hart (1955: 421/fn 1) argues that Reith over estimated the extent of help by confusing loans to help set up a force with loans to help quell public disorder. The high charge made for the services of men loaned from the Metropolitan Police deterred many watch committees, particularly in the smaller boroughs, from seeking outside help. There does however exist further evidence to show that they frequently sought to recruit Metropolitan Police

---

[19] Not all boroughs adopted the Metropolitan Uniform. One of the reasons for adopting the Metropolitan dress was that they could be bought second hand, thus keeping down the cost of uniforms. Constables were also expected to repair their own clothes: "PCs should repair their own clothes, except when Mr Chalk, Chief Constable, considers that repairs should be done at the city's expense" (Extracts Mins. York WC, Jan. 1849).

trained officers as chief officer (Wall, 1987, also see later).[20] In fact upon finding themselves without a chief officer upon the death of William Pardoe in 1841, York Watch Committee wrote to Commissioner Rowan asking if he could recommend a Metropolitan police officer to fill the position. Rowan replied, suggesting that the salary be increased and that if not successful, the person would be reimbursed for his travel. The recommended person arrived in York and was instantly engaged as chief officer; his appointment was confirmed two weeks later (Mins. York WC, 4/11/1836).

Whilst the personnel structure of the Metropolitan Police provided a practical working model of a full-time force of constables, the borough police reforms did not set out to imitate its management structure. Far from it, as one of the fundamental characteristics of the borough police was that they were not to be controlled by magistrates, rather by a local committee of elected people.[21] The watch committee was directed, under the Municipal Corporations Act, to appoint, dismiss and discipline the members of its force. It also took control over local policing policy, and documentary evidence from the minutes of the various watch committees[22] shows that they took operational control over the policing operations of their forces. The York Watch Committee minutes illustrate many instances where orders were given to the police that would today be described as operational. These orders ranged from giving quite detailed directions for "constables to be dispersed around the city and not walk two together" (Extracts York WC, Aug. 1836) to instructions "to take proceedings against infractions of the act for the suppression of betting houses" (Extracts York WC, May 1868).[23]

Under the 1835 Act, watch committees were vested with the same powers as the county chief constable under the County Police Act 1839. The consolidation of policing under one authority was quite a radical step for local government at the time, especially as stated earlier, it took powers away from the justices. The 1835 Act made no provision for a chief

---

[20] Interestingly, Peel's own valet, John Stephens, became the first chief constable of Newcastle-upon-Tyne in 1836.

[21] Eligibility to vote was based upon property ownership.

[22] See Bridgeman and Emsley (1989) for details of the location of such minutes. Also see literature such as Brogden (1982).

[23] These instructions were not unique to York, see the Devonport, Norwich and Southampton cases that are documented in chapter 3.

officer; it was probably assumed that the existing practice of designating one of the constables to be in charge would continue, as was the case with the various night and day patrols. It was certainly the case that there were few salaried officials in local government in the 1830s and therefore few precedents for appointing an officer with such a broad range of independent powers. The early borough chief officer was merely "the superintending or executive officer of the watch committee".[24] Underpinning this arrangement was a broader political strategy of passing the responsibility for the policing of disorder from central to local government. The use of the army was an unpopular action which tended to be both expensive and politically divisive. Writing to Leeds council in 1855, the Home Secretary reminded members that "a military force should not be relied upon as a substitute for the police ... it should only act in support of the civil power".[25]

Although the position of borough chief officer was initially quite tenuous, it developed during the course of the nineteenth century to resemble, but not imitate, the office of county chief constable. Indeed, the common use of the title by all borough forces, excepting Liverpool[26], and the confusion it created for the delivery of mail caused the Home Secretary, in 1897, to allow them to use the title chief constable.[27] Initially called superintending constables, most borough chief officers subsequently became referred to as head constables and then chief constables. Some boroughs, however, always used the title as it had previously been used to describe the constable in charge of the old day or night watch. Leeds, for example, used the title of chief constable from the eighteenth century onwards to describe the constables in charge of their watch (Clay, 1974: 8).

The main reason for the independent development of the *de facto* office of borough chief constable was the practicality of managing a police force whose role developed in both function, size and complexity. Quickly

---

[24] Chief Constable of Norfolk giving evidence to the 1855 Select Committee quoted by Critchley (1978: 143). Memorandum, October 29, 1858, HO 45/ 19774.

[25] Letter written on behalf of Sir George Grey to the Leeds Authorities, March 30, 1855 (Clay, 1974: 27).

[26] HO 45 9969/ X26632/6.

[27] The correspondence on this matter was typically from county chief constables who complained of the improper use of the term 'chief constable'. The letter from John Dunne, for example, suggests some considerable snobbery on the part of the county chief constables (HO 45 9969/ X26632/ 3 - May 7, 1892). See chapter 3.

after their introduction, most borough police forces acquired additional responsibilities for the fire brigade and later the ambulance service. These functions were performed by constables and overseen by the chief officer (see later).[28] A second, though more minor reason, was that there tended to exist in most watch committees a class divide between the middle and upper classes and the working class police. Thus, the chief officer also acted as mediator between the two, in much the same way as the previously mentioned visiting superintendent in the Metropolitan Police. A third reason was that the regular turnover of watch committee membership created a reliance upon the borough chief officer for information and continuity. So, the watch committee, being elected representatives with their own livelihoods or interests to pursue, often had neither the time nor the experience in police matters to manage their police force in the manner set out by the 1835 Municipal Corporations Act: it was simply not practical for them to do so. As the activities of the police became more complex, the watch committees tended to devolve many of their powers to a specially appointed chief officer:

> The exercise of all these powers has been found so disadvantageous, or so cumbersome that, in most of the larger boroughs, the watch committees have delegated it to the chief constables, but reserved a right of appeal to them against any decisions of the chief constable. In smaller boroughs, the powers of the watch committee are exercised directly (Nott-Bower, 1926: 319).

Importantly, as the watch committees delegated their powers to a chief officer, they found it hard to regain them.[29] Particularly as the broadening of the police role was to endear chief officers and their constables to the townsfolk, offsetting local opposition and often giving them considerable personal legitimacy that was independent of the local council. Consequently, in addition to becoming skilled managers of local emergency services, borough chief officers also became important and

[28] See the various local histories of the police, for example, Clay (1974), Swift (1988), Smith (1973), Richer (1990). Also Bridgeman and Emsley (1989).

[29] The minutes of York Watch Committee clearly show that the operational orders decreased during the second half of the nineteenth century and issues discussed came to relate to conditions of service etc.

well known individuals who could court much local respect and political currency.[30]

The first provincial police forces were very different in appearance from the Metropolitan Police; their uniforms were often designed locally and varied in both colour and style between the counties and boroughs. In the 1840s, for example, the borough police in Manchester[31] wore different coloured tunics from the County of Lancashire police who were stationed in the same town. The organisation of borough forces also tended to vary considerably between boroughs as they were designed around local models of management (Steedman, 1974). Many watch committees, like York and Leeds (Swift, 1988; Clay, 1974), found themselves involved in the middle of local political debates over the police and ended up making the type of compromises illustrated earlier whereby they simply ended up merging their night and day patrols to form the 'new' police force for their borough.

The progress of borough police reforms

The provisions of the Municipal Corporations Act of 1835 and the County Police Act of 1839 for the installation of police forces were not taken up immediately by some provincial police authorities, even though the former was compulsory. There is, however, some controversy over the immediacy of take up, especially in the boroughs. In her influential article "Reform of the Borough Police 1835-1856", which has since come to represent the conventional wisdom on the subject (see for example, Critchley, 1978), Hart used Parliamentary records to demonstrate that many boroughs were guilty of a "dilatoriness in fulfilling their statutory obligations" (1955: 415) and that the borough police reforms were slowly implemented (*HC Papers* 1847, xivii and 1854, liii). After establishing a case to show a slow take-up, she offers various "factors which retarded the reform of the borough police between 1836 and 1856" (Hart, 1955: 422), such as borough opposition to the idea of a paid public police, either because it was not reconcilable with traditional English liberties, or because of expense. Another factor was the difficulty that boroughs had "to get advice on the organization and running of a force except from the Metropolitan

---

[30] This tended to depend upon the individual.

[31] Formed under the Manchester Police Act 1839 until 1842.

police" (Hart, 1955: 422). In fact, a revised estimate of the take up of police reforms based upon a range of other contemporary and historical sources,[32] rather than Parliamentary returns,[33] finds that the borough councils started their police forces much more quickly and compliantly than she suggests.[34] Table 2 below contrasts Hart's figures with the revised estimates.

Table 2: The impact of the borough police reforms 1835-1853
(Number of independent borough forces)

Year	Hart*	Revised estimate**
1835	7	30
1836	83	137
1837	100	141
1838	105	144
1839	108	148
1840	114	150
1853	155	164

* Based upon Table B, Hart, op. cit. p. 417.
** Taken from Table A1 in the appendix.

Table 2 illustrates that by the end of 1836, over half of the boroughs (137) had started police forces in contrast to the 83 suggested by the Parliamentary records, and by 1840, 150 boroughs in contrast to 114 had started their forces. These findings reveal that the boroughs did not display "dilatoriness" in fulfilling their statutory obligations, it was more likely the case that they simply omitted to supply details of their arrangements to the Home Office. Moreover, the findings show that the boroughs were actually keen to establish a police force and that resistance to the idea was not as great as previously indicated. A complete list of the annual numbers of independent police forces in England and Wales are shown in Tables A1

[32] These are listed in chapter 1.

[33] Which Hart herself questioned (Hart, 1955: 417/ fn 4).

[34] However, the discussion in chapter 5 will show that compliance tended to depend upon whether or not the local authorities felt that it was in their interests to comply.

and A2 in the Appendix. Figure 1 plots the data from Table A2 to illustrate the differences in the annual number of borough and county forces between 1836 and 1996. It also demonstrates the impact of the various policies, referred to throughout this chapter, designed to reduce the number of small police forces.

Figure 1: The annual number of all independent police forces in England and Wales 1836-1996

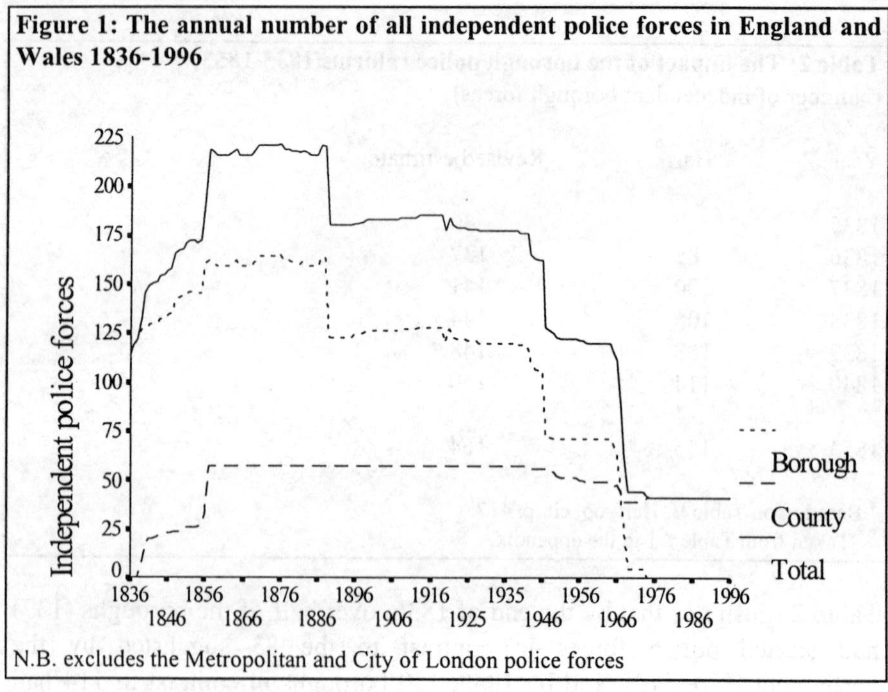

N.B. excludes the Metropolitan and City of London police forces

County police reforms

The county police reforms, like those in the boroughs, were also driven by the need to maintain order rather than prevent crime. However the government's first stumbling block was the fact that the idea of police reform in the counties was initially rejected by most of the Quarter sessions who were responsible for the administration of the counties. In 1839, the Royal Commission on Establishing an Efficient Constabulary Force in the Counties of England and Wales (1839, 169, XIX.1) concluded much along the same lines as the earlier Royal Commission on the County Rates (see earlier), namely that the old system was rendered inadequate by the wider changes that were taking place in society. However, it found that the unsatisfactory state of policing was not just the fault of an inefficient body of police, but a change in the very basis upon which the old policing system stood.

> The early constitutional principles of local responsibility for offences ... has been impaired: and that there does not exist an adequate local interest to ensure the adoption of efficient means for the prevention of crimes ... (Para 4.1).

The commissioners, Charles Lefevre, Charles Rowan and Edwin Chadwick,[35] believed that there were solid grounds to believe that crime could be reduced by the appointment of a proper force for the prevention or repression of crimes (*Report of the Royal Commission on establishing an efficient constabulary force in the counties of England and Wales*, 1839: Pt. 9 Conclusions). They countered the view that the police were antithetical to liberty by arguing that to leave the populace without police would be an even greater threat to liberty:

> the evils we have found in existence in some districts and the abject subjection of the population to fears which may be termed a state of slavery, which the objectors would endure from a groundless fear of loss of liberty, form a condition much worse in all respects than any condition that could be imposed by any government that could exist in the present state of society in this country (*ibid*).

Moreover, they argued that the "great mass of evil" indicated in their report was not ascribable to abuse of "beneficial powers" but to their neglect and disuse. Thus, the safe course for maintaining the freedom of the subject was not to render the authorities impotent, but to make them strictly responsible for the use of power. In contrast to the police forces abroad, implying France, the commissioners argued that the police act on arbitrary powers, whereas the force they propose could only act upon legal powers for which they would be responsible to the courts and to Parliament (*ibid*). They suggested that the best way to improve policing was to remove

---

[35] Lefevre was a country gentleman, Rowan was a Metropolitan Commissioner and Chadwick was Secretary of the Poor Law Commissioners and a well known advocate of utilitarian reform (Emsley, 1996: 38).

the responsibility for policing from the justices at petty sessions and introduce a regular paid constabulary force "trained, appointed, and organised on the principles of management recognised by the legislature in the appointment of the new Metropolitan police forces" (*idem*: Proposal 1). This force of constables would be part funded by the Treasury and it would be directed by commissioners of police appointed by the Home Secretary (*idem*: Proposal 2), but constables and their superintendents would report to magistrates at Quarter sessions, who would have the power to dismiss them. Basically, the Royal Commission sought to extend the Metropolitan police model to the rest of the country, although the commissioners themselves were not fully united on the mechanisms by which this would take place. Rowan and Lefevre disagreed with Chadwick's proposal to make the rural police responsible to the boards of guardians appointed under the poor law, preferring instead the more common view that the police should be under the control of the county magistrates (Emsley, 1996: 39).

The Royal Commission's report was not very well received by the various Quarter sessions and only a few were willing to accept the idea of an independent, full-time, and paid police force in their county because of the high cost. Nevertheless, the imminent threat of unrest by the Chartist movement led Russell to introduce county police reforms[36] on a voluntary basis. The County Police and District Constabulary Act 1839[37] empowered, but did not compel, justices in Quarter sessions to establish a police force for all or part of their county. Whilst some of the ideas put forward by the Royal Commission were retained, the idea of a centrally organised national police force was ignored, as was the idea to part-fund it from the Treasury.

In contrast to the comparative vagueness of the Municipal Corporations Act 1835, the County Police and District Constabulary Act 1839 was quite specific about the structure and management of county police forces. The Act stated that executive control over the police would rest with a specially appointed chief officer of police called a chief constable (Para IV). The Quarter sessions were given the responsibility of appointing a chief constable for their force but the chief constable would

---

[36] He also increased the army by 5000.

[37] Often referred to as the County Police Act 1839 and elsewhere as the Rural Police Act 1839.

be responsible for appointing, dismissing and disciplining the constables in the force (see chapter 4). The rates of pay and qualifications for office were set by the Home Secretary[38] and were largely based upon the Metropolitan police pay rates.[39] The prescribed minimum wage of the chief constable was to be more than six times greater than the constables' minimum wage and the maximum wage was nine times greater.[40] The pay of the various ranks in the county police was to be as follows:

> The chief constable's pay is to be not less than £250 or not more than £500 a year.
> The superintendent's pay not less than £75 or more than £150 a year.
> The inspector's pay not less than £65 or more than £120 a year.
> The weekly pay of a sergeant is to be not less than 19s. or more than 25s.
> The weekly pay of the constable is to be not less than 15s. or more than 21s.
>
> Source: (Home Secretary's Rules, 1840).

These differentials in pay were to be instrumental in determining the type of people who filled the posts as in the Metropolitan police.

The first county police officers were drawn from the labouring classes because it was assumed that they possessed the physical characteristics required for the job and, more importantly, had a clear knowledge of their place in the local social hierarchy and did not question it (Steedman, 1984). It would, however, be wrong to assume that they were agricultural workers, but were drawn from a variety of occupations; so varied, in fact, that Emsley and Clapson warn against too much generalisation from a single local experience (1994: 269). Like the first Metropolitan police officers, they were a very unstable occupational group. Most either resigned from the police or were dismissed within a short time of joining. The chief constables, as the following chapters will demonstrate, were drawn from very different backgrounds to the constables under their command.

---

[38] See chapter 3 for the Home Secretary's rules relating to the appointment of chief constables.
[39] Although the Home Secretary's rules under the County Police Act 1839 were for the county police many borough forces did tend to use them as a guide-line in their own forces.
[40] Today a chief constable's salary is roughly between three and four times greater than that of a constable.

The progress of county police reforms

Parliamentary records show that the implementation of the County Police Act 1839 was very slow. Just under half (27) of the 57[41] counties in England and Wales had fully installed forces before the Act of 1856 came into force. The annual establishment of county police forces between 1839 and 1857 can be found in Table 3.

Table 3: The impact of the county police reforms 1839-1857[42]
(Number of independent county forces)

Year	*Increase*	*Total*	*Year*	*Increase*	*Total*
1839	6	6	1849	0	24
1840	11	17	1850	0	24
1841	3	20	1851	2	26
1842	0	20	1852	0	26
1843	1	21	1853	0	26
1844	1	22	1854	0	26
1845	1	23	1855	1	27
1846	0	23	1856	6	33
1847	0	23	1857	24	57
1848	1	24			

Source: Table A1 in the Appendix.

[41] Including the Liberty of Peterborough.

[42] N.B. Includes the Liberty of Peterborough. These figures slightly differ from Critchley's 'tentative' estimates, see p. 89. They also differ from the figures given in *Returns of Police Established in Each Counties or Divisions of a County in England and Wales under the Acts of 3 Vict., c.93 and 3 & 4 Vict.*, c.88 P.P XXXII, and Table VII of the appendix to the *Report of the Select Committee on Police Superannuation Funds*, 1877, P.P. XV. The differences are one or two forces in any one year and are explained by inconsistent definitions. A number of counties only partially implemented the Act, of whom, some completed the official returns where as the others didn't.

There were a number of very practical reasons why police reforms in the provinces were slow to take effect. An important deciding factor, Emsley observes, was the overall level of unrest within the country (Emsley, 1996: 40-41), and the counties in which there was much unrest tended to implement the act. However, in the counties where the threat of unrest was not so imminent, three issues came to the fore to delay implementation.[43] Firstly, the intensity of crime and disorder was not perceived in the provinces to the same degree as it was in London. Next, there was some evidence of apathy on the part of local authorities to implement the police reforms, especially in the counties where there was little unrest. The Quarter sessions either felt that a police force was unnecessary for their county or that the cost would be excessive. In some counties the Quarter sessions chose to reform their police by expanding the existing network of constables and high constables under the Parish Constables Acts of 1842 and 1850. Finally, some local authorities simply could not reach a decision because of irreconcilable differences of opinion, thus adding fuel to the Marquis of Normanby's view that it was a "serious and almost fatal error" that the new county police were not more closely under government control (Critchley, 1978: 80).

A compulsory police for England and Wales

In 1853, the Select Committee on Police in the Counties and Boroughs examined the effectiveness of policing arrangements in England and Wales and sought to rationalise the organisation of the police. It found that crime had decreased where forces complying with the police reform acts were in operation and the police had efficiently replaced the army in controlling disorder. The Committee also found that the attempts to revitalise the old system had largely failed[44] and that the County Police Act of 1839 exceeded expectations, despite its piecemeal application (*Second Report of the Select Committee on Police in the Counties and Boroughs*, 1852-53:

[43] For an interesting account of the establishment of a county police force see Smith (1990: 3-23).

[44] Although the remnants of the old system remained operative for a number of years after the County and Borough Police Act of 1856, the office of High Constable remained on the statute books until it was abolished by the High Constables Act, 1869 (32 & 33 Victoria c.47).

163-164). The Select Committee commented that "the adoption of the rural police ... has proved highly advantageous to those districts, whether tested by moral, social or economic considerations" (*idem*: 163).

The Select Committee identified the main problems with existing policing arrangements as arising from a deficiency in personnel, a fragmented organisation of police forces and an unhealthy rivalry between borough and county forces. It gave Palmerston the backing he wanted by resolving that:

> it is most desirable that legislative measures should be introduced without delay by Her Majesty's Government, rendering the adoption of an efficient police force on a uniform principle imperative throughout Great Britain (*idem*: 164).

The subsequent Police Bill of 1854 was designed to increase central control over all forces whilst preserving local control over management. All forces in small boroughs with a population of less than 20,000 people were to amalgamate with adjoining counties, and the Home Secretary's rules for the government, pay, clothing etc., for police would also become applicable to the boroughs. Most of the watch committees' powers of control over their force were to be transferred to the officer in charge.

In the face of considerable hostility from the boroughs, who felt that their powers were being threatened, Palmerston's Police Bill was rejected by Parliament. An amended version suffered the same fate the following year. In 1855 Palmerston became Prime Minister, with Sir George Grey as Home Secretary. Grey successfully introduced a third Bill in 1855 which omitted the proposal to abolish the smaller borough forces,[45] and it became the County and Borough Police Act of 1856.[46] The Act compelled all Quarter sessions to establish police forces under the County Police Act of 1839; gave county police officers the same jurisdiction in boroughs as the borough police had in the counties; empowered the Crown to appoint three Inspectors of Constabulary to assess the efficiency of each force and present annual reports of their inspections before Parliament; gave a Treasury grant to all forces certified by the Inspectorate as efficient to

[45] One of motivating factors behind the third police bill was the anticipation of thousands of displaced unemployed soldiers returning from the Crimean war.

[46] Also known as the Police in the Counties and Boroughs Act 1856.

cover one quarter of the costs of clothing and salaries;[47] forced the small boroughs, with a population under 5,000, to make a choice between amalgamating with adjoining counties or paying the full cost incurred by their force; requested all police authorities to submit annual records of crimes, committed and solved in their area, to the Home Secretary. The Select Committee's plans to impose direct central control over policing were not realised. However, the Act did give central government a co-ordinating role and laid down a constitutional basis for increasing central control over policing which was to gain importance in early twentieth century police reforms.

The first HM Inspectors of Constabulary were men with military backgrounds and some police experience. Of the three, only Maj-General Cartwright had no prior police experience. Lt.-Colonel John Woodford had previously been chief constable of the Lancashire Constabulary and Captain Edward Willis had previously been chief constable of the Manchester City Police. Both had been directly appointed to those posts. Hence it is not surprising that force inspections tended to be limited to drill and appearance (Mins. York WC, 20/6/1894). Each inspector had equal status and each took responsibility for a district of England and Wales. Their reports of the late 1850s give an insight into the state of the 237[48] or so separate police forces that existed in 1857. Each force was assessed for strength, the degree of co-operation it extended to neighbouring forces and the quality of supervision exercised over the men (Parris, 1961: 123). In the first inspection, seven of the 59 county forces were not certified as efficient. However, by the next inspection all, with the exception of Rutland with an establishment of two, were certified efficient.

The borough forces were split into three categories: large forces in boroughs with populations of over 20,000; medium forces in boroughs of between 5,000 and 20,000; and small forces in boroughs with less than 5,000. The 65 small boroughs were not entitled to a grant and were not inspected. About half of the medium sized borough forces were not certified as efficient in 1857; but by 1870 only 19 (25 per cent) were still

---

[47] This, and a number of the other proposals had previously been suggested by the Royal Commission on Establishing an Efficient Constabulary Force in the Counties of England and Wales, 1839, [169]XIX.1 but rejected either on the basis of unnecessary interference in the running of the county.

[48] See Table A2 in appendix. N.B. Includes the River Wear, River Tyne, Metropolitan and City of London forces.

found to be inefficient. All of the 57 large borough forces except one were certified as efficient. Gateshead, Sunderland and Southampton resisted the County and Borough Police Act, but they were, nevertheless, inspected and of the three only Gateshead was found to be inefficient. Sunderland and Southampton rejected the grant that was offered to them but eventually succumbed to the lure of the government purse (Critchley, 1978).

The County and Borough Police Act of 1856 laid down an organisational structure within which the administration of the police took place for the next century. The Act introduced elements of central control over policing and laid the foundations for the future standardisation of police. It also recognised the need for a chief officer in the borough forces for the first time, although it did not give them any statutory powers.

Conclusions

This analysis of the origins of the provincial police reveals just how different and separate the traditions of policing the boroughs, counties and Metropolitan police were. Moreover, it demonstrates the very different bases upon which the respective offices of chief constable stood. Perhaps the most significant common factor was the considerable autonomy which the various local government legislation[49] gave to the local authorities. Troup believed that this was the result of "practical convenience rather than from any deep regard for the principles of local autonomy" and furthermore "had the local authorities been supine their powers might at one time have been taken over by the national Government" (Troup, 1928: 11). However, the local authorities were far from supine and they jealously guarded their powers over the police with the result that the emerging organisation of policing was characterised by three common factors. Firstly, there was a lack of a coherent concept of police professionalism. Whilst many historians have used the term professional to describe the introduction of a full-time paid police, professional they were not. Although they held the office of constable, they had no common understanding of policing or of police work. In addition to possessing a fairly insecure employment status as waged employees of their police authority, they underwent little, if any, formal training other than drill and

[49] Municipal Corporations Act 1835 and County Police Act 1839.

learned their policing skills on the job. They were valued more for their low cost, physical stamina and local knowledge. Secondly, to further emphasise the non-professionalism and amateurism of the early police, the management of forces was determined by local models of management. In the boroughs, these models were imported into the mechanisms of police governance by members of the watch committees and in the counties by the individual chief constables. These local models also determined the patterns of recruitment and appointment of the local chief constable. Thirdly, local policing priorities were largely determined by the local power élites: the watch committees in the boroughs and the chief constable and Quarter sessions /Standing Joint Committee in the counties.

3 The Development of the Police Organisation in England and Wales

Introduction

Since the mid-nineteenth century, the function, structure and role of the police have continually adapted to meet the encroaching demands made by the public and local and central governments. Consequently, the agenda for change was set by the tensions which existed between local and central government. The resolution of these tensions eventually caused a shift in the balance of power over control of the police, from the police authorities to the Home Office, and also towards the chief constable.

This chapter will explore the development of the provincial police since 1856. It will highlight the shift from the local to the central and will show that the changes in the police organisation have shaped both the nature and role of the chief constable. During this period, the police organisation has been shaped by four key processes: standardisation, centralisation, unification and, more recently, corporatisation.[1] Whilst each of these processes has been present to varying degrees since the introduction of the new police, it is also the case that each can be identified with a specific period in the development of the police. Consequently, the first part of this chapter will explore the various initiatives which sought to standardise aspects of police up to the end of the First World War. Part two discusses the attempts by the Desborough Committee and the Police Act 1919 to further standardise policing whilst introducing elements of centralised control over it. Part three looks at the unification of the provincial police by the Police Act 1964 and Local Government Act 1972. Both of which abolished the borough and county police and created a single model of police organisation. Part four looks at the continued centralisation and the growing trend towards a new corporate national

---

[1] Although these discussions largely focus upon the provincial police of England and Wales, it is assumed that most of the processes described in this chapter also apply /applied to all of the main police forces in the UK.

public model of policing. The implications of these changes for the role of chief constable will be assessed in the conclusion to this chapter. Importantly, it is against this backdrop that the changes in the appointment to chief constable will be viewed in the later chapters.

Beginning to standardise the police: 1856 and 1918

From the middle of the nineteenth century onwards, the police became part of British culture. The development of what Reiner has called the "English Policing Myth" (Reiner, 1992: ch. 2) gave the police a sacred status which remained intact until the middle of the next century (Reiner, 1995: 123). One of the reasons why the police became popular was, as stated earlier, that their role broadened to that of public protector. This role included responsibilities for the emergency services (fire and ambulance) and also the inspection of a range of commercial activities such as weights and measures, gasometers, bridges. The police effectively became an all purpose emergency service upon which the local townsfolk relied when in trouble. Initially, these emergency services were staffed by constables. However, towards the turn of the century many local authorities tended to employ individuals to work in only one of the services,[2] although the overall responsibility for all three nearly always remained with the chief constable. Consequently, models of local police organisation differed considerably in terms of both their size, function and purpose.

Following the County and Borough Police Act 1856 (see chapter 2) a series of minor legislation, mainly concerned with fine tuning the provisions of the Act, sought to standardise some of the idiosyncrasies in the organisation of policing. The rationale behind these attempts to standardise the police arose, initially, out of the bureaucratic inefficiency of having so many independent police forces, many of whom, did not feel obliged to respond to the Home Office's statutory requests for information

[2] York Watch Committee, for example, employed a mechanic "to reside at the engine house, and keep the engines, hose and appliances clean and in an efficient working order, charged ready at all times for immediate use". This person was initially a police constable (York City Diary 1884/5 p. 40 para. 2), but in 1889 this requirement was lifted and the engineer did not "necessarily be a police constable" (*idem*, 1894/5 p.75 para. 2).

under s. 86 of the Municipal Corporations Act 1835.[3] There were also a number of problems arising from the varying practices which occurred within forces, to which the Home Office would have to respond.

One of these problems was the common practice of watch committees making operational decisions, such as instructing constables as to which individuals to prosecute. Typically, these orders would usually relate to the owners of licensed houses.[4] Part of the problem here was that, not only did the legislation give such wide ranging powers to the local authority, or chief constable in the county forces (Troup, 1928: 11), but the Home Office, whether it be the Home Secretary or Permanent under-secretary, did not appear to have particularly strong views about the police until the turn of the century. In fact, successive Home Secretaries seemed reluctant to incur the formidable, political, wrath of the MPs who represented the many boroughs with independent forces. In addition, officials lacked an independence of thought and were reluctant to engage without guidance from their political masters (Pellew, 1982: 5-33). Parris observed that although Home Secretaries were guided by a number of understood principles as to the role of the police in society (for example, that they should not normally carry firearms),[5] there is no evidence that any of the Home Secretaries between 1856 and 1870 had many ideas as to the way that the police should develop (1961: 235). What was certain though, was that the Home Office, initially inspired by Maj-General Cartwright, one of the first Inspectors of Constabulary, clearly wanted to reduce the number of independent provincial police forces by amalgamating them with the county forces (Cowley, 1996: 26). But, no Home Secretary appears to have

---

[3] The Home Office were constantly frustrated by the reluctance of many forces to respond to their requests for statistics and information about their composition and activities (HO 158/1 March 5 1855). The many annotations to the files (HO 45 and HO 158) at the Public Record Office illustrate this point.

[4] HO 45/ 17278 - Correspondence between the Magistrates and Watch Committee of Devonport and the Home Secretary, as to the powers of the Watch Committee in the Control of Borough Constables, with a Case and Opinion of the Law Officers (Campbell, Attorney, Wilde, Solicitor, 1840), and a Case and Opinion of the Solicitor-General (Thesinger) and Mr Greenwood (1844). A similar issue arose in Norwich see *Reports of the Select Committee on Police*, (1st Report) HC 1852-1853, 603; (2nd report) HC 1852-1853, 715. Parris (1960: 251) and Critchley (1978: 67n) also cites the case of Newport (HO 43/63). This issue re-emerged in 1895 in Devonport and also in Southampton in 1901 (HO 45/ 17278).

[5] HO 45 OS7487 (Parris, 1961: n31).

made any determined effort to persuade them all to take this step (Parris, 1961: 235). The willingness of the Home Office to yield to the Parliamentary pressure exerted by the MPs is most apparent during the discussion over the Police Expenses Act 1874. This legislation increased the Treasury grant to cover half the costs of pay and clothing but, not surprisingly, failed to reduce the number of smaller boroughs.

The Home Office managed to make some headway on reducing the numbers of very small forces three years later, when the Municipal Corporations (New Charters) Act 1877 prohibited boroughs with populations of under 20,000 from forming new police forces. The main reason was that the representatives of the small boroughs were only concerned with protecting their existing interests, so they did not object so strongly to the new provisions. The debate over the small borough forces continued until the Local Government Act 1888 forced all boroughs with populations of less than 20,000 to amalgamate with their adjoining county force. The number of independent borough forces fell from 220 to 181,[6] although the overall figure rose again slightly to 185 by the First World War as new boroughs were created. Figure 1 (earlier) and Tables A1 and A2 in the Appendix, clearly chart the effects of the County and Borough Police Act 1856, the Local Government Act 1888, and other legislation, upon the annual number of independent forces.

By the 1890s, strong personalities like Edward Troup, later Sir Edward Troup, had joined the Home Office through the civil service open competition and were starting to make their strong views about policing known. Troup was a particularly important influence in the Home Office from around the turn of the century onwards. Having joined in 1880, he rose to become Permanent Under-Secretary of State in 1908 where he remained until 1922 (Troup, 1928: 12). Troup was an important player in that his fixed views upon the constitutional position of the police provided the Home Office with a level of consistency which lasted throughout his

[6] These were forces with superintending constables. A small handful of forces were so small in size that they did not have a chief officer. These forces disappeared after the Local Government Act 1888. Also in a number of situations, one of which was Cumberland and Westmoreland, the two forces might be commanded by one chief officer. In addition, there were the independent river police forces. These observations explain the differences between Tables A1 and A2 in the Appendix.

tenure of seven Home Secretaries[7] and which he developed in his successors. For example, Troup remarked in the margins of a letter received by the Home Office from the Clerk to the West Riding Council, in which they stated their wish to seek a private member's bill to transfer powers from the standing joint committee to the county council:

> I think that it is out of the question to allow the West Riding by a private bill to alter the general law of the land and establish in their county a police authority different from that of other counties. The well established policy of Parliament has for many years been opposed to all such local departures.[8]

Realising the political implications of the situation and also the need to be diplomatic, he concluded by stating that "[i]t may, however, be well for the Secretary of State to see and hear their case before giving a negative answer to their proposal".[9] Troup believed firmly that local autonomy over policing matters had been taken too far, and he deplored the "ignorant or meddling watch committees of the smaller boroughs". Furthermore, he claimed that only those watch committees of the "greater and stronger municipalities" could be relied upon to recognise the practical limits to their own jurisdictions (Troup, 1928: 15).

One of the products of the quiet revolution at the Home Office was the Police Act 1890. It was an important piece of legislation, which gave police officers the right to a pension after twenty-five years' service, or after fifteen years' service and with discharge on medical grounds. This was a significant development in the autonomy of the police officer, because prior to the Act, the decision to award a pension rested with the chief constable in the counties and the watch committee in the boroughs. Until the Act, pensions were sometimes denied to police officers, even though they may have contributed to the force superannuation fund throughout their working life. The pension provisions also increased the autonomy of the chief constables, particularly in the boroughs as it also gave them the right to a pension for the first time. This had the effect of allowing many of the older chiefs to retire: some had remained in office

---

[7] Gladstone 1905, Churchill 1910, Mackenna 1911, Simon 1915, Samuel 1915, Cave 1915, and Shortt 1919.

[8] HO 45 10348/145030/5 - September 12 1907.

[9] HO 45 10348/145030/5 - September 12 1907.

until their late 80s. What is more important is that it removed one of the watch committees' key instruments of control which they used to secure compliance from their chief officer. It is, therefore, no coincidence that the numbers of disputes between chief officers and their watch committees increased after the Act's passing.[10] One of the drawbacks with the 1890 arrangements was that they did not solve the problems created by the existence of different police pension funds. Each force had its own pension fund and transfer arrangements did not yet exist, thus discouraging the transfer of personnel between forces and the resulting exchange of ideas and practice.

Another function of the Police Act 1890 was to introduce a facility for providing mutual aid between police forces in times of emergency. It was a provision that was to gain renewed importance during the Miners' Strikes of the 1970s and 1980s. If a police force was found to be understaffed during an emergency situation, such as a public disorder, then a chief officer could call upon the chief officer of another force to provide reinforcements.[11] Critchley seemed surprised that by 1908 only sixty of the 200 or so forces had entered into such agreements (1978: 179). However, Morgan (1987) suggests that this number of agreements was much more significant than Critchley implies, not only because of their overall impact upon the quelling of disturbances but also because they were practical examples of the principle of mutual assistance between police forces.

An equally important event in police history was the debate leading up to the Police Weekly Rest Day Act of 1910. Until 1910, being a police officer was a seven-day-a-week occupation and, although most constables were given a day off every one or two weeks, leave was granted at the discretion of the chief constable. The Police Weekly Rest Day Act of 1910 granted police officers a statutory weekly rest day. It was the evidence that was presented to the Select Committee on the Police Weekly Rest Day Bill in 1908 that was, perhaps, more important in the long-term as the Act itself. It was the first time that policing issues, normally the domain of the individual chief constable or police authority, were discussed before

---

[10] These were disputes of all kinds but mainly related to the watch committee attempting to exercise operational policing functions. Typically, they would involve the licensing of public houses.

[11] See HO 158/6-8 for copies of the agreements. Also provided to chief officers were lists of forces that they could draw upon, plus some guidance on how to go about it.

Parliament. This was also the year when Troup became Under-Secretary for State at the Home Office. Whilst responding to a question from the floor of the House, the Home Secretary displayed considerable ignorance of the occupational or social origins of the chief constables of England and Wales. Furthermore, the evidence later presented to the select committee illustrated, for perhaps the first time, the high degree of discontent amongst police officers; discontent that was to spill over at the end of the First World War (Critchley, 1978: 171).

During the course of its deliberations, the Select Committee on the Police Weekly Rest Day questioned the methods by which chief officers were recruited (see chapters 4 and 6). In taking evidence, the Select Committee became aware of the manner by which chief officers dominated both the lives of the persons under their command and also their families. It will be remembered from the earlier discussion that the architects of British policing emphasised the importance of rigidly controlling the constable's private life. This was so as to diffuse the opposition that accompanied the introduction of the new police (Reiner, 1995: 123).[12] Whilst this opposition had long disappeared, the rigid control remained, partly to prevent scandals that might undermine the legitimacy of the police and partly through tradition. The chief constables, particularly those county chiefs with military backgrounds, were used to exerting such a high degree of control over their subordinates. Of particular concern to the Committee was the discretionary manner by which chief officers allocated rest days and it was suggested by the editor of the *Police Review*[13], John Kempster, that chief officers did not understand the needs of their men because they were removed from them, both socially and occupationally. The Select Committee heard that two major issues were the cause of

---

[12] A major bone of contention was the requirement in most forces for constables to apply to their chief constable for permission to marry. In 1899 the chief constable of Surrey further insisted that applications should be accompanied by "a recommendation or testimonial from a clergyman or a responsible person, who can guarantee the respectability of the woman the constable intends to make his wife". Such a requirement was practised until the 1970s in some forces in order to identify any potential conflicts of interest. In the Surrey example, taken from A short centenary of the Surrey Constabulary, 1951 (see Critchley, 1978: 174/fn 43) the chief constable was imposing his own moral view of the world upon his constables.

[13] It was initially called the *Police Review and Parade Gossip: Organ of the British Constabulary* and was later shortened to the *Police Review and Parade Gossip* then to *Police Review.*

discontent amongst the lower ranks. First, no formal mechanisms existed to enable police officers to express their grievances. All existing channels relied on the judgement of the very people who were the source of the complaint. The *Police Review* provided police officers with probably their only means to express grievances. Founded in 1893 by Kempster, a self-styled protector of police interests, the *Police Review* provided police officers in the lower ranks with an outlet to "ventilate their troubles" (1893: 171). Kempster rarely missed an opportunity to speak up on behalf of the interests of police officers. Second, as stated earlier, central government did not take a particularly strong stance over policing policy, especially on the question of rest days and had made no attempt to find out the views of police officers. It also had little interest in the problems of the police and had even reduced the number of HM Inspectors of Constabulary from three to two. Within the Houses of Parliament few members were willing to champion the police cause, with the result that the police remained fairly low on the political agenda.[14]

By the end of the First World War, grievances over leadership and representation were brought to a head by the extra demands placed upon policing by the First World War. First, the number of laws that required police intervention was increasing and placing many new duties upon the police. Between 1900 and 1908, for example, sixteen such laws were passed.[15] Secondly, the incidence of public unrest around the turn of the century placed many new demands on police resources. The increase in the number of suffragettes who were arrested following demonstrations highlighted a general lack of provision for dealing with women offenders. Furthermore, the first decades of the century had also been witness to a series of industrial strikes. The Miners' Strike of 1910 was the most remembered of these strikes, because of the infamous Tonypandy Riot where the police, supported by the army, were used to quell the disorders. Thirdly, the rising popularity of the automobile created logistic problems for a foot-patrol based policing system by placing extra demands on police resources to enforce traffic regulations and match the mobility of

---

[14] Policing did, however, feature quite regularly on the political agenda, particularly with regard to riots. See Morgan (1987).

[15] It was a small number when compared with the large number of laws requiring police intervention that were passed in later decades. Between 1960 and 1976, 160 laws were passed that required the intervention of the police (Whittaker, 1978).

motorised criminals (Critchley, 1978: 176). It also brought the police into contact, and conflict, with the middle and upper classes for the first time as they were the only people who could afford such luxuries.[16] Finally, the (First World) War-time emergency powers placed many new duties upon the shoulders of the police, such as arresting aliens, performing air-raid duties, guarding vulnerable locations, and enforcing lighting restrictions. These additional duties were not popular and forced war-time police officers to work longer hours and sacrifice their rest days and holidays. Moreover, many regular police officers had left their forces to join the war effort and created a personnel shortage and extra workloads for those who were left (*Police Review,* 1915: 633). The war also enticed a number of (mainly county) chief constables back to their old regiments, leaving their forces without proper leadership. The *Police Review* could not resist the temptation, in keeping with its internal recruitment campaign (see later), to enquire as to whether or not chief constables were necessary. Their proposition was based upon the mischievous observation that most of the forces which had lost their chief constables to the war effort ran perfectly well without them (1918: 229).

Each complaint arose out of the inadequacy of the police organisation to deal with the rising demands made of it since the latter half of the previous century. The manner in which policing in England and Wales was organised was the root cause of most of the problems that were experienced by police forces. Little communication and no co-ordination existed between borough, county and the Metropolitan forces. It was only during wartime that a serious effort was made by the Home Office to co-ordinate the activities of borough and county police forces through a series of chief constables' district conferences. The chief constables' conferences were the first occasion that borough and county chief constables had met within an official framework to exchange views and opinions (*Report three of the Committee of Inquiry on the Police, 1979*, Appendix II: 106-109). Previously, both borough and county chief constables' associations had existed since 1858 and 1896 respectively, to encourage social intercourse between chief constables (*idem*: 106. para 1). Little more than gentlemens' clubs, they were nevertheless forums for chief officers to meet and share ideas and experiences. However, little communication took place between

[16] Punch cartoons regularly featured the poorly educated police officer in encounters with the motoring upper classes.

the two bodies as the county chief constables regarded the borough chiefs as their inferiors.[17]

Before continuing, it is worth exploring the separation of the two bodies in further detail, because this division was not just based upon differences of opinion, it was a manifestation of the different social status of the individuals within each group. The issue of separate identities came to a head in the late 1890s when the Home Office decided to end any confusion over their title by referring to them as the chief constable of [their city or borough] (see chapter 2 and also later). Ever conscious of their status, the formal adoption of the title of chief constable by borough chief officers did not go down well with the county chief constables, who sought to further differentiate themselves from their opposite numbers. Once that strategy failed, they then sought to make themselves appear different and, under the aegis of the County Chief Constables' Association, Captain E. Showers, the chief constable of Essex, commissioned a uniform design that would be appropriate for their station.[18] Whilst borough chief constables usually wore a uniform based upon that of a superintendent, there was no uniform specified for a county chief constable to wear, either for everyday wear or for dress occasions.[19] Most would not wear a police uniform, other than upon dress occasions, where it tended to be either their own design, or an adaptation of their predecessor's.

The new uniform, (see illustration) was a collaborative effort between the chief constables and King Edward, who suggested a number of small changes to the design. It was mainly intended for dress occasions and was designed to accord with court protocol, along the lines of the uniform worn by the assistant commissioners of the Metropolitan police. Although it was subsequently adopted by a number of county chief constables, it was, however, extremely expensive to make and some county police authorities either simply refused to pay for them, or asked the Home Office for increased resources to cover the cost. The Home Office did not pay the cost, and in 1913 a circular informed county chief constables that the

---

[17] See for example the tone of the acrimonious exchange between Col. Anson the Chief Constable of Staffordshire and David Webster, Chief Constable of Wolverhampton (*Police Review* 1922: 8).

[18] See the correspondence on Chief Constables uniforms 1901-1908 in HO 45 B36765.

[19] Henry Knight, chief constable of the small Beverley force between 1870 and 1877, is reputed to have designed his own uniform which cost £50 to make. At the time, this was approximately equal to the salary of a constable.

uniform was optional.[20] The debate over chief constables' uniforms also revealed the hierarchical nature of each group of chief constables, as the chiefs of the larger borough and county forces also wanted their own uniforms to differentiate them from their colleagues in the smaller forces.[21]

The county chief constables' new uniform (HO 45/B36765)

The formation of the chief constables' conferences also paved the way for the Home Office to adopt a new role as: "a general clearing house for the exchange of ideas and experiences and to make its contribution to fostering the well being and sense of common purpose that invests the whole police service" (Critchley, 1978: 183).[22] However, this role was short-lived as any co-operation between the two associations ceased once the First World War ended, although the district conferences did continue as the recognised channel for collective representations from chief officers, both with regard to their executive duties, on pay and conditions of service and also for the election of the representatives to serve on the Police Council created by Desborough (*Report three of the Committee of Inquiry on the Police, 1979*: Appendix II: 106, para. 4). The two groups of chief constables did not meet together again in an official capacity until 1948, when the Oaksey Committee refused to receive separate representations. Critchley succinctly described the organisation of policing in the first part of this century.

> The police institution on the eve of the First World War was still a collection of Victorian bric-a-brac. There remained fifty forces with a strength of fewer than fifty men. Little co-operation existed, and there were no common standards of pay and other conditions of service. Foot patrolling was the basis

[20] See the correspondence on chief constables' uniforms 1908-1919 in HO 45 10689/228489. Particularly HO 45 10689/228489/6: "[t]he existing uniform designed by the chief constables and approved by the King is felt to have been designed on far too magnificent and expensive a scale".

[21] Note dated 20/3/13 (HO 45 10689/228489).

[22] Critchley quoting Sir Frank Newsham.

of all good police work, though bicycles were appearing in the 1890s and senior officers toured their area by horse and trap (Critchley, 1978: 176).

The policing crisis at the end of the First World War was brought to a head in 1918 and 1919 by two police strikes. This unrest within the police was instrumental in bringing about police reforms and driving future policing policy. In 1916 an unofficial police officers' union, the National Union of Police and Prison Workers, was formed. Initially a London-based organisation, the Police Union made several demands of the government but received little response. The attitudes of government and police management were negative and dismissive, not surprisingly, at a time when the government were engaged in a systematic campaign of discrediting labour related organisations as Communist revolutionaries (Weinberger, 1986: 9; Lustgarten, 1986: 44). On Tuesday, 27th August 1918, the Police Union threatened strike action unless the Home Secretary increased police pay, reinstated a sacked member and officially recognised the union by midnight the following day. The demands were not met and almost 6,000 police officers, mostly Metropolitan, came out on strike. The strike was effective in so far as it brought the issues to a head and forced the Government to respond. Although it could be argued that they were bought off with the promise of a pay rise for the Metropolitan police and a half promise to recognise the Police Union once the war was over, the promises were lost when the Commissioner of the Metropolitan Police became a scapegoat and was forced to resign. At the end of the First World War, the Police Union was not officially recognised, as previously promised, and instead a representative board of all police ranks, with direct access to the commissioner, was proposed. Some months later, at the end of July 1919, the Police Union, fighting for survival, called a second strike to which 2,364 men from seven forces responded. The strike was a failure, it lasted 24 hours and received little support from other unions. Chief officers were merciless and dismissed the strikers, leaving them without hope of reinstatement. Perhaps the most significant aspect of this episode was the fact that, once again, the problems of the police which led to the strike, were perceived, in part, as being related to the quality of senior officers.

The centralisation of police policy: The Desborough Committee

The general unrest that existed within the police, during and following the First World War, was instrumental in bringing about the appointment of a committee, chaired by Lord Desborough, in March 1919 to advise the Home Secretary on police pay and conditions of service. Its official brief was to consider: "and report whether any, and what, changes should be made in the method of recruiting for, the conditions of service of, and the rates of pay, pensions and allowances of the police forces of England, Wales and Scotland".[23] The urgency of the matter was apparent in the personal note by the Home Secretary to Lord Desborough. Edward Shortt stated that he was "desirable that the Committee should report at as early a date as possible and for that reason should meet frequently".[24] Towards the middle of May 1919, the Committee indicated to the Home Secretary that it would be recommending a substantial rise in pay, to be standardised throughout all forces and a mechanism through which representations could be made to the Home Secretary. In July 1919, the Home Secretary pre-empted the Committee's report by introducing a Police Bill that would, amongst other things, legislate to prevent police officers from joining a trade union and to set up an alternative form of representation that would not take the form of a union. Prompted by fears of Bolshevism within the police ranks, the Bill became the Police Act of 1919 the following month. It prohibited police officers from entering into any trade union activity and proposed the formation of a Police Federation to represent the interests of the ranks of inspector and below (ss. 1-3). In addition, a Police Council was to act as a consultative body for the Home Secretary on police matters (s. 4(2)) and finally, the Home Secretary was to be given the power to regulate police pay and conditions of service of all police officers (s. 4(1)). It was the latter proposal that was to have an important and lasting effect on the relationship between the Home Office, police authority and the police. Most of the Desborough Committee's recommendations were subsequently enforced through these regulations.

---

[23] HO 45 /15605, minute signed by Edward Shortt, dated March 1 1919. Also to be found in the front of the *Report of the Committee on the Police Service of England, Wales and Scotland*, pt. 1, 1920).

[24] Letter from Edward Shortt, Home Secretary to Lord Desborough, KCVO, dated February 21, 1919 (HO 45/15605).

The Desborough Committee's first report, published in July 1919, recommended that police pay and conditions of service should be improved, standardised and centrally determined by the Home Secretary. It also recommended a substantial increase in police pay, and for the first time since the Metropolitan Police Act of 1829, police pay ceased to be comparable with that of an agricultural labourer. The Committee's second report, published in January 1920, made recommendations on police recruitment, training, promotion, discipline, control over policing, the merging of small borough forces and the appointment of chief constables.[25]

The Desborough Committee's recommendations (see chapter 6) symbolised a change in the official perception of policing towards the idea of a standardised police service. It also symbolised the beginning of the decline of the effective powers of police authorities and an increase in the respective powers of the Home Secretary and chief constables. The Committee sought to standardise, and centralise, many aspects of the police, a process which effectively led to a decrease in the powers of the police authority. Rather ironically, it had previously rejected, on the grounds that it would prejudice the intimate relations between the police and their localities, a suggestion made during the hearing of evidence, that the police should become a national police force. Perhaps the greater irony was that these views were at the centre of the debates that took place three-quarters of a century later, during the early 1990s, over the reform of the police (see later). The reforms proposed by the Desborough Committee created four groups of influential legal and bureaucratic mechanisms which altered the balance of what later became known as the tripartite relationship.

An increase in the role of the Home Office in formulating central policing policy. The Police Act 1919 extended the Home Secretary's powers to regulate the pay and conditions of service of the borough police. The Home Secretary's influence therefore increased considerably through his ability to make rules and regulate police pay and conditions for the whole

[25] For a more detailed overview of the Desborough Committee report see Critchley (1978: 190-198) and Morgan (1987: 84-87).

of the police.[26] These powers included prescribing the conditions upon which officers were lent from one force to another. The increase in the Home Secretary's powers was augmented by a rise in the Treasury grant to cover one half of all policing costs and by the introduction of a permanent police department at the Home Office to help carry out the new duties more effectively. To make the inspection of forces more effective, the number of HM Inspectors of Constabulary was restored to their previous strength of three.

The real increase in the influence of the Home Office arose as the direct result of the quiet revolution that had taken place in the Home Office since the late 1880s (*supra*). Not only did the Home Office now have a clarity of vision about the role of the police, this had existed independently of Desborough for some time because of Troup and his colleagues, but the use of rules and regulations was made even more effective by the increased use of the circular. The Home Office circular had been used regularly since the 1830s, but its use had proliferated during Troup's ascendancy within the Home Office.[27] Initially, they were used to suggest good practice or to inform, but after the First World War and notably after the Desborough Committee, the circulars became much more formal and assertive. Furthermore, they were a device which increased the influence of the Home Secretary and Home Office over the police to this day. Importantly, circulars are an interesting form of regulation in public law. They are sometimes referred to as quasi-legislation (Ganz, 1987), because they act as though they are legislation, even thought they are technically not subordinate legislation and are therefore not subject to Parliamentary scrutiny (Lustgarten, 1986: 105).

A revision of the philosophy towards police personnel. The Desborough Committee's greatest impact, from the point of view of this study, was its revision of the police personnel structure. It envisaged that a new type of police officer, a "scientifically" trained police officer, would staff the new integrated police service (*Police Review*, 1919: 181). Furthermore, the managers of the new style police service would have extensive experience as professional police officers and, preferably, have served as constable.

---

[26] The Police Regulations of the 20th August 1920 made by the Secretary of State under section 4 of the Police Act 1919 (Statutory Rules and Orders 1920, No. 1484).

[27] See HO 158/ 14-21.

This idea of internal recruitment had gained momentum during the past two decades and is the focus for the discussion in later chapters. At the time, a number of borough, and almost all county chief constables, were recruited directly from outside the police. The Desborough Committee, rather controversially, proposed that all persons who were appointed as chief constable should have experience of serving in a police force, thus threatening the traditional independence of the police authorities to appoint whoever they wanted as chief constable (see chapter 6).

A change in the position of borough chief constables. Whilst the proposal to place borough chief constables on a similar statutory footing to that of county chief constables failed because of opposition from local municipal authorities (Morgan, 1982: 87), their position was nevertheless strengthened by the increased influence of the Home Office over the police and the formalisation of the title of chief constable for all borough chief officers. Lustgarten quite rightly argues that the formalisation of this policy increased substantially the symbolic appearance of the post of borough chief officer (Lustgarten, 1986: 44), a point which can be demonstrated by the fact that the practice of referring to borough chief officers as chief constable, had by the turn of the century, become common practice. The Home Office had, since 1897, adopted the policy of referring to borough chief officers as "Chief Constable, Borough [or City] Police"[28] and by this time all borough chief officers with the exception of the Liverpool head constable were usually referred to as chief constable.

The formal position of the borough chief officers continued to become more independent through the continued delegation of powers to them by the watch committee over the day to day running of the police. It was also strengthened by improved links between the borough chief constables and the Home Office via the Chief Constables, Boroughs and Cities Association and the Police Council. The statutory independence of the borough chief constable was further increased by the Police (Appeals) Act 1927, which made the decision of the Police Authority to dismiss a chief constable subject to the approval of the Home Secretary (*Police Review* 1942: 295).

---

[28] HO 45 X26632/6. Memorandum from H.B. Simpson to the Assistant Under-Secretary. C.S. Murdoch, initialled by all officials and copies circulated to departments D, P and J. Dated March 22, 1897.

The development of police representative machinery. The development of police representative machinery during the 1920s introduced a forum through which the ideas and views of police officers on policing could be voiced. Whilst the Police Act prevented police officers from joining a trade union, it did provide for the formation of organisations to represent the interests of police officers on the negotiating table. The Police Council, replaced in 1964 by the Police Advisory Board, was a central advisory body to the Home Secretary and comprised of representatives of police authorities and all ranks of the police. It was organised by the Police Department of the Home Office and was chaired by either the Home Secretary or a senior Home Office official. In Council, the ranks of inspector and below were represented by the Police Federation, superintendents by the Superintendents' Association and the chief constables, including assistant and deputy, by the Association of Chief Police Officers (ACPO). Before 1947, the borough and county chief constables were represented by separate associations: the Borough and County Chief Constables' associations (see earlier). The new framework for representation also allowed an exchange of ideas on policing to take place between the ranks as well as creating the potential for the development of informal contacts between police forces. The fact that the police did not align themselves with the labour movement during the general strike of 1926, as they had in the strikes of 1918 and 1919, is taken as a measure of the success of the representative framework, and indeed of the effectiveness of the Desborough Committee's recommendations in general.

These mechanisms amounted to an early incarnation of what Rhodes (1996: 658) has referred to as a policy community. Through careful and strategic management this network effectively by-passed the perceived, undesirable aspects of local government. These undesirable aspects of local government were described by Troup as "undue interference by an ignorant or meddling Watch Committee" (1928: 15). Troup believed the relationship between central and local government was "in practice a successful reconciliation of the two principles of central guidance and control and of local initiative and responsibility" (1928: 18). Of particular interest is the fact that while all efforts had been aimed at eroding the position of the borough authorities, the militaristic nature of the county forces remained untouched (Morgan, 1987: 87). Furthermore, it is established later that the county police authorities were successful in resisting central attempts to influence the appointment of chief constables (see later chapters).

In order to support the new centralised approach towards policing policy, legal theory was introduced (Morgan, 1987: 87) into the debate over the constitutional position of the police. The legal officers of the Home Office had on a number of occasions been called to decide upon the legal position of the borough chief constable,[29] and from the time of Desborough onwards, the Home Office began to "popularise the theme that the keeping of the King's Peace was a 'Royal prerogative as old as the monarchy itself'" (Morgan, 1987: 87).[30] This ideology of constabulary independence was to be later strengthened by caselaw (see Lustgarten, 1986: 62).

The Inter-War Years

The years between the two World Wars were an important, but somewhat under-documented, period in the development of the police. Lustgarten notes that "unlike the Victorian period, which has yielded a rich historical literature, the inter-war years have largely remained uncharted territory. An important study begs to be written" (1986: 43). They were a period during which the recommendations of the Desborough Committee, through the Police Act 1919, effectively placed existing practices on a statutory footing and brought police legislation up to date. In doing so, they provided a framework for the creation of a uniform police service with a high degree of central co-ordination.

During the late 1920s and early 1930s, a number of concerns were voiced publicly about the quality of senior police officers. For example, in the late 1920s a series of scandals brought about a crisis of confidence in

---

[29] With regard to Devonport, Newport, Norwich and Southampton in 1901 See HO 45/17278 in the above notes.

[30] See the evidence of Leonard Dunning to the Desborough Committee. *Report of the Committee on the Police Service of England, Wales and Scotland*. Part II, p. 665 (Morgan, 1987: 88, fn 46).

the police, and there were a number of quite widely publicised cases involving disputes between chief constables and their police authorities. In the first, the Monmouthshire Standing Joint Committee tried, unsuccessfully, to dismiss its autocratic (county) chief constable, Victor Bosanquet, because he refused to give an undertaking to Labour members of the Standing Joint Committee that he would not proceed with the further prosecution of miners' leaders, even though their cases had already been heard and dismissed by the magistrates (*Police Review*, 1926: 418, 531). The Home Secretary intervened and threatened to stop the Treasury grant unless Bosanquet was reinstated. Rather than face the possibility of the Treasury grant being withdrawn, the standing joint committee duly reinstated Bosanquet as chief constable. In the second case, the chief constable of the borough of St Helens, A.R. Ellerington, was asked to retire by the watch committee after allegedly insulting one of its members who had attempted to talk with a constable regarding a dispute with Ellerington's senior officers (*Police Review*, 1927: 780). Ellerington refused to retire and an inquiry under the Police Appeals Act 1927 led the Home Secretary to reinstate him (*Police Review*, 1927: 827).

A year or so later, the Royal Commission on Police Powers and Procedures was appointed in the aftermath of the Savidge case when Irene Savidge and Sir Leo Money were arrested in Hyde Park after the gates had been closed (*Royal Commission on Police Powers and Procedures*, 1928-1929: 127). Allegations were later made in Parliament that Ms Savidge had been mistreated by the police whilst she was under arrest. An inquiry was set up and failed to agree. The resulting public outcry led to a Royal Commission being appointed (*idem*). The Royal Commission made recommendations about police powers and procedures. Whilst these recommendations are not particularly relevant here, the Commission did venture beyond its brief to discuss the appointment of chief officers (see chapter 4). Three years later, in 1932, the question of whether the small borough forces should be merged was put to the Select Committee on the Amalgamation of Police Forces. All recent attempts to force the amalgamation of the smaller borough forces had failed.[31] In common with the Royal Commission of 1929, the 1932 Select Committee also went beyond its brief to comment upon the qualities that chief constables should

[31] The Police Act 1919 did, however, provide for the voluntary amalgamation of the smaller borough forces. Only eight took that course during the 1920s and 1930s.

possess; another point that is developed later. It was quite common practice whenever police practices became problematic to blame the problem on the quality of police management. The structure of the police organisation was not seriously reviewed until the 1960 Royal Commission on the Police, and even then the outcome was muted.

The impact of the Second World War upon the police

The Desborough Committee's ambitions to create a framework for increasing the standardisation of many aspects of police work were not quickly realised, because the legislators had underestimated the extent of local government resistance (see chapter 6), particularly with regard to the proposals for the appointment of chief constables. This resistance remained until the regulations[32] of the Emergency Powers (Defence) Act 1939 gave the Home Secretary control over provincial chief constables and police authorities "in the interests of public safety, the defence of the realm, the maintenance of public order and the efficient prosecution of war". Regulation 39(1), for example, specifically empowered the Home Secretary to instruct chief officers to assist other police forces where necessary. By increasing central control over the police, the Defence Regulations acted as the catalyst for a number of organisational and administrative changes.

More specifically, the regulations resulted in two significant changes to the tripartite relationship. Firstly, they led to the weakening of the traditional powers held by local police authorities over the police and permanently changed the relationship between local and central government, especially after the Defence (Amalgamation of Police Forces) Regulations 1942 made under Orders in Council, under the Emergency Powers (Defence) Acts 1939 and 1940, empowered the Home Secretary to amalgamate forces if necessary "for facilitating naval, military or air operations" (Critchley, 1978: 241).[33] Secondly, the war-time Defence Regulations also, formally, strengthened the link between the Home Secretary and the chief constables, increasing the power of the former over

[32] Regulation 39 of The Defence (General) Regulations, 1939(b) (Statutory Rules and Orders, No. 927).
[33] Rescinded by the s. 13, Police Act 1946.

the latter. This also resulted from the 1942 Orders in Council which enabled the Home Secretary to retire chief constables in the interests of efficiency if necessary (*Police Review*, 1942: 98). So, the war-time regulations not only reinforced the concept of a nationally co-ordinated police service, but they also changed the culture which underpinned the bureaucracy of policing. Consequently, they resulted in new working practices which reduced the possibility of returning to the pre-war arrangements. Evidence of this development can be found in the tone of the Home Office circulars for this period[34] which seek to direct, rather than suggest, as was the case with those issued during the First World War. Moreover, both the volume of circulars and also the same directing tone continued after the war.

It is likely that these regulations might not have had such a permanent impact, had the two war-time Home Secretaries, Sir John Anderson[35] and Herbert Morrison, not been sympathetically minded towards both the police viewpoint and also the Home Office's bureaucratically driven centralising philosophy. Anderson, Home Secretary between September 1939 and October 1940, had succeeded Troup in 1922 as Permanent Under-Secretary at the Home Office, and continued the philosophy which had been established during Troup's tenure of office whereby the Home Office were to take on a "steering", policy, role whilst leaving the "rowing" to the local authorities who had previously performed both functions (Troup, 1928).[36] Morrison, who held the office between October 1940 and May 1945 was, in contrast to many of his predecessors, the son of a police officer.[37]

In 1944, Morrison set up a committee to discuss the post-war reconstruction of the police service and prepare it to deal with the

---

[34] See HO 158 files 31-61.

[35] Later 1st Viscount Waverley.

[36] Troup clearly distinguished between these functions (1926 and 1928), although he did not use Osborne and Gaebler's (1992) terminology.

[37] Also very significant during this period was the role played by Sir Arthur Dixon, who had been secretary to the Desborough Committee and was in charge of the Home Office police department during the inter-war years. Dixon had developed the police department along the steering philosophy. He was an autocrat and "did not like troubling ministers" for which we can read: if they did not agree with his view. Sir Philip Allen summed up Dixon by citing a verse by Ross: "Arthur Lewis Dixon, Said the plural of fox was vixen, And in spite of all protestations, Put it in the police regulations" (Allen, 1982: 28).

problems of policing a post-war society. The Post-War Reconstruction Committee was composed of representatives of the chief constables and Home Office officials and was briefed to look into the organisation of local police forces; particularly with regard to training, promotion, management, buildings and communications. The Committee produced four reports which formed the basis for the Police Act of 1946. The first considered higher training and recommended that a new police college be created to improve the quality of command. The remainder dealt with the organisation of the police, buildings and welfare, the responsibilities of the higher ranks and the organisation of the special constabulary. These proposals formed the basis of future legislation.

One of the central themes in the discussion leading up to the Police Act 1946 was the recurring question of what to do with the smaller independent borough forces. All previous attempts to reduce the number of borough forces, with the exception of the Local Government Act of 1888, had been unsuccessful. However, the comparative ease by which the Police Act 1946 passed through Parliament clearly indicates the shift of the balance of power within the central /local divide. Under the 1946 Act, all of the existing 47 non-county borough forces, with the exception of Peterborough,[38] were forced to amalgamate with their local county force. This reduced the overall number of provincial police forces, and chief constables, from 181 in 1939 to 124 in 1960 (see Figure 1 and Table A1 in the Appendix). The passing of the Police Act of 1946 was mainly due to the large Labour majority in Parliament. However, its path was eased by the decrease in the powers of provincial local government authorities that arose from the exercise of the war-time regulations and also the precedent created by the forced amalgamation of borough forces in seven counties during war-time helped to reduce opposition. The principal sacrifices during the subsequent amalgamations were made by the displaced chief constables, who either opted for early retirement or took reduced rank in the new force (Critchley, 1978: 241).

Whilst the Police Act of 1946 solved some of the problems that were emerging in the organisation of the police, it did little to quell the disquiet amongst police officers over pay and conditions, a scenario reminiscent of the pre-Desborough era. A pay increase was awarded in 1946 with the promise of a review in 1950, but rising inflation devalued the pay rise

[38] Peterborough had a population of over 50,000 people.

within two years. To prevent a repetition of the events of 1918 and 1919, the government brought forward the promised review and in 1948 the Oaksey Committee was appointed to:

> consider in the light of the need for the recruitment and retention of an adequate number of suitable men and women for the police forces in England, Wales and Scotland, and to report on pay, emoluments, allowances, pensions, promotion, methods of representation and negotiation, and other conditions of service (*Report of the Committee on Police Conditions of Service*, 1948-9: pt. 11: 379).

The Committee produced two reports. The first, published in April 1949, dealt with police pay, pensions and various other conditions of service. The second, produced seven months later, dealt with a variety of issues that ranged from the appointment, training, promotion and discipline of police officers, to police housing, amenities and the establishment of negotiating machinery to replace the consultative framework established by Desborough. The police did not get the increase in pay they had hoped for on the premise that a large rise would contravene the government's pay policy. Rather, the Oaksey Committee hoped that improved conditions of service and other changes in the occupation would dampen down the disquiet over pay levels. Police wages increased over the next seven years, but always fell behind the levels set by Desborough. The low level of police pay reduced the attractiveness of the police as an occupation and police forces found difficulty in finding suitable recruits to fill their vacancies. Some forces lowered their height limits in order to increase the pool of potential recruits. In 1954, the Police Council for Great Britain, whose authority had been increased by the Oaksey Committee became a negotiating body. It raised wages, but failed to keep up with inflation.

The failure of the Oaksey Committee to resolve the dispute over low pay was not the only problem faced by the police during the late 1940s and early 1950s. A noticeable divide was growing between the police and the public, especially the affluent young. New policing initiatives were designed to win back public support and re-legitimise the police - team policing methods were introduced to make policing more efficient and a national crime prevention campaign was launched. In addition, new supposedly realistic, media images of the police were being presented to the public such as George Dixon, the star of the television programme

Dixon of Dock Green. Dixon and his colleagues were modern bobbies who combined modern policing techniques with the traditional role of the police officer (Reiner, 1992: ch. 2). The programme made the public aware of the functions performed by the police and presented to the public a particular image of police work which hid both the problematic constitutional position of the police and also the inadequacy of police organisation to cope with the demands made of the police in the 1950s.

The effect of these new re-legitimisation strategies was soon negated by a series of public scandals, during the 1950s and 60s, which involved a number of chief constables. In 1956, disciplinary action was taken against the chief constable of Cardiganshire after it was alleged that his force was not being properly administered (Critchley, 1978: 270). During the following year the chief constable and other senior members of the Brighton force were charged with corruption. The chief constable was acquitted, although he was later dismissed from office, and two of his senior officers were imprisoned. His appeal against dismissal was later upheld by the House of Lords on the grounds that natural justice had not been done (*Ridge v Baldwin*). Later in that year, the chief constable of Worcester was convicted of fraud and sent to prison (Critchley, 1978: 270). These scandals, and others in the Scottish police, served to worsen relations between the police and the public by lowering public confidence in both the police and also in the office of chief constable. However, it was the constitutional implications of two further public scandals which were more influential in bringing about demands for a large-scale reform of the police.

The first case illustrated uncertainty about the constitutional position of the chief constable. It involved a dispute between the chief constable of Nottingham, Captain Aethelstan Popkess, and his watch committee. Popkess was suspended by the watch committee on the grounds that he was unfit for office. Popkess believed that some members of the city council had acted in a corrupt manner and referred the case to the Director of Public Prosecutions (DPP). The DPP advised Popkess to pursue his enquiries, and he engaged the Metropolitan Police to carry these out. On receipt of the report, the DPP decided to take no further action. The watch committee then instructed Popkess to report to them about the inquiry. Popkess refused, claiming that it was his job and not that of the watch committee to enforce the criminal law. The watch committee exercised their powers under the Municipal Corporations Act of 1835, as amended in 1882, and suspended him on the grounds that he was not fit for office. The Home Secretary intervened in the dispute and argued that the maintenance of law and order was the chief constable's responsibility and not that of the watch committee and therefore the watch committee had acted wrongly. Popkess was reinstated but retired at the end of the year. The Popkess affair illustrated the changes that had taken place over the years in the constitutional position of the police, a constitutional position that was perceived to be quite different from that envisaged in the original legislation passed a century earlier. The respective roles of the chief constable and Home Secretary in the governance of the police had gradually become more prominent, at the expense of the police authority.

The second scandal, in 1959, involved the stopping of Brian Rix, the actor, by a P.C. Eastmond for a possible motoring offence. A third party became involved and was allegedly assaulted by P.C. Eastmond. The third party sued the Metropolitan Commissioner for the assault and received damages out of court. During a House of Commons debate which followed, MPs were angered at their inability to raise questions about the police from the floor of the House. The incidents led to the appointment of the Royal Commission on the Police in 1960 whose purpose was "sufficiently wide ranging to require it to examine afresh the fundamental principles on which the service always relied" (Critchley, 1978: 267).

The unification of the provincial police: 1964 - 1973

The terms of reference of the 1960 Royal Commission on the Police were: to review the constitutional position of the police throughout Great Britain, the arrangements for their control and administration. They were to consider: the constitution and functions of local police authorities; the status and accountability of members of police forces, including chief officers of police; the relationship of the police with the public and the means of ensuring that complaints by the public against the police are effectively dealt with; and the broad principles which should govern the remuneration of the constable, having regard to the nature and extent of police duties and responsibilities and also the need to attract and retain an adequate number of recruits with proper qualifications (*Final Report of the Royal Commission on the Police*, 1962: para. 140).

The Royal Commission was the first time that the principles, organisation and constitutional position of the police had been examined publicly.[39] It was a watershed in police history as it revised many of the existing principles of policing and brought them into line with current practices. The main report was published in 1962[40] and sought to secure: a system of control over the police that achieved maximum efficiency and the best use of manpower; adequate means of bringing the police to account; and proper arrangements for dealing with complaints (*idem*). The Commission did not think that the present system achieved the first two objectives and that dissatisfaction existed with the third. Whilst it felt that no fundamental disturbance of the existing system was necessary, the Commission thought that the main problem lay with the local forces which needed to be brought under more effective central control (*idem*: para. 22).

All of the Royal Commission's recommendations were based upon three fundamental conclusions reached by the Commission about the nature of policing. Whilst it was not without its critics and controversies, for example, Hart criticised its lack of concern for particularities, its "verbiage and hollow phrases" and its excessive respect for the past (Hart, 1963; Morris, 1981: fn. 28), it became an influential document. First, the Commission decided that, constitutionally, the constable was an office whose authority is original, not delegated, and therefore exercised by virtue of the office.[41] Secondly, the Commission favoured the retention of a system of local forces but with increased central co-ordination.[42] The Commission proposed to increase the size of forces and reduce the overall number of forces to allow for a more efficient administration at local level.

---

[39] The constabulary commissioners had looked at the constitutional position of the police in 1839 (see chapter 2).

[40] There had been an interim report in 1960 to recommend an increase in pay etc.

[41] This has been debated by Marshall (1965), Jefferson and Grimshaw (1984) and Lustgarten (1986). The Royal Commission based their observation that the constable was neither a servant of the Crown nor of his police authority on examples of case law (See Lustgarten, 1986) and did not consider the occupational reality of being a police officer, the effects of bureaucratic control or occupational culture on the exercise of the powers of the constable.

[42] One of its members, Dr A.L. Goodhart, believed that a national police force would be more politically accountable and issued a memorandum of dissent which was published as part of the report.

Thirdly, and importantly, it asserted that the problem of controlling the police was the problem of controlling chief constables (discussed later).

The Royal Commission's report underpinned the Police Act 1964, which still determines the structure of the police service today, although it was consolidated by the Police Act 1996. The 1964 Act faithfully followed most of the Commission's recommendations and brought the legislation into line with existing practices. The first part dealt with the organisation of police forces and replaced the old borough and county police authorities, the standing joint and watch committees, with police authorities whose composition included two-thirds elected representatives and one-third magistrates.[43] The powers of the new police authorities were far inferior to those of their predecessors, particularly in the boroughs, where the watch committee used to exercise considerable control over their force.

The Act placed a duty upon the police authority to maintain an efficient police force for its area, but gave the authority no operational powers over the force. Whilst the police authority did retain a responsibility for appointing the senior officers, the chief, deputy[44] and assistant chief constables,[45] from a Home Office approved shortlist and also retained a power to force their chief constable to retire in the interests of efficiency, both powers also required the approval of the Home Secretary. Similarly, the Act gave the police authority the power to request a report, separate from the chief constable's annual report, on matters relating to policing in their area, but then it gave the chief constable the right to refuse such a request if he or she believed that disclosure of the information was not in the public interest. In this, the chief constable effectively became the guardian of the public's interests. In cases of stalemate between a police authority and a chief constable, the Home Secretary was to make the final decision.

Part II of the Police Act 1964 defined the functions of the Home Secretary. The Act gave the Home Secretary a duty to promote the efficiency of the police (section 28) through a new range of powers which would enable this duty to be carried out. Many of these powers were

---

[43] Elected by the Quarter sessions in the counties and local board of justices in the boroughs.

[44] This rank was abolished by the Police and Magistrates' Courts Act 1994.

[45] The latter in consultation with the chief constable.

already exercised in a limited form under the original police legislation, but the new Act widened and extended them to cover all forces. They fell into two categories: powers over the chief constable and powers to regulate the government, administration and conditions of service of the police service. Under the Police Act, the Home Secretary had, and still has, to approve a police authority's choice of chief constable[46] and can require a chief constable to retire in the interests of efficiency or suspend him /her pending the outcome of an inquiry. The Home Secretary could and still can also request a report from chief constables on policing matters, has the right to make grants for expenses incurred for police purposes and can institute a local inquiry into the policing of an area. Furthermore, the Home Secretary, as has been the practice since 1857, appoints the HM Inspectors of Constabulary who have a responsibility to report on all matters concerning the police. They inspect each police force and, once certified as efficient, its police authority then receives a treasury grant to cover two thirds of the total cost of policing for its area. The Police Act effectively rearranged the distribution of power within the tripartite arrangement of control over policing to make the Home Secretary and chief constables the dominant partners and the Police Authorities the subordinates.[47]

The most visible effects of the Police Act 1964 upon the police organisation were the force amalgamations, which reduced the number of independent provincial forces from 116 in 1965 to 44 in 1969 (see Figure 1 and Table A1). The chief constables whose jobs were reduced by the amalgamations were given immediate assistant chief constable status in the new force, but their contract ended after three months if no job was found for them in the new force. In his autobiography Robert Mark[48] described the prospects of a borough chief constable whose force was destined to be amalgamated into the county force:

> I had fondly imagined Leicester, which was then over 500 strong, to be immune but it was not to be. Oddly enough, I had earlier fought hard on a

[46] The police authority now chooses their chief constable from a Home Office approved list of candidates. See *Chief Officer Appointments in the Police Service: Guide-lines on Selection Procedures* which accompanies HOC 52/96 - Chief Officer Appointments in the Police Service, 2 December 1996.

[47] The third part of the Police Act 1964 dealt with representative organisations and the fourth dealt with complaints against the police.

[48] Later Sir Robert Mark, Commissioner of the Metropolitan Police.

> committee to prevent a shameless and dishonourable attempt by the Home Office to worsen the terms of compensation for chief constables displaced by amalgamation without ever imagining that I would be liable to benefit from our eventual victory, which led to a special section being inserted belatedly into the Police Act (Mark, 1978: 78).

Moreover, the amalgamations created a surplus of individuals who were used to their own independence:

> When the amalgamation programme was announced the bottom fell out of my world. After ten happy years' association with a force I believed to be both contented and efficient I was to go out on my ear. The county force was larger, the value of the county rate was higher, it was bound to have a majority of seats on the joint police authority and to support its own chief constable, even though he was then already entitled to retire. The prospect of serving as second in command is not attractive to anyone who has exercised command for ten years (Mark, 1978: 78).

Where a combined force was to be created, preference was given to the chief constable of the larger force to command the new force. Just as the force reorganisations were being finalised, the Local Government Act of 1972 re-defined local authority boundaries and caused a number of police areas to be redrawn and some forces to be reorganised. The Local Government Act created seven metropolitan police areas and the large city police forces that survived the first wave of amalgamations became part of the new metropolitan police forces. The overall number of independent provincial police forces fell from 44 to 41, the number that exists today.

From centralisation to police corporatisation: 1974-1996

Whilst the number of independent provincial police forces now remains the same as it did in 1974, the police organisation, the police, and indeed, police officers have undergone a number of changes. The public police model today has a somewhat contradictory nature because, not only has it become increasingly pluralistic, especially through the expansion of the private police,[49] but police policy, and also the police organisation, have

[49] Not discussed here (see Johnston, 1992).

become increasingly centralised. Furthermore, the formal levers of power over the police have also been placed in more hands, such as the customers of police services and to some extent, the reconstituted police authorities. Yet, the impact of this diversity is contestable, as we have also experienced the re-configuring and the structuring of the central police policy making process, which, in the 1990s, has shown signs of an increased corporatisation. It will be argued, that as we reach the next millennium, this corporatisation will increasingly come to mark the next era of the public police.

In the late 1970s and early 1980s, the police became an integral part of Conservative law and order policy. The increased resources, made available to the police through the Edmund Davies agreement, increased police wages and against the backdrop of rising unemployment had the effect of attracting officers from a broader social background. This contrasted with the limited social origins, mainly skilled working class (Reiner, 1978), of their predecessors. In addition to the increased resources was a series of legislation which impacted considerably upon the police by not only centralising police and police policy, but also laying the foundations for the new police corporatisation mentioned above.

The Police and Criminal Evidence Act 1984 (PACE) increased police powers over search, entry and seizure and arrest by placing existing police practices on a statutory footing, whilst simultaneously increasing the rights of the suspect against the abuse of police power. It increased police accountability by creating a new independent body to deal with police complaints - the Police Complaints Authority. More importantly, PACE impacted upon police management by transferring some supervisory roles from the ACPO ranks to inspectors and sergeants, further removing the responsibility for operational police work from the higher ranks and placing effective operational power in the hands of the middle management and front-line supervisors. It was one of a series of legislation passed in the 1980s and 1990s which sought to structure and make police decision making more transparent.

Two years later, the Public Order Act 1986 gave police officers greater control over policing unrest. At street level officers have greater powers of arrest where behaviour is unruly. The Public Order Act also gave the senior ranks greater powers to supervise public gatherings forcing them to make political decisions and increasing the political profile of the police.

The Criminal Justice Acts 1991 and 1992, whilst not addressing police organisation directly, placed increased pressure on the police role as gatekeeper to the criminal justice system by formalising contents of Home Office circular 60/1990 which encouraged the police to caution offenders and thus divert them away from the courts.

Other legislation has impacted upon the internal structure of the police organisation, some in minor ways, others more significantly. The Prosecution of Offences Act 1985 removed the power of prosecution from the police and passed it on to the independent Crown Prosecution Service. The responsibility for prosecution had previously rested with the chief constable. Police officers who prosecuted offenders did so on behalf of their chief constable. This broke the practice, conducted since the late 19th century, of the police carrying out their own prosecutions, although in practice, the police still make recommendations as to whether or not they think that a person should be prosecuted following their investigations.

During the 1990s, the Royal Commission on Criminal Justice (1993), the White Paper on Police Reform (1993) and the Sheehy Report (1993), followed by the Police and Magistrates' Courts Act 1994 (PMCA) have been the most influential engines of recent change to the police structure.[50] The PMCA compacted the rank structure by reducing the overall number of police ranks and it placed senior (ACPO rank) officers on fixed term contracts. It also restructured police authorities by almost halving their size[51] and by introducing lay representatives who are appointed locally from a Home Office approved shortlist[52] (see later).

The cumulative effect of the policy debates and the legislation has been to centralise both the police and, in the case of that legislation which

---

[50] Also of considerable importance were the influential reports of the Audit Commission (see later) and reviews of core police skills and competencies.

[51] Although the sized of police authorities varied. Most had between 30 and 40 members.

[52] Following the PMCA 1994, advertisements for lay representatives were placed locally by police authorities and centrally by the Home Office. Local police authorities drew up shortlists of a maximum of 20 and submitted the names to the Home Office who then reduced the list by half. The local police authority then selected its members from the 'short' shortlist. Although there were allegations of party political interference, it is not correct to say that these are central appointees (From correspondence with Tim Newburn, March 3 1998).

calls for the (central) issue of codes of practice, also policing policy. But, this final move towards the centralisation of police is not just legislative as it has been accompanied by an important, cultural, change in the overall philosophy, even rationale, behind police management. The urban unrest of the early to mid-1980s, combined with the Miners' Strike, led to the development and operation of the centrally controlled national reporting centre which co-ordinated policing actions nationally. Secondly, underlying the legislative changes since the late 1970s and early 1980s has been the growing influence of new public management, or new police management (Leishman *et al.*, 1995: 11). This is a social market philosophy (Loveday, 1995: 281) which seeks to make public organisations more economic, efficient and effective. It impacted upon the police through Home Office circular 114/1983 and was subsequently articulated through a series of Audit Commission reports and through the introduction of Financial Management Initiatives which have led to quite a large scale internal restructuring of police organisations. Its main impact has been to rationalise the bureaucracy of the police and has led to the centralisation of many previously local functions. Another of its impacts has been to civilianize many, and privatise a few, of the hitherto state police functions (Johnston, 1992). The combination of strict financial controls, increased consumerism and targeted resources has created a hybrid style of management which presents a service style of policing which is not only very legalistic in approach (Reiner, 1992), but is also increasingly specialised. Consequently, by the late-1980s and early 1990s, both police and policing were centralised to a point at which we had a *de facto*, although not a *de jure* national police force (Reiner, 1995).[53]

Since the early 1990s there have been four subsequent, centralising, pressures which have led to the development of what is effectively becoming a *de jure* national police force. First, was the rationalisation in the overall number of the regional crime squads following the setting up of the National Criminal Intelligence Service (NCIS) in 1991. NCIS later became defined by the Police Act 1997 (pt. I). Second, linked with the above was the creation of the, operational, National Crime Squad following the Police Act 1997 (pt. II). Third, was the broadening of the

[53] Newburn places a slightly different spin on this argument. Whilst he does not dispute the power and influence of ACPO in the 'steering' of the police, he does argue that the level of 'steering' varies from force to force (*idem*).

role of the security services by the Security Service Act 1996, which amended the Security Service Act 1989 to allow the Security Service (MI5) to gather intelligence with regard to serious crimes so as to assist the police. At the time of writing, the Foreign Office have also announced their intentions to draw upon the Intelligence Services Act 1994 in order to extend the role of Secret Intelligence Service (MI6) in order to assist the police by gathering intelligence about serious crimes:

> Our diplomatic, aid, law enforcement, and intelligence assets will all be targeted at fighting the international drugs trade. This is one of the new tasks for the Intelligence Services envisaged in the 1994 Intelligence and Services Act; now that the Cold War is over, this is a very high priority for these resources.[54]

Fourth, the increasing desirability on the part of central government during the late 1980s to have a single police voice on a range of issues relating to police and policing policy. ACPO has subsequently become the main forum for the articulation and formation of police policy (see conclusion).

An audit of changes in the police 1856-1996

Before concluding, we will first conduct a brief audit of the major changes in the organisation of the police over the past 160 years which have affected the role and nature of the office of chief constable. There are six specific trends which are of interest. First, the nature of the *police role* broadly determines the types of decisions that chief officers have to make. It also positions them within their locality. Second, the number of *independent provincial police forces* determines the overall number of individual chief constables. Third, the *number of police officers*, determines the size and complexity of the chief constable's command and also their salary. This, in turn, has influenced both the social profile of recruits for chief constable and also the degree of their mobility between forces. Fourth, the *personnel structure* of those forces, as indicated by both the pool(s) from which police officers are recruited and the principles

[54] Speech by Foreign Secretary, Robin Cook, to the Malaysia Institute of Diplomacy and Foreign Relations, Kuala Lumpur, August 28, 1997.

which underlie promotion, also determines the nature of the relationships between chief officers, their subordinates and also their colleagues. Fifth, formal and informal structures of accountability affect *chief constables' independence* from control over their decisions. They also determine the nature of their relationship with their police authority and the Home Secretary. Sixth, there is the state of the balance of power within the *tripartite relationship*, between the chief constable, the police authority and the Home Secretary /Home Office. This balance determines who is in overall control of the police. The following paragraphs summarise these broad changes that have take place in the police since their inception.

Police role. The nature of the police role determines the types of decisions that the chief officer has to make. After the introduction of the police their role expanded to include a broad range of emergency services. Their primary policing function throughout the main part of the nineteenth century was to maintain order. The role of detecting crime is a characteristic of the latter part of the century. By the First World War the police role had expanded fully, with police constables still performing the broad range of emergency services as well as maintaining order and dealing with crime. At this time, the local police also performed a range of civil functions such as inspecting weights and measures, the gas system, highways, bridges and so on. On top of these functions were the responsibilities added by the war-time situation.

During the inter-war years the police role began to narrow as many of these additional functions were shed. Whilst the chief constable tended to also be chief officer of the fire brigade, the actual tasks of fire-fighting were performed by specially employed fire officers and not constables. The same applied to the ambulance service. The inspection of weights and measures was increasingly devolved to non-police officers and so on. After the Second World War the police role continued to narrow towards the professional crime-control model of policing that we recognise today.

Force numbers. In the late 1850s there were about 230 or so independent local police forces in England and Wales. Some of these had no more than two or three constables and were forced to amalgamate with the nearest force by the Local Government Act 1888. Between 1889 and the outbreak of the Second World War the annual number of separate forces was about

180. During the Second World War, the Home Secretary, using emergency powers, forced some amalgamations, but it was the Police Act 1946 which reduced force numbers to about 120. This remained the average annual number until the Police Act 1964 and Local Government Act 1972 forced the borough, and some county forces to amalgamate to form the 41 provincial forces which exist today. These decreases in force numbers took place against a backdrop of a gradual increase in the numbers of provincial police officers.

Police numbers. A clearer picture of these changing dynamics can be obtained from Table 4, which compares the growth in the numbers of provincial police with the growth in relative force size.

Table 4: Growth in provincial police numbers and force size[55]

year	no. of forces	no. of police	increase	mean force size	increase
1850	190	7.5k	0%	39	0%
1860	220	12k	60%	55	38%
1870	225	17k	127%	76	91%
1880	220	20k	167%	91	130%
1890	180	24k	220%	133	238%
1900	180	27k	260%	150	280%
1910	180	29k	287%	161	308%
1920	180	36k	380%	200	407%
1930	180	37k	393%	206	421%
1940	175	39k	420%	223	465%
1950	120	44k	487%	367	829%
1960	120	50k	567%	417	956%
1970	41	75k	900%	1829	4534%
1980	41	86k	1047%	2098	5214%
1990	41	97k	1193%	2366	5893%

N.B. i) Full-time police only, does not include specials. All numbers are rounded.
ii) Force numbers taken from the Appendix.
iii) Police numbers calculated from Parliamentary returns and HMIC reports and rounded.

The actual size of individual police forces has always varied dramatically. In the 1880s, for example, the largest provincial forces, Liverpool City and

[55] N.B. these estimations indicate broad trends only.

Lancashire, with establishments of about 1500, were between three and four hundred times larger than the smallest borough forces, which had only a handful of officers. Even today, force sizes differ, Dyfed Powys for example, is about seven or eight times smaller than the Greater Manchester force. The last two columns on Table 4 show that since 1850 the overall number of the provincial police officers has increased twelve fold, while the average size of police forces increased sixty fold. So, not only have the number of positions at the level of chief constable decreased, but the relative size of the command has increased dramatically. Until the end of the Second World War, it can be seen that the average force size grew more or less in line with the rise in the numbers of police, not surprisingly, because the annual number of police forces remained roughly the same. After this time, the average force size increased as forces amalgamated and the police establishment increased. These trends are important because not only does the size of a police force determine the chief officer's salary and therefore influence the profile of recruits for the job, but it also concentrates more power in the hands of fewer people as well as determining the nature of the role of the chief constable.

Personnel structure. The personnel structure of the police determines the nature of the relationships between chief officers and their subordinates. It is also important if the body of police officers is to continue to be the pool from which chief constables are recruited. Recruitment into the police for the first century and a half was mainly of people with working class backgrounds (Reiner, 1978, 1982). This was a deliberate policy for the reasons outlined earlier and the social profile was maintained by relatively poor police wages. The 1979 Edmund Davies agreement (see earlier) increased police salaries and made the police attractive to the more educated middle classes. Today, entrants into the police have attained greater educational success than their predecessors.

The chief constables' independence. The chief constables' individual independence places them in a situation whereby they are not directly accountable for their operational actions over policing matters, other than to the law. This is in contrast to previous years, when borough watch committees regularly steered the operations of their police force. Unlike other local public service officials, chief constables are in full control of the operations of their force and are free from local control over their actions. A series of case law ranging from *Fisher v Oldham Corporation* through to *R v Secretary of State for the Home Department, ex parte Northumbria Police Authority* has been used to establish this point.

Other case law such as *R v Chief Constable of the Devon and Cornwall Constabulary, ex parte CEGB* has further established the independence of the chief constable to make operational decisions. Alderson, the chief constable concerned, was determined to retain his independence of judgement, despite pressure to act otherwise.

> I refused to arrest people although the CEGB wanted us to and was taken to court. I also told my officers not to give the CEGB the names and addresses of the people so that they could slap injunctions on them. It was because I thought that the people were not wrong.[56]

Alderson believes that the judgement in the case, which was in favour of the chief constable, has subsequently had a broader impact upon the policing of industrial disputes. "It's paid off in Thames Valley, where the police have treated the motorway protesters with velvet gloves. It has caused a lot of younger men to think about their roles."[57] More recently, chief constables' independence has further been strengthened by the decision in *R v Chief Constable of Sussex, ex parte International Trader's Ferry Ltd.*

Whilst it is widely accepted, although frequently contested, the doctrine or ideology of constabulary independence (Jefferson and Grimshaw, 1984; Lustgarten, 1986) ensures the chief constable's freedom from local interference in policing. It does not, however, mean that chief constables are not accountable for their actions. A brief analysis of their accountability reveals that they are accountable in different ways to different bodies. Firstly, chief constables are accountable to the courts and the Home Office. Such accountability is the obedient and subordinate model of accountability (see Reiner, 1995) and failure to account satisfactorily could lead to either prosecution and /or removal from office. Secondly, chief constables are accountable to their police authorities, the media, public, colleagues and subordinates in a different way. This

---

[56] Interview with John Alderson, April 17, 1997.

[57] *Idem.*

accountability is not the obedient and subordinate model of accountability that characterises their relationship with the courts or Home Office, or indeed which characterised the accountability of the early Victorian chief constables, especially in the borough forces, where they could be summarily dismissed by their police authority for not effecting their policies correctly. Rather, it an explanatory and co-operative model of accountability (Marshall, 1979: 61-3) whereby chief constables are mainly account-givers rather than account-takers (Reiner, 1995a: 81).

The tripartite structure and the new police authority. The first police authorities were very much in charge of their own police areas, and indeed, determined the type of person that *they* felt should be chief constable. They generated policing policies for their police force and frequently interpreted the law. In many cases these were local bylaws which members of the authority, in their capacity as local councillors, may have had a hand in creating. The local police authorities retained their independence throughout most of the nineteenth century, which, for various reasons, outlined elsewhere in this book, they gradually lost. Although it is arguable that the cultural divide between the borough and county forces was weakened as the amalgamations caused borough and county police officers to mix, they nevertheless remained statutorily different until 1974, when the watch committee /standing joint committee models were replaced with a single model of police authority, although they did carry over some of their provincial characteristics. Since then, three variations of the police authority have existed. First, are the single county police forces who were administered by a police authority which functioned as a committee of the county council (Jones and Newburn, 1995: 449; 1997). Second, are the police forces which covered more than one county. They were administered by combined police authorities which consisted of councillors and magistrates in equal proportions from each of the constituent areas. Finally, are the metropolitan provincial police forces that were administered by joint boards composed of district councillors and magistrates from the constituents of the metropolitan areas (Jones and Newburn, 1995: 449). Following the Local Government Act 1972, the police authority, whose average size ranged from about 30 to 40, consisted of two-thirds elected councillors and one third serving magistrates from within the force area.

The Police and Magistrates' Courts Act 1994 (PMCA) radically changed the composition of the police authorities. It almost halved their size to 17, and changed their composition (see earlier), so that just over half (nine) are elected councillors, three are magistrates and the remaining five are local persons, nominated by the police authority, but appointed by the Home Office. The dual purpose of reducing the authority's size and then appointing local people was, firstly, to make their decision making capacity more effective and, secondly, to increase the police authority's local policy making role. Kenneth Clarke, then Home Secretary, thought that these changes would encourage decentralisation. But, whilst there certainly is some evidence to demonstrate that the decision making capabilities of the new police authorities have been strengthened, rather than weakened (Jones and Newburn, 1997), this increased effectiveness has arguably taken place at the expense of the police authority's local, democratic, representation (Loveday, 1995). Yet, any prior claims by police authorities towards local democracy were quite weak anyway, because of their size, and also because of the fractious nature of local politics (Jones and Newburn, 1995: 449; Reiner, 1995). These links were further weakened by the gradual professionalisation of policing and its increased technological and legal complexity. Together, these reasons explain why police authorities have rarely used their existing powers to the full.[58]

The overall change in the position of the police authority within the tripartite structure can be illustrated by drawing upon Osborne and Gaebler's distinction between the functions of "steering" and "rowing" (1992). This metaphor, although oversimplified, is useful because it illustrates the intended direction of a policy (Crawford, 1997: 221). Once the main source of police policy, the police authority traditionally steered the police within their areas, whilst their chief constables and police forces carried out the rowing function. Over time, this steering function has been transferred to, or captured by, depending on the version of events, central

[58] At the time of completing this text two examples of police authority action took place which suggested that police authorities might be becoming more assertive. In January 1998, the West Yorkshire Police Authority refused to appoint a new chief constable from the Home Office shortlist (however, it subsequently reversed its decision). Also in the same month the North Yorkshire Police Authority refused to allow its chief constable to remain in office so that he could appeal against allegations brought against him following his alleged mis-handling of a sexual harassment case brought against male officers by a female officer.

government and the debate over police authority powers has now shifted to negotiations over their role within the rowing function. So, any claims of increased effectiveness on the part of the new police authority must be understood in terms of this increased demarcation of (central) steering and local (rowing) functions.

Although the new police authorities arguably forge stronger alliances with central government, given that the Home Secretary now appoints five of the authority's 17 members, any relationship, if it exists at all, is largely one way, emanating from the Home Office towards the police authority. This gives weight to the argument that the PCMA has further increased the centralisation of control over police policy (see Savage, Charman and Cope, 1996; Charman and Savage, 1998). Furthermore, the preceding analysis of the changes illustrates that control over the police is no longer the zero-sum equation that it was once assumed to be. So, any gain in power by the police authority does not necessarily mean that the other two players, Home Office and chief constables have necessarily lost power. In a limited way, the PMCA empowered police authorities to develop, along with the Home Office, local policing plans which are to determine the "what" of policing.[59] The chief constables, in contrast, are supposed to be responsible for the "how". However, in practice, even this possibility fell short of expectations, as Jones and Newburn found in their study of the new police authorities. The reason was two fold, partly because of the "compliance culture", which they found evidence of, in which members either found it difficult, or did not wish to challenge the chief constable (1997: 207). However, more significantly, it was because the national policing objectives have been so broadly defined and local policing plans have come to be largely dominated by the police. Therefore chief constables have found themselves to be in a stronger position to determine both the "what" and also the "how" (Jones and Newburn, 1997: 205). So, if the intentions behind the PMCA were to encourage effective partnerships between the police authority, the Home Office and chief constables, they were not realised and even if a working partnership is established, it is unlikely that police authorities will become anything more than junior partners.

---

[59] They were made budget-holders in order to facilitate this role.

Conclusions: the development of an increasingly corporate police model

The chief constables' milieu has changed considerably over the past 160 years. The "Victorian bric a brac" described by Critchley (1978: 176) of small independent forces run locally by a local police authority has developed into a centrally co-ordinated set of standardised police organisations. In essence, the police organisations have changed from a set of small local autocracies, to a series of large regional bureaucracies, in so far as most police areas now have little local meaning, either in the old borough or traditional county sense.

Once a multi-purpose emergency service, the police today have become much more narrow in focus and yet more complex in function. All this is set against the backdrop of a broader public policing model, which has become multi-tiered and pluralistic. This increasing complexity of the police has impacted upon both the quality and quantity of the decisions that have to be made by the chief constable. Consequently, chief constables make their decisions in a professional decision-making environment which requires a much different type of decision-maker from that of old. In the 1990s, the chief constables' work involves mainly the management of resources, the making of general policy decisions and, importantly, the management of the appearance of law enforcement within their police area (Manning, 1977).[60] At the head of a professionally trained management team of senior officers, chief constables are now professionally trained police managers whose art lies in their application of management skills, a stark contrast to their predecessors.

As the growth in size and administrative complexity of police forces gradually removed chief constables from operational police work, their managerial role changed from being warrior /leader to being administrator /leader to becoming a chief executive. The notion of the professional manager, trained in management, with an ability to manage any organisation runs counter to the police occupational culture which requires that chief constables must have risen through the ranks of the police service. The existence of the Police Staff College (see chapters 6 and 7)

---

[60] The former and serving chief constables who were interviewed were asked about this function. Most thought that this was a cynical view of the chief constable's role but they nevertheless conceded that it was *one* of the many roles performed by the chief constable.

bridges the gap between these contradictions and will continue to do so in the future.

As chief executives at the head of the management team of a large bureaucratic public service organisation, today's chief constables are mainly account-givers rather than account-takers and are therefore not accountable for their actions in the conventional obedient and subordinate way (Reiner, 1995a: 81). Following the PMCA and other changes in policing during the early 1990s, such as, the introduction of fixed-term contracts for chief constables and the establishment of performance indicators, it was anticipated that the explanatory, or account giving, accountability would be replaced by a more calculative or contractual form (Reiner 1995a: 92). Some years on, there are few signs that this is happening (Jones and Newburn, 1997) and they continue to be comparatively free from any stringent formal accountability, although they are subject to a number of forms of informal or semi-formal accountability (see chapter 10). It will be argued in the forthcoming chapters that the rigorous selection procedures and lengthy socialisation period that they go through prior to appointment, means that probably the most effective form of accountability that they experience is to their peers (the police). Without peer recognition, it is unlikely that they would rise to a position to be appointed as chief constable. Whilst such informal accountability provides some protection against the appointment of extremely politically motivated or even simply dangerous individuals, it nevertheless raises further concerns. Most specifically, it will be argued later that chief constables have effectively become a self-selecting élite and one which, through ACPO, has a direct link to the process which makes the key decisions over police policy, including the qualities of the individuals who become chief constable.

It is ACPO which is engendering the emerging police corporatisation. Not only has it become the collective police voice on issues of police policy, but the recent introduction of the principle of "in favour of compliance", which requires dissenters to ACPO policy to put their reasons in writing to the ACPO president, creates a mechanism which binds all ACPO members to the collective ACPO decision (Savage and Charman, 1996: 15; Charman and Savage, 1998: 8). Thus, it is probable that the chief, and other ACPO, officers of the 41 English and Welsh independent provincial forces, plus those in the Metropolitan, City of

London and Scottish, Northern Irish and other police areas will increasingly come to think and act as one. Add to this corporatising structure the new national police organisations and we have both a *de facto* and, in effect, a *de jure* national police service. As the corporatising police structure develops in the millennium, then it is likely that chief constables will emerge more as directors of local, or regional, police services rather than as chief executives of large police organisations, particularly if the new private forms of policing become regulated by central police policy.

The history of policing, especially during the twentieth century, has been the history of creeping, or incremental, centralised control over the police organisation. This centralisation has taken place largely in the absence of a formal statutory framework and has largely bypassed the formal democratic process for the formulation of policy. This outcome was attained through four main processes: standardisation of policing; centralisation of policing policy; the unification of the various policing traditions; the more recent corporatisation of the police. Central to these processes were a number of devices or agencies of which the ability to determine the type of individual who becomes chief constable (recruitment), their training (selection) and appointment were of crucial importance. The following chapters illustrate the operation of these devices.

4 The Recruitment and Selection of Chief Constables Before Desborough

Introduction

Before the Desborough Committee reported in 1920 there existed no centrally determined policies to govern the appointment of chief constables.[1] It was not until the after recommendations of the Desborough Committee were published that policies to govern the selection of all chief constables came to be centrally formulated. Indeed, even these only established who were not to become chief constables, such as those without any prior police experience. To put this into perspective, it was as recently as the mid-1950s that a number of counties, Cornwall was one, appointed their first "professional police officer as Chief Constable" (see chapter 6).[2] Other than having police experience, the new rules did not say anything about what competencies a chief constables should possess. So, prior to Desborough, the selection processes comprised of local variants of time-honoured practices: this was the truly the age of amateur policing and of management by the 'gifted amateur', which for almost a century, had been the principle underlying many public appointments. Policing was seen as a function of local government, and one in which central government was not keen to become directly involved, with perhaps the exception of providing a national framework of mutual assistance for the maintenance of order. In the absence of formal policy, or even central guidance, the selection and appointment practices of police authorities tended to be governed by a combination of formal and informal practices. These practices will become the focus of this and the next chapter.

---

[1] There did exist some vague rules which stipulated basic criteria. They are described later.

[2] HO 287/289. Comment in a note from HM Inspector of Constabulary, F.T. Tarry to Francis Graham-Harrison at the Home Office regarding the attitudes of the Standing Joint Committee. The Cornwall Constabulary had only four chief constables during its first century of existence, they were Col. W. R. Gilbert (1857-1896), R. M. Hill (1896-1909), Lt. Col. Protheroe-Smith (1909-1935) and Major E. Hare (1935-1956).

It was established in chapter three that prior to 1974, two traditions of police existed in provincial England and Wales. Each police authority was defined by a separate Act of Parliament.[3] In the boroughs, the watch committees were both created and informed by the Municipal Corporations Act 1835: later amended by the Act of 1882. In the counties, the quarter sessions were informed by the County Police Act 1839. The Local Government Act 1888 later transferred the responsibility for policing the county to a standing joint committee of the county council composed partly of justices and partly of elected county councillors. This Parliamentary compromise was designed to appease those who wanted it to be made up of elected councillors and also those who wanted it to be organised entirely of magistrates, but it had little immediate impact because, it will later be established, the elected members of the police authorities were of the same social stock as the justices in quarter session. Indeed, the individual social characteristics of the members of police authorities in both the boroughs and counties were important factors in shaping their selection practices. These social characteristics began to decrease in importance soon after the turn of the century, as principles of promotion by merit gained popularity and also because of the centralised appointment and promotion policies which followed Desborough. They nevertheless remained important factors until the Second World War.

The first and second parts of this chapter will, respectively, consider the nature of the composition of the police authorities who were responsible for the appointment of chief constables in the boroughs and counties. The second and third sections look at the mechanics of selecting a chief constable before Desborough in the borough and county forces, in particular at who the candidates applying for the job were, the ways in which prospective chief constables prepared themselves for office, and who was selected for the short list.

---

[3] The general powers of police authorities were described earlier in Chapters 2 & 3.

The appointing bodies of county chief constables: quarter sessions and standing joint committees

The County Police Act 1839 (2 & 3 Vict. c. 92 & c. 93) empowered the justices in quarter sessions to appoint and dismiss a chief constable for their county.

> And it be enacted, that as soon as any rules, as finally settled, shall have been received from the Secretary of State, the justices of the county in general or the quarter sessions assembled, or at any adjournment thereof, shall, subject to the approval of the Secretary of State, appoint a person duly qualified according to the rules to be chief constable of the county, and in every case of vacancy of the office shall, subject to the like approval, appoint another fit person in his room ... and every chief constable so to be appointed may hold his office until dismissed by the justices in general or quarter sessions assembled, or at any adjournment thereof (*idem*, s. 4).

The Home Secretary's rules under the County Police Act of 1839 were quite specific about the characteristics of police officers up to the rank of superintendent, but they were less decisive about the educational qualifications or training required of chief constables. The Home Secretary's Rules of December 1, 1840 gave a list of four qualifications a chief constable must possess:

> His age must not exceed 45 years.
>
> He must be certified by a medical practitioner to be in good health and of sound constitution, and fitted to perform the duties of the office.
>
> He must not have been bankrupt, nor have taken the benefit of the Insolvent Act.
>
> He must be recommended to the Secretary of State by the magistrates, in whom the appointment is vested, as a person of general good character and conduct (Home Secretary's Rules, 1840).

These qualifications were revised after the County and Borough Police Act 1856, to bring them in to line with existing practice (HO Circular,

3/2/1857).[4] This revision was, in part, designed to appease the counties with police forces who had previously disregarded the ruling. It was also very conveniently timed so as to curry favour with those county authorities who had been resistant to the idea of a full-time police. Grey's predecessors had tended to approve appointments of chief constables who often fell outside the rules. This raised questions as to the legality of the appointments. However, the Law Officers of the Crown, who were consulted on this matter, were of the opinion that whilst the justices of a county can only appoint a person duly qualified according to the rules, the approval of the Secretary of State for the appointment of a chief constable not so qualified will nevertheless be valid (*idem*). While there is a strong sense that Grey had given in to the county police authorities over this matter, he nevertheless remarked pointedly that the revision was made "owing to any doubt as to the expediency of requiring these qualifications which I am of opinion ought as a general rule to be insisted upon" (*idem*).

The revised rules of 1857 were even less specific about the qualifications of chief constable and gave the quarter sessions a virtual free rein over the appointment. Candidates had to satisfy two broad requirements, they:

> must be certified by a medical practitioner to be in good health and of sound constitution, and fitted to perform the duties of the office.

In addition they:

> must be recommended to the Secretary of State by the police committee in whom the appointment is vested as a person of general good character and conduct. (Home Secretary's Rules 1857).

Although the appointment still had to be approved by the Home Secretary, this was largely a formality and interventions were rare. The Home Secretary was more likely to disallow an appointment on the grounds that the appointee was also "in the commission of the peace for the county", an office which Grey considered to be incompatible with service in the police

---

[4] Circular from the Home Secretary, Sir George Grey, to the Clerks of the Peace in the counties, dated February 3, 1857. Reported in the *Justice of the Peace* (1857: 201-202).

(HO Circular, 3/2/1857).[5] The quarter sessions could, in effect, appoint whoever they wanted as chief constable so long as they satisfied the broad requirements of the Home Secretary's rules. The Home Secretary's rules were revised in 1866, 1873 and 1886, but the qualifications for chief constable remained the same. In fact they remained unchanged until the rules made in 1920 under the Police Act 1919 (Home Secretary's Rules 1920).[6]

Once appointed, a chief constable took command of policing the county, but the quarter sessions still retained some control under the last clause in Section 6 of the County Police Act which said that the chief constable shall be,

> ... subject to such lawful orders as he may receive from the Justices in General or quarter sessions assembled, or at any Adjournment thereof, and to the Rules established for the Government of the Force (2 & 3 Vict. c. 92 & c. 93).

However, whilst the quarter sessions may have used this direct power during the period when the county forces were being established, it seems to have rarely been used afterwards. It will be shown in this section, that in practice, the quarter sessions had little cause to use this power because the persons they appointed held a similar outlook to themselves. Steedman (1984) and Wall (1987; 1994) found that professional (military) commanders with gentry backgrounds and proven experience in disciplining and managing men were chosen to run the first county forces. Drawing upon Steedman's work, Lustgarten rightly argues that this was because: "men of social standing equal to the justices themselves could not be treated as menials, and conversely could be assumed to be reliable" (Lustgarten, 1986: 41).

---

[5] This position would at first appear to contradict with the experience of the Metropolitan Commissioners who were magistrates. However, the Commissioners were ex-officio magistrates and, importantly, they were not sworn constables.

[6] After 1857 the Home Secretary's rules were published in Home Office circulars. They are located as follows: March 1866, (HOC/HO 158/2); April 1873 (HOC/HO 158/3); April 12 1886 (HO 158/3); 1920 (HOC/HO 158/21).

The social composition of the county police authorities

The justices in the quarter sessions were in charge of law enforcement in the counties. Smellie described the nineteenth century county magistracy as: "the rear guard of an agrarian oligarchy" (Zangerl, 1971: 113). Keith-Lucas saw them as "the most aristocratic feature of English government", which "in default of specific instruction from Parliament could establish and enforce general rules in accordance with which they would interpret the statutes of common law under which they acted" (Keith-Lucas, 1962: 85).

The justices in quarter sessions were presided over by the Lord Lieutenant of the County and were the mechanism through which the justices governed the county. The Lord Lieutenant was, in addition to being the Monarch's representative, the military commander and chief magistrate of the county. Between quarter sessions, the magistrates would administer justice and many other aspects of local government in their own petty sessional divisions.

The qualifications required of magistrates were suggested by the Duke of Wellington in 1838, who believed that they should be "gentlemen of wealth, worth and consideration and education; that they should have been educated for the bar, if possible; and that, above all they should be associated with, and be respected by the gentry of the county" (*Hansard,* 1838, vol. 3: 1280). Although Wellington valued education and legal experience, he effectively welcomed into the magistracy anyone who earned a reasonably large income, displayed the values of the landed classes and were accustomed to a genteel lifestyle. The emphasis upon the latter was highlighted when the social composition of the magistracy is examined. Zangerl (1971: 115) compared the *Returns of Justices of the Peace* between 1831 and 1887 in order to look at the degree of continuity in the social composition of the county magistracy over that period (Table 5). It is clear from Table 5 that the gentry formed the single largest group of magistrates, however, the aristocracy held the more important county positions. For example, in 1875 over 90 per cent of Lord Lieutenants came from the aristocracy. The internal relationship between the aristocracy and the gentry was complex and often ambivalent. The great wealth, influence and position of the peers in the House of Lords enabled them to move easily within central Government and actively participate in national policy making. The quarter sessions on the other hand, acted as a forum through which the Lord Lieutenant and titled magistrates could discuss matters of common interest with their gentry associates (Zangerl, 1971: 117).

Table 5: The social composition of the county magistracy*

	Aristocracy	Gentry	Clergy	Middle-Class	other
1842	8%	77%	13%	0%	1%
1887	6%	68%	5%	15%	5%

Number of Magistrates in 1842 = 3090 / Number of Magistrates in 1887 = 2570
* Source Zangerl (1971: 115).

Zangerl found that whilst the county magistracy in the 1840s was dominated by the gentry and the clergy, by the time the first county council elections were held in 1889, the percentage of middle class magistrates had increased from zero to 15 per cent; replacing the clergy.[7] He argued that the apparent increase in the social fluidity of the county bench was the result of a self-preservation exercise by the aristocracy to retain control over law enforcement in the counties at a time when wider social changes were taking place in society. The administration of the counties was threatened by the rising 'nouveau riche' middle classes and a shortage of people considered suitable to sit on the county bench. Thus class barriers did not disappear, they were merely lowered as a response to changing social conditions. By assimilating the aspiring middle class into the magistracy rather than disturbing the established order of social relations, the landed classes reinforced and preserved their value system (Zangerl, 1971: 125).

It must be noted that the social composition of the county magistracy did vary between areas and that Zangerl's analysis was based upon a study of all county magistrates. In his study of the Black Country, Phillips found that the composition of the county bench changed during the 19th century from being dominated by the land-owning classes to being dominated by

[7] Zangerl made the assumption that the areas which contributed to the returns were representative. He did not take regional variations into account.

the industrial/entrepreneurial classes (1977). In contrast the county bench in the East Riding of Yorkshire, a very rural area, continued to be dominated by the landed classes (Buckle, unpublished). Sillitoe's experiences in the East Riding, during the 1920s, provide evidence to support this view (1955: 53) (see chapter 8).

The Local Government Act 1888 sought to democratise the government of the counties, but the newly elected county councillors in 1889 were found to be disproportionately from the land-owning classes (Buckle, unpublished). Not surprisingly, following the elections, the social composition of the standing joint committees was very similar to that of the old quarter sessions. The standing joint committees were composed of equal numbers of justices, who were appointed by the quarter sessions, and county councillors appointed by the county council. It therefore follows that local attitudes towards policing and towards the selection of the chief constable did not change much after the Local Government Act of 1888.

The appointing bodies of borough chief officers: the watch committee

The Municipal Corporations Act 1835 (5 & 6 Guliemi IV, c. 76) required the newly elected borough councils to appoint: "... for such a time as they may think proper, a sufficient number of their own body, who, together with the mayor of the borough, for the time being, shall be and be called the watch committee". The watch committee was vested with similar powers to the county chief constable, there was no statutory borough equivalent of the county chief constable. One reason for this omission was the fact that the employment of salaried officials was, even in the 1830s, fairly uncommon. The watch committee, as established earlier in chapter two, was expected to accept responsibility both for policy, administration and also what today would be termed operations, but were forced to delegate responsibility for the latter two functions to a trusted member of the force for the very practical reason that it did not possess either the time or expertise to do so. The chief constable of the borough force became known as the superintending constable and later the head or chief constable. Towards the latter part of the nineteenth century many borough chief constables had formally adopted the title chief constable,[8] which caused much disquiet amongst the county chief constables who believed that they were superior officers. A number of county chief constables complained to the Home Secretary about the confusion created by the borough chief officers holding the same title and suggested that the borough officers were given the title head, rather than chief, constable.[9] The Home Office declared that the two groups should be referred to a chief constable, but that the county chiefs be referred to as the chief constable of a particular county force and the borough chiefs as chief constable, borough or city police "emphasising the fact that they are not statutory officers, merely the highest officers of forces appointed and governed by Watch Committees".[10] The chief officers of the borough forces gained a statutory footing under the rules established under s. 4 of the Police Act 1919.

The social composition of the watch committee

Little information is available to provide a comprehensive profile of the social composition of watch committees, but the little information that does exist indicates that it was not only less consistent, but also quite different from that of the county police authorities because of the varying nature of local economies and party politics. However, some broad trends can be identified.

In his study of the social composition of borough councils between 1835 and 1914, Hennock (1968: 315) found that whilst the political complexions of borough councils differed considerably, they nevertheless tended to be dominated by the local economic élite. He also observed a decline in the numbers of councillors with business interests and an increase in councillors from the professions and trades. These observations

---

[8] Forces such as Leeds had always referred to their chief officer as chief constable (see previous chapters).

[9] See for example, the letter from John Dunne, Chief Constable of Cumberland and Westmoreland, to the Right Hon. H. Matthews, M.P., Home Secretary (HO 45/9969/X26632/3). These views were countered by charges by borough chief constables that they were employed as chief constable (letter from F.H. Mardlin, Chief Constable of Northampton to Sir Philip Manfield, M.P. HO 45/9969/X26632/5).

[10] Home Office internal memo (HO 45/9969/X26632/6).

broadly fit in with the findings of Brogden (1982), who studied the social composition of the Liverpool watch committee during the nineteenth century. Brogden found that between 1836 and 1910 the domination of the watch committee by the mercantile classes and gentlefolk decreased whilst the percentage of tradespeople and manufacturers increased (*idem*).

The members of the watch committees were elected from the borough council and local party politics played a very important part in the attitude of the watch committee towards the policing of their area. Local politics in the counties, on the other hand, tended to be more covert and class based. Brogden found that mercantile domination of the watch committee meant that police work tended to be centred around broader issues such as urban social engineering and hygiene and not what is known today as police work (*idem*: 60). As the mercantile domination decreased towards the end of the nineteenth century there was a decline in the general direction of the police force by the watch committee. Brogden believes that whilst the potential for intervention still remained with the watch committee, the chief constable had obtained a high degree of autonomy from intervention by the turn of the century.

The watch committee was one of the most prestigious of the borough council committees and tended to be dominated by the local municipal élite. The borough police were a symbol of civic pride and their reputation became attached to the watch committee through the chief constable. Because all of the borough chief constables' powers were delegated, their relationship with the police authority was different to that found in the counties. Constitutionally, the borough chief constable was in a similar position to that of other specialist council managers, for example, town clerk, city engineer, or city architect. However, this does not necessarily imply that the borough chief constable was always the direct servant of the watch committee, but it does suggest that watch committees would tend to look for candidates who would be sympathetic to their view of the world and sought individuals that they could trust.

In both the boroughs and counties, the chief constables were an integral part of the process of local government. On the one hand they acted as mediator between the main body of police officers and the police authority, interpreting instructions, managing, appointing and dismissing. One the other hand they acted as a public symbol of police-work. Both types of police authority were dominated by the local economic élite and sought chief constables whose backgrounds and social qualities were similar to that of their members.

The police authorities of the Metropolitan and City of London forces

Although this book is concerned with the provincial police, some brief mention, by way of contrast, should be made of the police authorities of the two other major English police forces to highlight their different traditions of management, recruitment, selection and appointment.

Under the City of London Police Act of 1839, the police authority for the City of London is the Court of Common Council, which is also responsible for administering the city. The Council, according to Nott-Bower who was Commissioner between 1901 and 1926,[11] held "that most potent of all powers - the power of the purse; but even that power is now subject in many respects to the sanction of the Home Secretary" (Nott-Bower, 1926: 173). The Commissioner of the City of London Police was, and still is, more autonomous than any county chief constable and like the Metropolitan Commissioner can only be appointed and dismissed from office by Royal Warrant,[12] although in practice the dismissal warrant would be served if the Home Secretary wished it to be. Nott-Bower described the independence of the Commissioner of the City of London Police once appointed:

> In matters of Police Administration and Discipline, having once selected a Commissioner, they [the Court of Common Council] have no authority over him. He holds his appointment subject to dismissal by the Crown; or by the Court of Aldermen (the Magistrates of the City), for 'misconduct' or other reasonable cause; and his duties for which he is responsible to himself alone and his powers are regulated by statute (1926: 173).

The Common Council had a membership of 230 persons in Nott-Bower's day, compared with the watch committee's 15 to 20.

In contrast to the provincial and City of London forces, the Metropolitan Police do not have a locally elected police authority. The

---

[11] After his period of office as head constables of the Liverpool force.

[12] The process by which the Commissioner of the City of London Police is selected is described later in this chapter.

police authority for the Metropolitan police is the Home Secretary. This situation is a historical remnant from the time of the Metropolitan Police Act 1829. At the time there existed no London council, so it was left to the Home Secretary to take on the role of police authority. Since the introduction of elected councils for London,[13] one of the arguments for retaining the Home Secretary as the singular police authority has been that the Metropolitan Police District crosses the boundaries of the neighbouring counties and an elected body would create problems for the administration of policing. Another, often quoted, argument has been that the Metropolitan Police plays an important role in the defence of the capital. The Metropolitan Commissioners have until recent years been political appointees by the Home Secretary and their qualities tended to reflect broad political themes of the time. For example, the appointment of a Civil Servant, Sir Harold Scott, by the post-war Attlee government, broke the tradition of drawing the Commissioner from the upper echelons of the armed forces in order to re-emphasise the civilian nature of police-work. Although Scott was a civil servant, he had previously been involved with the administration of the RAF in the Ministry of Aircraft Production. This experience may have been important in his selection, given that the two previous Commissioners had also come from the RAF. Concerned that Scott would be able to perform the symbolic functions of the office Herbert Morrison's, now legendary, first question to him prior to offering him the post was "Can you ride a horse?" (Scott, 1970: 7).

Until 1976, the Commissioner of the Metropolitan Police was not a constable. In his autobiography, Sir Robert Mark, a former Commissioner, described the relationship between the Commissioner, the Home Office and the Home Secretary, as being an odd one. The Commissioner is appointed by the Sovereign on the recommendation of the Home Secretary and therefore ceases to be a constable upon appointment. Prior to Mark's term of office, the Commissioner was also an ex-officio magistrate, but this peculiar constitutional position disappeared when Lord Hailsham abolished all ex-officio magistrates (Mark, 1978: 152).[14] Importantly, the

---

[13] The elected council for Greater London was disbanded by the Conservative administration 1979-1997. At the time of writing there was some talk of reinstating an elected council.

[14] It will be remembered from Chapter Two that appointing the Commissioners as justices appeased the magistrates who had opposed the police bill in the late 1820s.

Commissioner "not being a police officer enjoys no security of tenure, unlike provincial chief constables who enjoy a measure of protection for arbitrary dismissal under the Police Act 1964" (Mark, 1978: 152). But a measure of protection is gained from the high profile of the position, so that dismissal for any reason would be likely to attract the attention of Parliament, and yet, if the Home Secretary feels that there is a strong enough case, then he/she has the right to dismiss the Commissioner. The Commissioner's orders are also subject to the approval of the Home Secretary, although in practice such approval is rarely sought. On operational matters, the Commissioner, like a chief constable, is not in theory subject to orders from anyone (Mark, 1978: 152-153).

Selecting county chief constables before Desborough

The formal process of selecting a chief constable has not changed very much over the years and was, until very recently, not much different to that which was practised during the 19th century. Upon finding the post of chief constable for their police area vacant, the police authority, or a sub-committee, formed to deal with the appointment and would meet to decide the qualifications of the chief constable they wanted to appoint before advertising it.[15] Typically, such qualifications would include age and residency, for example, they may have sought a candidate within a specific age bracket and who lived within a specified distance of the police headquarters. A typical advertisement for the post, from 1894, can be found in Figure 2.

Applicants would respond to the advertisement and be short-listed by the police authority's appointment sub-committee. This committee would then ballot its members on their choice of applicant after the interviews with candidates. The police authority's choice of chief constable was then sent to the Home Secretary for approval.

[15] Appointments were not always advertised, for example, where the police authority wanted to appoint a deputy who had been appointed by the previous chief constable. These were typically external appointments (see chapter 6).

Figure 2: A typical advertisement for a chief constable, 1894

"CHIEF CONSTABLE FOR EAST SUSSEX."

Candidates (who must be officers serving in the army or navy, or who have retired from those services, or persons who have had police experience) for the appointment of CHIEF CONSTABLE, which has become vacant, are requested to address their applications in writing (marked "Chief Constable") to the Standing Joint Committee of the quarter sessions and County Council, under cover to me [the clerk of the standing joint committees], not later than the 24th April instant ...

Source: *Police Review* (6/4/1894)

The advertisements for chief constableships attracted many applicants from all walks of life, despite their being fairly specific about who would be eligible for the job. Upon receipt of the applications, the appointing sub-committee would draw up a shortlist of those they felt were most suitable for the post. Although the advertisements could be very general and invited applications from a wide sector of society, the appointing body had a preconceived notion of the type of person they wanted as their chief constable and looked for that person among the applicants. The shortlist would contain between five and ten of the most suitable applicants and short-listing was accepted elsewhere as a qualification of suitability as a candidate for the post of chief constable, even if the candidate was unsuccessful. Once short-listed, it was the common practice for candidates to canvass support from the members of the appointing body, usually by any means at their disposal even though the rules of application may have prohibited such action. Here the patronage system came into its own and the candidates, who eventually came to be appointed, tended to be those who could wield the most influence over enough members of the police authority to win the ballot.

The dynamics of the selection and appointment process are best explained by observing an actual example derived from a secondary analysis of Wilson's painstaking description of the appointment of a new chief constable in Buckinghamshire in 1896 (1987: 39-44). This example, and also the others which follow, not only describe the selection and appointment procedures, but also illustrate the various hidden, social agendas which were in play and which form the focus of discussion in later chapters.[16]

Captain John Charles Tyrwhitt Drake had been chief constable of Buckinghamshire since 1867, having been appointed directly after his service as a career army officer. After the post became vacant upon his resignation in May 1896, William Crouch, Clerk to the Justices of Buckinghamshire constructed a job description for the new chief constable. He had no personal experience to draw upon, so he consulted the Home Secretary's Rules (1886), which were, as stated previously, generally unhelpful in that they only required that the new chief constable be under forty six years of age, unless promoted from within the police, have been transferred from elsewhere or be able to claim some special circumstances. In addition, the applicant also had to be certified as being in good health, and to have been recommended to the Home Secretary by the magistrates as a person of good character. Most importantly, the new chief constable did not have to be a police officer (Wilson, 1987: 39) and the rules did not expect such experience.

Secondly, Crouch wrote for advice to counties who had recently appointed a chief constable,[17] for example, Shropshire in 1889, Devon in 1891, Warwickshire also in 1891, Nottinghamshire in 1892, Monmouthshire in 1893, East Sussex in 1894 and Herefordshire in 1895. The answers he received showed that salaries that had been offered ranged from £300 in Herefordshire, to £460 in East Sussex. In addition, successful candidates were given allowances of between £100 and £150 to provide a horse for their use. Some counties had included special conditions, Shropshire for example, barred bankrupts from applying while others required residence in or near the county town. Only one county, Monmouthshire, had specified that no-one without police experience would be appointed (Wilson, 1987: 40).

The post was advertised in the *Buckinghamshire Herald* and the *Times* at £300 per annum, plus £150 horse allowance and rent free accommodation. The salary was only £50 above the £250 minimum prescribed by the Home Secretary in the rules of 1886 and £100 below

---

[16] This is one of a number of examples given here. The degree of overlap in the issues covered is deliberate as it establishes the commonality of the themes raised.

[17] N.B. Many of these appointments were to replace the second or even the original chief constables who had held office for over thirty years.

Drake's final salary. Personal canvassing, by candidates, of members of the committee was strongly deprecated (*Police Review*, 1896: 259). The implication, regarding the small salary, is that the new incumbent would have his own private income with which to supplement the salary. This desired social characteristic is apparent when the social and professional profiles of the sixty two applicants for the post are examined (see Table 6).

Table 6: The composition of the applicants for the Buckinghamshire post*

Military backgrounds		
Lieutenant	3	5%
Captain	19	31%
Major	24	39%
Colonel	1	2%
Commander	2	3%
Non-military backgrounds		
no military rank	9	15%
Superintendent	3	5%
Total	61**	100%

*Source: reworked from figures given by (Wilson, 1987: 41).
**The details of one applicant are missing.

The applicants were mainly middle ranking military officers (80 per cent), a further 15 per cent had no military rank, but "stressed their local connections and friendships with councillors" (Wilson, 1987: 41), and the final 5 per cent were serving police personnel. They were very well to do and were typically from the upper-middle, and upper classes. This social profile can be demonstrated by an analysis of the sources of the testimonials supplied by the twenty applicants from which the shortlist was drawn. They included two field marshals (Lord Roberts and Sir Donald Stewart), twenty seven major generals, thirty five lieutenant generals, three brigadier generals, one hundred and two colonels, thirty five lieutenant colonels, fifteen majors and six captains. Also included were testimonials by a Duke, two Marquises, seven Earls and ten Lords. Plus testimonials from a variety of professional people. Twenty testimonials came from chief constables (Wilson, 1987: 41).

Of tremendous importance to the appointment process was the role played by the clerk to the county who administers the event. Wilson observed, from Crouch's annotated list, that he struck out applicants who did not supply testimonials, those whose testimonials were undated, those over the recommended age, those giving no age at all (this included a serving police officer). Crouch's actions were based upon his estimations of the expectations of the members of the standing joint committee. Not surprisingly then, the revised list of applicants were of a similar social standing to the members of the standing joint committee. It consisted of 30 members, half of whom were appointed by the justices in quarter sessions and half appointed from the county council. The former group included the Earl of Buckingham, Lord Cottesloe, a clergyman, a member of Queen's Council and three army officers.

Crouch narrowed the applications to twenty, which he marked as good and from which the standing joint committee chose the shortlist. All five of the shortlisted candidates were military officers; four were majors and one was a commander. None had police experience, although several had worked in chief constables' offices "with a view to qualifying for the office of chief constable" (Wilson, 1987: 41). That Crouch "mobilised the agenda" (Lukes, 1974: 16), was apparent and the way that he did it was interesting. He understood the social profile of the person whom the committee would feel comfortable with as chief constable, but he also appeared to have some sympathy with the view that the chosen person should have some police experience. Of the five candidates who were interviewed, Major Otway Mayne was appointed. He was the only candidate to have been supported by a chief constable and he had also been supported by the chairman of a standing joint committee. Mayne provided a unique combination of some basic policing experience, or experience of police forces, and the preferred social profile for the post as evidenced by his social connections. His testimonials were supplied by a county chief constable who made reference to Col. Edward Bradford, Commissioner of the Metropolitan Police; Robert Gordon the chairman of the Norfolk County Council and former county MP; Sir William Ffolkes, vice-chairman of the Norfolk County Council and also a former MP, and from his commanding officers, Colonels Perry, Burton and Shepard (Wilson, 1987: 41).

Further examples of appointment to county chief constableships

Here, the previous careers of some more appointments are described in order to illustrate further the dynamics of the appointment process and, importantly, the impact of appointments upon the overall field of candidacy. The examples complement the example given earlier of the appointment of the chief constable of Buckinghamshire and show/confirm how narrow the actual pool was from which candidates were drawn, they describe the candidates' backgrounds and give a flavour of the local politics involved. They also illustrate the careers of chief constables whilst they were at the level of chief constable, they demonstrate their length of tenure, movement from smaller to larger forces and the knock-on effect that this movement had upon other appointments. Finally they indicate the breadth of activities carried out by chief constables. The examples given here were well documented and were reported in the *Police Review* in 1908, a fairly typical year which was chosen because it was the year in which the issue of who should become a chief constable was first discussed at a governmental level. It also signified the middle of a period in which local police authorities appeared to have most independence in their choice of chief constable.

On the 23rd of January 1908, Captain Robert Sterne RN, the chief constable of Wiltshire, resigned. He was 75 years old and had been chief constable for 38 years. Prior to his police career, he had served in the Royal Navy for 24 years where he had the unenviable distinction of being the first English officer to be wounded in the Crimean War. The standing joint committee advertised for a successor at a salary of £500 per annum with £150 for expenses. The expenses were to cover all services rendered by the chief constable, including those as Chief Inspector of Diseases of Animals.

The advertisement stated that candidates must not be more than 45 years old. Applications were to be accompanied by not more than six testimonials and be delivered to the office of the clerk to the county. The age limit effectively excluded serving police officers from applying. The response to the advertisement was impressive and the 182 initial applications were reduced to 33 at a meeting of the standing joint committee on February 24th. The *Wiltshire Times* noted that one of the applicants for the post was Lord Heytesbury, a Wiltshire nobleman and a major in the Wiltshire regiment. Lord Heytesbury inherited the title on the death of his elder brother, but the family's fortune went to his brother's wife. Heytesbury was 45 years old and had been preparing for the position by working under the retiring chief constable, who gave him a good testimonial. The *Police Review*, in pursuance of their policy of internal recruitment, sent copies of their prize essay "The Appointment of Chief Constables" (see chapter 5) to the principal newspapers circulating in Wiltshire. On the 29th of February the *Wiltshire Times* reproduced the essay for its readers in full.

The *Wiltshire Times* reported on the 13th of March 1908, that a shortlist of seven was drawn up for interview and that their selection clearly had exposed a raw nerve. The seven candidates were Lord Heytesbury, formerly adjutant to the Wiltshire volunteers; Captain Callard of the Dragoon Guards; Major Lafone of the Kent Constabulary[18]; Mr Llewellyn, DSO, RN ex-District Commandant of the South African Constabulary; Major Thessinger of the Metropolitan Police; Captain Thresher of the Rifle Brigade; Major Wilkinson of the Durham Light infantry and a relative of the Earl of Pembroke who was the Chairman of the standing joint committee (*Police Review*, 1908: 140). The *Police Review* reported on the 20th of March that although applications were invited from all persons, the standing joint committee had no intention of appointing a person who had proved themselves as a police officer. Lord Heytesbury was the favourite for the post and the *Wiltshire Times* described the social composition of the standing joint committee and questioned its impartiality over the selection of the chief constable:

> So far as we can gather, the standing joint committee have no intention to give this prize of the profession to a police officer of known capacity. Social standing may possibly count, practical experience is hardly likely to be a

[18] Where no police rank is given, the candidate had been serving a placement in the office of the relevant chief constable and was not a member of the force. It is possible that some of these 'gentlemen' may have sworn the oath of constable.

> factor in their choice. With 'Lansdowne', Lord Lieutenant, 'Bath,' Chairman of County Council; 'Pembroke', Chairman of the Standing Joint Committee, 'Radnor', Chairman of Territorial Force; and 'Heytesbury', Chief of Police, Wilts, our county, will have a list of well known names concerned in local government (*Police Review*, 1908: 140).

Lord Heytesbury was not appointed as chief constable, instead the standing joint committee chose a war hero, Mr Hoel Llewellyn, as its chief constable. Llewellyn was 37 years old and had spent about 15 years in the Royal Navy. During the latter part of his service Llewellyn had fought in the South African War where he won the DSO. He had also been nominated for, but did not receive, the Victoria Cross. Llewellyn left the Navy on being appointed a District Commandant for the Lichenburg Police District and a Justice of the Peace for the Transvaal colony. He returned to England in 1903 and was attached to the office of the chief constable of Hertfordshire for a year, and later the offices of the Commissioners of the City[19] and Metropolitan police, for eight and two months respectively. In 1906, Llewellyn was short-listed, successively, for the chief constableships of Shropshire and Devon.

During the same year, the chief constableship of Somerset became vacant following the retirement of Captain Charles Alison who had been chief constable since 1884. The appointment processes had similar characteristics to that of Llewellyn's appointment at Wiltshire. The standing joint committee advertised for a successor to Alison, offering a salary of £500 per year, with £100 to cover expenses and travelling. Candidates other than those at present in the police service were to be not more than 42 years old, a condition that was different to the Wiltshire advertisement, and applications were to be accompanied by only three recent testimonials. The *Police Review* sent copies of its prize essay to the principal papers circulating in Somerset. Many applications were received, from which a shortlist of seven candidates was drawn up. The candidates on the shortlist were: Captain E. Napier of New Scotland Yard; Mr R.L. Williams, the chief constable of Exeter; Captain Gwyne of the Royal Fusiliers; Captain Thresher of the Rifle Brigade; Major Dunlop, the chief constable of the East Riding of Yorkshire; Captain Metcalf, the chief constable of the West Riding, of Yorkshire and Major Teale, the chief

[19] By coincidence Nott-Bower's office.

constable of Eastbourne. Of the seven candidates only Mr R.L. Williams, the chief constable of Exeter, had spent his whole career in the police.

Captain Herbert Metcalf, the chief constable of the West Riding of Yorkshire, was duly appointed as the new chief constable of Somerset at the advertised salary of £500 per year, with £100 travelling expenses and rent free accommodation at Glastonbury. Metcalf's salary was less than he had received in the West Riding, but in his letter of resignation to the West Riding standing joint committee he gave the poor health of his family as the main reason for taking up the new appointment. Before becoming chief constable of the West Riding, Metcalf had been chief constable of West Suffolk, a post he commenced shortly after leaving the army. The *Police Review* described Captain Metcalf as being 6'3" tall and 44 years of age, two years over the prescribed age limit. The Somerset appointment was his third appointment as chief constable in three years. Almost uniquely, for it was the usual practice for chief constables to move from smaller to larger forces (see chapter 8), it was a smaller, but less demanding position than that in the West Riding. This appointment was to cause vacancies in two other forces.

On finding themselves with a vacancy to fill, the standing joint committee of the West Riding advertised the post of chief constable of the county at £700 per annum with expenses. Candidates for the post were to be between 35 and 42 and must reside within one mile of the Wakefield boundary. The advertisement stated that canvassing, either personally or through friends, was to warrant disqualification. Proposals made to the standing joint committee to raise the age of applicants to under 52 and to include serving members of the force were ruled to be out of order on the grounds that they were made after the initial resolution was passed.

A total of 80 applications were received from which a list of five of the most likely candidates was drawn up. Those on the shortlist were: Major L.W. Atcherley, chief constable of Shropshire; Captain J.G. Mignon of the Leicestershire regiment who was attached to the City of London Police; Captain Henry Ramsden of the Royal Artillery reserve; Captain C.E. Rich, the deputy Governor of Wakefield Prison; and, Mr Henry Riches, the chief constable of Middlesborough. Riches was the only person on the shortlist to have risen through the ranks and to have served as a career police officer. Of the 35 members of the standing joint committee present at the selection, 21 voted for Atcherley and twelve voted for

Riches, two of the other candidates got one vote each. Major Atcherley was 38 years old and had served in the army for 16 years, before being appointed chief constable of Shropshire in 1905,[20] his departure left the Shropshire chief constableship vacant.

The Shropshire standing joint committee advertised the post and selected a shortlist of seven applicants. The *Police Review* did not say who the applicants on the shortlist were, only that a Captain Gerald Lysley Derriman of Eaton Square, London, was appointed as the new chief constable of Shropshire. Captain Derriman had served in the Grenadier Guards for nine years and for the past three years had been secretary to the RSPCA.

Another vacancy in 1908, was the chief constableship of Rutland, the smallest of the county forces with a police establishment of only 15. The vacancy arose due to the retirement of Mr William Keep at the age of 83 after 62 years police service. Keep had been chief constable of Rutland since 1871. His successor was Superintendent William Wilson, the deputy chief constable. Wilson had joined the Rutland force in 1872 but left in 1880 to join the civil service, where he remained for eight years. On rejoining the Rutland police, Wilson became inspector and was appointed as superintendent and deputy chief constable in 1905. The men appointed to the chief constableships of the larger county forces, West Riding and Somerset, were ex-army officers with experience of commanding a county police force, but not experience of being a police officer. The appointments in the few small county forces, like those in the borough forces, tended to go to trusted police officers. By and large, the pattern of recruitment throughout the county forces remained much the same during the nineteenth, and early twentieth, centuries.

Selecting borough chief officers before Desborough

Appointments to the larger borough or city forces

The case studies described above, especially the Buckinghamshire appointment, find a resonance in the autobiographical experience of Sir William Nott-Bower, in which he described his appointment to each of the

[20] Atcherley became an HM Inspector of Constabulary in 1919 and retired in 1936.

three police forces he commanded during his 47 years as a chief police officer (Nott-Bower, 1926: 24). The first two were as chief constables of the Leeds and Liverpool city forces and the third was as Commissioner of the City of London Police. These experiences provide a useful insight into the interplay between the formal procedures and the informal mechanisms in the appointment process in a large borough force and show how these positions were seen to be the preserve of the local power élite.

Sir John William Nott-Bower
(*Police Review*, 1893: 43)

As a contrast against the appointments to the large borough forces, which as will be shown, bore many characteristics of the county process, some examples of appointments to the medium and smaller borough forces are given later on.

Frustrated by his lack of prospects in the army Nott-Bower disliked the idea of leaving it:

> ... but I could see no prospect of real service and still less of any promotion which might promise a satisfactory career ... So I seriously pondered over future plans, with the result that I concluded that, next to the army, a police career was probably what would suit me best, and I determined to use every effort to obtain a start in the police (Nott-Bower, 1926: 24).

Nott-Bower contacted his father's old friend, the Minister for Education, for help with his choice of career and joined the RIC as a Gentleman Cadet.[21]

> My father's old friend - the Right Honourable W.E. Forster - at the time Minister for Education, gave me, towards the end of 1872, a letter of introduction to Lord Hartington, then Chief Secretary for Ireland. The result was to procure for me, in a very few weeks, a nomination to a cadet-ship in the Royal Irish Constabulary, which seemed to offer the most likely, and

[21] Under the RIC Gentleman Cadet Scheme the successful applicant would spend six months under a course of instruction at the training depot before being posted as sub-inspector to take command of a district. Entrance by competitive examination was later introduced after Nott-Bower's time.

> sure, approach to a successful career. These nominations were very eagerly sought after, and needed some influence for an Englishman to secure, so I was specially fortunate in receiving one so promptly (Nott-Bower, 1926: 26).

Without the right connections from the outset, it is very unlikely that Nott-Bower's police career would have got off to such a promising start. Nott-Bower stayed in the RIC for five years and whilst he was serving as a district inspector he heard that the chief constableship of Leeds was about to become vacant. Nott-Bower's background was typical of a number of borough chief officers, but not all, as will be established in later chapters. He used his Leeds position to gain the experience that would qualify him for the more prestigious appointments at Liverpool and the City of London. The salary at Leeds was less than he was receiving in the RIC, when all of the expenses were taken into consideration, but he saw an opportunity to further his police career. "I realised that an important command, such that it was, was just the necessary stepping stone towards a successful police career, and I therefore decided to become a candidate" (Nott-Bower, 1926: 39). Once he had made the decision to stand for the post, he required the support of enough members of the Leeds watch committee as it needed to ensure his election.

> To secure a chance of election, a pretty strenuous canvass was necessary, and I succeeded in my efforts mainly owing to the strong, and friendly, support of Sir E.H. Carbutt, then Mayor of Leeds, of M.W. Thompson (an old friend of my father's, a director of the Midland Railway, and formerly M.P. for Bradford), and of Colonel Gunter of Wetherby (my old militia commanding officer) who had one or two tenants who were members of the Leeds Town Council. So, in May 1878, I commenced my police life in England, as Chief Constable of Leeds (Nott-Bower, 1926: 39).

Nott-Bower had experience of policing, but his influential connections, not his ability as either a police officer or as a manager, secured his election as chief constable. This state of affairs was fairly commonplace at the time. Nott-Bower's credentials were impeccable, but his appointment did not meet with the approval of all of the watch committee and one councillor, a local fruit trader, strongly objected to the chief constable being paid a large salary and (unsuccessfully) moved an amendment to reduce his salary by £100.

> The office of chief constable isn't worth the figure. We'd 'ave lots of applicants if we put it at 'alf the wages. We don't want one of these 'ere Gentlemen, who can play lawn tennis and go a-fishing, or make a nice bow in the Major's drawing room, or say 'Ow-d'ye-do without dropping 'is H's. What we want is a man as can catch a thief when a chap's 'ouse is broken into (Nott-Bower, 1926: 41).

Nott-Bower stayed at Leeds for three years before he heard about a vacancy at Liverpool, the largest police force in England and Wales outside the Metropolitan Police. He felt that the Head Constableship of Liverpool would offer him the opportunity of some "really important police work". So, he:

> ... at once decided to become a candidate for the position. Again, vigorous 'electioneering' became necessary if there was to be any chance of success. The Leeds Magistrates and watch committee most generously and cordially recommended my application, and I again had the warm support of many friends. Mr M.W. Thompson (Chairman of the Midland Railway), who helped me so much at Leeds, again gave me valuable aid. I owed very much to the unstinted and influential help of Mr Alfred Turner (a Liverpool Magistrate, and leading merchant, and a brother of Mr Bickerton Turner, Agent to the Bank of England in Leeds), and to Sir James Bourne, Bart., of Liverpool. With their weighty support, and that of many other friends, I found myself duly elected, on the 30th August, 1881, to be Head Constable of Liverpool (Nott-Bower, 1926: 55).

Nott-Bower was 32 years of age when he became the Head Constable of Liverpool and once again his appointment was due to the strength of his influential allies and friends in high places, little mention was made of his ability to do the job in question.

Nott-Bower remained Head Constable of Liverpool for 21 years until 1901, when the Commissionership of the City of London Police became vacant upon the resignation of Sir Henry Smith KCB. It was the second most important police position in the country[22] and in Nott-Bower's own words was *secundus inter pares* with the Metropolitan Commissioner. After applying for the post and being short-listed, he found himself, once

[22] The highest was, as it still is, the Metropolitan Commissioner.

again, in the position of having to canvass support in order to secure his new position.

> I have referred before to the (very undesirable) 'electioneering' necessary for the obtaining of an appointment as a chief officer of police. And if such electioneering was necessary in the case of a chief constableship it was still more so in the case of the City Commissionership, for in the former case the electing body was a watch committee, composed of fifteen or twenty persons, whilst in the latter it was the Court of Common Council, composed of 230 persons. So that (I am happy to say for the last time) I found myself in the position of being compelled to 'canvass' and 'solicit' votes (Nott-Bower, 1926: 171).

The process of appointing the City Commissioner was very different from that of chief constable.

> In the first place, it is not enough that a candidate should 'apply' for the appointment, he must be nominated by a member of the Court of Common Council (I was nominated by Alderman Sir James Ritchie, Bart.) Then election is not complete (as it is in the boroughs, as soon as the vote has been taken), but requires the formal approval of His Majesty the King. And finally, a declaration of acceptance of office, etc., must be made before a Judge of the High Court before the duties are taken up (Nott-Bower, 1926: 173).

Nott-Bower and the four other candidates on the shortlist were present whilst the interviews and ballot were taken.

> It was somewhat of an ordeal for the candidates. We had to take our places on the dais, next to the Lord Mayor, and were questioned as to our qualifications, then a vote by ballot was taken, and (in our presence) each paper was openly read out on removal from the ballot box, and the vote recorded. Then the count was taken, and the result announced ... Whilst the votes were being taken, an amusing remark was made to me by the candidate to whom I was sitting next. He said: 'I never expected to win, and I really think you ought to, but I never knew before how many damned liars there are in the Court of Common Council. I had double the number of promises than I have votes (Nott-Bower, 1926: 172).

It is of interest that the formal process changed little over the next seventy years, as Alderson recently described:

> There was Jim Page, the sitting tenant [acting commissioner], and myself who had been talked about in police circles. So we went along in morning dress, we were put under the Guildhall in a kind of dungeon and a flunky said 'just wait in there gentlemen and I shall come for you when they are ready'. So we were in this room pacing about like lions.
>
> 'Mr Alderson' ... he said, 'when we go in go to the centre isle, bow to the mace, walk down the isle and when you get to the mace, bow again, go up round by the steps to the microphone and the Lord Mayor will ask you some questions.' Seated in the hall were about a hundred people, each with a vote ... So, anyway, I go in and bow, walk down, bow again ... I just stood there and the Lord Mayor had this paper with the questions on. I found the questions not too bad and at the end he said 'thank you very much Mr Alderson' and I bowed again facing the altar and as I walked back through the hall a polite applause rippled through the chamber.
>
> They fetched Jim up and I could hear a loud applause as he came back and we stood there in this dungeon until the flunky came back and said 'er, Mr Page'. So he goes up and gets the job ... That is how they appointed commissioners. I didn't get one question that I could have used to get into debate.[23]

Nott-Bower's accounts of his appointments give us a rare insight into the workings of the Victorian patronage system as it applies to the process of selecting a chief officer of police, patronage is discussed in greater detail in the next chapter. Nott-Bower's account augments that of his predecessor as Commissioner of the City of London Police, Sir Henry Smith KCB. Smith's autobiography is a detailed account of the way in which this patronage system worked (Smith, 1910).

Like Nott-Bower, Smith had been born into the upper classes. He retired from the army on half pay whilst aged in his early forties and went to live with his mother in Alnmouth in Northumberland. Here, he lived the life of a country gentleman - hunting, fishing and playing golf - mostly in the company of his friend Major Browne. It was Major Browne, former chief constable of Northumberland, who introduced Smith to the idea of pursuing a career within the police. Smith gives a rare glimpse of how the chief constableship of the county was regarded by the gentry.

---

[23] Interview with John Alderson, April 17 1997.

> Driving one morning with him to Shiply Lane End, a favourite 'meet,' he said: "How would the Chief Constableship of the county suit you?" He had held the appointment himself before succeeding to a fortune. "Nothing in the world", I replied, after a moment's reflection, "would suit me better."
>
> "Well," he continued, "I think that may be arranged. Allgood has completely broken down and can't last long now" (Smith, 1910: 82).

Allgood's health recovered and he stayed in office for another twenty years.

Browne may have appeared casual and confident towards his friend because he once held the post but it is nevertheless clear from the exchange that the post was regarded as the preserve of the gentry alone.[24] The chief constableship of the county was a convenient post for the younger sons of the gentry to hold for it allowed them to retain status within county society and also gave them power at a local level, in much the same way that the army and cloth had done in previous years. "Becoming head of a county force might enable a man to consolidate and extend an existing social position and wed himself into the upper reaches of the county hierarchy" (Steedman, 1984: 47). Which was precisely the manner in which Smith approached it.

Although Smith did not become the chief constable of Northumberland, his mind was firmly set upon a police career, so he went about gaining the experience that would help him achieve his ambition. His anecdotes give an insight into the freedom a serving chief constable had in choosing the extent to which he became involved in the policing of his area. Smith obtained an introduction to the chief constable of one of the largest Scottish county forces and presented himself "one December evening".

> To say that I was received with open arms is to put it mildly. My superior for the time being had served in one of the crackest of Highland regiments, and was, it goes without saying, a very strict disciplinarian, albeit eminently convivial. He had a warm heart and a cool cellar, and before the evening was over - he promptly asked me to dinner - we were sworn friends. "I'll teach you all I know," he said to me confidently, "in three months time." About midnight he addressed me severely: "Parade every morning, remember,

[24] However, compare this vignette with St Johnston's experience of being approached about the chief constableship of Oxfordshire in chapter 6.

> Sundays included, my office, ten punctually." "I won't be late sir," I replied. Next morning I was there to a moment, and was received by the superintendent, who furnished me with the Scotsman. "Queer thing, sir," he said, "the Captain's late this morning." Queerer still, the Captain was late every morning (Smith, 1910: 83).

The life of a county chief constable in the last century was very relaxed.

> When he arrived, "any letters?" was his first query. "No letters sir," was the stereotyped reply. "Suppose we go along to the club," the Captain would say, and along we went. "Two small whiskies" was the order promptly given and promptly executed. After disposing of them we played billiard, or took a walk till luncheon time then back to the office. "Any letters?" "None this afternoon, sir." In fact there seldom were any (Smith, 1910: 84).

The purpose of the placement was to give Smith experience of police work and a testimonial as to his competence in police work. He left the Scottish force after three months with a favourable testimonial from his genial host. Smith stated that he did not believe in testimonials and like Nott-Bower professed his abhorrence of the patronage system, favouring a more democratic approach. But his feelings did not stop him going to elaborate lengths to obtain testimonials from his influential friends. In one passage he describes how he got his friend, the Earl Grey, to give him a testimonial.

> One day, when staying at Doxford, three miles from Howick, I jumped on a pony, and cantered over to show him my testimonials. Instantly he was all attention, and began to read them carefully.
>
> "I say, my dear fellow", he remarked, on coming to a rather elaborate one, "this is the best testimonial I ever read in my life."
>
> "I am very pleased indeed", I replied, "to hear your opinion of it, for I wrote it myself".
>
> "What's that you're saying? - what do you mean?"
>
> "This is what I mean", I answered. "If a man has not the intellect enough to write a testimonial in his own favour, and the energy enough not to stand over a good friend till he signs it, he's not fit for the position I aspire to".

> "By Jupiter !" said Grey, with a laugh, "there's little doubt you're right" (Smith, 1910: 91).

After gaining experience of the workings of a county police force, Smith sought experience of an English borough force.

> On my return to Northumberland I immediately made for Newcastle to serve under the chief constable there, being introduced to him by an intimate friend, then High Sheriff of the county (Smith, 1910: 84).

Captain J. Nicholls, the chief constable of the Newcastle force[25] gave Smith the run of his office.

> He gave me the run of his office; told me there was work twenty four hours a day if I wanted it; cautioned me against several members of the force, and finally promised me a testimonial should he, from his own observation and the reports of his superintendents, find I deserved one (Smith, 1910: 84).

After serving at Newcastle for a month, a possible vacancy arose when the post of superintendent became vacant in the detective department at Liverpool. Smith wrote: "by Captain Nicholl's advice I applied for the appointment. I had very powerful backing, and when I arrived on the scene of action I found myself first favourite" (Smith, 1910: 85). Smith did not get the job and doubted, in hindsight, that he could have done it. He then returned to Alnmouth in Northumberland only to receive a message from Major Bowman, Chief Superintendent of the City of London Police, who "having heard of my defeat in Liverpool, wrote to me saying that he should like to see me should I happen to be in London" (Smith, 1910: 85).

Bowman told Smith, in confidence, that he would be retiring shortly, that Smith was just the man to succeed him, and that Colonel Fraser, the Commissioner, would appoint the person that he recommended. The second appointment in the City of London Police was in the gift of the Commissioner. Smith had to wait six years for Bowman to retire and in

---

[25] Appointed at the age of 30 in 1869, Capt. Nicholls served as Chief Constable of Newcastle upon Tyne until 1899 when his resignation was called for. His force was in open revolt against him and a petition from local ratepayers and inhabitants called for his resignation (Evans, 1988: 78).

1885 after "living like a late noble duke on hope" (Smith, 1910: 87), he succeeded Major Bowman as Chief Superintendent and second in command of the City of London Police. Smith did not say why he waited six years to succeed Bowman and did not apply for a post elsewhere. After serving for five years as second in command he became Commissioner on Colonel Fraser's retirement.

The autobiographical accounts of Nott-Bower and Smith provide an interesting and valuable first-hand description of the process of selection and of the attitudes held by the landed gentry to senior police positions. The degree to which their individual experiences were typical of the appointment of other chief constables is hard to estimate, especially as their experiences were recorded as memoirs. However, their similarity to the biographies of many other chief officers depicted in the *Police Review* suggests that the processes they described were fairly representative of the manner in which appointments to the larger borough and county forces and the Commissionership of the City of London Police were made.

Appointments to the medium sized and smaller boroughs

The appointment of chief officers to the medium sized and smaller boroughs were qualitatively different to appointments to the larger forces. Here, some examples from 1908 are illustrated. In contrast to the county appointments, all of the appointments of borough chief constables in 1908 were of men who had risen through the ranks of the police. Borough chief constableships were not always advertised as it was very often the case that watch committees wanted to appoint the post to an internal candidate; for example, when the post of chief constable of the Dover force became vacant in 1908 the deputy, a man with many years service to the watch committee, was automatically appointed without the job being advertised.

Another borough chief constableship that became vacant in 1908 was at Devonport. The post was advertised by the watch committee and a shortlist of seven candidates was drawn up from the many applicants. All nine candidates were serving police officers; Mr William Bestwick, a superintendent from the Newcastle-upon-Tyne force; Mr G. Bridle, an inspector in the Brighton force; Mr A. Bruce, a detective in the Metropolitan police; Mr R.S. Eddy, the chief constable of the Barnstaple force; Mr C. Greenstreet, chief constable of the Ryde force in the Isle of Wight; Mr F. Hatch, the chief constable of the Banbury force; Mr Ingram, an inspector from the Southport force; Mr D. Rankin, the detective chief inspector at Cardiff; and Mr J.H. Watson, the chief constable of Congleton. Four of the seven candidates were chief constables of small borough forces wanting to gain command of a medium sized borough force. In 1908, Devonport had an established strength of about 83 police officers. Banbury (Hatch) had 13 officers; Barnstaple (Eddy) had 14; Congleton (Watson) had 11; Ryde (Greenstreet) had 14.[26] The others were applying for their first appointment as chief constable.

A further meeting of the watch committee narrowed the field down to three candidates: Watson, Bridle and Ingram. Watson was appointed as chief constable, he was 36 years old and had been chief constable of the Congleton force for six years. Prior to his appointment at Congleton he held the rank of chief inspector in the Hyde borough force. The notes describing Watson's career state that he had achieved his first post of chief constable less than ten years after joining the police and had experience in every department of the service. His career was very similar to that described in chapter 5 by 'Boro CC'. J.H. Watson was educated at Skipton Grammar school and worked in a manufacturer's office until he joined the police at the age of 21. His two brothers, J.P.K. and T.M. Watson were also chief constables of borough forces.[27]

The appointment of Watson as chief constable at Devonport left the Congleton force without a chief constable. The post was not advertised and a local police officer, one sergeant Ingles, was appointed to succeed him. Ingles had previously been station officer under Watson's predecessor and had at times taken control over the force. He was appointed as sergeant in 1906 and became chief constable in 1908 when he was 39 years old. In 1914, Watson became chief constable of the Bristol force, where he remained until 1930.

The examples of appointments given here have tended to date around the turn of the century. The process of open appointment, a format that was

[26] Table II: Ranks, Numbers and Rates of Pay, *Report from the Select Committee* on the Police Forces (Weekly Rest Day) Bill, with the Proceedings of the Committee, Evidence, Appendix and Index; HC 1908 Cmd. 353, 354 ix. 679.

[27] J.P.K. Watson was chief constable of Peterborough (1909-1915) and Preston (1917-1937), and T.M. Watson was chief constable of Kidderminster (1931-1933) and Walsall (1933-1953).

loosely based upon that which took place in the counties was not, however, always adopted. It only developed as the office of borough chief constable (see chapters two and three) developed and the police under their charge became integrated into Victorian municipal life. Before concluding this chapter, one final case study will be illustrated to demonstrate how the appointment process in the medium and small borough forces changed between the introduction of the borough police and the end of the First World War.

A case study of the recruitment, selection and appointment of the chief officers of the York City Police 1836 to 1918

Between 1836 and 1918 the York City Police, a typical medium sized borough police force, were commanded by eight chief officers. Here the appointments of each are described. The example illustrates how the process of selecting and appointing chief officers was shaped by a combination of existing practice and external influences. For the first fifty two years of the force's existence the watch committee appointed the city's first four chief officers as they saw fit.

Daniel Smith (1836) had previously served as captain of the York City night patrol that was created under the Improvement Act of 1825. The watch committee took control of the night patrol and temporarily appointed Daniel Smith as head constable pending investigations by the committee as to how to proceed in forming a police force (Mins. York WC, 18/5/1836).[28] Smith was demoted later in 1836 to being inspector in charge of the night patrol, his previous role, because of his untoward "night" activities. In addition to running several brothels, Smith had also introduced a scheme whereby complaints against crimes were only followed up after a payment of a fee of 4*s* to 5*s*. Despite these practices, he remained in office as the new chief officer's deputy. He was eventually dismissed from the force in 1841, after Pardoe died, for being absent from duty and for falsifying records of his duties (Mins. York WC, 4/7/1841).

[28] Weekly minutes of the watch committee.

William Pardoe (*1836 - 1841*), the head of the old day patrol, replaced Smith as Superintendent and chief officer of the York City police force (Mins. York WC, 3/11/1836: 114; Swift, 1988). Pardoe was charged with implementing the recommendations of the Metropolitan Inspector who had been hired by the Council to advise on the installation of a police force (see chapter two). There was no formal appointment process.

Pardoe served as Superintendent for five years until his death on the 24th September 1841 (Mins. York WC, 18/9/1841). The watch committee resolved to "supply the vacancy occasioned by the death of Mr Pardoe by advertising in the newspapers, and also by communicating with the Commissioners of the London Police and police officers in other principal towns" (*idem*). On September 30 the Lord Mayor of York wrote to Colonel Rowan, one of the Metropolitan Commissioners, to see if he would recommend "a fit and proper person" to fill the post (Mins. York WC, 7/10/1841). Rowan promptly replied on October 5 to say that he had received the letter but wanted an assurance before recommending anybody that if the person was not appointed then the watch committee would pay their return expenses (*idem*). Once this assurance had been given Colonel Rowan replied, on October 8, to say that he thought that an "efficient" person could be found to fill the position for about £150 per annum rather than the £120 originally suggested by the watch committee (Mins. York WC, 9/10/1841). Rowan stated that this increased salary would be necessary because:

> ... the active and deserving men of the Police of the Metropolis, have all superior situations in their own establishments, to which they may hope to rise, and they have the advantage of a superannuation allowance when worn out, which they of course are unwilling to give up (Mins. York WC, 18/10/1841).

Rowan was simply trying to point out that his men were experienced and did not come cheaply. The increase was approved and a Metropolitan police officer was sent to York. There is no evidence that the suggestion made after Pardoe's death to advertise the post and inform police in other forces took place.

Robert Chalk (1841 - 1862) was the officer recommended by Col. Rowan and he arrived in the city on October 16 with a letter of introduction from the Commissioner. Chalk was immediately placed in charge of the force "until further notice". The watch committee minutes do not suggest that any other candidates were considered; moreover they show that Chalk was not even formally interviewed for the post. Just over two weeks later his appointment as Superintendent of Police was confirmed (Mins. York WC, 4/7/1841). Chalk remained in office for 22 years until 1862, when he resigned stating that he no longer had the strength to continue as chief constable (Mins. York WC, 26/5/1862).[29] During his period in office, Chalk had seen the York police increase in number and the police role broaden considerably to include many inspecting functions, the operation of a fire engine and other ancillary services.

Samuel Haley (1862 - 1888), the superintendent in charge of the night shift, was appointed as chief constable on June 6 1862. Once again, the watch committee were happy to appoint someone they felt that they could trust to do the job. Haley was to receive an annual salary of £150 with clothing, which comprised of £125 from the watch committee and £25 per year from the Board of Health Committee as inspector of nuisances (Mins. York WC, 4/6/1862). Haley served as chief constable for 26 years and resigned "on account of his failing health and long service" (Mins. York WC, 15/8/1888). He had been with the force for a total of 33 years.

Towards the end of the nineteenth century the practice of open appointment became the norm throughout public appointments. So, the vacancy left by Haley's departure was, in contrast to previous appointments, advertised by the watch committee "in the local newspapers and in certain London and provincial newspapers" (Report of WC to York Council, 1/10/1888).[30] The advertisement (see Figure 3) illustrates the increasing complexity of the police role and ran as follows:

The watch committee received 39 applications and shortlisted four. They were: Jas. Cumming, chief constable of Bacup; Edward Emery, chief constable of Chesterfield; Frank C. Froest, detective department, Metropolitan police; and G.W. Whitfield, chief constable of Shrewsbury (*idem*). With the exception of Froest, who was Superintendent and head of CID at Scotland Yard, the candidates were all chief police officers who

---

[29] Note that the office was now referred to as chief constable rather than superintendent.

[30] These were monthly reports made by the watch committee to York City council.

were either seeking a more prestigious or larger, and more remunerative post.

Figure 3: Advertisement for a borough chief constable, 1888

CITY OF YORK - APPOINTMENT OF CHIEF CONSTABLE

"The Corporation of York invite Applications for the Appointment of CHIEF CONSTABLE of the City. Salary £300 per annum inclusive. No residence provided. The Police Force numbers 67 men, and as the force acts as the City Fire Brigade. The Chief Constable will, if required, be appointed as Superintendent of the Brigade.

"The Chief Constable will have to conduct proceedings before the Justices in all ordinary Police cases, and generally discharge all the duties devolving upon a Chief Officer of Police, or which may be required by the Corporation and Watch Committee. Population of City about 70,000; area 3,553 acres.

"Applications (marked on the outside 'Chief Constableship'), stating age and present occupation and experience in Police and Fire Brigade duties, and accompanied by recent Testimonials, to be addressed to me the undersigned, not later than TUESDAY, the 18th September inst.

"Applicants should state when they can enter upon the duties.

"GEORGE McGUIRE,
"Town Clerk.

G.W. Whitfield (1888 - 1894) was appointed chief constable. He had previous experience of commanding the smaller Shrewsbury force which had an establishment of 35 officers, compared with York's 72 (Mins. York WC, 19/9/1888).

Although Whitfield's appointment may have been more democratic than that of his predecessors, it was not the most successful of choices because, unlike his predecessors, he did not appear to have got on very well with either his watch committee or the townsfolk. He did, however, appear to have got on well with his officers. In the September following his appointment, several officers who had taken an injured person to the county hospital, for the police also provided the local ambulance service, were accused of being drunk and being incapable of performing their duty properly. Whitfield was reprimanded by the watch committee for not going to the hospital with the injured person and for not personally making an immediate inquiry of the charges against his officers (Report of WC to York Council, 9/11/1889).

G.W. Whitfield
(*Police Review*, 1893: 535)

This was one of a number of such incidents. In 1894, Whitfield was accused of not acquainting the magistrates with the fact that two witnesses were available to give evidence against the police in a case which involved a sergeant of the force "exceeding his duty". A subsequent inquiry found that it was common practice for the colleagues of officers, who were fined for misconduct, to hold a collection in order to pay the fine. The watch committee resolved "that in the opinion of this committee, the Chief Constable no longer retains its confidence in the position he occupies and that he be requested to resign" (Mins. York WC, 3/8/1894).

Whitfield promptly tendered his resignation in which he stated that "any mistakes I have made have been occasioned by failing health, and not from any thought or desire other than to please the committee ..." (Mins. York WC, 8/8/1894). He also pleaded for a pension to be granted on the basis of his previous service and on account that he had no other profession or business. Accompanying his resignation on August 7, 1894, was a medical report in which Dr Reynolds concluded that Whitfield was no longer fit for further duty (*idem*). The committee resolved to grant a pension in accordance to the Police Act 1890 and to contact the other police authorities, under which he had served, to contribute towards the pension. Upon hearing that he would be granted a pension, Whitfield agreed to run the force until a successor was appointed. The committee also resolved to advertise the vacancy.

The advertisement described the position as per Figure 3, with the additional requirement that applicants should be no more than 45 years old. A total of 32 applications were received and a shortlist of six was drawn up. They were: Andrew Amour, chief constable of Windsor; J.W. Farmery, chief constable of Canterbury; E.T. Lloyd, Barrister-at-law and late of the Indian Civil Service; D.A. McNeil, private secretary to Lord Derwent, late of the Queensland (Australian) police; W.G. Morant, chief constable of Reigate; W.G. Kelly, district superintendent, Renfrewshire (Mins. York

WC, 5/9/1894). All the candidates, excepting Lloyd, had prior police experience and were looking to either secure a commanding position, for example McNeil, or to gain command of a larger force.

E.T. Lloyd (1894 - 1897) was chosen as the next chief constable. This appointment was very much against the grain, as for the first time since its commencement sixty years previously, the watch committee chose a person who was not a serving police officer. Moreover, Lloyd was not only of a similar social standing to the watch committee, but he was Oxford educated and was a barrister. It is highly likely that this was a deliberate appointment strategy given the scandal that had occurred when Whitfield was in command.

E.T. Lloyd
(*Police Review*, 1897: 450)

There were allegations relating to the previous administration in the local press of corruption and collusion which, substantiated or not, damaged the local credibility of the police force with the townsfolk.[31] An independent disciplinarian was therefore sought. The *Yorkshire Herald* stated that "mere Police knowledge is easily acquired, but the habit of formal discipline and the ability to command do not come by nature, nor are they readily picked up. The school in which they are best got is that of the Army" (*Police Review*, 1894: 426). It was thought that Lloyd's social and educational position, plus his military experience, would distance him from the men under his command and enable him to reform the force, thus re-establishing the force's local credibility. Lloyd stayed at York for three years tendering his resignation on account of his having been appointed as a Resident Magistrate in Ireland (Report of WC to York Council, 4/10/1897).

The vacancy for chief constable and superintendent of the fire brigade was advertised locally and also in the *Police Review* and the *Police Chronicle* (Report of WC to York Council, 9/11/1897: Accounts section).

[31] A number of other departures from the York police followed Whitfield's resignation.

Twenty seven applications were received and a shortlist of four was drawn up. They were: Pelly, a superintendent in the Devon county constabulary; Joseph Farndale, chief constable of Margate; W.B. Jones, chief constable of Grantham; Reeve, a chief inspector in the Doncaster force (*Police Review*, 1897: 473).

Joseph Farndale (1897 - 1900) was appointed chief constable. He was 33 years old and had previously served as the chief constable of Margate (establishment of 35 as opposed to 79 at York) since he was 28 years old. He had joined the police at the age of 19 as a constable.

Joseph Farndale
(*Police Review*, 1897: 546)

All candidates were serving police officers and all, with the possible exception of Supt. Pelly, had served in the police throughout their careers. It was a common practice in the county forces for the chief constable to appoint people with military backgrounds as superintendent. Once again the candidates possessed similar profiles to those found in previous shortlists. They were career police officers with experience of commanding smaller forces who were looking for a larger, more prestigious and more remunerative command.

The watch committee's choice of a police officer for chief constable was quite significant. Whilst Lloyd performed his duties and was popular with the watch committee, his approach was mainly that of an administrator, and had a smaller local profile to his predecessors. Given the lack of trust in the police after Whitfield's resignation, this is exactly what had been wanted. However, the choice of Farndale as Lloyd's successor was probably driven by the watch committee's realisation that they needed to have, and be seen to have, an experienced police officer in charge of such a relatively small force. It is also the case that there was a wider backlash over the appointment of a non-police officer, for example, arising from the *Police Review*'s campaign to encourage police authorities to appoint police officers as chief officers (see later). Farndale was young, ambitious and he stayed at York for three years before tendering his resignation on June 30, 1900, upon his appointment as chief constable of the larger Bradford city force (Mins. York WC, 10/7/1900).

The vacancy for Chief Constable and Superintendent of the Fire Brigade was advertised through the usual outlets, but with an increased salary of £350 and 26 applications were received; five were shortlisted for interview. They were: J. Burrow, chief constable of Kendal; J. Metcalfe, chief constable of Reigate; T.T. Earnshaw, superintendent and deputy chief constable at Wigan; J. White, probably chief inspector or superintendent at Bradford; R.J. Carter, chief constable of Windsor (Mins. York WC, 31/7/1900). As with previous candidates, all were either in command of smaller borough forces or were in the senior ranks of larger borough forces.

James Burrow (1900 - 1918) was appointed to the post. He was 34 years old. After working as a clerk in a manufacturing works he joined the Wigan police at the age of 20, becoming assistant clerk in the chief constable's office. Four years later, he moved to Cambridge as inspector and clerk rising to superintendent and deputy chief constable. In 1899 he became chief constable of the small Kendal force. Burrow remained as chief constable of York until he retired aged 52 in May 1918 (Report of WC to York Council, 4/3/1918).

James Burrow
(*Police Review*, 1900: 450)

He appears simply to have lost interest in the job, however, he had managed the York City force through the excessive demands created by the First World War and also through considerable tensions that occurred within the police force itself. It was at this point in time when the police in medium borough forces performed their broadest range of functions. The watch committee minutes list the endless reports on matters ranging from the sale of petroleum to the inspection of gas supplies.

The gradually changing process of recruitment, selection and appointment reflect contemporary attitudes towards the role of the police and also towards employment practices. The watch committee relied upon existing models of management and therefore of appointment. In the early years of the police they simply appointed people who proved that they could be trusted, if not by proof of loyalty to the committee, such as in the case of Smith, Pardoe and Haley. Later on they trusted the recommendation of a 'gentleman', Commissioner Rowan, when they appointed Chalk. These were common practices in most borough appointments during the early nineteenth century.

It must be understood that the society which the York borough force policed was socially stratified in a way that does not exist today. An insight into the make-up of the local power élite is given by Sir William Nott-Bower, who was born in York in 1849. In his autobiography, Nott-Bower describes society in mid-Victorian York as being "ridiculously stiff, and most comically 'exclusive'". There existed two main groups of 'society' in York, there were upper classes which consisted of the "'Superior' Clergy, those who, like my father, were closely associated with them, a few of the County families immediately around York, the Officers of the Cavalry regiment quartered around York and a few others". Outside the "charmed" circle of the upper classes were the professional classes "'Inferior' Clergy, doctors, solicitors, bankers, etc.," (Nott-Bower, 1926: 2). The watch committee were mainly members of the former group, but some were members of the latter. This was a world of patronage and favour.

It was only in the latter half of the nineteenth century that principles of meritocratic self-help[32] gained popularity and acceptance, and importantly, applications for appointment started to be considered solely on the basis of their merits. So we see the appointments taking place after Samuel Haley's retirement in 1888, as being of people who were recruited from a broader pool, who were selected for interview on the basis of their proven abilities and were appointed on their relative merits.

Conclusion

This chapter has shown that the provincial police authorities were dominated by the respective local power élites and that the police were an integral part of the Victorian system of local governance. Therefore, the police authorities were careful about who they gave the relatively powerful position of chief constable to. To assist them they had an almost free reign to appoint whomever they wished, although the county authorities had to

[32] Made popular by Samuel Smiles, see Smiles, (1860).

keep within the very vague and broad framework prescribed by the Home Secretary.

The autobiographical accounts, examples and cases studies, presented above, show that the county and large borough police authorities tended to appoint persons who shared a similar social outlook to their own. They were antithetical to police occupational culture and sought to avoid any conflict of interest by appointing persons who would appreciate their own viewpoint (Wall, 1987). Thus, the informal agenda of the selection process was more important than the formal process of selection in so far as the candidate with the most influential family or personal connections tended to get appointed. The example of the medium to small boroughs was slightly different, as the watch committees tended to seek individuals whom they could trust to effect their orders. They were often more interested in promoting a trusted servant as a reward for service than seeking the best socially qualified candidate. However, whilst there appear to have been considerable differences between the structure and composition of the borough and county police authorities, the basic informal agendas were nevertheless the same: all types of police authority actively sought qualities other than police experience in their chief constables in order to exercise as much control as was possible over the local police and the policing of the locale.

These important informal agendas, especially the debate over internal and external recruitment and the dynamics of patronage, are the subject of the next chapter.

5 Past Debates over Selection and Appointment

Introduction

Until the inter-war years, the management of the police was not only amateur, in the localised and pre-professional manner described in earlier chapters, but the external recruitment of police managers was a widely accepted practice. Furthermore, where internal recruitment did take place, it was not often on the basis of the principle of promotion by merit. Patronage played a very important role in both the promotion and selection process, as the autobiographical accounts in the previous chapter demonstrated. So, in order to explore the genesis of the development of the idea of internal recruitment this chapter will look further at the various debates that took place around the turn of the century (and since) over both the external recruitment of police managers and the role of patronage in the appointment and promotion process, especially the role of freemasonry. It will be shown in later chapters that these debates were equally as contemporary to policing at the turn of the century as they are today. The first part of this chapter will look at the debate over direct appointment versus promotion by merit. The second part will look at patronage versus promotion by merit, and the third part will evaluate the century long debate over freemasonry and its effect upon appointments and promotions within the police.

Direct appointment versus promotion by merit

After the turn of the century relations between the most senior and lower ranks were much the same as they were three quarters of a century previously, in so far as they were still class based. Yet, the society within which the police operated was changing, and new demands were being placed upon the police to fall into line. One such change was the increasing political importance of the labour movement and ideas relating to equality of opportunity. Police officers in the lower ranks were aggrieved at not being eligible for appointment to the highest ranks in the police service, and also at the way in which many appointments took place.

Writing in the 1920s, Nott-Bower thought that although contemporary practices of appointing chief constables had been effective during the early years of the police service, they were no longer a viable means of gaining the most efficient chief constables. Ironically, Nott-Bower had, himself, been a successful product of the very same system that he was attacking and would probably not have become a police officer if the reforms he advocated had been introduced earlier. He, nevertheless, felt that the efficiency of the police service depended upon the quality of the individuals who filled its higher administrative offices, but no system had then been introduced to ensure that the best persons were appointed to those offices. “And yet”, he argued, “during the ninety years in which police forces have been working in this country no suggestion, even of a system, securing the appointment of the most highly qualified men to these important offices, has ever been fully considered” (Nott-Bower, 1926: 323).

When police forces were first established, police authorities had no choice other than to appoint men they thought would be able to do the job efficiently. The initial choice of men for the office of chief constable was, Nott-Bower argues, correct and the:

> ... progress and increasing efficiency of the police during the ninety years of its existence is a testimony to the good service rendered by these officers, and to the general soundness of the selections made. And the system of selection was practically the same as then existed in all public services - army, navy, civil service, etc. - one necessarily redolent of nepotism, and one which any democracy must necessarily disapprove. It has now been discarded in all those services, save in the police alone, for which no definitive system has yet been substituted (Nott-Bower, 1926: 324).

The appointment of non-police officers to command a police force created discontent amongst serving police officers, who complained that they “... have to teach them their work, and suggest (even though the comparison is hardly accurate) that it is the same thing as if a policeman were appointed to command a regiment or a ship” (Nott-Bower, 1926: 324). Nott-Bower was referring here to the campaign by the *Police Review* to open up the most senior ranks and fill chief constableships from within the police, a view that became one of the primary demands of the police union in the early 1900s. But Nott-Bower did not think that the appointment of chief constables from within the police would provide the requisite quality of command. He believed that:

> it has led to the demand by the Police Federation that all appointments to these higher ranks should be made from the ranks of the Police Forces, a solution which, in my opinion, would be far more detrimental to the efficiency of the Police Service than even the old system, indefensible as that undoubtedly is (Nott-Bower, 1926: 323).

Instead, he thought that the qualifications required for the efficient discharge of the higher administrative duties of the police service should be as follows:

> It is clear that full knowledge and comprehension of the details of police work is very desirable. It is even more important that such duties should be discharged by men of a liberal education and training, giving them a breadth of outlook, an independent judgement, a power of grasping and assimilating facts, of lucidly expressing views, and of holding their own with persons of high official, or social position (Nott-Bower, 1926: 325).

He advocated a policy of equality of opportunity, but not along the same lines as those favoured by the *Police Review* (see later) and later the Police Federation. Whilst both Nott-Bower and the *Police Review* were in accord over the idea of equality of opportunity in the appointments to the upper ranks, each approached the issue from opposite sides. The former wanted equality of access to allow the best qualified outsiders into the police service, whereas the latter wanted equality of opportunity to allow career police officers to become chief constables. Nott-Bower believed that the type of person qualified for the higher ranks was not generally to be found within the ranks of the police forces. However, whenever he found a subordinate who he considered to be fit for command, he accelerated their promotion. But, he complained that such people were a rare occurrence as nearly all of the constables had little more than elementary education, and the constables with secondary education were dulled after many years in the lower ranks.[1]

---

[1] See 'Proved It' later in this chapter.

Nott-Bower favoured the civil service system of open competition to attract the right recruits to the higher ranks of the police service, claiming that the "days are past when being the cousin, the nephew, or the friend of a man of influence, should carry the smallest weight in the making of those appointments" (Nott-Bower, 1926: 326). His vision was to create an "officer class" of police officers trained in command who would enter the system by an open competition that was open to all. "The son of a working man, winning a scholarship to a secondary school, thence to university, would have equal opportunity with the son of an aristocratic father; it would be brains, not blood, that would secure the prize" (Nott-Bower, 1926: 327).

Before the Desborough committee reported in 1919, one of the main grievances of the lower ranks was their ineligibility, on their merits as police officer, for promotion through the ranks to chief constable, particularly in the counties. The only national forum for discussing their feelings was through the *Police Review*, which, from its inception in 1893, orchestrated a campaign for promotion to, rather than direct appointment of, chief constables. The *Police Review* became known as the voice of the constable and through its columns the editor, John Kempster, sought to represent the interests of the police officer. He allowed police officers to use his correspondence column to air grievances and discuss issues affecting their work. In the late 1890s, Kempster embarked on a crusade in pursuit of equality of opportunity for his readers. The *Police Review*'s crusade followed three courses of action. The first was to stimulate discussion of various controversial issues, such as freemasonry in the police service and its effect on promotions. The second was to lobby police authorities whenever a vacancy for chief constable was advertised, with the intention of getting them to appoint a serving officer as chief constable. The third course of action was to take the police cause to the public and inform relevant Parliamentary Committees of the views of police officers.

In 1897, the *Police Review* held an essay competition and invited its readers to contribute an essay entitled "The Appointment of Chief Constables" in which they were to discuss "the advantages of appointing gentlemen of long practical police service and experience to the chief constableships of the United Kingdom" (*Police Review*, 1897: 451). The essays were judged:

> ... with regard to cogency of argument and quality of style, and generally to the persuasive and convincing character of the essays, and of their favourably influencing the minds of the police authorities ... The last named consideration being of great importance to the object we have in view in the possible wider publication of one or more of these articles (*Police Review*, 1897: 451).

The essay competition and prize of two guineas was won by a person writing under the pen name 'Veritas' (*Police Review*, 1897: 451-452), whose view disputed the contention, later articulated by Nott-Bower, that there were not enough intelligent individuals to be found in the police who were fit for command. The basic thrust of 'Veritas's' argument was that all chief constables should be defined by statute and be drawn from the ranks of the police. 'Veritas' revived a debate raised three years previously by the chief constable of the Bristol force, Edwin Coathupe, on his resignation. Coathupe had maintained that borough chief constables should have all of the powers currently vested in county chief constables (*Police Review*, 1894: 558). 'Veritas' further maintained that the decisions to appoint chief constables were "made for the benefit of the governing classes rather than in the interests of good government and Police efficiency" and he put forward a case for increased professionalism in the police service and for increased professional control over policing matters generally (*Police Review*, 1897: 451).

The basis of 'Veritas's' argument was that those chief constables, who had served their apprenticeship within the police ranks, were much better able to discharge the responsible duties of the office than those who learned their role after their appointment. First, 'Veritas' believed that the law must be administered with considerable discretion, otherwise hardship may be inflicted where it is not deserved and only experience can teach "men how to exercise that discretionary power for the public good while upholding the dignity of the law" (*Police Review*, 1897: 451). Second, the experienced chief constable is in close sympathy with his officers and is likely to understand the difficulties and temptations they have to contend with. Third, experienced chief constables will have extensive "knowledge of the criminal classes, their habits and *modus operandi*, and be able to instruct how to circumvent their subtle arts and track them down when they have made a haul" (*Police Review*, 1897: 452). Fourth, an experienced chief constable "must in the course of his experience have gained many practical ideas for increasing the usefulness and efficiency of the Force" (*Police Review*, 1897: 452). Fifth, their experience promotes "a better understanding between the Police and the public, and till placed in power he has not the opportunity for giving full effect to his experience" (*Police Review*, 1897: 451-452). Furthermore:

> The system of appointment by patronage or favour, apart from being unwholesome in itself, is calculated to engender discontent and kindred evils throughout the ranks. There may be examples of good men appointed by such a system but that forms no justification of the system (*Police Review*, 1897: 451-452).

Sixth, the public interest is inseparable from the highest attainable efficiency of the Force, and promotion by proved merit and ability is the only system conducive to that end.

'Veritas' believed that if the conditions of the Service excluded outsiders from being appointed to the highest positions in the police, then more educated people would think it worth their while to join the police. Moreover, it would give a stimulus to all ranks to improve their opportunities and a higher standard of intelligence would be created throughout the police forces "and the public would benefit accordingly". 'Veritas's' prize essay became a formidable weapon in the *Police Review*'s campaign, and it was sent to all relevant parties whenever a chief constableship fell vacant, as demonstrated in the Wiltshire example illustrated in the previous chapter. Although it failed, in that instance, to persuade the police authority to choose a serving officer, it did probably help to prevent Lord Heytesbury, the favourite candidate, from becoming the new chief constable.

The *Police Review*'s claims to be "favourably influencing the minds of the police authorities" appear to have been somewhat exaggerated, but it did bring the issue to public attention through its contacts with local newspapers. Certainly, it will be shown later, there was a slight increase in the number of chief constables who were appointed with prior police experience after the turn of the century, but these men did not rise through the ranks of the police. They were young army officers who were not likely to see any active service or get promotion, who had entered the upper ranks of the police as a feasible alternative career. They either had gained informal experience of police matters with a friendly chief constable or had been appointed directly into the upper ranks. The *Police Review* maintained its campaign, and on more than one occasion John Kempster gave evidence to Parliamentary Select Committees on police related matters. By 1908, the *Police Review* had become the voice of the ranks as Kempster explained in his evidence to the committee.

> I have received upwards of 2,000 written replies to questions which appeared in the *Police Review* and that those answers also represent the views of the correspondent's comrades.
> *Chairman*: Your newspaper, as you have stated, is a medium for the force to express their complaints which it is possible they might be afraid to do to their immediate superiors. They are communicated to you, as you suggest, as the only means of giving vent to them
> *Kempster*: That is so (*Police Review*, 1908: 553).

Kempster pointed out to the Select Committee that because chief constables tended to be ex-soldiers they could not understand their men properly.

> *Chairman*: Do I understand that the chief constable of the county comes as a rule from the ranks of the police?
> *Kempster*: No I am speaking of superintendents. A very large majority of chief constables are military men.
> *Chairman*: Do you know how many chief constables have risen from the ranks?
> *Kempster*: I have the figures, I can supply them (*Police Review*, 1908: 556).

Kempster had the figures because earlier in the year he had, in pursuit of another matter, conducted an investigation of the origins of chief constables with the help of his readers. The Home Secretary had been asked in the House of Commons, by the MP for Glasgow University, how many chief constables had risen from the ranks and replied that he did not know but thought that it was a large number. In contrast to the assumptions of the Home Secretary, Kempster demonstrated that in England only three of the 44 county chief constables had risen from the ranks; 33 were ex-army officers and the rest were a combination of colonial police officers and county men. By comparison, half of the twelve Welsh county chief constables were career police officers, the rest were ex-army.[2] The careers of borough chief constables were very different; 105 (85 per cent) out of 123 had risen through the ranks. Only one Welsh borough chief constable had not risen through the ranks.

Kempster continued his crusade and took the views of his readers to a wider audience. In an article for the *Penny Pictorial* entitled "Our home protectors" Kempster colourfully described the despotism of the ex-military county chief constables.

> County chief constables are largely representative of the class known as 'officers and gentlemen' not only of spotless reputation but, for the most part, of excellent blue blood, in every way qualified to dine with their patrons and dance with their patron's daughters. And it must be admitted that these favoured sons of fortune do in many cases take kindly to their work and mature into benevolent despots and efficient chief constables.
>
> In other cases the spirit of the martinet dominates and the dragooning process prevails; not only to the domination of the men under them but to the defiance of the standing joint committee which is supposed to be their controlling authority (*Police Review*, 1909: 387).

Kempster also went on to support a bill by Sir Charles Schwann MP, which would have assimilated the powers of watch committees with those of standing joint committees: the bill failed.

Later in 1909, Kempster invited his readers to enter another essay competition. This time the subject of the essay was "How to rise in the Police Force". *Police Review* readers were asked to submit their views on the best way to rise to the top. The two winning essays are of interest because they were autobiographical and illustrated a range of contemporary attitudes towards police management. More important, they were written from two contrasting viewpoints. 'Eureka' was a borough chief constable and 'Proved It' was a senior officer in a county force (*Police Review*, 1909: 634). 'Eureka', the borough chief constable, recommended a few years' work in a solicitor's office in order to gain clerical skills and experience of the Police Courts. During his time in the solicitor's office the recruit should become qualified as a weights and measures inspector, a qualification that would help him later. 'Eureka' also

[2] Two thirds of the Scottish county chief constables had risen through the ranks.

suggested that a few years' experience in the territorial army would be a valuable additional qualification for a prospective police officer as it would accustom him to drilling and the habits of discipline. At twenty-one years of age the candidate should then join "one of the larger provincial forces with the intention of performing 2 or 3 years of street duty". 'Eureka' said that this experience would not be easy to acquire but that confidence will come with experience:

> If the future holds a chief constableship in store for him, his training and experiences at this stage will equip and help him as a chief later on to adjust to the doubtful balance of right and wrong, when a young officer appears before him for some alleged dereliction of duty (*Police Review*, 1909: 634).

After experiencing street duty 'Eureka' thought that the recruit should decide in which branch of police work he could make best headway and then look out for relevant openings at headquarters. Promotion lay in experience of the clerical branch and not out in the field:

> ... as a general rule promotion lies through the clerical branch. Two years experience on the Headquarters staff should make him eligible to start the promotion ladder. First, a sergeant-ship (preferably in the same force) then look out for an inspectorship in a small force where he would be second in command. Such an appointment would be a good stepping stone for the higher ranks (*Police Review*, 1909: 634).

'Eureka' explained that a combination of experience would afford him the opportunity to become a good all round man and a move to a smaller force would allow that skill to develop: "speaking generally, larger forces produce expert men in their particular departments, but it is in the smaller towns where the best all round men are found" (*Police Review*, 1909: 634). About four years as second in command, combined with the administrative experience gained in a larger force, plus experience in weights and measures, should qualify the candidate for a chief constableship: "he should apply for every likely chief constableship which becomes vacant and after a few unsuccessful attempts he should obtain his berth and reach the summit of his ambitions" (*Police Review*, 1909: 634).

'Proved It', the senior officer from a county force, gave ambitious police officers a rather different set of career instructions. His advice was also autobiographical, but in contrast to 'Eureka's' self-help message, 'Proved It's' advice consisted solely of duty, service and deference to authority. A constable's first duty was to obey orders, even when the constable was aware that the order given to him was not wholly proper. "It is", warns 'Proved It', "his duty to obey".

> The efficiency of the county force depends chiefly on the maintenance of discipline. Therefore he should be obedient and respectful to his superior officers at all times ... There is nothing which helps a constable through his duty like civility ... He must remember that he is appointed as a peace officer, and it is his duty to protect not oppress the public (*Police Review*, 1895: 15).

The rest of 'Proved Its' advice was basically for the constable to keep his nose clean, not to swear, to be fair and honest in court, improve his education and not to get involved in any religious or political affair. 'Proved It' makes no mention of practical or administrative experience.

The contrasting essays show different sides of the police service just after the turn of the century. To 'Eureka', chief constableships were a prize to be won through personal effort and stealth: in contrast, 'Proved It' saw it as a reward for dutiful service. Such a contrast was understandable as 'Proved Its' message was based on the experience of working in a medium to large sized county force where it was impossible for an ordinary constable to rise to chief constable and where promotions were often made as a reward for seniority or length of service. That is why 'Proved It' made no mention of the value of administrative experience. In contrast to the county experience, 'Eureka' showed that it was possible for a borough constable to rise through the ranks. However, 'Eureka' did not mention either the means by which he found out about vacancies or the fact that he had much more educational experience than the average constable. Neither did he mention the canvassing process that was described earlier by Nott-Bower. Finally, in order to have mapped his career out in the manner that he described he must have had some family relative inside the police service to guide his early career decisions.

During the 25 years between 1893 and 1918, the *Police Review* played a very important role in articulating police opinion and was instrumental in developing the debate over internal recruitment. Although it acted in an unofficial capacity, it was nevertheless formidable and scrutinised every appointment of chief constable and where it could, because not all appointments were open, it exposed what it saw as the moral wrong of external appointments and also the various forms of patronage that were employed at the time.

Patronage versus promotion by merit

In the examples of the appointment process, illustrated in the previous chapter, the exercise of patronage was commonplace, but not always overt. Forms of patronage ranged from nepotism through family connections to patronage through social connections that are fostered through membership of secretive organisations.

Nepotism

A number of father /son dynasties can be identified where the fact that the father had held office probably influenced the appointment of his son. In Carmarthenshire, William Phillips and his son William Picton Phillips had a combined 65 years tenure as chief constable of the county.

William Phillips
Police Review, 1894: 403

In Glamorganshire, Lt-Col. Henry Gore Lindsay and his son Capt. Lionel A. Lindsay ran the county force for 69 years.[3] In Anglesey, L. Prothero and his son R.H. Prothero were chief constables of the county for 55 years.[4] In the Beverley borough force Henry Knight was succeeded by his son George Knight. Together they commanded the borough force for 42 years. In Blackpool the Derhams held office for a total of 41 years, and there were the Eddys at Barnstaple who

---

[3] See Morgan (1987) for a description of Lindsay's conduct as chief constable.

[4] Prothero's other three sons also served in the police. One was later killed in the First World War, another, John, served in the Metropolitan Police and the third, Fred, was chief of the New York Dock Police (*Police Review*, February 21, 1919).

held office for 28 years. More examples exist both where the father and son or uncle and nephew held office in the same, or in different, forces (see chapter 9). Police authorities were more prepared to appoint people they knew and the son of a chief constable, particularly with police experience, would be especially favoured.

In other cases, wider family links were found to have influenced the appointment, such as in Kent where the new chief constable, Lt-Col. Henry Warde,[5] also happened to be the son-in-law of the chairman of the standing joint committee. His brother, Major St. Andrew Warde, was chief constable of Hampshire and his brother-in-law was also chief constable of another county force. In Radnorshire, an even more interesting chain of events indicated the occurrence of nepotism. In 1892, Capt. James E. Lloyd became the new chief constable, a post that his father had held between 1868 and 1873. Not only had Lloyd's father previously served as chief constable of the force, but upon his retirement he became a local JP and also a member of the county's standing joint committee. In the same county, three years after Lloyd resigned as chief constable in 1897, the Hon. Maj. Charles E. Walsh became the chief constable. Walsh was the son of Lord Ormathwaite, the chairman of the county's standing joint committee.

Such family links were not restricted to the county forces. A similar type of family based link was found in the Brighton borough force, not far from the Wardes' domain. Henry Solomon was appointed as Brighton's first chief constable in 1838. His brothers-in-law Levy Cohen and Hyman Lewis were well known local dignitaries. Lewis was one of the 10 town commissioners who appointed Solomon to his post.[6] Not only was Lewis probably the first practising Jew to be elected to local government in the UK, but Solomon was also probably the first practising Jew to become a chief police officer in the UK. Solomon is also notable for the fact that he was also the first, and possibly the last, chief constable to have been murdered in his own office (*Police Review* 1938: 488-489).[7]

---

[5] Son of General Sir, Edward Warde KCB, Royal Horse Artillery.

[6] I am very grateful to Rabbi Leonard Book of Malmo, Sweden, for this interesting information.

[7] Solomon's headstone states that he was murdered on 14th March 1844 at the age of 50. He had a public funeral and the townspeople raised £500 for his widow and children. His grave is adorned with Hebrew text which describes him as a martyr, one of "the holy".

A century ago, patronage was a fairly widely accepted practice in local civic life,[8] whereas today it is regarded as alien to the meritocratic philosophy behind modern appointments. The patronage system worked through the procurement of testimonials and favours from influential persons, and any available means were used to achieve support in the appointment process. The autobiographical experiences of chief constables, shown earlier, particularly those detailed descriptions given by Nott-Bower and Smith (see earlier), illustrate that the exercise of patronage was an integral, though informal, part of the selection process. Until the practice of canvassing was officially ended, shortly after the turn of the century, it was quite acceptable for candidates to canvass openly members of the police authority through any means that were available to them. However, the point at which it declined as a common practice is hard to identify. The (circumstantial) evidence that does exist suggests that it became more covert as the police became more professionalised. The *Police Review* (3/10/1941) was critical of "wire pulling" and the general practice of soliciting votes in support of a candidacy. In Manchester, during the Second World War, a candidate for a senior post had sought to canvass watch committee members for their support. The *Police Review* then went on to criticise the giving of testimonials by Home Office officials whose recommendations were expected to carry great weight. The article concluded that such practices could jeopardise the impartiality that Home Office officials were supposed to exercise.

Social Patronage: Freemasonry and Police Promotions[9]

The source of patronage that has probably sparked off the most debate within the police during the past century, has been freemasonry. The very fact that the issue has not gone away necessitates the need to understand it further, for if the allegations were true, then they would undermine the rational analysis of the recruitment, selection and appointment of chief constables.

---

[8] Although at a national level, the army and civil service had sought to eradicate its influence by introducing open competition.

[9] Parts of this section are adapted from Wall (1994a: 257-266).

The following analysis of historical and current literature on freemasonry, complemented by original material, illustrates that the century old debate over freemasonry and police promotions has not progressed substantively. Furthermore, it suggests that this may either be due to the fact that the silence of freemasons has prevented further enquiry or that the wrong questions are being asked. The rather diffuse organisation of freemasonry makes the full extent of its effect upon society hard to evaluate, and this is probably why the subject has such appeal; we just don't know! The vacuum created by ignorance provides a fertile environment for rumour, gossip and speculation, regardless of any facts that may arise to the contrary. It is therefore important to put freemasonry into perspective (Wall, 1994a). However, for these very reasons, this is not an easy task and will no doubt incur the scorn of those involved in both sides in the argument.

The issues are simple. Upon joining a masonic lodge, an individual swears oaths of allegiance towards 'the craft' and to fellow freemasons. If these oaths of allegiance are broken then violent retribution will, allegedly, follow. The basic concern regarding police membership of the freemasons is that a conflict of interests arises whereby an officer's pledge of allegiance to the Crown becomes secondary to their allegiance to freemasonry. Two further concerns arise. The first, is a concern that freemasons within the police will use masonic favouritism in order to gain promotion in preference to non-freemasons. The second, is a concern over the impartiality of police officers when dealing with fellow freemasons who are outside the police service and whose interests conflict with the goals of police work.

Many books and articles about freemasonry have been written by authors who claim to be privy to inside information. Some are merely descriptive, whereas others discuss the effects of masonic influence upon society, including the police service. This latter group have sought to identify specific cases where masonic influence is alleged to have affected police impartiality. Alleged cases are further dramatised by the mystery of freemasonry whereby unexplained phenomena are assumed, by default, to be the result of masonic secret action. Yet, this view contrasts sharply with recent attempts by the freemasons to go public and de-mystify their craft as being, for the main part, mundane and not worthy of such public attention.

Freemasonry within the police during the nineteenth century

Allegations of corrupt and unfair patronage through the secret influence of freemasonry within the police service first emerged in the letters column of the *Police Review* during the early 1890s and have reappeared regularly ever since. Examination of this debate reveals much about the police service and of relations between the police ranks. In 1894, for example, a correspondent writing under the alias 'Chinne Strappe' incensed masonic readers of the *Police Review* by asserting that the promotion system within the police service was corrupted by freemasonry. Non-masons in the police, he alleged, could not achieve promotion past the rank of sergeant and that as many as nine out of ten inspectors in his force were freemasons. In response to 'Chinne Strappe', a mason called 'Fidelity' claimed that he did not know of one uniformed inspector who was a fellow mason and that favouritism rather than freemasonry was the problem.

In January 1895 'Equity', a member of a provincial county force, gave one of the more informed descriptions of the dilemmas into which membership of the freemasons placed police officers[10] and of the way in which freemasonry operated in the police service (*Police Review*, 1895: 15). 'Equity' stated that he merely wished to show that freemasonry worked a gross injustice and had a pernicious effect which extended to the public. He indicated that whilst his chief constable was not a freemason, the superintendents in his force were. All promotions in his force were made by the chief constable on the recommendation of the superintendents, who in turn, made their recommendations on the suggestions of the inspectors who were also freemasons. Freemasonry provided a medium through which influence could be exerted in favour of members of the brotherhood.

'Equity' asked of 'Unigrander' (a correspondent who became a freemason after being promoted to inspector) why he became a freemason and whether his superintendent was a freemason? 'Equity' also questioned the motives of superintendents who remained freemasons once appointed. The reason for continued membership, he claimed, was that they:

[10] In the late nineteenth century freemasonry, like the police, was (and some argue still is) an exclusively male (non-Roman Catholic) world where women are kept on the periphery.

> ... had either to please, or receive the favours of, the gentry who monopolise the county bench or to 'serve the testimonials of freemasonry and the licensed victuallers association'(sic). How can the superintendent serve two masters and still be impartial? (*Police Review*, 1895: 15).

He further maintained:

> ... that freemasonry totally unfits a policeman for that faithful discharge of his duties, without partiality, in accordance with the oath he took on joining the force ... All I ask is a fair field and no favours (*Police Review*, 1895: 15).

'Equity' went on to suggest that freemasons rose more quickly through the police organisation than did non-masons:

> I have also noticed in the 'Biographical Sketches of past and present chief constables' that where they rose rapidly to those positions they became freemasons early in their police careers, thereby serving the assistance of that all-powerful organisation (*Police Review*, 1895: 15).

The chief constables that 'Equity' alluded to were mostly in charge of borough forces. At that time, county chief constables were typically ex-military personnel with gentry backgrounds who were directly appointed to their positions (see later). He failed to mention any other reasons, such as education, family connections or class background, that were also indicated in the biographical sketches and that may have been equally important in determining promotion.

The replies to 'Equity's' letter were polarised. The pro-freemasons disputed the validity of his statements and questioned his character, whereas the anti-freemasons applauded his stance. In the issue of January 25 1895, John Kempster, the *Police Review*'s editor, suddenly closed all correspondence on the matter with a final letter by 'Chinne Strappe' who stated that his intention had not been to attack freemasonry as a body of individuals but only the system of obtaining promotion by means of influence. In his closing remarks on the subject Kempster wrote: "(This must close the correspondence on the subject with a verdict of 'Not guilty - and don't do it again' - ED)".

It is hard to assess the real significance of freemasonry in police appointments and promotions in the late nineteenth and early twentieth centuries. In the few cases that are described below, freemasonry appears to have influenced senior police appointments. Yet, these cases are hardly out of character with the times. Freemasonry was popular and a senior police officer's involvement with freemasonry was frequently mentioned in the *Police Review*'s biographical sketches and obituaries. Many chief constables were quite candid about their association with freemasonry as it was an accepted part of civic life. In 1885, it is estimated that as many as three quarters of borough chief constables were freemasons, although by the turn of the century the number identified as members had fallen to one third (see later).[11] From there on it became harder to detect membership. This apparent reduction was caused by a number of factors. Firstly, there was an increase in the overall secrecy of the organisation due to unpopular allegations of masonic interference within local government made by the rapidly growing pro-equality movement, although as recently as 1913 police correspondents to the *Police Review* complained that their police instruction books contained orders prohibiting them from belonging to any political society or to any secret society except that of the freemasons.

> Our friend takes no exception to freemasonry, but wonders why that society is singled out while Good Templary, for example or any other society for promoting the good fellowship and the moral advancement of its members, is condemned (*Police Review*, 5/9/1913).

Secondly, the anti-freemasonry campaign, inspired by the above, received wide support from the lower police ranks. These processes led to freemasons within the police becoming more reluctant to reveal their membership, in some cases ceasing their involvement. They also deterred some, but not all, from becoming members.

The borough chief constables who were freemasons tended to be in local lodges, usually becoming Worshipful Masters of that lodge at some point during their career (see later).[12] Take, for example, the case of R.S. Eddy who succeeded his father as chief constable of the small Barnstaple force in 1905, after serving as a sergeant in the Metropolitan Police. Eddy was a Master Mason and became Worshipful Master of his lodge in 1917,

---

[11] These estimations were based upon a relatively small sample of chief constables, although the sample was much larger around the turn of the century than at other times (Wall, 1989).
[12] See Knight (1984: 2) for a description of the different types and degrees of freemasonry.

whilst holding the office of chief constable. However, the evidence, slender though it is, suggests that borough chief constables were likely to have been freemasons and that their membership probably assisted their rise through the ranks. Furthermore, it is by no means a clear case that their freemasonry actually assisted their appointment as chief constable and nor is it necessarily the case that they remained active members of their lodge once they held office. Rather, freemasonry appears to have been more influential in the middle of the organisation than at the top, and the lists of freemasons who attended major functions, where they can be found, provide us with a fruitful source of information to test this hypothesis. Examination, for example, of the printed souvenir of the installation of the Right Worshipful Provincial Grand Master of West Yorkshire at Leeds in 1893 (Provincial Grand Lodge, 1893) shows that of the 400 or more listed names of active freemasons from lodges throughout the country, only one, that of the chief constable of Leeds[13], tallied with the names of chief constables and superintendents listed in the *Police and Constabulary Almanac* as serving between 1891 and 1894.

The few county chief constables, in contrast, who are known to have been freemasons, also seem to have been associated with the higher degrees of freemasonry in either the Grand Lodge or Provincial Grand Lodges. Some achieved quite high positions, for example, Edward Holmes, the chief constable of Leicestershire between 1889 and 1928, became Post-Grand Master of the Provincial Grand Lodge on the death of Earl Ferres in 1913. Holmes was nominated for the office by the Grand Master, the Duke of Connaught. The Leicester temple is still named after Holmes.

Whilst freemasonry could have played a part in promotion and/or selection by enabling candidates to become known to senior officers, or in the case of chief constables, key members of appointing committees, there were other factors that also had to be taken into consideration which could have influenced the appointment just as much. Edward Holmes for example, mentioned above, was also a devoted cricketer and was heavily involved in the administration of sport. Sporting prowess was just as, if not more, likely to have brought a person to the attention of a senior officer or members of the appointing committee as would membership of a lodge.

[13] Even then only Webb's first and last name matched. His middle initial was not printed. To cast further doubt upon the link, he was listed under a Doncaster, rather than Leeds, lodge.

Freemasonry within the police: The twentieth century

On balance, only a few cases are documented where freemasonry can be seen to have had a direct influence on either appointments or dismissals. Most are little more than circumstantial as in the case of Eddy above. One interesting example where influence can clearly be seen to have been exerted was in the case of Evan Lewis, the chief constable of the small Neath borough force. Lewis became chief constable of Neath in 1900 having previously served as a sergeant in the Birmingham City force (*Police Review*, 1900: 581). In 1905, the watch committee asked him to resign because of his "unsatisfactory conduct". He tendered his resignation and it was accepted. However, a number of local groups, including Good Templars and freemasons, wrote to Neath Town Council in support of Lewis, arguing that it would not be in the interest of the town if Lewis were forced to resign (*Police Review*, 1905: 484). The council acceded to the request and reinstated Lewis on a six-month trial, the watch committee were not allowed to vote on the matter. Lewis was dismissed after the trial period.

The subject of freemasonry became a regular feature in the *Police Review* and was mentioned on least twenty four occasions between 1894 and 1936. There have also been many instances since then.[14] However, despite its regular occurrence, the structure of the debate remained largely unchanged, at least until recent times. Typical was a 1972 *Police Review* article by a Sergeant Wellings who claimed that he had become increasingly aware of the number of police officers who were freemasons. He had previously thought that most freemasons were in the senior ranks of the service but had been mistaken. The influence of freemasonry permeated all ranks and:

> manifested itself in the instruction one would sometimes receive regarding members of the public who held prominent positions in public life and who committed infringements, if only minor infringements of the law (*Police Review*, 1972: 560).

[14] *Police Review*, 19/10/1894, 26/10/1894, 2/11/1894, 23/11/1894, 14/12/1894, 11/1/1895, 25/1/1895, 13/10/1905, 5/9/1913, 9/4/1914, 17/1/1919, 24/1/1919, 7/3/1919, 14/3/1919, 14/9/1923, 7/3/1924, 27/3/1925, 3/4/1925, 24/4/1925, 1/5/1925, 5/8/1927, 26/8/1927, 3/2/33, 7/2/36.

He claimed that this was a legacy of the old system where the police authority controlled the police force through its purse strings, and it was therefore important for senior officers to have close contact with committee members at a social, as well as a professional, level. He said that the influence of freemasonry had not disappeared and was an important factor in the promotion of young officers. Through membership of a lodge, he believed that young freemasons were able to canvass support for promotion from senior officers. Wellings was worried that membership of freemasonry was increasing to a point of saturation, where it could bring into question the impartiality of the police. He thought that the Home Office and Police Federation should discourage police officers from becoming freemasons. Wellings concluded his article by asking readers: what benefits do the freemasons gain from having police officers as members, and what do the police officers gain from being members? (*Police Review*, 1972: 560).

In common with 'Chinne Strappe', Wellings provoked a massive response from *Police Review* readers. Yet no one, as in previous debates, provided any evidence to substantiate the allegations. Interestingly, one of the replies to Wellings was from the President of the Christian Police Association, the former-chief constable of Northampton and father of the then chief constable of Cumbria, John Williamson, who "did not think that freemasonry was that powerful for I made my way through the ranks to become chief constable of Northampton at 33" (*Police Review*, 1972: 759).

The depth of feeling aroused by Wellings's article eventually forced the editor of the *Police Review* to follow his predecessor, back in 1895, and close the correspondence on that issue by concluding that whilst he was sympathetic to Wellings's point of view, he felt that the influence of freemasonry had fallen off because of what he terms, the "liberalisation" of the police service: which he appears to understand as police officers changing their views on the matter in line with broader public thinking on the subject. Any freemasons who remained in the police service were therefore to be found in the more senior ranks, as young men were not interested in the pseudo-religiosity of the masonic movement.[15] He claimed that masonic nepotism was still a factor in promotions, but was decreasing in importance. What was still an important matter was that freemasons, Rotarians, Lions and Round-tablers tend to expect favours

---

[15] No evidence was given to support his arguments.

from fellow members who are police officers. He gave the final word on the matter to Wellings, whose reply paraphrased 'Chinne Strappe' eighty years before. Wellings said that he was against the secrecy of the masonic movement, secrecy which gives rise to suspicion whether it is well founded or not because "there should be no secrecy in the police service. It should be above suspicion" (*Police Review*, 1972: 954).

In early 1988, the row over freemasonry broke out once again, but with a slightly different pitch than before. A serving police officer, Chief Inspector Brian Woollard, alleged masonic bias within Islington Council, within the police force that was investigating the handling of corruption charges against masonic officials within the council and also within the office of the Director of Public Prosecution (*Police Review*, 1988: 420, 425, 788, 1124-5, 1158, 1412). In the wake of the scandal that followed, Woollard was suspended from duty, but his case was championed by the national press who campaigned against the secrecy of freemasonry. Although this case did not specifically relate to the appointment of senior police officers, it nevertheless broke the mould of previous allegations in a number of different ways. It gained nation-wide media attention, it raised the issue of masonic links between the police and non-police, and finally it caused the government to express its concern over freemasonry in public service, even if the Home Secretary did conclude that there was no need for a major inquiry. A number of years later, the Home Affairs Committee took the opposite stance and investigated freemasonry within the police (see later).

Moving back to the issue of freemasonry and senior police appointments, Stephen Knight[16] and Martin Short have both investigated this link. Knight (1983: 2017) alleged that the appointment of C.J. Page (a mason) instead of John Alderson (a non-mason) as Commissioner of the City of London Police in the 1970s was the result of pressure on the Court of Common Council by freemasons. Knight further alleged that the appointment of Page as Commissioner was both unpopular and unexpected amongst the City Police and had disastrous consequences for that force. Knight (*ibid*) stated that Page had supported an officer whom he had

---

[16] Stephen Knight died of a brain tumour in 1985, but not as the result of masonic retribution as has been frequently rumoured. Martin Short took over Knight's much criticised work and his 1989 book 'Inside the Brotherhood' is both well researched and very readable.

recruited to the force, over a disciplinary matter, despite the recommendation of other senior officers, including the assistant commissioner, for dismissal. The validity of Knight's claim was, however, questioned by Andrew Munday (*Police Review*, 1984: 581), one of Page's relatives who was not a freemason. In the article Munday accused Knight of "what he arrogantly accuses others: of seeing a masonic conspiracy where there may be none" (*ibid*). It is therefore significant that Alderson himself does not believe that his failure to be appointed as Commissioner was the result of masonic interference. He believes that the explanation is altogether more simple: the sitting tenant got the job.

> It was a close run thing. They had a short list of about seven of us, and they boiled it down to two, myself and Jim Page, the sitting tenant [acting Commissioner], and myself who had been talked about in police circles. So it was between me and Jim Page ... [h]e was acting commissioner at the time. He had become a mason, but I wouldn't have put it down to that because to boil it down to two they could have picked anybody else. I was simply not in a terribly strong position ... The Commissioner (Met) Sir John Waldron, at that time was annoyed with me for applying. I had then been [Commandant] at Bramshill for only two years ...[17]

It is an interesting fact that few, if any, of the many autobiographies[18] of senior police officers have mentioned freemasonry. In fact the subject is fairly conspicuous by its absence and also because of the strength and passion that have lain behind many of the allegations. Allegations which were coincidentally made during the same time period covered by the autobiographical accounts and also about the same forces which the authors commanded (Nott-Bower 1926; Smith 1910; Sillitoe 1955; St-Johnstone 1978; Mark 1978; McNee 1983). Clearly, these individuals either consciously omitted to mention either their own freemasonry or that of others or they simply did not see it as an issue. This latter possibility is a curious one because not only has the issue of freemasonry been a running sore in the police world for so long, but there is evidence from a number of

[17] Interview with John Alderson, 17 April 1997. Upon Page's death a few years after his appointment, Alderson was asked to apply once again for the job of Commissioner of the City of London Police.

[18] Stalker's autobiography (1988: 169) is one exception and coincidentally Anderton's biography does discuss freemasonry (Prince, 1988: 108, 269).

different quarters to suggest that despite all of the adverse publicity, only a minority of senior police officers are freemasons.

In 1984, Knight attempted to compile some quantitative data about senior police membership of the freemasons and wrote to all of the 43 serving chief officers asking them if they were members. Whilst none admitted to being freemasons, one third (14) replied to say that they were not. He interviewed an ex-chief constable about his freemasonry and was told that he had allowed his membership to lapse because of the contradictory position it placed him in.

> I've not stood back because I've got any guilt complex or conscience at all about masonry, if one is in the position to (a) influence promotions and (b) take decisions on discipline, then quite obviously one is open to the allegation that masonry is a factor in one's decisions (Knight, 1983: 2017).

Four years later, Short (1989) followed in Knight's footsteps and again wrote to chief constables asking them if they were freemasons. He obtained a numerically similar response to Knight but they did inspire him to point out the dangers of assuming an involvement in freemasonry where no response was given. Knight had assumed, quite wrongly in many cases, that his non-responses were due to chief constables reluctance to admit being freemasons.

Almost a decade later in 1997, evidence placed before the Home Affairs Committee's investigation into freemasonry within the police and the judiciary (see later) by the ACPO executive stated that between five and ten serving chief constables were freemasons (*Home Affairs Committee,* 1997, *Guardian*, 30/1/1997: 6).[19] This figure is less than the findings of Knight and Short and whilst it indicates a fall in membership amongst chief constables, it still suggests that about a fifth may still be members. A freemason, who kindly commented on a draft of this chapter believed that the figure was much less, possibly as low as one. Of course,

---

[19] There was some disagreement as to the actual number. Paul Whitehouse, chief constable of Sussex and vice-president of ACPO, said that he thought that ten, just under a quarter (23 per cent), of the 43 chief officers in England and Wales were freemasons, whereas Ray White, chief constable of Dyfed-Powys police and President of ACPO thought that "only five or so chief constables were masons." Interestingly, White's percentage corresponds exactly with the estimate of senior judges who are thought to be freemasons (30 out of 130, *The Independent*, 1997: 4).

until the Grand Lodge's very recent decision to allow masons to resign, a major problem was to identify which of the masonic chief constables were still active within the organisation. It was previously the case that a person remained a mason for life once they became a member.

The official response to freemasonry within the police

There has long been concern within the higher echelons of the police and government about the effect of masonic involvement on police appointments. As long ago as 1919, one of His Majesty's Inspectors of Constabulary expressed disquiet over the grounds upon which appointments to chief constable were made in both the counties and boroughs. Giving evidence to the Desborough Committee he said that he thought that chief constables were appointed: "not on their merits as policemen, especially in the smaller boroughs" (*Report of the Committee on the Police Service of England, Wales and Scotland Pt. II*, 1920: para. 87). A prevailing concern, although not explicitly stated, was that masonic links between senior police officers and members of their police authorities were subverting Home Office attempts to standardise and centralise the police.

In recent years, senior police management have expressed concern over police membership of secret organisations, but they have always stopped short of banning membership. In 1985, the then Metropolitan Police Commissioner, Sir Kenneth Newman, chose to discourage rather than ban constables from becoming freemasons on the grounds that it is not compatible with being a police officer. *The Principles of Policing*, issued to Metropolitan Police officers since 1985, outlines the problems a police officer may face on becoming a freemason:

> The police officer's special dilemma is the conflict between his service declaration of impartiality, and the sworn obligation to keep the secrets of freemasonry. His declaration has its statutory obligation to avoid any activity likely to interfere with impartiality or to give the impression that it may do so; a freemason's oath holds inevitably the implication that loyalty to fellow freemasons may supersede any other loyalty (Newman, 1985: 37).

The code then goes on to give a warning to officers who are either considering becoming, or are already, freemasons:

> the discerning officer will probably consider it wise to forego the prospect of pleasure and social advantages of freemasonry so as to enjoy the unreserved regard of all those around him. It follows from this that one who is already a freemason would also be wise to ponder, from time to time, whether he should continue as a freemason; that would probably be prudent in the light of the way that our force is striving, in these critical days, to present to the public a more open and whole-hearted image of itself, to show a greater readiness to be invigilated and to be free of any unnecessary concealment or secrecy (Newman, 1985: 37).

Newman's advice did not, however, prevent the formation of a police lodge[20] opposite New Scotland Yard after its publication. This lodge has been described, on the one hand, as a snub to his attempts to restrict freemasonry, but on the other hand it has also been seen as a way of allowing masonic police officers to safely practice their craft without being exposed to the potentially corruptive influences of outsiders. It was a picture of the members of this lodge proudly displaying their regalia, which Chris Mullin MP showed to one of Newman's successors, Sir Paul Condon, after he had given reassurances to the Home Affairs Select Committee (see below) that all was well in his force. "Mullin pulled out the picture and told him: I thought you might like to have a look at your alternative command structure" (Davies, 1997: T2).

During the latter part of 1996 and early 1997, the Home Affairs Committee investigated freemasonry within the police and the judiciary. It heard evidence from a wide range of bodies and called for a public register of members to be set up, in order to overcome a "general feeling of unease" that existed over the membership of the police, and also judges, magistrates and Crown Prosecutors in secretive organisations. The Home Affairs Committee (1997) argued that measures were necessary in order to end the: "public perception that Freemasonry can have an unhealthy influence on the criminal justice system" (*Daily Mail*, 26/3/1997: 17). The police representative organisations were split over the issue. ACPO

[20] Masonic Lodge number 9179, known as the Manor of St. James, was founded 11 years ago on January 27, 1986, for the exclusive use of Scotland Yard officers who worked in the West End of London (Short, 1989; *Guardian*, 29/1/1997: T2).

welcomed the requirement to disclose membership: "not because it has evidence that Freemasonry is still a problem in today's police force, but because it will help to dispel a public perception that it is" (Topping, 1997: 63). Furthermore, ACPO indicated its commitment to dealing with the issue by promising that it "will pursue speedy implementation of this policy" (ACPO press release 24/8/1996).[21] The response from the other staff associations was less than co-operative as both the Police Federation and the Superintendents' Association argued that requiring disclosure of membership would be: "an unwarranted interference with the private lives of officers" (*Police Review*, 15/11/1996; Topping, 1997: 63).

Putting freemasonry into perspective[22]

Traditionally, there have been two schools of thought about freemasonry, the sympathetic pro-mason, and the conspiratorial anti-mason approaches. It will be argued here that these traditional approaches each carry political, emotional, personal and ideological baggage which colour their perceptions of the phenomenon and therefore fail to be objective about freemasonry. To understand fully the effect of freemasonry a third, realist, position has to be adopted which attempts to place freemasonry into perspective.

The sympathetic pro-masonic stance is complementary to freemasonry. It presents freemasonry as a unifying force and states that being a freemason is primarily about having an enjoyable social life in which one can experience a comradeship of trust with fellow-masons. In addition, they also feel that they benefit the community by funding various charitable causes, whilst providing security for their dependants in case of hardship. One of the main attractions of membership is the prospect of self-improvement and increasing their social standing.

---

[21] Although not all ACPO members were in accord. David Wilmot, the Chief Constable of Greater Manchester, for example, disagreed with the ACPO line on the grounds that "it would be an 'infringement of personal liberty' and contrary to natural justice" (letter to Ian Westwood, vice-chairman of the Police Federation, *Daily Telegraph*, Feb. 28, 1997:13. Also see for the same day *The Guardian*, p. 7; *The Independent*, p. 2).

[22] This section is based upon a small number of unstructured and informal interviews with both police and non-police freemasons, personal contact with freemasons, and observations based upon the experience of working as a waiter at lodge 'ladies' nights.

The pro-masonic stance is encouraged by a closed culture and is maintained by pro-masonic literature which is supportive of the movement, thus reaffirming its internal normative structure and legitimating its function. In opposition, stands the conspiratorial anti-masonic stance, which quite expectedly, views freemasonry as a dark force that exerts unfair patronage through its anti-egalitarian philosophy, which is both élitist and divisive. Its secret allegiances provide a fertile environment for over-riding existing structures of accountability and thus allowing potentially corruptive relationships to develop and conspiracy to germinate. Adversarial in its approach, anti-masonic literature seeks to build up a case against freemasonry. In contrast to both perspectives, is the realist approach towards freemasonry, adopted here, which is inquisitorial by nature and, whilst respecting some of the traditional propositions, looks towards the dynamics of freemasonry and at its situational reality. It presents a slightly different picture of freemasonry, a picture that looks at the reality of freemasonry and assesses its practical implications.

Freemasonry is a mainly a haven for the self-employed and middle management, and is attractive to those in closed organisations (such as the police or the various trades) where normal social activities can be affected or otherwise dominated by the nature of the occupation. Membership is driven by self-interest, but often for social reasons rather than for occupational self-advancement; although it is often hard to delineate between the two. Those who joined specifically to further their own interests were often disappointed and were also despised by fellow masons. In addition, freemasonry is not as homogeneous an organisation as is often assumed, despite its pretensions of being a brotherhood. Its organisational components are found to be heterogeneous, and it is socially, racially, sexually, and religiously divided (and divisive). There are even divisions within the lodges, between those who join for the social life and those who use their membership to promote their businesses (Wall, 1994: 264).

Whilst freemasonry is unique in so far as it involves ritual initiation, swearing oaths of allegiance with the threat of violent retribution for transgression of the rules of membership, there is little evidence to show that the retribution has ever been carried out to the letter.[23] Furthermore,

[23] The bloodthirsty penalties were removed by the Grand Lodge in 1986. There were suggestions that the death of Calvi the banker was due to masonic revenge by the Italian P2 (a non-approved) lodge, but this has never been proven. The issue of European

none of the loudest voices against freemasonry has ever produced hard evidence that could result in decisive action against the organisation.[24] Whilst there have been some documented cases of suppression of information (Knight, 1984; Short, 1989), it is also the case that there has been a tendency on the part of authors to look for masonic membership and to assume conspiracy at the highest level. Whilst the available literature (Graef, 1988; Knight, 1984; Stalker, 1988, Prince, 1988; Short, 1989; Wall 1994a, and see earlier) did identify some masons in the upper echelons of the professions, it also suggests, by default, that there are many, if not more, people in top management who are not involved in freemasonry. Furthermore, the majority of the known examples of masonic influence do not involve people at the top of their professions, rather, they are in the middle. So, it is arguable that freemasonry is most potent within an organisation: although on such slender evidence it might be imprudent to go as far as Foxcroft, who claimed that freemasonry is the "Mafia of the mediocre" (see Short, 1989: 674, n. 5).

This view is, however, given some substance by the opposing stances taken by ACPO and the Superintendents' Association and Police Federation on the issue. The latter two staff associations, it will be remembered, opposed the disclosure of membership. However, before reading too much into this observation, further research would need to be carried out into police officers' membership and conduct within a number of other types of social groupings that can be said to help individuals to further their self-interest in order fully to substantiate the argument: such as links developed through family connections; the education system or through business; membership of a number of secretive Christian organisations such as the Roman Catholic *Opus Dei* and the Knights of Columbus; an individual's prowess in a sport or membership of a sports-related organisation, which involves both participation and involvement in social, extra-sport, activities; membership of charitable or benevolent organisations which demand active participation in social events, such as the Round Table, Lions and St John's Ambulance.

Freemasonry is not discussed here but would be a very interesting topic in light of the reduction in cross-border controls between the European countries.

[24] The conspiracy theorists would see this as hard evidence of the all pervasive power of the organisation.

The more the issue of freemasonry and the police is explored, the greater is the weight of argument against it being an important factor in senior police appointments. The first of the arguments to support this view is that being a member of a lodge can be an extremely time-consuming, if not extremely expensive, business. This point was not lost on some of the *Police Review* correspondents who observed the logistic dilemma faced by freemasons who aspired to high office, whereby they had to make a choice over whether to spend their spare time learning the secret rituals, or in studying for the police examinations which police officers, masons or not, still had to pass. Following on from this, is the (second) argument, that as both the system and criteria for promotion within the police have become more open and bureaucratic, then the potential of freemasonry to interfere with the normal course of police promotions must have reduced. Furthermore, there is a greater emphasis today upon demonstrable competencies and, of course, the major decisions about senior police appointments are made both centrally and bureaucratically, to the point that personal references or recommendations are no longer valued (see chapter 6).

The third argument is that freemasonry is simply not as secret as it is often believed, rather it is one of life's great "open secrets" and there is available much substantive literature that describes masonic ritual and secret information (Wall, 1993: 22-23). To further this point, there has, since the mid-1990s, been a proliferation of information about freemasonry on the World Wide Web.[25] What is more, freemasons themselves appear to be very willing to talk about their involvement in freemasonry, despite the supposed veil of secrecy. Investigative authors such as Knight, Short, and Graef seem to have had few problems in getting freemasons to talk to them. "If there is one secret in Masonry, it is that there are no secrets" (Whalen, 1958; Short, 1989: 10). However, whilst the secrets may be fairly open,[26] the list of members is not.

---

[25] On October 29, 1997 an *Alta-Vista* simple query on the word "freemason" revealed over 700 different sites from all over the world relating to freemasonry. Some were bookshops, others were the web sites of national freemason organisations, even some masonic lodges have their own web pages. A further group of pages disseminate general information about freemasonry.

[26] See Knight (1984), Short (1989) on the Her Majesty' Inspectors of Constabulary and Home Office membership of Freemasonry.

Perhaps the most important observation to be made from the point of view of this study, is that within fairly closed organisations such as police forces, there tends to be a fairly widespread knowledge about who is and who is not a freemason. When combined with the above factors, and the necessity for modern chief constables to possess qualities of personal openness and integrity, this point would suggest that the likelihood of senior police officers becoming freemasons will fall rather than increase, particularly in the light of the recent ACPO policy on the matter and the growing body of public concern towards freemasonry within the police.

The debate over police membership of the freemasons is now over a century old. Yet, few of the many allegations regarding its influence upon police promotions that have been made over the years have been substantiated and most have been based upon circumstantial evidence providing no firm basis for action. In the past century freemasonry was an important part of municipal life and acknowledgement of membership was open and even revered. Since then, adverse publicity associated with membership has deterred police officers from joining and police policy, whilst varying regionally, is now to discourage police officers from membership but not to ban it. And whilst there does exist some evidence to show that this non-mason policy is being actively resisted, police membership of the freemasons appears to have declined as other social organisations have gained popularity. It is arguable that nowadays a police officer's golf handicap or other sporting prowess is as, if not more, important than being a freemason. This very point was affirmed in many conversations with masonic police officers in a northern police force during a two year period in the late 1980s. Although, a degree of caution may be observed, as this is precisely the sort of argument that masonic police officers make to justify their involvement in freemasonry: "police officers who want to be corrupt can make bad friendships through golf clubs or Round Table dinners, and that the lodges have no special influence" (*Guardian,* 1997: T2). And yet, perhaps this is just another example of the way that freemasonry is driven by self-perpetuating myths which, once seeded, germinate allegations of masonic corruption in the dark corners of the unknown and feed the public's insatiable desire for conspiracy theories. Myths which engender paranoia, and then continue to feed that paranoia.

Generally speaking, the traditional explanations of freemasonry fail to consider its situational reality, pro-masons celebrate their own self-importance through continuing the secretive nature of freemasonry, whilst the anti-masons, intending to expose the "truth" about masonic conspiracy, inadvertently mythologise its conspiratorial nature and perpetuate the myth. When freemasonry is brought into perspective it becomes quite clear that its impact is probably more limited than we are led to believe. It neither lives up to the expectations of some insiders, nor does it probably merit the paranoia of some outsiders. The weight of argument appears to favour the view that it is not an important factor today in the appointment of chief constables, in fact given the current climate it may even hinder the applicant. And yet, the very fact that freemasonry is still being talked about with such passion means that it shapes public opinion of the police, and the criminal justice system, and impacts upon its legitimacy. Therefore, regardless of whether or not freemasonry has any impact upon police promotions, action has to be taken to make membership more transparent.

Conclusion

The issues of freemasonry and the police, of promotion by merit and also of internally recruiting chief officers were, through the correspondence columns of the *Police Review*, the first major policing issues to be debated by police officers as a whole. Importantly, these issues helped to gel police opinion, even though police views were split a number of different ways. The debate over freemasonry was important, not just because of its own substance, but also because it sensitised the police to the broader practice of externally recruiting chief constables. Furthermore, once the principle of internally recruiting chief officers was accepted then it provoked debate over whether the route by which senior officers rose through the ranks should be the product of promotion by patronage or merit. The principle of promotion by merit won the day.

6 Towards the Internal Recruitment of Chief Constables

Introduction

Before 1919 there existed no central policy to specify the professional origins of chief constables. The Home Secretary's rules, outlined in chapter 4, were extremely vague and were mainly concerned with establishing the social bonafides of candidates. After the First World War, a time when the Home Office sought to increase its influence over policing, a policy of recruiting chief constables from within the police was introduced. This policy was given neither the force of primary legislation, nor was it embraced by all parties involved. In fact, there was considerable resistance towards it. So, from that time onwards, the Home Office adopted a two fold strategy. Firstly, under the Home Secretary's Rules (1920), they became more assertive over the processes governing the selection (shortlisting) of candidates and their appointment (approval). Secondly, they sought to develop various recruitment strategies to encourage the recruitment and development of individuals with leadership potential who would later fill the higher ranks. These strategies are dealt with in the next chapter.

This chapter will look at the processes of selecting and appointing chief constables since 1919. Part one will focus upon the debates that arose over the selection of chief constables as the result of the Desborough Committee's recommendations. Part two will look at the procedures of selecting and appointing chief constables between 1919 and 1964 and will then discuss, both the outcome of that debate and also the enforcement of the idea of internally recruiting chief constables from within the police. Part three will explore the continuing debate over internal recruitment and will look at the way that procedures became standardised after 1964, before contrasting the appointment of todays' chief constables with their predecessors.

The policy of internally selecting and appointing chief constables

By 1919, the debate over the selection of chief constables had been simmering for a couple of decades, having been brought to the boil by the *Police Review's* long standing campaign. The debate, briefly, became a political issue during the Select Committee on the Police Weekly Rest Day in 1908 when the Home Office were embarrassed to admit that they did not know the origins of serving county chief constables (see chapter 3). This event did not have a direct impact on policies for selecting new chief constables, for it soon became overshadowed by the First World War. It did however, cause the Home Office to reflect seriously upon the qualities that a chief constable should possess and was the first time that the issue had been raised at an official level and took it beyond the pages of the *Police Review*.

One of the root causes of the police unrest during and after the First World War was understood to be the varying quality of senior police officers. At the root of this "problem of senior command" (Davies, 1973) was the idiosyncratic way in which chief constables were selected. These idiosyncrasies applied to both county forces, which had been the focus of the *Police Review* campaign, and also the borough forces. Although most borough chief officers had prior police experience, in their case it was regarded by many watch committees and police officers as a reward for dutiful service to the committee (*Report of the Committee on the Police Service of England, Wales and Scotland*, 1920, Part II; para. 137). It will be remembered from earlier chapters, that one of the HM Inspector's of Constabulary remarked in his evidence to the Desborough Committee that he felt that borough chief constables were often appointed: "not on their merits as policemen, especially in the smaller boroughs" (*idem*: para. 87). Thus, patronage, rather than promotion by merit, still prevailed. These conclusions led to the first real review of the processes by which chief constables were recruited.

The Desborough Committee and Regulation 9

The Desborough Committee (see chapter 3) inquired into the appointment of chief constables and was presented with conflicting arguments from those who favoured the retention of the existing system and those who wanted a fully 'professional', self-contained police service.[1] Quite predictably, the representatives of the county police authorities and their serving chief constables, believed that service in the lower ranks was not necessarily the best training for chief constables. They argued that experience gained in the armed forces was a better training for the job. The representatives of the police themselves argued precisely the opposite viewpoint and suggested that all appointments should be confined to persons with experience in all ranks of the police service. Underlying these two perspectives was the Home Office's agenda to become more actively involved in centrally determining police policy, whilst leaving its implementation to the local authorities who had previously been performing both functions (outlined in chapter 3). This latter view would have appeared to swing the opinion of the Committee, whose recommendations were very much a compromise. In their deliberations, they acknowledged the contradictory nature of the problem of senior command. On the one hand, they accepted the increasingly popular principle that all chief police officers should possess police experience, preferably gained from UK police forces. In fact seventeen out of twenty witnesses before the committee were in favour of confining appointments to people with full police experience.[2] On the other hand, they also accepted that there tended to be a shortage of individuals with the requisite qualities serving within the police: "but", stated the committee:

> after full consideration we recommend that no person without previous police experience should be appointed as chief constable in any force unless he possesses some exceptional qualification or experience which specially fits him for the post, or there is no other candidate from the police service who is considered sufficiently well qualified (*idem*: para. 139).

This recommendation was incorporated verbatim into the rules that the Police Act 1919 empowered the Home Secretary to make to govern the appointment, pay, and conditions of service of the police (Home Secretary's Rules, 1920).[3] Issued in 1920, it became known as "Regulation

---

[1] These two concepts are, of course, quite different, but they were frequently confused in the debates that took place over policing at the time.

[2] See statement by Supt. Tanner to the Police Council March 5, 1924.

[3] The Police Regulations of the 20th August 1920 made by the Secretary of State under section 4 of the Police Act 1919 (Statutory Rules and Orders 1920, No. 1484).

9"[4] and was the first time that an attempt had been made to impose upon police authorities the 'professional' qualities that they should look for in a chief constable:

> Every appointment to the post of Chief Officer of Police in any county or borough police force shall be subject to the approval of the Secretary of State, and no person without any previous police experience shall be appointed to any such position unless he possesses some exceptional qualification or experience which specially fits him for the post, or there is no candidate from the police service, who is sufficiently well qualified. (Regulation 9, Home Secretary's Rules, 1920).

In addition to Regulation 9, was a stipulation under Regulation 7(1)(2), that candidates must be "of good character" (7(1)) be aged under 40 years of age (7(2)) unless they "had previous service in a police force or [were] otherwise entitled to reckon previous service as approved service for the purposes of pension" (7(2a)) or could claim "special circumstances" (7(2b)) that would be approved by the Home Secretary. In addition, they must have been over five feet eight inches tall (7(3)) and they must be certified as fit (7(4)).[5]

It is important to note here that, although the rules and regulations (secondary, or quasi-legislation) changed, the framework of primary legislation for the appointment of chief constables remained very much as it was in the 1830s. The framework for the appointment of county chief constables was still defined under statute by s. 4 of the County Police Act 1839[6] (see chapter 4). Similarly, the statutory framework for the appointment of borough chief constables remained unchanged in so far as there was no statutory provision which directly conferred powers upon the watch committee to appoint a chief constable. However, s. 4 of the Police Act 1919 applied the Home Secretary's rules to *all* police forces and not just the county forces as was previously the case, which meant that watch committees had a *de facto* power to appoint chief constables, because,

---

[4] Regulation 9 of the Home Secretary's Rules (1920) (HO 158/93).

[5] In addition they must also satisfy the conditions for the appointment of a constable which required them to not be involved in certain business activities or be related to anybody who is (Regulation 8).

[6] As amended by s. 30 of the Local Government Act 1888 which replaced the Quarter Sessions with the Standing Joint Committee.

under s. 191(1) of the Municipal Corporations Act, 1882[7] they had the power to appoint borough constables and, under the Police Regulations 1920, the chief constable had become one of the ranks of constable.[8]

The agenda underlying the new regulation was to encourage all police authorities to look towards appointing career police officers as their future chief constables. This strategy would, in theory, appease the police lobby, reduce some of the variations in the quality of senior officers, and increase the overall influence of the Home Office over the police in general.[9] At first sight, these new regulations appear to have been successful in achieving their goal. An examination of the occupations of chief constables prior to their first command reveals that the percentage of county chief constables with prior police experience increased dramatically after the introduction of Regulation 9. Furthermore, after 1919 there was a definite move by police authorities towards selecting chief constables with experience of police work. Most of the 15 county chief constables who took up office between 1919 and 1939 were appointed from police related occupations: three came from the Royal Irish/Ulster Constabulary[10]; four from the Indian police; three from the ranks of the police; and five from elsewhere (see Figure 4).

However, further examination found that although the chief constables appointed after Regulation 9 came into force had more policing experience than their predecessors, they had similar, if not identical, military career patterns and similar social backgrounds. The truth of the matter was that most the police authorities greatly resented the intrusion of central government upon their independence. Evidence of this resentment emerged during a meeting in June 1920 of the Conference of Representatives of Police Authorities and led to a widely supported

---

[7] Which replaced the Municipal Corporations Act 1835.

[8] "Except where the title Head Constable is used" (Regulation 1).

[9] A number of subsequent attempts were made to insist that all individuals who were appointed chief officers of police had "full police experience" The Police Federation, for example, proposed to the Police Council in 1924, that "no person shall be appointed or promoted to any rank above that of inspector unless he has completed seven years service in a public police force". (Minutes of a Meeting held at the Home Office March 5, 1924 - HO 158/24).

[10] The Royal Irish Constabulary became the Royal Ulster Constabulary in 1922. See Walker, (1990: 105).

resolution "that the appointment of a chief constable shall remain a matter for the local police authority as heretofore".[11]

Figure 4: Chief constables appointed without UK police experience - after 1919

1919 - Lt-Colonel (later Sir) F. Brook became the chief constable of Southport (ex Custom and Excise officer and soldier).

1926 - Captain (Later Sir) A. Hordern became the chief constable of the East Riding of Yorkshire. He was ex army, but he had commanded the civil police in Nigeria. Sir John Anderson regarded him as possessing exceptional qualifications and experience (HO 287/388,074/43).

1928 - Lt-Colonel T.R.P. Warren became the chief constable of Buckinghamshire. He had experience in the administration and control of the military police in Egypt and Gallipoli during the First World War. He had also been a resident Magistrate in Ireland. Sir John Anderson expressed the view that it would have been preferable for a police candidate to have been chosen, but Col. Warren possessed exceptional qualifications and Anderson recommended that his appointment be approved (HO 287/388,025/33).

1928 - Major S.H. Van Hook became the chief constable of Norfolk. He had previously been the chief constable of the War Dept. Constabulary.

1929 - Commander E.R.B. Kemble RN was appointed the chief constable of Warwickshire. He had no police experience other than organising and supervising the ship police on a battleship.

1929 - Captain A. Popkess became the chief constable of Nottingham. He was an ex-Provost Marshal of the Corps of Military police at Aldershot and ex-intelligence officer in Ireland. He was considered to have exceptional qualifications and experience which fitted him for the post (HO 287/388,160/26).

1929 - Major J.C. Chaytor became the chief constable of North Riding of Yorkshire. He had commanded a detachment of civil police in South Africa and was closely associated with the Metropolitan Police.

1931 - Major L.H. Morris became the chief constable of Devon. Morris was the former Governor of Dartmoor prison. He was regarded as having outstanding personality and ability (HO 45 388,035/77).

1937 - Lt-Commander W.J.A. Willis became the chief constable of CC Rochester. He had 23 years Navy service. There were no outstanding candidates from within the police for this post. The appointment attracted criticism within Parliament and elsewhere, including the Police Review (HO 287/ 388,172/51/52/53).

1939 - Captain S.M.E. Fairman appointed as chief constable of Herts. He was the divisional accidents officer at the Min of Transport and had previously worked with the police in Cairo and Alexander (HO 287/825,253/1).

---

[11] Proceedings of a Conference of Representatives of Police Authorities held at Caxton Hall, Caxton street, Westminster, London on Friday, 25th June 1920. (HO 45/15605/376689/75).

Four months later, feelings were even stronger when Neville Chamberlain MP led a deputation of representatives of the Conference of Representatives of Police Authorities and Association of Municipal Corporations to meet with the Home Secretary, Edward Shortt and his civil servants, who included Sir Edward Troup. They complained bitterly about the Home Secretary's attempts to interfere with their power to control their own police forces[12] and expressed their resentment over the removal of "that which they have most jealously guarded and prized most highly, namely, the right to govern themselves and manage their own affairs".[13] Shortt provided curt replies to the deputation's statements arguing that "you must have in every aspect of life a certain amount of central control - a certain amount of central advice and regulation".[14] Troup, who appears to have chaired much of this meeting following Shortt's early departure, firmly believed that the police authorities were over-reacting, having not observed "that the Regulations cannot take away the power given by Act of Parliament to the Watch Committee".

The deputation gained no concessions, however, the strong feelings of local police authorities about the changes that were being pressed upon them became expressed through their subsequent circumnavigation of the regulations, especially Regulation 9. They were assisted in this task by the rather vague wording of the regulations and the Home Office's own vague internal definition of approved service and special circumstances. In the case of the latter, Sir John Anderson, permanent under-secretary of state in the Home Office, appeared to be slightly more liberal than his predecessor, Sir Edward Troup,[15] in his interpretation of these concepts when approving appointments.

So, although Regulation 9 was a milestone in the development of the police as a centrally co-ordinated service, it was, nevertheless, a compromise and its loose wording allowed police authorities, particularly in the counties, to interpret it 'creatively' and minimise its intended impact. Some idea of the extent to which police authorities evaded Regulation 9 can be illustrated when the occupational origins of chief

[12] The main focus of this deputation was to complain about the borough chief constable becoming the force disciplinary authority although there was much discussion over the appointment of the chief constable. (HO 158/22, October 13 1930).

[13] Mr Lovell Dunstan, Major of Plymouth to the Home Secretary, p. 5 (HO 158/22).

[14] Home Secretary's reply to Mr Dunstan, p. 8 (HO 158/22).

[15] See HO 287/29 section 5.

constables serving in 1908 are compared with those serving in 1939. John Kempster, editor of the *Police Review*, informed the 1908 Select Committee on the Police Weekly Rest Day that only three of the 44 English county chief constables had spent their careers in the police. Of the remainder 33 were ex-army officers and 8 were a combination of colonial police officers and gentry, all with army experience. In contrast, only 15 of the 123 borough chief constables had *not* risen through the ranks of a British police force (*Police Review*, 1908: 307). By 1939, 31 years later, there had been little change as only four of the 42 English chief constables, one more than in 1908, had been in the police throughout their careers. Similarly, only six of the 117 borough chief constables had *not* risen through the ranks (Police Advisory Board, 1967: 8). The resistance of the local authorities to what they perceived as central government interference in their affairs was also met by another strategy. At the level below chief constable, they would tend to appoint ex-army officers directly as assistant or deputy chief constable - appointments that were traditionally "in the gift" of the chief constable and were not covered by the regulations. Having served as an assistant chief constable, that experience could be claimed as prior police experience in order to qualify for candidature as chief constable whenever a vacancy arose.[16]

Both the statutory framework for the appointment of chief constables and also the wording of regulations 7 and 9 remained unchanged until 1964.[17] However, patterns of recruitment, selection and appointment did change substantively before then. The remainder of this chapter, therefore, focuses upon the processes by which, in the absence of a statutory force, the changes took place.

---

[16] An interesting example of this was the appointment of Capt. G.W.R. Hearn as the chief constable of the East Riding of Yorkshire in 1934. The appointment was not approved by the Home Secretary. However, the following year Hearn was appointed assistant chief constable of Staffordshire and later became its chief constable in 1949.

[17] Regulations 7 and 9 became known in the Police Regulations 1952 (SI No. 1704) as rr. 5 & 6 respectively. They were repealed by Police (Amendment) (No. 2) Regulations 1964 (S1. No. 831) 9 June 1964. Circulated by HOC 151/1964 and which followed the Police Act 1964.

The procedure for appointing chief constables: 1919 to 1964

Throughout the period 1919 to 1964, the procedure for appointing chief constables gradually became standardised. First, a vacancy would be advertised by the police authority in both the press and also various police journals. Secondly, upon becoming aware of a vacancy,[18] the Home Office would send out a letter reminding police authorities that it wished to give an opinion about the qualities of the candidates who had been shortlisted - to ensure that no well qualified officers were overlooked by the police authority. Six copies and 14 days' notice were required. Thirdly, these shortlists were sent to the HM Inspector of Constabulary for observations. Prior to this, it was not unknown for police authorities to have sent their list of applicants to the Home Office for comment. The HM Inspectors of Constabulary would comment upon the candidates and possibly suggest some others to be considered. The Commissioner of the Metropolitan Police would be also consulted for an opinion on any Metropolitan Police officers who were included. Finally, a summary of all comments would be prepared by the relevant department in the Home Office, and the clerk to the police authority would then be informed as to which of the shortlisted candidates would be approved if appointed. Occasionally, where there were difficulties, the clerk or representatives of the police authority might have met to discuss the shortlist.

The interview process would often take two days and would involve a combination of formal and informal activities. The formal interviews tended to be conducted by the whole of the police authority. A common method was to give the candidates a card on which a number of questions were written:

> I was asked to come into meet the full committee [about forty people]. There was one seat next to the chairman which I sat in. In front of me was a card with some questions on it. I had to read out the questions and was given ten minutes to answer each. To be quite honest it is quite a good filtering system because some candidates dry up after a few minutes. I had no problem with it and could speak and engage the audience.[19]

[18] For it would appear that they were sometimes unaware of vacancies until quite late in the appointment process.

[19] Interview with CC5.

Sometimes candidates might also have undergone additional interviews with various sub-committees of the police authorities.

Procedures did, however, vary between forces as they tended to be based, certainly before the Second World War, upon local models of appointing officials. In describing his appointment in 1923 as chief constable of Chesterfield, Sillitoe indicated that social and personal acceptability featured very highly on the agenda. After being persuaded to pursue the job at Chesterfield by his father's neighbour, Reggie, he found himself on a shortlist.

> Much to my surprise I was invited to Chesterfield a few days afterwards - I was on the shortlist of final applicants. There were six of us, all the others experienced senior police officers. [N.B. Sillitoe was a former colonial police officer] The members of the watch Committee heard me with admirable patience as I stated my qualifications for the job. The Chairman then asked: "Captain Sillitoe, what are you doing now?". I answered that I was reading for the bar, but that to be frank, I was one of the unemployed (Sillitoe, 1955: 50).

Sillitoe's reply seemed to amuse the watch committee, and he was given the job. The post-war practice of regularly involving the regional HM Inspector of Constabulary in the appointment process tended to shift the emphasis away from social acceptability towards police experience and made the process increasingly more professional.[20]

A very important part of the appointment process was the series of informal meetings, especially the formal dinners and receptions, which were designed to enable members of the police authority get to know more about the candidates. This informal vetting process was commonly referred to as 'ordeal by dinner' and was a common feature of the appointment procedure until the 1990s.[21] It was described by a successful ex-interviewee.

---

[20] Attendance by an HM Inspector is currently prescribed practice. It gradually started to become the practice during the war years and thereafter, but only where difficulties were anticipated with the appointment. And, of course, upon invitation of the police authority.

[21] Ordeal by dinner was discouraged by para. 49 of the Home Office in the *Chief Officer Appointments in the Police Service: Guidelines on Selection Procedures*, which accompanies HOC 52/96. It states that: "Previous formal contacts with applicants, especially in the form of social functions involving candidates and panel members, are not

> Ordeal by dinner is usually a very decorous affair with a carefully worked out routine where the members stay still and the candidates rotate and some of the members keep notes of the questions they want to ask.[22]

No doubt, to assess their social characteristics and acceptability. Another respondent observed that the questions could sometimes be pointed.

> We had two dinners along the way, on each of the evenings. We changed places between each of the courses and questions like are you a Freemason seem to figure in my memory quite a lot. [INTERVIEWER - Was that important?] No, I don't think that it was important at all, but it was the sort of thing that they were interested in.[23]

But 'ordeal by dinner' did not always go the way that the organisers had planned:

> Ours was absolute bedlam. No fault on the part of the police authority. We'd all sat down for dinner and given our orders to the waiter, à la carte, and so we'd been served with our starter which was perfectly agreeable. But as with all of these dinners, we were rotated, and when the maître'd came back into the room ... he started serving à la carte orders to the wrong people in the wrong places. It was absolute pandemonium, but it was a wonderful ice-breaker.[24]

After the shortlisted candidates were interviewed, they would return to a waiting room where they would wait for the "clerk to the police authority ... to invite the successful candidate to join the police authority. He never says you are successful".[25] Upon acceptance, the police authority would submit the name of the successful candidate to the Home Office for the approval of the Home Secretary. If approval was not given, the police authority would have been informed of the reasons in a confidential communiqué. The police authority was then invited to submit the name of

---

an effective means of assessing candidates and it is recommended that they should be avoided" (para. 49).

[22] Interview with CC2.

[23] Interview with CC3.

[24] Interview with CC2.

[25] Interview with CC2.

another candidate. If approval was given, the HM Inspectors of Constabulary and MI5 were informed.

Effecting the policy of internal recruitment and selection

The Desborough recommendations did little to change the prevailing views. Contemporary sources, such as the evidence given to the 1929 Royal Commission on Police Procedure and to the 1934 Select Committee on Police Forces (Amalgamation), demonstrate quite clearly that ten years or more after Desborough, there were still considerable divisions over which approach should be taken to deal with the problem of senior command. On the one hand the Home Office and police establishment were behind the policy to recruit internally career police officers for senior positions. Political opinion, however, still lay with the traditional point of view, no doubt because of the political clout held by the parliamentary representatives in whose constituencies the independent police forces were located.[26] An example of the manner in which local political opinion conflicted with that of central government (Home Office) can be found in the report of the Royal Commission on Police Powers and Procedure 1929. Although the remit of the 1929 Royal Commission did not extend to the selection of chief constables, the issue of senior command arose as it was thought that the events which led to the Commission being formed were a consequence of the poor quality of personnel within the higher ranks of the police. The Commissioners asked that "we may perhaps be permitted to make a few general observations upon these matters in so far as they have an effect upon the investigation of crimes and offences" (*Report of the Royal Commission on Police Powers and Procedures*, 1928-1929: para. 49). The Royal Commission was impressed by the Royal Irish Constabulary cadet system and thought that it could be extended to the provincial police. The formation of a central police staff college was also suggested. Contrary to the spirit of Desborough, the Royal Commission observed that:

> (X) Long experience and good service in the lower ranks are not the only, nor even the most important, qualifications for higher posts. It would be inimical

[26] During the Labour Government of the late 1920s and early 1930s.

> to the police interest to limit appointments to the higher posts to those who had entered the police as constables. Such posts should be filled by the best men available, irrespective of the source whence they are drawn (*idem*: 114).

This view contrasted with that of Mr C. de Courcy Parry, one the HM Inspectors of Constabulary in his report of the same year:

> ... with the ever increasing difficulty of police administration and criminal investigation, one realises that such appointments must now place the man of inexperience in a very difficult position, and if he has had no previous training or experience in police administration he must of necessity be for some considerable time entirely in the hands of his subordinates. There is probably no other profession in the country where a man of no experience can be placed in such a responsible position (*Report of His Majesty's Inspectors of Constabulary 1929*, Mr de Courcy Parry).

The 1932 Select Committee on Police Forces (Amalgamations) was a significant turning point in the debate over the selection of chief constables. Although discussion of the origins of chief constables was not within the Select Committee's terms of reference it, like the Royal Commission 1929 before it, felt that the issue was too important to be excluded. However, unlike the Royal Commission, it identified the external recruitment of chief constables as being a source of "dissatisfaction amongst all ranks in the police service" (*Report from the Select Committee on Police Forces (Amalgamations),* 1931-32: para. 51). Furthermore, it went on to criticise those police authorities which had evaded the spirit of the Desborough Committee's recommendations and warned that:

> ... unless the spirit of the regulation is adhered to in the future more strictly that it appears to have been in the past, the advantages that they hope will be gained from carrying into effect of the recommendations they have made will be in some degree counterbalanced by the dissatisfaction in the service (*idem*: para. 51).

The issue arose when the Select Committee considered the possibility of abolishing the small non-county borough forces, previously the stumbling block of many policies. One of the arguments heard in defence of the small non-county borough forces was that they were actually training grounds for future chief constables. Some forces, such as Leamington and Chesterfield, developed a reputation as training grounds for chief constables (see illustration).

The Leamington Springboard

Source: *Police Review,* 1942: 522

This was the view taken by the representatives of the Chief Constables' Association (Cities and Boroughs), who told the Committee that merging the small forces would reduce the facilities for the training of chief constables. They felt that their experience in, and promotion through, the lower ranks of the police constituted both training and also a qualification for command. In addition, it would also have wider implications for morale.

> The Chief Constables' Association of the Cities and Boroughs views with much apprehension the retrograde and injurious effect the suggested merging of 68 Borough Forces will have upon ambitious Police Officers who seek to obtain the higher posts in the service (Statement by J.A. Wilson, *idem*: Appendix 4: 3).

Clearly, the borough chief constables believed that training could only be obtained in-service and were very critical of the tradition of the county police authorities in appointing 'untrained' military men as their chief constables. Their major concern was their lack of police experience:

> we submit the larger portion of their number was appointed to their post on Army or Naval records, and not as Police officers with a knowledge of crime and the maintenance of the public peace by good will and the law (*ibid*).

Finally, they were very critical of any proposed attempts to merge the boroughs with the counties on the grounds that most borough chief constables would leave the police rather than become subordinate to a county chief constable, which indicates the strength of feeling between the borough and county forces (see chapter 3). The county police believed themselves to be superior to the borough forces, which the latter resented.[27] A number of the former chief constables interviewed during this project confirmed this strength of feeling. It is, for example, apparent that a county chief constables' club still existed in the late 1960s as a private club: "They would meet at the Savoy in white tie and tails. As late as 1968 they would not admit the borough chief constables".[28] Quite predictably, the borough chief constables, who gave evidence to the 1932 Select Committee, favoured the merging of the county forces with the large borough forces, a viewpoint which contrasted sharply with that of the county chief constables who proposed precisely the opposite.

After taking into consideration the evidence put before it, the Committee recommended that the principle of promotion from within the service be established and in order that:

> ... there may be an adequate supply of candidates from the police forces with proper qualifications for the higher positions within the service, your committee recommends that steps should be taken to organise the discovery of administrative capacity within the service by the selection and training of suitable men (*idem*: para. 51).

This recommendation was a wise solution to the problem of senior command but it was forged out of compromise. It reaffirmed the principle of the internal recruitment of chief constables on their merits, but at the same time accepted the concerns raised by police authorities (and Nott-Bower, 1926) that there were not enough potential chief constables to be found within the police service. Furthermore, it clearly stated that police experience was not *de facto* training for senior command. This principle

---

[27] CC1, CC4, CC5.

[28] Interview with CC5.

was instrumental in the development of the Hendon Scheme (see chapter 7).

Enforcing the policy of internal selection and appointment

Whilst the 1932 Select Committee sorted out the conceptual issues regarding the problem of senior command, it was the Second World War which enabled the Home Office to implement finally the policy of internal recruitment. The war-time emergency placed new demands upon the police, notwithstanding the loss of many officers to the war effort. It was therefore considered to be crucial that the police forces were run as effectively as possible. In order to increase this effectiveness, the Home Secretary's powers over the police were increased, which in turn increased Home Office control over the appointment process. It will be remembered from chapter 3, that during the Second World War the links were strengthened between the Home Secretary and the chief constables and that the Home Secretary became the dominant partner in the tripartite relationship. An Order in Council made in 1942 under the Emergency Powers (Defence) Act 1939, "regularised" the Home Secretary's practice since 1939, of requesting the retirement of a chief constable if any of the clauses of the war-time emergency regulations were contravened, or if any of the chief constables were considered to be "unfit to perform their duties in the conditions which prevail or may be expected to prevail in his Police district" (*Police Review*, 1942: 98). This power was in addition to the regulations which enabled the Home Secretary to give chief constables instructions over a range of matters.

A very interesting demonstration of the impact of the changes that had taken place in the recruitment and selection process by the time of the Second World War is to be found by contrasting two personal examples of recruitment as chief constable. The first was illustrated in chapter 4, and describes the recruitment of Sir Henry Smith as a potential chief constable of the Northumberland County police by a member of the local ruling élite, who had himself previously been chief constable before receiving an inheritance. Contrast this example with the recruitment of St Johnston as chief constable of Oxfordshire, half a century later.

> I was patrolling in Kensington when I met, by chance, Colonel Halland ... one of Her Majesty's Inspectors of Constabulary. I had not seen him for some time and we stopped to talk ... Out of the blue Colonel Halland asked, "How would you like to be Chief Constable of Oxfordshire?" I was dumfounded but delighted at the prospect. Colonel Halland went on to explain that ... the force had been lagging behind in war preparation and policing in general and only that week he had persuaded the Chief Constable to resign ... To me it was a wonderful suggestion, opening out vast possibilities. I said as much and Colonel Halland promised he would see the Commissioner the next day and broach the matter at the Home Office (St Johnston, 1978: 62).

The important change here is the shift in influence from the local to the central. It demonstrates the increased involvement of the HM Inspector of Constabulary over the appointment process. It also illustrates the development of an internally constructed pool of recruits (see chapter 7).

Consequently, there was a marked increase in the number of chief constables who left office following the introduction of the Defence (General) Regulations, as Table 7 illustrates. In contrast with the chief constables who left prior to the war through natural wastage, most were encouraged by the Home Secretary either to retire 'in the interests of efficiency' or to amalgamate their forces with the local county force.[29] Many were already beyond the retirement age of 65 years.[30]

Table 7: Turnover of chief constables (leaving office)

	Boroughs	Counties	Total	Amalgamations	Actual turnover*
1929-1933	55	18	73	0	73
1934-1938	37	20	57	-1	56
1939-1943	71	23	94	-12	82
1944-1948	69	26	95	-19	76

* Adjusted for decreases in number of forces through amalgamations.

Of great significance was that, in contrast to their predecessors, the chief constables appointed to replace those who retired were, with but one

[29] The *Police Review* contains many examples of forced retirement between 1939 and 1946.
[30] Under certain circumstances, chief constables had been permitted to serve beyond their statutory retirement period.

exception,[31] individuals who had prior home (UK) police experience (see chapter 8). So, the increased influence of the Home Office over policing matters remained even after the relevant Emergency Defence Regulations ceased to be effective. One reason for this was the increased use of the Home Office circular, which as illustrated in chapter 3, became a very important instrument in the exercise of Home Office influence over policing during, and between, both periods of war. It will be remembered from chapter 3, that circulars are a form of regulation in public law that are technically not subordinate legislation and are therefore not subject to formal scrutiny by Parliament. Furthermore, they have a peculiar constitutional position in so far as they are basically little more than strong declarations of government policy and yet have come to be treated as though they are binding in law (Lustgarten, 1986: 105). Moreover, being subject to the 30 year rule, they are instruments of policy that are not made publicly available.

During the Second World War, the volume of circulars not only increased to cover every aspect of police life, organisation and activity but they also changed in tone, which shifted from suggestion to direction. Together with the continued pervasiveness of the idea of internal recruitment, or ideology, as it had now become, these circulars changed the nature of the bureaucratic relationship between the police and central government. By the end of the war the internal recruitment of chief constables from within the police was broadly perceived as a natural or logical assumption.

Even so, once the war-time emergency regulations were lifted, the Home Office went to great pains to ensure that police authorities did not continue to exploit loopholes in the regulations as they had done before the war. They became much more closely involved in the shortlisting process and as recently as 1964, the Home Office[32] would carefully monitor the appointment practices of those police authorities who were reluctant to appoint serving police officers as their chief officers. An illustration of the continued resistance of some local police authorities, to what they saw as

---

[31] In 1946, Brig. J.N. Cheney became the chief constable of the East Riding of Yorkshire. He had previously served as senior assistant chief constable in the War Department constabulary, service which qualified him under regulation 5 of the Police Regulations. The HM Inspector recommended that the appointment not be approved, but it was.

[32] F1 Department.

central government dicta, are illustrated by the circumstances leading to the appointment of a new chief constable of Cornwall. In 1956 the chief constableship of Cornwall became vacant after the departure of the fourth chief constable Major Edgar Hare MC.[33] The post was advertised and forty seven applications were received. Applicants came from all walks of life and ranged from the owner of the Wellington Hotel in Crowthorne, to various retired service people, to many serving police officers. This latter group included a number of officers at superintendent and ACPO rank, plus the chief constable of West Sussex, a small county force, and about 12 serving borough chief constables; none of the latter were shortlisted.[34] An internal memo remarked that:

> It seems fairly clear that the Police Authority have set their faces against the appointment of a borough chief constable and are determined to appoint an officer of the type of those included on the list.[35]

Consequently, the Home Office commented, in its letter to the Clerk to the County approving the candidates, that it was "felt that the list was not very strong and that it might be strengthened by the inclusion of a couple of borough chief constables".[36] This advice was ignored, as was the information given about the preferences of the HM Inspectors of Constabulary. The committee appointed R.B. Matthews, an assistant chief constable at East Sussex, who was a "county man" and had entered the police through the Hendon Scheme (see later). An appointment such as this was a partial victory for the Home Office, because, although its advice about the shortlisted candidates was ignored, it had nevertheless mobilised the agenda with regard to the compilation of the short-list. The list of applicants indicated a few individuals who had similar non-UK police profiles to the chief constables appointed during the inter-war period, experience which would have met the Police Regulations and could have led to their appointment had the Home Secretary so approved.

---

[33] Hare had been chief constable since 1935. He had no police experience other than serving for just over a year with the South African Police in Rhodesia before joining the Army in the First World War (Police Review, 1935: 242).

[34] Although the Assistant Chief Constable of Newcastle was.

[35] Almost all of those shortlisted were Hendon graduates, March 9, 1956 (HO 287/298).

[36] Letter from F. Graham-Harrison (Home Office) to Mr Verger, Clerk at County Hall, March 16, 1956 (HO 287/289).

Eight years later in 1964, just before the Police Act of that year, the post became vacant once again. During those eight years a considerable change had taken place in the way the appointments were conducted. Although many of the applicants and appointing personnel were the same, this time the police authority had no hesitation in appointing K.M. Wherly, a serving borough chief constable.[37] Not only was the Home Office advice considered this time, but so were the HM Inspector of Constabulary's opinions about the shortlisted candidates.[38] This shift was the result of two processes. The first was a review of appointment procedures which was conducted following the 1950s scandals (see later) and which looked for the first time at the processes and issues involved in the appointment of chief constables. It was also the first time that the Home Office would appear to have collated records of recent appointments to inform future actions.[39] The second was the impact of the report of the Royal Commission on the Police, which stated quite categorically that the "problem of controlling the police can, therefore, be restated as the problem of controlling chief constables" and placed the initiative further away from the police authorities (*Report of the Royal Commission on the Police*, 1962: 34, para. 102). The recommendations of the Royal Commission in 1962, and the subsequent Police Act 1964, radically restructured the process of appointing chief constables. It is, therefore, necessary to reflect upon the changes that standardised the bureaucratic procedures of the appointment process between 1919 and 1964.

Standardising the selection and appointment process

Between 1919 and 1964, many aspects of the process of selecting and appointing chief constables were gradually brought under central bureaucratic control by the Home Office, which led to their standardisation. These aspects were as follows.

---

[37] Mr K.M. Wherly, chief constable of Walsall.

[38] Letters from the HMIs to the Chief HMI, dated January 1964 (HO 287/289).

[39] Memorandum on Appointment of Chief Constables in England and Wales, April, 1959 (and updated until 1965) (HO 287/29).

Causing all vacancies for chief constableships to be advertised. A common practice of police authorities was to refrain from circulating information about their vacancy in order to restrict the field of candidates. Alternatively, they might only advertise in places where they felt that they would attract the type of candidates that they wished to appoint, because the smaller the field, the greater the say they would have in whom they appoint, given that the principle behind the rules was to appoint the best person for the job. The Home Office, therefore, became increasingly concerned that police authorities advertise broadly so as to attract as wide a field of candidates as possible. In fact, until 1939 it was not always common practice to advertise the appointment. Until war broke out the Home Office found this practice to be reasonable, but after the outbreak of hostilities, it encouraged the advertisement of all vacancies to attract as wide a field of candidates as possible. This practice was reviewed at the end of 1941[40] when it was decided to require police authorities to advertise every vacancy. In special circumstances they could apply for dispensation,[41] for example, when individuals had been asked to take over forces and it was felt inappropriate then to advertise the post.[42] In other cases police authorities would appoint their deputy chief constables with the support of the HM Inspector of Constabulary.[43]

Merely advertising the post was not enough, as police authorities would sometimes restrict their advertisements to specific, non-police sources, for example in 1958 the clerk to the North Riding Standing Joint Committee only advertised its vacancy for a chief constableship in the *Times* and the *Justice of the Peace*. The Home Office believed that the advertisement "did not come to the notice of the Police service generally" and the police authority was advised to re-advertise in the *Police Review*

[40] HO 45/400518/97.

[41] HO Circular HO 158/ 33, dated December 27, 1941.

[42] For example, in 1940 when Tarry (Exeter) took charge of Southampton when its chief (Allen) was sick. Allen resigned from the force and Tarry became chief constable in 1941. A Superintendent Rowsell then became CC of Exeter in Tarry's place without applications being invited. Some years later, in 1957, Rowsell, by co-incidence, took over the Brighton force when its chief was suspended from duty then dismissed. Rowsell was appointed without the vacancy being advertised.

[43] For example, in 1952 the Tynemouth watch committee wanted to appoint the deputy as chief constable and the Home Office allowed them to do so without advertising the post. Again, in 1957 the same happened in Bradford and the HMI thought the deputy was most capable and the Home Secretary approved the appointment.

and *Police Chronicle*. Alternatively, an advertisement might not be phrased as clearly as it might or indeed might be deliberately misleading. For example, in 1956, the Standing Joint Committee of Monmouthshire advertised its vacancy and required that candidates must have "previous service in a county force". A similar case occurred a year later, when the Lincoln watch committee wanted to give preference to candidates with "previous municipal experience". In both cases, the police authorities were advised by the Home Office not to give such preference.

Discouraging local canvassing for appointments. The practice of canvassing for appointments generally became outlawed and in 1965, canvassing members of the police authority or council on matters "concerning the force" became a disciplinary offence. This included matters relating to the appointment of a chief constable. But it only related to the appointment within one's own force. It was, seemingly, still legitimate to canvass members of the council or police authority in another force.

The main problem with canvassing was, as illustrated in chapter 5, establishing that it had taken place. This task was complicated by the fact that not only can it take a number of different forms, but it mainly takes place in secret. Furthermore, where it was observable, it was often hard to distinguish from other recognised practices. In 1947, the Oaksey committee recognised that whilst canvassing took place, it was a practice that was difficult to prevent by formal regulation. But it, nevertheless, discouraged the practice and hoped that police authorities and chief constables would continue to condemn it (*Report of the Committee on Police Conditions of Service*, 1948-49: para. 233). There have been a number of examples of action being taken against those who canvassed support for their candidacy. In 1941, an assistant chief constable at Scarborough was proceeded against by the watch committee for canvassing members of the council in relation to his not being included in the shortlist for chief constable. A more interesting case took place in 1958, when Superintendent J.R. Jones was appointed chief constable of Mid-Wales. The Inspector of Constabulary subsequently found that he had canvassed the police authority over his appointment, but no proceedings were taken because no-one would give evidence. This did not, however, stop the Home Office encouraging police authorities to state in their job advertisements that canvassing would lead to disqualification. This appointment was not approved on the grounds that Jones did not have any experience of serving in another police force (*Police Review*, 1958: 710).[44]

Standardising the terms of appointment of chief constables. An increasing function of the Home Office between 1919 and 1964, was to examine the terms upon which chief constables were appointed by their police authorities. It was usual for chief constables to be offered terms of appointment which set out the salary, payment of allowances and other matters, but the Home Office criticised police authorities when they made terms on matters that were already covered by the Police Acts and Regulations. The Home Office were conscious that some police authorities would set terms that went beyond the Police Acts and regulations and could compromise the personal, geographical or constitutional independence of the chief constable.

The more serious of these constraints were those which challenged the constitutional independence of the chief constable. For example, some police authorities attempted to write into their employment contracts terms that were outside the law, such as making "the appointment be subject to it being terminable by three months notice on either side." This happened in the case of the appointment of the chief constable of Staffordshire in 1960. The Home Office stated that it had no objection to the provision requiring the chief constable to give not less than three months notice, as it was fairly common practice, but expressed doubt as to the legality of whether a police authority could give notice to a police officer.[45]

Another condition that police authorities would typically seek to require, was that chief constables should spend their whole time in the duties of the office. This was no doubt a necessary condition of service, due to the fact that many county chief constables spent much of their time socialising with the local gentry.[46] However, police authorities would also attempt to stipulate what the duties of the office of chief constable should

---

[44] Jones later became the chief constable of the Carmarthen-Cardiganshire constabulary in 1960 (*Police Review*, 1960: 202).

[45] POL 2043/2/3 (also in HO 287/29).

[46] Local county police histories are replete with stories of the bygone times when their chief constable would be more likely to be found on the grouse moor than in the office. Also see for example, Sillitoe's account of his resistance to this expectation of the chief (1955).

be,[47] or make it a condition of employment that the chief constable should carry out such duties as the police authority or local council may require.[48] The Home Office, ever vigilant of the attempts by police authorities to control their chief constables, changed the clause to "such other duties that may be assigned to him by the Standing Joint Committee".[49]

Other stipulations, such as hours of duty, as in the case of the Wigan appointment in 1946, were frowned upon by the Home Office; as were the conditions on the means of obtaining legal advice and assistance. In the latter case, a number of situations arose where police authorities attempted to require their chief constable to instruct the county or town clerk to act as their solicitor when they needed legal advice or assistance with regard to the duties of their office.[50] The Home office pointed out that:

> Because of the constitutional position of the chief constable as an officer of the Crown ... it is essential for the chief constable to take legal advice, or employ a solicitor, without reference to the Town Clerk or indeed to his police authority.[51]

In addition, chief constables were entitled to consult the Director of Public Prosecutions[52] whenever such advice was deemed desirable.[53] Interestingly, the Home Office did not object to the police authority exercising control over the financial expenditure incurred in obtaining legal advice.[54]

Police authorities would occasionally try to impose other conditions, such as requiring the chief constable to attend meetings of the county or city council and/or the police authority. Home Office policy was that chief constables should not be required to attend the county or city councils, but that they should attend meetings of their police authority. Some police authorities imposed distance limits upon residence, others argued that a

---

[47] As in the appointments in Kent 1939, Lincoln City 1940, Berkshire 1953, Lincoln City 1957.

[48] For example, in Lincoln City in 1940.

[49] As in the case of Buckinghamshire in 1952, Berkshire 1953, Luton 1964.

[50] Lincoln City 1957, Burnley 1962.

[51] POL 2134/2/3.

[52] Under Regulation 6(i)(e) of the Prosecution of Offences regulations, 1946.

[53] Cases of difficulty had arisen in Kent 1943, 1946, Berkshire 1953, 1958 and Kent 1939, Lincoln City 1940, Wigan 1946, Oxfordshire 1954.

[54] POL 2134/2/3.

chief constable should be responsible for alterations repairs etc., in relation to the chief constable's house. Many of these conditions were minor and petty, but could restrict the independence of the chief constable. Moreover, if the rules were infringed the chief constable could be made to answer disciplinary charges.

The Home Office endeavoured to persuade police authorities to remove what it believed were restrictive clauses, many of which were not meant to be obstructive and probably reflected traditional local employment practices. Other practices were more serious, such as the condition that the appointment of the chief constable should be subject to the approval of the city or borough council. In some areas, it had been common practice for the whole of the Town council to select the chief constable, such as in 1923, when the Northampton Town Council selected the chief constable, who was subsequently appointed by the watch committee.[55] In 1930, the opposite scenario happened when the Accrington watch committee made the selection but then referred their final choice to the Town Council for confirmation.[56] A number of similar cases also occurred around that time, indicating that such practices had been fairly commonplace but had only come to be detected once the Home Office's purview of the appointment process had increased.

If the local authorities were restrictive about conditions of service, they were equally strict about their chief officer's personal circumstances: as was the practice with any of their police officers.[57] In 1953, for example, the chief constable of Norwich proposed to marry a woman who held the directorship of a large licensed hotel in the city. The Home Office advised against the marriage under regulation 4 of the Police Regulations 1952.[58] The woman subsequently gave up her directorship and married the chief constable. Whilst these conditions of employment were usually minor, if not petty, they could compromise the chief constables' independence at a time when the Home Office were actively promoting the idea of constabulary independence (Morgan, 1987).

---

[55] POL 388,158/16/17.
[56] POL 388,077/14.
[57] Under regulation 8 Home Secretary's Rules (1920).
[58] SI 1952/1704 POL 2142/2/1.

Improving disciplinary procedures. Until 1952, there were no clearly defined procedures for dealing with allegations of misconduct by chief constables. The system was overhauled by the Oaksey committee and statutory regulations were made for dealing with disciplinary matters. The police authority was the disciplinary body, but chief constables could appeal to the Home Secretary.[59] It is therefore interesting, that during the decade or so after the introduction of these disciplinary regulations, six or seven chief constables were subject to an inquiry, which does beg the question about the previous conduct of local policing.[60]

Discouraging the appointment of local candidates. One of the main reasons for discouraging canvassing was to prevent unhealthy, or even corrupt, alliances taking place between the chief constable and members of the police authority. Underlying this discussion was the broader issue of appointing local candidates who had no policing experience outside their force. It became an issue of concern following the police scandals of the 1950s. It was felt that chief constables should have police experience in more than one police force. Before 1939, the Home Office appears to have only objected to one appointment, on the grounds that the candidate was local. This happened in Sheffield in 1926, during a period when there were many problems with local gangs.[61] The Home Secretary refused to approve either the appointment of the deputy or any other officer from the force. Although the correspondence to the police authority does not say as much, it was clear that there existed concerns that internal candidates might be on close terms with various undesirables within the area.

---

[59] They had this right since the Police (Appeals) Act 1927, but the 1952 Disciplinary Regulations made the procedures less opaque.

[60] These cases are cited elsewhere in this book but include: 1952 - Peterborough, charges of mis-using the police staff car etc. 1955 - Mid-Wales, charges of oppressive and tyrannical conduct. 1956 - Cardiganshire, charges of misconduct made by the SJC. 1957 - Brighton, charges of conspiracy to defraud (Chief constable acquitted but dismissed). 1958 - Worcester, charged with theft. Chief constable found guilty and imprisoned. 1958 - Nottingham, The Popkess affair (see chapter 3). 1964 - Sheffield, Rhino Whip enquiry. 1965 - Southend, Chief Constable charged with fraud and the investigation found substance, charges were brought and chief constable imprisoned.

[61] The deputy chief constable was shortlisted for the then vacancy and the Home Secretary stated that since the deputy was 60 years old he wouldn't approve his, or the appointment of any other officer from the force. Capt. Percy Sillitoe, from the East Riding of Yorkshire, was appointed (Sillitoe 1955).

From 1939 onwards, the Home Office wanted more efficient (obedient) forces and actively discouraged the appointment of local candidates. This time, the issue was not so much the fear of corruption, rather it was that local candidates were not felt not to have sufficiently wide experience and would therefore not bring a sufficiently critical outlook to bear upon the policing of the area. However, there is some evidence to show that the Home Office was still very concerned about close links between candidates and local people. In 1943, for example, the town clerk of Norwich was advised that although the Home Secretary could not refuse to approve the appointment of the deputy chief constable as chief constable, there were concerns about the fact that he (the deputy chief constable) had been living with a woman who was not his wife. Similarly, a year later in 1944, the Home Secretary refused to approve the appointment of a local candidate for the chief constableship of Wolverhampton, because there had previously been irregularities in the force and that it was felt that a fresh face was necessary in order to restore public confidence in the local police.[62]

Basically, the Home Secretary's rule of thumb was that if there was a record of recent trouble in the force, then approval tended to be denied, similarly if there had been a succession of local appointments to the post.[63] In most cases, approval would only be refused if something was also known to the detriment of the candidate. There was until the 1960s no rule about the non-approval of local candidates, because the underlying principle was that the local person might be the best for the job. The view that chief constables should be appointed from outside the force was given impetus by the dismissal from office, and imprisonment, of the chief constable of Worcester and the subsequent dismissal of the chief constable of Brighton, both of whom, had spent their entire careers in one force. In addressing the 1958 ACPO conference, R.A. Butler, the Home Secretary, criticised the appointment of local candidates on the grounds that it discouraged the flow of ideas across forces.[64] This mood swing subsequently led to approval being refused for a number of local

---

[62] HO 287/29.

[63] Where there had been no trouble the applicants tended to be approved, although often with some reluctance: Portsmouth (1958), Exeter (1958), Liverpool (1958).

[64] A copy of the speech was circulated to clerks of police authorities as HO Circular 90/1958.

appointments because of their limited experience. Those refused were in Gateshead, Blackburn and Mid-Wales in 1958, Nottingham in 1959, Barrow-in-Furness in 1961, Gateshead in 1962, and Glamorgan in 1963. In each case the main reason for refusal to approve the appointment was not that something was known to the detriment of the candidate, as in the past, but that their experience was limited to one force.

The problem of local appointments was solved by the Police (Amendment) (No.2) Regulations 1964 which followed the Police Act of that year. They stated that:

> No person shall be appointed chief constable of a police force unless he has had at least two years experience in another police force in the rank of inspector or above. For the purposes of these regulations 'experience in some other force' means experience in a home force.[65]

Prohibiting the appointment of candidates without police experience. Although, as discussed above, no candidates without police experience were appointed after the Second World War, the position on their appointment was not as cut and dry as perhaps the Home Office tended to make out to police authorities. In fact, the memorandum on the appointment of chief constables noted that "It may of interest to record that prior to the Police (Amendment) (No.2) Regulations, 1964 coming into force, the position of candidates without police experience was not so definite".[66] It will be useful at this point to briefly recap on the rules for appointing a chief constable: firstly, candidates over 40 years of age might have only been appointed if they had served in a police force in Great Britain, or there were special circumstances that could be taken into consideration. Secondly, candidates under 40 would have only been appointed without the need for other conditions to be satisfied, if they had police experience anywhere in the world. Thirdly, candidates without any police experience could only be appointed if they had exceptional qualifications or experience, or there were not sufficiently well qualified candidates from within the police service. Consequently, the successful

[65] HO Circular 151/1964 containing the Police (Amendment) (No.2) Regulations 1964 (S1. No. 831).

[66] Memorandum on Appointment of Chief Constables in England and Wales, April, 1959 (and regularly updated until 1965) (HO 287/29).

implementation of the policy of internal recruitment relied upon the definition of what was understood by "police force", what was meant by "special circumstances" and what counted as "exceptional experience".

The Legal Adviser of the Home Office expressed the view that the expression "police force", in Regulation 5 meant a police force to which the empowering enactment, the Police Act 1919, applied.[67] This interpretation restricted the provision to service within a police force in England and Wales and Scotland, in so far as a candidate over 40 years of age was concerned. But, previous service in another force outside the UK would, however, make the applicant eligible if it was reckonable as pensionable service and this could be interpreted fairly broadly. Under the provisions of Section 10 of the Police Pensions Act 1912, approved service could be as a civil servant, or office of the staff of the Metropolitan Police, or in a number of differently funded police forces.[68] For candidates under 40, the restrictions did not apply. The Legal Adviser held that the understanding of the term "police experience" did not have the restricted meaning that 'police force' had in Regulation 5. It was taken to mean police service in any part of the world.[69]

As for the interpretation of "special circumstances", a Home Office memorandum[70] stated that there had been "no occasion where it has been necessary to consider how it should be defined." But, it was thought in practice that the Home Secretary would expect the police authority to make out a strong case before approval. They would have to show in particular that the candidate was outstandingly well qualified and suited to the particular post in relation to candidates from police forces of Great Britain.[71] "Exceptional circumstances" were, for example, a proven background in criminal justice administration as in the case of the appointment in 1931 of the former governor of Dartmoor prison, Major L.H. Morris, as the chief constable of Devon. He was regarded as having

---

[67] POL 2001/2/2, POL 2037/2/3, POL 2032/2/3.

[68] In a police force with a salary paid out of the police fund. In a police force with a salary wholly paid by parliament. In a police force with a salary partly paid by parliament. Services within the War Department Constabulary count. Regulation 28(e) of the Police Pension Regulations, 1955, also included service in the RUC.

[69] POL 2001/2/2.

[70] HO 287/29 and POL 2012/2/2.

[71] HO 287/29 and POL 2012/2/2.

outstanding personality and ability[72] and the appointment was approved by the Home Secretary.

So, until 1964, candidates without any police experience were able to apply, regardless of their age, for a post as chief constable. It was demonstrated earlier, that even as recently as 1956, people with no police experience were applying for chief constableships. But it was also illustrated above that their appointment became increasingly unlikely and they were not even shortlisted after the beginning of the Second World War. At least four appointments were not approved between 1919 and 1940.[73]

Preventing the appointment of candidates with police experience outside United Kingdom. Under the Police Regulations 1952, individuals over 40 years of age and with no service in the United Kingdom, but with service outside the United Kingdom, could have been appointed in special circumstances approved by the Home Secretary.[74] There were a number of examples of such appointments, but not since the Second World War.[75]

---

[72] HO 45 388,035/77

[73] In 1925 Lt-Colonel A.J.N. Bartlett, 41 years of age, was appointed as the chief constable of Cumberland and Westmoreland. He had studied the workings of the police for three years with the chief constable of Oxfordshire. The Home Secretary declined with great reluctance to approve the appointment. In 1932, Captain R.D. Busk, 36 years of age, was appointed chief constable of Montgomeryshire. He had military service in the First World War and also in Ireland where he had acted in charge of the RIC. He was subsequently attached to the Birmingham police to study police methods. The Home Secretary met with the chair of the standing joint committee and a local Member of Parliament before declining to approve the appointment. In 1934, Captain G.W.R. Hearn, 40 years of age, was appointed the chief constable of the East Riding of Yorkshire. He had military service in the army and had worked closely with the Commissioner of Police in Mandalay. He had also co-operated with local police in Ireland. The standing joint committee could not show exceptional experience. As stated earlier, in 1935 Hearn became assistant chief constable of Staffordshire and became its chief constable in 1949. In 1940, Lt-Commander, the Hon, R.D.C. Coleridge, 34 years of age, was appointed as chief constable of Bedfordshire. He had served in the Royal Navy for 20 years. He had some instruction in police work from the chief constable of West Sussex. (HO 287/29).

[74] SI 1952/1704.

[75] In 1923, Capt. Percy Sillitoe of the Rhodesian Police was appointed Chief Constable of Chesterfield (POL 388107/27). In 1926, Mr C.E. Lynch-Blosse of the Bombay Police was appointed chief constable of Montgomeryshire (POL 388053/25). In 1927, Mr J.C. Lloyd-Williams of the Indian police became chief constable of Montgomeryshire upon Lynch-Blosse's departure to become assistant chief constable of Lancashire. Lynch-Blosse became

However, the unlikelihood of appointment did not in fact prevent applications from individuals with experience outside the UK. These were typically of officers either from colonial forces, the RUC or the Garda Siochana. For example, six of the nine candidates for the Dorset vacancy in 1954 were colonial police officers. The clerk was informed that if any of the candidates were appointed, who were over 40 years of age, then the standing joint committee would have to show special circumstances.[76] There were further examples from the 1950s of individuals with police experience outside the UK applying, who would most likely have been appointed two decades previously. In 1956, Mr K.I. McCrea applied for the post of chief constable of Monmouthshire. He was a deputy chief constable of the Air Ministry Constabulary, and had previously served in the Indian police between 1927 and 1947. The standing joint committee were advised by the Home Office that Mr McRea would not be approved.[77] Two years later Mr N.P. Hadow, Commissioner of the Uganda police, was shortlisted for the appointment of chief constable of Gloucestershire. The clerk to the standing joint committee was informed that they would have to demonstrate special circumstances if Hadow were appointed. Hadow was strongly supported by Sir William Johnson, the HM Inspector of Constabulary, who said that he had known Hadow for years and that he had a high reputation. He said that Hadow could not be excluded from consideration on the grounds that colonial police forces were organised and administered along lines that were similar to those of the UK police. Furthermore Hadow had attended courses at the National Police College in 1952. Johnson suggested that it might be necessary to reconsider the current attitude towards the appointment of colonial police officers in appointments to chief constable. The standing joint committee took heed of the Home Office advice and Hadow was not appointed.[78] Four years later,

---

chief constable of Leicestershire in 1929. In 1929, Mr Freeman Newton of the Indian police became the chief constable of Hereford (POL 388130/33). He subsequently became the CC of Herefordshire in 1929. In 1942, Mr G.E. Banwell of the Indian Police in Burma became chief constable of the East Riding of Yorkshire. He had previously been an assistant inspector of constabulary between 1941 and 1942. He became the chief constable of Cheshire in 1946 (POL 825103/7).

[76] Lt-Col R.B. Greenwood, assistant chief constable of Lincolnshire was appointed as chief constable (POL 2012/2/2).

[77] POL 2012/2/3.

[78] POL 2018/2/49.

in 1962, Sir Kerr Bovell, previously Inspector General of Police in Nigeria, applied for a post of Chief Constable. He was 48 years of age, had no police service in the UK, and would have to have shown special circumstances. He was not shortlisted.[79]

These cases typically involved former colonial police officers, whose numbers were increasing as the various colonies were granted independence. In 1964, the Home Office were formally approached by Lord Boyd, chairman of the overseas resettlement bureau, who wanted to know about the position of former colonial police officers applying for posts of chief constable. He was told that the Home Office felt that their appointment to senior positions in the UK police forces was generally undesirable.[80] Lord Boyd was told: firstly, that police work abroad is very different to that in the UK and that it was becoming increasingly difficult for officers who had never served in a UK police force to take effective command without first hand experience of the knowledge and methods used. Secondly, their appointment would make the police service a less attractive career to recruits. Furthermore, it was the unanimous view of the HM Inspectors of Constabulary that any temporary benefits that might be gained from appointing former colonial police officers either as chief constable or to the posts below would be offset by the adverse effect upon morale. Thirdly, to appoint such officers would conflict with the policy set out in the 1961 White Paper on Police Training (*Police Training in England and Wales*, 1961). This policy towards former colonial officers was confirmed by Mr Brooke, Home Secretary, in a speech to recruits. He said that: "In the years ahead of you there will be many senior posts to be filled. They will all be filled by men who have, like you, joined the police service as constables".[81]

Reforming the process of selecting and appointing chief constables

Between 1958 and 1964 there was a considerable mood swing with regard to chief constables. The aforementioned scandals during the 1950s reduced

[79] POL 50/2/15. There were a number of other cases which illustrate similar circumstances and are therefore not listed here. See *Absorption of Ex-Colonial Police Officers into United Kingdom Police Forces*, (POL50/1/42 also in HO 287/29).
[80] The letter did, however, state that officers who were aged under 30 were welcome to join the lower ranks of the police.
[81] Section 11, HO 287/29.

public confidence in both the office and the police service in general. They excited the agenda for reform that was apparent in the speech of R.A. Butler, Home Secretary, to the 1958 ACPO conference. Butler believed that the senior ranks of the police were parochial and not equipped to take the police into the next half of the century. This shift in opinion and other events (see chapter 3) helped to fuel the 1960 Royal Commission on the Police, which was underpinned by the principle that police forces were a reflection of those who commanded them. In addition to increasing central controls over chief constables, it also recommended that "there should be freer interchange between police forces at higher levels" (*Final Report of the Royal Commission on the Police*, 1962). So, the new vision of the most senior police positions was as a self-contained professional group of trained police managers: effectively, a criminal justice élite group with a degree of autonomy from both central and local government. The consequence of these events was the overhauling of both the statutory and regulatory framework for the selection and appointment of chief constables. The new rules were fairly wide sweeping and many of the issues, illustrated earlier, simply disappeared. Parallel to the reformed structure, was a programme of Higher Police Training, which is the subject of the next chapter.

The Police (Amendment) (No. 2) Regulations 1964[82] substituted the old regulation 6 (formerly 9) with new wording and considerably different meaning:

> 6. Every appointment to the post of chief constable shall be subject to the approval of the Secretary of State and, without prejudice to the Regulations 4 and 5 of these Regulations, no person shall be appointed to such a post in a police force unless he has at least two years experience in some other force in the rank of inspector or a higher rank.[83]

All future chief constables, therefore, had to have served in a UK police force, there were no exemptions, and they had to have served in more than one force at a senior rank: the rank of inspector was later replaced with that of assistant chief constable.[84] A provision was subsequently brought in

[82] SI 1964/831 (also in HO Circular 151/1964).
[83] SI 1964/831, reg. 6.
[84] SI 1995/215, reg. 13a. Also see HOC 78/1965, para. 1.

during the amalgamations which allowed service in a combined police force to count as service in another police force, but this was rescinded in the mid-1970s.[85]

Another significant change was that appointments to all ACPO ranks, including deputy and assistant chief constables, became subject to the approval of the Home Secretary[86] and the police authorities, who made the appointment, had to consult the Home Office about the suitability of candidates, as they previously did for the post of chief constable,[87] in order further to promote the "freer interchange between police forces at higher levels" that was encouraged by the 1960 Royal Commission on the Police. Arrangements were also made to facilitate the transfer of officers between Metropolitan and Provincial forces.[88] In Home Office circular 78/1965, the Home Secretary, Roy Jenkins, made it quite clear that he regarded it as vital, in the interests of the police service, that there should be the fullest opportunity for those who attend the senior staff course to gain experience in the highest ranks.[89] In order to circulate information about vacancies, so as to increase the interchange, the Police Council, in March 1965, agreed that police authorities should be advised that all vacancies for posts in the ACPO ranks should be advertised.[90] The Police Council also agreed that one in three of vacancies in other ranks down to and including that of chief inspector should also be advertised.[91]

In 1976, following the amalgamations of 1974, the Home Office issued circular 176/1976, essentially to remind police authorities of the need to introduce new blood into their forces in the interests of efficiency. This circular becomes significant because of the almost cajoling tone it took, in comparison to the suggestive or even directive tones of previous circulars. One possible reason for this change in tone, is that the circulars

---

[85] The special circumstances were no longer justified. HOC 176/1976. Chief, Deputy Chief and Assistant Chief Constables: Requirements for Appointments (also 76/1981 as amended by letter to Clerks of Police Authorities 13 April 1989).

[86] Schedule 2 of the Police Act 1964 (Commencement No.1) Order, 1964. See HOC 78/1965 Senior Appointments in the Police Service.

[87] See HOC 171/1965.

[88] Para. 5, HOC 78/1965.

[89] Later called the senior command course and subsequently the strategic command course.

[90] Arrangements were also made to facilitate the transfer of officers between Metropolitan and Provincial forces (paras. 2-3, HOC 78/1965).

[91] Paras. 2-3, HOC 78/1965.

increasingly became the product of a network of policy-makers which comprised of ACPO representatives (the chief constables), Home Office civil servants and often, Home Office ministers. It states forcefully, that it is important to bring "new blood into forces which might otherwise have tended to become inbred ... there is unmistakable advantage in requiring those officers who seek to rise to the highest posts to gain experience in other forces: and it is hoped that a clear statement of intent will be helpful in securing this result" (*idem*: para. 2).

The circular went on to describe how the recent amalgamations caused the disappearance of the borough and smaller county forces and diminished the opportunities for individuals gaining command of a small force, which had been regarded as training experience in preparation for a larger command. Consequently, the only way that preparation for command could be made was by working as a deputy chief constable. The Home Office therefore introduced a general practice that no officer should be appointed consecutively as assistant, deputy and chief constable (*idem*: para. 3). The circular also changed the minimum rank for qualifying service in another police force from inspector to superintendent. Finally, the circular reminded police authorities of both the benefits of consulting and their requirement to consult with the Home Office regarding all of their appointments at ACPO rank, also reaffirming the need to advertise appointments. Procedurally, this circular was reaffirming many practices that already existed, but presented them with a *fait accompli*. On the issue of consultation it stated that:

> ... the Home Office will then indicate to the police authority if the Home Secretary would not be prepared to approve the appointment of any applicant, and will also indicate, for the confidential information of the authority, which candidates, appear to him to be well qualified and deserving of interview. The police authority will then be able to select the short-list (*idem*: para. 8).

Another example is found in paragraph 5, which states that: "The Home Secretary hopes that police authorities will agree to adopt the practice he proposes. For his part it will be his intention to apply them when giving his approval to appointments" (*idem*: para. 5). The outcome of this circular was to restrict considerably the police authoritys' powers to appoint a senior police officer. The circular was accompanied by a covering letter which rehearsed many of the arguments. It then impressed upon the clerks to the police authority that the Home Office wished "to develop further the partnership between police authorities and the Home Office in the whole matter of senior police appointments and to advance our joint interest in obtaining the best man for the job".[92] Clearly, the Home Office were still experiencing hostility from local authorities who, in comparison to today, still expressed greater control over their local police. Some five years later, in 1981, circular 76/1981 reminded clerks to the police authorities that the circumstances outlined in circular 176/1976 were the only basis upon which appointments would be approved by the Home Secretary.

During the late 1980s and early 1990s, the selection and appointment of chief constables was reviewed again. This time, the emphasis was upon the training qualifications held by the candidate. As from January 1 1992, circular no. 98/1991, which followed the recommendations of the Home Affairs Committee's inquiry into Higher Police Training and the Police Staff College (1989), made it a compulsory requirement for all applicants for the ACPO ranks to have completed the senior command course at the police staff college.[93] This shifted the ball further away from the police authorities towards the Home Office, in so far as the key issues in selection and appointment were concerned. It placed new emphasis upon the extended interview system by which individuals were selected for admission onto the special course and also on to the strategic command course (see next chapter). Although the extended interview panels do include some non-police personnel, it is clearly the case that the agenda is set by the police. Many of the key decisions in the appointment process are now made by police officers. Decisions, which range from whether or not an individual is acceptable through the extended interview system to whether or not they are likely to be approved by the Home Office and HM Inspectors of Constabulary. In this way, not only has the Home Office removed control over the selection and appointment of chief constables from the police authorities, but it has effectively devolved much of the key decision making back to the police. Whilst it could be argued that there exist perfectly justifiable reasons for these actions, the point being made here is that this policy was being introduced, and enforced, without the use of primary legislation. It was the exercise of power through bureaucratic

[92] Letter dated November 12, 1976 accompanying HOC 176/1976 (POL/66 50/1/13).

[93] There were some exceptional circumstances, such as the person has been accepted for the next course.

means and without the full sanction of law or having gone through the full democratic process. Of course, this is not to imply that the activity was in any way illegal, just that there is a strong argument that policy which has profound implications for public life should be openly debated within Parliament.

Appointing today's chief constables

The most recent review of the selection and appointment process took place in 1993 and resulted in the publication in late 1996 of best practice guide-lines on the selection procedures of chief officer appointments in the police service (*Chief Officer Appointments in the Police Service*, 1996). These guide-lines result from a Home Office working group, established in 1993, to review the current arrangements for the appointment of chief officers (ACPO and above) to police forces in England and Wales. The members of the working group included representatives of the, then, police authority associations,[94] the police staff associations,[95] the HM Inspectors of Constabulary, and the Equal Opportunities Commission (*idem*: para. 1).

The 1996 guide-lines map out in considerable detail what has been accepted by the working group as the best practice for appointing a chief constable. The instructions clearly state that they are not prescriptive and suggest that police authorities might want to vary them according to local situations, but they are also warned to be aware of the potential difficulties and pitfalls if they are to avoid complaints of unfairness or discrimination, whilst at the same time selecting the most suitable candidate for the post (*idem*: para. 2). Police authorities are advised that without declared equal opportunities policies and procedures, unsuccessful applicants will often feel unfairly treated and the fairness and credibility of the organisation will be undermined. Therefore, procedures must be visible in order that fairness of intent and action are perceived by both applicants and also the serving staff (*idem*: para. 3). The opaqueness of the previous procedures gave rise to misunderstandings and resentment. One of the chief constables interviewed outlined their frustrations with the previous system:

---

94 The Association of Metropolitan Authorities and Association of County Councils.

95 The Association of Chief Police Officers, the Superintendents' Association, the Police Federation.

> You would apply for a job and you would be told that you would not be called for an interview, but there was a restriction on them telling you and which prevented you from finding out why. So you didn't know whether it was the Home Office who was not supporting you or whether the police authority just did not call you for interview, and you just could not get to know and certainly following the time of the Alison Halford case, and maybe [the Chief HM Inspector of Constabulary] was going to do it anyway, but certainly since that time you are told if the Home Office didn't support you and if they don't support you, you now know why they weren't supportive and you are now given objective feedback about your interview with the police authority if you are not selected. But that has only been during the last three or four years. Before then it was very much a lottery.[96]

A commonly held assumption is that the new guide-lines were driven by the Alison Halford case. However, both Sir John Woodcock and Sir Geoffrey Dear, respectively HM Chief Inspector and HM Inspector of Constabulary, have independently pointed out that elements of the new best practice guide-lines were already in the process of being implemented and had already been adopted in some forces.[97] It will be remembered that during the early 1990s, the police were undergoing considerable review by the Audit Commission: this was the age of the professional managerialist. Woodcock believes that the review was more about professionalism and about removing any uncertainties that existed.

> These are fairly important people, assistant chief constable and above, so they have made good progress in the service and they deserve the best professional advice about how they are doing. ... If you actually tell somebody as to where their shortcomings are then you will find that they already know and it rarely takes them by surprise.[98]

However, whilst the new system irons out many of the idiosyncrasies that previously existed, Woodcock is not so sure, however, whether or not "it achieves the same analytical honesty in relation to people's capabilities. It

---

[96] Interview with CC4.

[97] Interview with Sir Geoffrey Dear, May 30, 1997 and interview with Sir John Woodcock, June 11, 1997.

[98] Interview with Sir John Woodcock, June 11, 1997.

does bring into vogue the tendency to make more people into swans than they otherwise are".[99]

The new procedures for shortlisting and interview are very similar to those described earlier, for example, the advertisement of the vacancy to ensure that every eligible officer becomes aware of it, Home Office vetting of the applicants, Home Office assistance with the short-list, interview and approval by the Home Secretary. The main differences today lie generally, in the level by which the process is standardised, in the depth of detail provided by the best practice guide-lines, and in the principle of giving feedback to applicants.

More specifically, the new procedures actively discourage the practice of informal interviewing, particularly 'ordeal by dinner', and focus instead upon the objective appraisal of the candidates' professional competencies, so it is common, for example, for police authorities to run briefing events either before or after the short-listing process. The short-listing process itself has been revised, so as to be more open than it previously was, but it is also more peer-oriented than before.

Applications for chief constableships. Applications are submitted to the clerk to the police authority. However, the applicant's chief constable is required to complete a form (E.1), using set criteria,[100] to assess the candidate's suitability for the post (*idem*: para. 18). This form, as with other assessments, is shown to the candidate. The HM Inspectors of Constabulary draw upon this form and any other relevant sources of information about the candidate, such as their performance during extended interviews, to award a mark that is based upon a predetermined scale.[101] They also prepare a narrative assessment about the candidate's suitability for the post. This assessment is subsequently returned to both the applicants and their chief constables for possible discussion if there is any disagreement.

---

[99] *ibid.*

[100] Judgement, Self-confidence, Strategic perspective, Achievement focus, Communication, Information search, Team building, Influencing others.

[101] Grade S1 means ready for this post and also capable of commands larger and more difficult: Grade S2 means ready now to undertake this post, no substantial reservations: Grade S3 means ready now but some reservations, which may include the view that the next rank appears to be the limit of the candidate's potential: S4 means not ready yet: S5 means probably at the limit of the candidate's capabilities.

As soon as the closing date for applications is reached, the list of applicants is sent to the Police Personnel and Training Unit at the Home Office. The police authority are then told if any of the applicants would not be approved by the Home Secretary if they were appointed. Candidates who are not approved, are informed by their HM Inspector of Constabulary, who also lets them know the reasons.

References. In keeping with Equal Opportunities Commission recommendations, selection should be carried out by reference to an open set of criteria in order to reduce the possibility of subjective assessment, which could lead to unlawful discrimination (*idem*: para. 29). Because of the level of subjectivity which is found in references, they are to be used with great care. The guide-lines suggest that they may not, in fact, be required since the selection panels will have access to full assessments from a range of different sources.

Short-listing. Independently of the Home Office assessments, and to assist the selection panel in the short-listing process, candidates are assessed by the appointing police authority in terms of their personal specification criteria. Not only are panel members to be trained for this process, but the regional HM Inspector of Constabulary is also to be available in order to advise upon the short-list, but not as a part of the panel. Short-listing has to be structured and objective, therefore the selection panel have to agree both the level and type of experience needed in each of the areas of competence to warrant invitation to interview. They are required to assess the applicant on eight criteria: judgement, self-confidence, strategic perspective, achievement focus, communication, information search, team building, influencing others. "Applicants should be independently evaluated by panel members for appropriate levels of evidence and then collectively reviewed before a consensus decision is reached" (*idem*: para. 33). The panel's short-list should be a minimum of three and a maximum of six and the Home Office is informed of the choice, but as the candidates' levels of approve-ability have been already assessed, then any further work by the Home Office would be duplicated.

Interviewing. The most popular method of assessment is the interview, but the guide-lines warn that it can be highly unreliable as a selection tool unless objectives are clear, interviewers possess good interviewing skills, and questions are appropriately structured. The most important part of the interview is that all applicants are assessed against previously agreed competencies criteria. It is important that interview panels can draw upon the advice of professional police officers and the relevant HM Inspector of Constabulary is invited to be present to act as adviser. Where presentations are used, all candidates should be given the same topic in advance. Previous informal social contacts with applicants are now recommended to be avoided because of their potential to introduce bias into the interpretation of the candidate's performance (*idem*: para. 49).

Post-interview procedures. As stated earlier, the final decision has to be made against structured and objective criteria with an overall mark set against an agreed scale.[102] The guide-lines warn against basing judgements upon potentially unlawful discriminatory considerations such as family or domestic arrangements, or unlawful positive discrimination in favour of candidates from minority groups. When a final selection has been made and the candidate has accepted, the clerk to the police authority submits the recommended appointment to the Home Secretary for approval.

Feedback to unsuccessful applicants. Unsuccessful applicants are given the opportunity to find out about their performance during the selection process. On completion, the selection panel prepare a short report on each applicant's performance, outlining strengths and weaknesses. It is for the applicant to decide whether or not to read this report or discuss it with a member of the interviewing panel, or their chief constable or regional HMIC.

Monitoring. A record of the number, gender, race and age of people applying for each chief officer post, of those shortlisted and those selected is kept and the information is available upon request.

In sum, these new procedures formally create a structured appraisal of candidates' professional competencies. This is in contrast to the more

[102] Q1, highly qualified for the post; Q2, more than qualified for the post; Q3, qualified for the post; NQ, not qualified for the post. (*Chief Officer Appointments in the Police Service: Guidelines on Selection Procedures*, which accompanies HOC 52/96: 9, para 51).

personal or subjective evaluations that existed previously and in stark contrast to the evaluations of candidates' social position (in the county forces) and trustworthiness (in the borough forces) of bygone years. In these latter assessments, any notion of professional competence played a very minor role, if at all. In contrast, the new procedures are clearly driven by the need to make the assessment process more transparent and less contested. But, there is evidence in the explanatory notes of an obvious wish to avoid litigation under the Equal Opportunities legislation, and there is also a desire to avoid the negative media coverage which politicises police management, damages the reputation of the police service and questions its legitimacy. This criterion brings to mind Manning's (1977) observation that one of the many roles of the police chief is to "manage the public appearance of law enforcement" in order to maintain the legitimacy of policing methods or protect the public mandate of the police (see earlier). This also highlights the changed role of the modern police authority in the appointment of the chief constable. Whilst the recruitment and selection functions are now firmly in the hands of the Home Office, the police authority does still appoint the chief constable. A committee of the police authority does interview all candidates and its members chair the various appointment panels. It could therefore be argued that the function of the modern police authority, when appointing their chief constable, is to choose the most appropriate or credible personality for the post.

By concentrating upon professional competencies, the new procedures for appointing police chiefs may effectively prevent the appointment of chief constables with any radical political or religious views. Important here is the fact that all chief constables will have passed through the senior /strategic command courses and the majority will also have passed through the special course earlier in their careers (see chapter 7). Entry onto both courses is dependent upon passing through an extended interview procedure which, depending upon the course in question, is a two or three day series of high pressured interviews during which candidates are closely observed and assessed against a range of criteria. These processes are possibly the most important hurdles to any aspirant police chief and therefore the extended interview becomes an important, if not the most important, tool in the selection process. So, each candidate who is approved for selection will have been assessed and re-assessed in terms of their relevant competencies (see earlier). In many respects these competencies demand from a modern police manager qualities that are almost precisely the opposite of those required of their predecessors a century, or so, ago. The most obvious difference is that the concepts of leadership and management have replaced the concept of command. Modern chief constables are in charge of organisations with budgets of up to, and beyond, a third of a billion pounds, and therefore have to work closely with colleagues in their management team, with whom they are *primus inter pares*. In Lukesian terms, there has over time been a shift from the coercive first dimension of power, through the second dimension in which chief constables had to 'mobilise agendas' to achieve their goals, towards the third, 'ideological', dimension of power (Lukes, 1974).

Modern police chiefs are expected to influence their management team rather than control them, and are judged on their leadership qualities, especially their ability to build teams around them. They are also judged on their strategic perspective which places their force within the national framework of policing: their predecessors tended to adopt a purely local perspective.[103] Furthermore, they are expected to set objectives that will enable them to achieve their strategic aims and be able to carry our those strategies with self-confidence. They also are judged on their communication skills, which require the flow of information in two directions and which also require them to seek the sources of information that will enable them to reach informed decisions and, importantly, to make sound judgements about both people and also situations.

Today, the Home Office exerts almost complete control over the selection and appointment process. They are aided in their task by the HMICs who "occupy the critical space between central government, chief constables and, on occasion, police authorities" (Lustgarten, 1986: 106). In addition to acting as the eyes and ears of the Home Office, and as a conduit for disseminating its policies, they play a dominant role in shaping and co-ordinating policing practice throughout the country. Perhaps their greatest role, within the context of this study, is the key role they play in head-hunting the next generation of chief constables (Lustgarten, 1986: 107).

---

[103] It could be argued that this perspective did tend to change temporarily, during times of industrial unrest. See Morgan (1987).

Conclusions

Over the past 160 years the selection and appointment process has changed dramatically. Qualities once revered are now reviled, and the scientific appraisal of chief constables means that no matter who the police authorities appoint, they will be acquiring a certain pre-determined set of competencies. This is a far cry from the days when police authorities wanted someone they could trust to command their force as they wished, whether it be a social equal in the counties, or a trusted servant in the boroughs.

This chapter has illustrated the mechanisms which have driven the changes in the selection and appointment processes. The most important of these mechanisms was the utilisation of secondary or quasi-legislation (Ganz, 1987), through the Home Office circular. These "declarations of government policy" (Lustgarten, 1986: 105) are neither primary nor subordinate legislation and are exercised in a bureaucratic framework which effectively causes them to be treated as if they are binding in law. Practically speaking, the circulars help the Home Office deal with the contradictions that arise out of the local-central debate, in so far as policing is essentially still a function of local rather than national government; although the changes in the constitution of the police authority in 1985 and 1994 obfuscate the constitutional position of the police somewhat. Basically, the quasi-legal function of the circular enables the Home Office to fulfil a steering role whilst the independent police forces row, in this sense they are carrying out Troup's (1928) vision of the Home Office role forged during the early decades of this century. In practice, the police, through ACPO and the HM Inspectors of Constabulary, are actively involved in the formulation of policies which are expressed by the circulars (chapter 10).

The main concern surrounding the form of quasi-legislation which effected this particular policing policy, is that it raises a number of constitutional problems. First, whilst the processes of appointment are themselves now transparent, the mechanisms which control them are not. For example, they are not currently published in a publicly available form and although individual Members of Parliament might ask questions about them in the House of Commons, as they relate to the policing of their constituency, they are not otherwise subject to direct Parliamentary scrutiny. At the time of writing, they are covered by the 30 year rule, although issuing departments within the Home Office will, under the Code of Open Government, release most circulars to the public. The main problem, therefore, is not so much getting hold of the circulars but actually getting to know about their existence. The second concern with the use of quasi-legislation to achieve, what is in its effect quite major change, is that were the overall political structure to change radically in complexion, then it is possible that even further, radical, change could be effected outside the democratic process. It will be remembered that, initially, the policy of the internal recruitment, selection and appointment of chief constables went against the popular will and was not widely supported, primarily because of the Parliamentary support of constituencies containing independent police forces, thus demonstrating that the sharing of power is just as important a safeguard as the manner by which that power is exercised.

Whilst this chapter has illustrated the mechanisms which have driven the changes in the selection and appointment processes it has not considered the processes which led to the change being sustained, this is the purpose of the next chapter.

7 Higher Police Training: Strategies for Sustaining the Internal Recruitment of Chief Constables

Introduction

For many years following its introduction, one of the weakest aspects of the policy of recruiting chief officers from within the police was concern by the Home Office and the HM Inspectors of Constabulary over the overall quality of potential candidates who were serving in the various forces. In order to address this problem, various recruitment programmes were developed to encourage the recruitment and development of individuals with leadership potential who would later fill the higher ranks. These programmes also identified any late developers with leadership potential who were already serving within the police. It will be argued in this chapter that these strategies were responsible for reinforcing the bureaucratic enforcement of the selection and appointment policies. Not only did the recruitment strategies maintain the policy of internal recruitment, but they also assisted in entrenching an ideology of internal recruitment.

This chapter will look at the various recruitment strategies that have been introduced to solve the problem of senior command. Part one will look at three, quite different, models that were proposed during the 1930s to produce senior officers from the police ranks, before charting the development of the successful scheme, the Metropolitan Police College, and evaluating its long term legacy. Part two picks up on the discussion over the Post War re-construction of the police service and the various plans for taking forward the idea of higher police training. It then explores the roles of the National Police College and the Police Staff College at Bramshill. Part three focuses upon the advanced promotion schemes provided at Bramshill and looks at recent debates over its role in the police service.

Three proposals to solve 'the problem of senior command'

During the 1920s the quality of senior police management became an issue and by 1932 two schemes were suggested to solve the problem of senior command. A third scheme was proposed in 1933. These schemes are examined below.

Open competition. The first scheme to create police managers from within the police service was Nott-Bower's idea to develop an 'officer class' within the police into which all candidates would enter by civil service type open competition (Nott-Bower, 1926: 328) (see chapter 5). The candidates would be examined after a two-year course of training in all branches of police work at Scotland Yard and successful 'cadets' would be automatically given the rank of assistant chief constable in a small provincial police force. From there on, they would have to reach higher office through the normal promotion channels. Nott-Bower's scheme was unpopular within the police because it would have legitimised the non-commissioned/commissioned divide that was already the source of much disquiet. However, the principles behind the scheme were reinforced by the Royal Commission of 1929 which was impressed by the number of distinguished chief constables who had started their careers in the Royal Irish Constabulary's gentleman cadet scheme. The Royal Commission of 1929 stated that "it is a matter of regret that this supply no longer exists".

The Dixon plan. During the period between the Royal Commission of 1929 and the 1932 Select Committee, the Home Office considered a number of methods by which to train serving police officers in the principles of command and favoured a national police college. The idea, known as the Dixon plan (Critchley, 1978: 205; Dixon, 1966: 52), was the brain child of Sir Arthur Dixon, assistant Under-Secretary, and was proposed in 1929 by the Home Secretary. The central theme of the Dixon plan was:

> to develop more effectively and bring to the front the men of exceptional qualifications and personality who enter the police service in the normal way, and to attract to the service and, so far as possible, to equip for higher posts

> men of superior education and wider outlook than those who ordinarily joined as constables.[1]

The objectives set out in the plan were to be achieved through a two-year course in police related subjects at the proposed police college. A third function of the police college was to become a centre for police research, where new ideas relating to police work would be examined. The successful graduates of the scheme would be appointed to the rank of inspector and would then occupy staff posts in the headquarters of the police forces. In contrast to the idea of open competition, all of the students to the police college were to be drawn from within the ranks of the police. The principles that lay behind the Dixon plan were very similar to those of the advanced promotion scheme (formerly the special course) that is currently operated through the Police Staff College.

When the Dixon plan was proposed to the Police Council in 1930, it was clear that the Home Secretary considered the existing arrangements for selecting chief officers to be grossly inadequate (Davies, 1973: 303). A sub-committee of the Police Council supported the Dixon plan but representatives of the two Chief Constables' Associations and the Association of Municipal Corporations questioned its economic feasibility. The economic depression of the 1930s meant that police authorities would have difficulty in meeting their share of the costs, even if supported by a Treasury grant. The Dixon plan was finally rejected by the central conference of the Police Federation in November 1930 on the grounds that it was too much of a short cut for a favoured few at the expense of the many.[2] The idea of educated police was clearly a novelty, see for example the following verses from *Punch* which E.V. Knox wrote to commemorate Dixon's idea for a police college.

> There shall our boys, for evermore,
> Matriculating, seek their solace,
> Under the great Vice-Chancellor,
> The very learned Edgar Wallace.
>
> Here on the thrice-enchanted ground,
> Conversant with Gaboriau's hints,

---

[1] (PRO/HO 45/544255) cited by Davies (1973: 302).
[2] (PRO/HO 45/544255/28) Nos. 34-296.

Shall pious benefactors found,
A Faculty of Finger-Prints.

Source: Pulling, (1964: 222)

The Trenchard, or Hendon, scheme. The third proposal came from the Commissioner of the Metropolitan Police, Lord Trenchard, in 1933 (*Report of the Commissioner of the Metropolis,* 1933). In his annual report for 1932, Trenchard argued that the Desborough recommendations had not improved the quality of recruits into the police service and that the educational attainment of recruits in 1932 was as low as that of recruits in 1919, yet the overall number of people receiving secondary education had quadrupled since the turn of the century. He stated that:

> the idea that too much mental development was likely to make a policeman discontented with his job is obsolete ... it seems to me no longer possible to shirk the problem of how to secure a steady supply of the best brains from every available source (*Report of the Commissioner of the Metropolis,* 1932).

Trenchard felt that there existed three main problems with the police service. Firstly, there was a lack of potential recruits for the command positions. Secondly, there was a low *esprit de corps* in the lower ranks arising from inadequate opportunities for promotion and from poor quality command; and thirdly there was a lack of incentive on the part of those who had missed the opportunity for promotion. Trenchard's priority was then to improve the overall quality of senior command in the Metropolitan Police by introducing new blood into the force. He proposed to recruit young men[3] with suitable educational qualifications and characteristics and give them a special course of training at a Police College. The idea of a college that was specifically designed to train future senior officers was based upon the success of a similar idea which he introduced in the RAF in the early 1920s.[4] Successful completion of the course would guarantee accelerated promotion to inspector. He also proposed to get a large number of officers onto the beat quickly by introducing a ten-year short-term

[3] Women were not considered.
[4] Trenchard was one of the founders of the Royal Air Force.

contract to encourage large numbers of young people who did not necessarily want to pursue a permanent police career.[5]

The three proposals were very different from each other. Nott-Bower's scheme was very élitist in nature and was very contradictory, given that the solution was widely perceived to be the cause of the initial problem. The Dixon plan was designed to serve the police as a whole and would have provided a long-term solution to the problem of finding senior officers from within the police, but it fell victim to constraints created by the financial climate of the time. Trenchard's officer class scheme contained elements of both Nott-Bower's officer cadet scheme and also the more generic Dixon plan, but applied to only the Metropolitan Police. It proved a cheaper alternative to the national scheme and Trenchard's own personal prestige ensured that his plan was successful.[6]

The Metropolitan Police College at Hendon

When the Home Secretary reported to the Cabinet in March 1933, he made it clear that he considered reform a matter of the greatest urgency as the discipline and morale in the force was bad and its efficiency was low. He was nevertheless aware of some of the shortcomings of the scheme, especially the potential for criticism over it being a step in the direction of militarising the police service and also as an anti-democratic scheme that was based on class interest (Davies, 1973: 308). But he felt that this was a relatively small price to pay, given the urgency of the situation. Trenchard's proposals quickly passed through Parliament to become the Metropolitan Police Bill 1933. It took only 16 months from the appointment of a committee by the Home Secretary to examine the financial implications of the project, to the actual opening of the Metropolitan Police College at Hendon. The college became colloquially known as 'Hendon', and entry was to be through three channels.

---

[5] Trenchard's plans made no provision for women and did not appear to consider the possibility of training women for command positions.

[6] The idea of short term contracts was rejected.

- Open Examination for all men aged between 20 and 26 from the Metropolitan Police or from outside, who passed a competitive examination which roughly corresponded to the schools' certificate examination.

- Open (Direct) Entry to men in their early, to mid-twenties, either from the Metropolitan Police or from outside, who were of a high educational standard. Typically, they would be those who had qualified for a university degree, the administrative class of the civil service, or for entry into the military colleges of Woolwich, Sandhurst or Cranwell.

- Reserved Vacancy for men, up to 28 years of age, who were serving in the Metropolitan Police and who did not qualify for entry under the previous categories, but were considered likely to qualify for promotion after completing the course at the Metropolitan Police College.

The Metropolitan Police College course lasted 15 months. Students who entered from the Metropolitan Police underwent 8 months of pre-course training that was adapted to their individual needs (Davies, 1973: 311). The non-police entrants spent a period of time in uniform before undertaking their studies. One of the primary qualifications required of recruits was their potential as 'officer material' and once in the police, their officer status was established by a number of procedures. Firstly, the Metropolitan Police Act of 1933 excluded the Hendon recruits from taking up membership of the Police Federation. Secondly, when they were accepted onto the course, students were given the newly created rank of junior station inspector. They could expect to be promoted to station inspector upon successful completion of the course. Thirdly, perhaps the most controversial aspect of the scheme was the suspension of the promotion of ordinary recruits into the Metropolitan Police, who joined whilst the scheme was in progress, in order to enable its graduates to rise rapidly through the ranks. Consequently, a commissioned /non-commissioned divide developed between the Hendon recruits and the rest of the force. This division reflected Trenchard's poor opinion of both the structure of the police organisation and also the quality of the existing senior officers: a view that was not surprising given that Trenchard's background was in the upper echelons of the armed forces. Accordingly, he tried to apply a military model of organisation to the police.

The recruits to the Metropolitan Police College were quite different from the ordinary recruits of the Metropolitan Police. Robert Mark, a standard entrant into the police, observed that "the mixture of which Hendon was composed, ranged from the university graduate to the public schoolboy with one 'O' level or its equivalent, in woodwork or some other subject not requiring marked intellectual capacity" (Mark, 1978: 90). They were the very people, a century earlier, whose background Peel had thought (see chapter 2), would render them inappropriate for service in the police (Mark, 1978: 88).

Opposition from within the ranks of the police towards Trenchard's scheme was fierce, particularly as it contradicted the meritocratic philosophies that had become practice within both the police and elsewhere in the public sector. The main opposition to the scheme came from the Police Federation, which was incensed both by the exclusion of the Hendon recruits from its membership and also by the freeze in promotions. Davies questioned the quality of a leadership within the police "which could ignore the representative machinery of the vast majority of the force some 13 years after its foundation" (Davies, 1973: 314).

The media reaction to the Hendon scheme was much the same as that a few years earlier with the Dixon plan. They had a field day with what they saw as the novel, almost ridiculous, idea of having an educated officer class of police officer. Ronald Frankau wrote and sang the following in the music halls.

> We'll be reading police-craft at Oxford,
> And attending the new rozzer-course,
> Our knowledge of classics will be quite unique,
> And to prove to the crooks all the lingos we speak,
> We'll warn 'em in Latin and charge 'em in Greek,
> When you've fellows like me in the Force.[7]
>
> (Source: Pulling, 1964: 224)

The subject also became popular with cartoonists as the illustration from the *Police Review* demonstrates.

---

[7] Published by Peter Maurice Music Co. Ltd.

The patent Hendon collegiate moulder

Source: *Police Review*: 1935: 220

In addition to introducing what were effectively commissioned recruits into the Metropolitan Police, Trenchard also created a number of new senior posts to strengthen disciplinary control over the force. He filled these posts with outsiders who were typically commissioned officers from the armed forces who were known to him personally. One such appointment was of his old staff officer, Colonel, the Honourable, Maurice Drummond, CMG, DSO, as a chief constable (Met).[8] The post was 'in the gift' of the commissioner and the appointment of Drummond understandably generated great hostility from within the police.

The Metropolitan Police College opened on the 31st of May 1934 at Hendon and was appropriately situated in the grounds of an old country club. In accordance with the 'officer class' philosophy upon which the college was based, the commandant was Lt-Col. G.H.R. Halland, an ex-chief constable of Lincolnshire, who had previously served in the armed forces. The first intake of 32 recruits consisted of 20 serving officers from the Metropolitan Police (12 by open examination and 8 through reserved vacancy) and 12 direct entrants. One of the early students on the course

[8] The title chief constable (Met) was used in the Metropolitan police because for many years they were the highest rank of constable within the force (see chapter 2).

was Eric, later Col. Sir, T.E. St Johnston, who subsequently became chief constable of Oxfordshire, Durham, Lancashire, and Her Majesty's Chief Inspector of Constabulary. St Johnston was from an upper-middle class background, educated at public school and read law at Cambridge, where he also read for the Bar. Upon graduation, he joined the Solicitor's Department of the Metropolitan Police and later applied, successfully, for a place by open competition at the Metropolitan Police College. At Hendon he won the baton of honour as the most outstanding student on the course and became the chief constable of Oxfordshire at the age of 29 (St Johnston, 1976: 61). His background was typical of many, but not all, of the recruits who came to the college from outside the police service, although few had such a colourful career.

The legacy of Hendon

In 1935, Trenchard was succeeded as commissioner by Sir Philip Game, a former senior RAF officer and his former colleague, whom he had recommended for the position on the condition that the Metropolitan Police College was left untouched. It was, however, clear from the outset that Game held very different views from Trenchard. In particular, he thought that practical experience of policing was more important than educational or social background and that the special qualities required of chief officers could not be identified without them having first served in a police force. In the face of mounting tension within the Metropolitan Police, caused by Trenchard's promotion block and also by the inadequacies of the candidates who were entering by open competition, Game was forced to reconsider Trenchard's original plans. Trenchard's complaints that Game had departed from the spirit and letter of their original understanding were ignored, and yet they were modifications rather than sweeping changes (Boyle, 1962). Game thought that the Metropolitan Police College had been generally successful, but that its principles needed revising. He planned the following changes.

- To reduce the number of direct entrants to about six a year and only allow them to enter the Metropolitan Police College after they had completed one year of duty as a constable.

- To raise the upper age limit for the selection of entrants within the Metropolitan Police to 30 years in order to improve the eligibility of serving constables who had passed the promotion exam to sergeant.
- To abolish the rank of junior station inspector.
- To allow entry to officers from the provincial forces and increase their upper age limit to 35.
- To change Trenchard's rules regarding eligibility for promotion elsewhere in the Metropolitan police. All serving officers in the Metropolitan Police were to be given an equal chance of promotion to the higher ranks.
- To increase the intake from 32 students to 90: nearly treble that of the original course.

The most sweeping change he planned was the inclusion of officers from the provincial forces. It was a move which gained wide-spread support and the Home Office persuaded the Treasury to pay three-quarters of the cost of fees for students from the provincial forces.[9] Unfortunately, the changes were never fully implemented because the college was closed at the outbreak of war.

Considering the relatively short period in which the Metropolitan Police College existed, its legacy as a source of chief police officers was considerable. Two quite contradictory issues stand out: on the one hand, any success that the Hendon scheme had achieved in creating future senior officers was offset by the fact that it took place at the expense of the rest of the police. Not only did morale drop within the Metropolitan Police during its existence, but the quality of recruits entering by normal procedures also fell. Consequently, it is likely that the scheme may not have been sustainable in the long term. On the other hand, the Hendon graduates provided provincial police authorities, particularly the county standing joint committees, with a source of potential chief constables who possessed (social) qualities that they recognised as traditionally being required for senior command, but, they also came with the relevant experience of police work that was required by the revised police regulations. By appointing Hendon graduates as their chief constables, provincial police authorities

---

[9] HO 809164/4. 30. p. 317. cited by Mark, (1978: 90).

could avoid the criticism that they had previously received over externally recruiting their chief constables.

Of the 197 students who attended the seven courses held at the College, 141 were from the Metropolitan Police, of whom 123 took up reserved vacancies for sergeants or constables, 13 passed the open examination and five passed the open selection procedure. The 56 remaining students were direct entrants, 32 entered through open examination and 24 by open selection. Table 8 shows the composition of each course held at the college.

Table 8: Entry into the Metropolitan Police College

Course number	1	2	3	4	5	6	7	All
Metropolitan Police								
reserved vacancy	20	20	19	18	17	20	9	123
open examination	2	-	2	1	3	3	2	13
open selection	-	3	1	-	-	1	-	5
Direct Entry								
open examination	10	-	6	8	4	2	2	32
open selection	-	6	4	3	5	4	2	24
Total	32	29	32	30	29	30	15	197

Adapted from the *Report of the Commissioner of the Metropolis, 1965*, section by Webb.

Of the 197 original entrants, 7 resigned, 3 were required to resign and 3 died during the course. A further 5 did not return to their force after graduating. A total of 179 students graduated from Hendon, of which, 19 were later killed in the Second World War and 39 resigned from the police during the ten years after the demise of the college. Most of the latter were direct entrants to the scheme. In 1949, 116 graduates were still in the police and of the 99 serving in the Metropolitan Police, 2 had reached the rank of superintendent, 9 chief inspector and 28 sub-divisional inspector. The remaining 60 were still at the rank of station inspector. Seventeen graduates had left the Metropolitan Police to take up senior posts in provincial forces. They had all reached high rank, 15 were chief constables and 2 were superintendents. By 1959, the 59 graduates still serving in the Metropolitan Police were all in the higher ranks and none was still below the rank of chief inspector. The Metropolitan Commissioner and two assistant commissioners were graduates of the Metropolitan Police College as were five commanders and 45 superintendents. Only six had remained at the rank of chief inspector. By 1959, 38 'Hendon' graduates had moved out to provincial forces and all were in high positions; 29 were chief constables (21 in counties and 8 in boroughs), a further 8 were assistant chief constables and 1 was a superintendent.

Table 9: The progress of the Police College Graduates

	1949	1959	1965
Metropolitan Police			
commissioner	-	1	1
dep./asst. commissioner	-	2	5
commander	-	5	5
chief superintendent	-	12	5
superintendent	2	33	11
chief inspector	9	6	1
sub. divisional. inspector	28	-	-
station inspector	60	-	-
total Met. Police	*99*	*59*	*28*
Provincial forces			
county chief constables	15	21	19
borough chief constables	-	8	6
assistant chief constables	-	8	3
superintendent	2	1	1
total provinces	*17*	*38*	*29*
HM Inspector of Constabulary	-	-	5
total (all graduates)	116	97	62

Adapted from the *Report of the Commissioner of the Metropolis, 1965*, section by Webb.

The full legacy of the Hendon scheme was felt in 1965, when all of the top positions in the police service were occupied by its graduates. The commissioner, deputy commissioner, five assistant commissioners and five commanders of the Metropolitan Police, plus five of Her Majesty's Inspectors of Constabulary were all Hendon graduates. Furthermore, in the provincial forces 25 graduates were chief constables (19 county and 6 borough). A breakdown of the progress of the 'Hendon' graduates is shown in Table 9, and the attainment of those still in the police in 1965 by mode of entry is shown in Table 10.

Table 10: Attainment in the police service by mode of entry to the Metropolitan Police College of senior police officers serving in 1965

	Entry from the Met. Police		**Direct entry**			**Total**
	reserved vacancy	open exam	open selection	open exam	open selection	
Attainment in the Metropolitan Police						
comm/dep./asst/	3	-	1	2	-	6
commander/dep	3	-	-	1	1	5
ch. superintendent	4	-	-	1	-	5
superintendent	5	1	1	3	1	11
chief inspector	-	1	-	-	-	1
total Met. Police	15	2	2	7	2	28
Attainment in the provincial forces						
county ch. const.	8	1	1	3	6	19
borough ch. const.	5	1	-	-	-	6
Asst ch. const.	1	2	-	-	-	3
superintendent	1	-	-	-	-	1
total provinces	15	4	1	3	6	29
HM Insp. Const.	4	-	-	1	-	5
total	34	6	3	11	8	62

Adapted from the *Report of the Commissioner of the Metropolis, 1965*, section by Webb.

From Table 10 it can be seen that a disproportionate number of the county chief constables who were direct entrants had entered the college via the open selection procedure, whereas the direct entrants serving in the Metropolitan Police tended to enter by open examination. More specifically, seven out of the 9 direct entrants still serving in the Metropolitan Police had entered via the open examination whereas 6 out of the 9 county chief constables who were direct entrants were selected through the open selection procedure. This finding confirms, that the pool of Hendon graduates enabled the provincial police authorities, particularly in the counties, to select people with similar social qualities to those of their previous, externally appointed, chief constables and at the same time comply with the principle of appointing career police officers. This point is further emphasised when the provincial destinations of the graduates are examined, they occupied almost a third (31 per cent) of the 197 county appointments, compared with less than ten per cent (17) of the 195 borough appointments. All told, a fifth (79) of the 392 chief constableships filled between 1939 and 1975[10] were Hendon graduates.[11] The 42 individuals involved, represented a quarter of all the graduates from the short-lived Hendon scheme. The impact of the Hendon scheme is shown in Figure 5.

The Trenchard scheme clearly had a considerable impact upon senior police positions beyond the Metropolitan Police. However, this impact was largely unintended. Further analysis suggests that this outcome was the product of two events. Firstly, the pool of candidates from which standing joint, and some watch, committees, had recruited their chief constables had diminished in size as they joined the armed forces after the outbreak of war. Secondly, were the traditional pool of candidates to have been available, then they would have been unlikely to have been appointed because of the increase in the Home Secretary's powers over the police authorities through the war-time defence regulations. So, the Hendon graduates, such as St Johnston (see earlier), whose personal qualities, education and backgrounds, were similar to those which the county police authorities traditionally accepted as being requisite for command were an attractive alternative, especially as they had acceptable police experience.

---

[10] The dates of the appointment of the first and last Hendon graduates to become chief constables.

[11] The 79 chief constableships were held by 42 individuals.

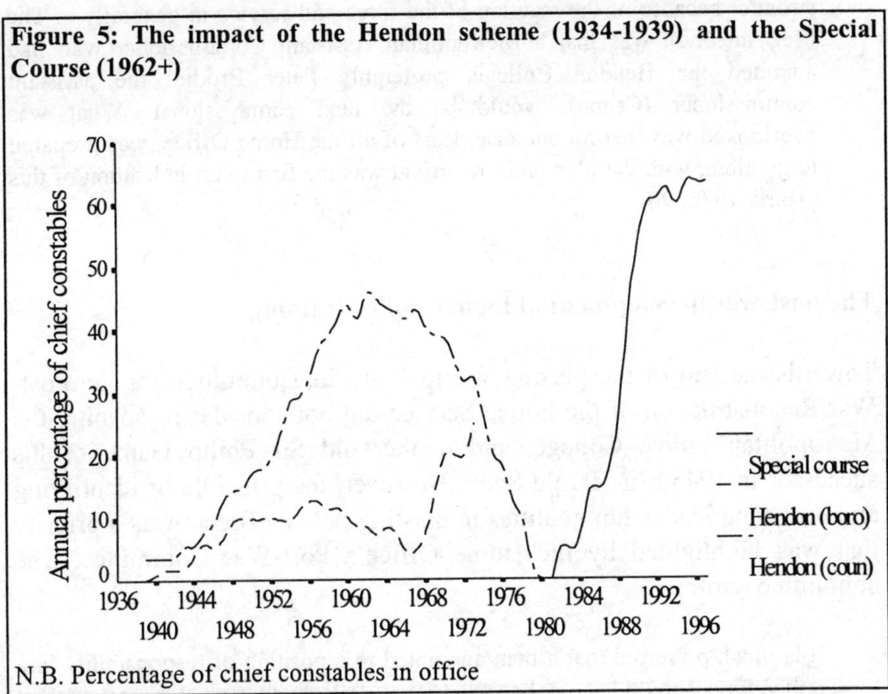

Figure 5: The impact of the Hendon scheme (1934-1939) and the Special Course (1962+)

N.B. Percentage of chief constables in office

So, the Trenchard scheme unintentionally provided a palatable compromise, but it did not solve the problem of senior command, rather it provided a short-term solution, and commentators such as Sir Robert Mark, an ex-provincial chief constable and former Commissioner of the Metropolitan Police, argued that the collegiality of Hendon may have established personal networks that may have not been in the best interests of the police and were very divisive. He described how the Hendon graduates dominated the senior ranks of the Metropolitan Police at the time of his appointment as assistant commissioner[12] and that he constantly had to be aware of their allegiances to Hendon trained colleagues.

[12] Mark was one of the first assistant commissioners to have been appointed for many years who was not a Hendon graduate and it was for this reason that Roy Jenkins, the Home Secretary, appointed him. The commissioner Sir Joseph Simpson did not, apparently, approve of Mark's appointment.

> The sense of group loyalty amongst the Hendon 'graduates' was all the stronger because of the reaction of the force and service in generally ... The Met. intention was that a Metropolitan Assistant Commissioner who had attended the Hendon College, preferably Peter Brodie, the assistant commissioner (Crime), would be the next commissioner. What was overlooked was that no one else, least of all the Home Office, was prepared to go along with the plan and my arrival was the first overt indication of this (Mark, 1978: 90).

The post-war development of higher police training

Towards the end of the Second World War, the Committee for the Post-War Reconstruction of the Police Service did not consider re-opening the Metropolitan Police College, and neither did Sir Philip Game or his successor in 1945, Sir Harold Scott. However, the principle of identifying and nurturing leadership qualities in existing police officers was a priority that was highlighted by the Home Office's Post-War Committee. The committee wrote:

> It is much preferred that a man appointed to a position of responsibility in a police force should have police experience. Policemen carry out most of their work alone, and a police inspector, for example, has not the same opportunity of watching his men's work as, say an army subaltern. It is therefore all the more important that officers in control of policemen should have served as constables themselves (*Police Post-War Committee, Higher Training for the Police Service in England and Wales*, 1947).

The Post-War Committee's re-affirmation of the principle of internal recruitment was very important for police morale as it healed the wounds that had been opened by the Metropolitan Police College scheme. It also re-introduced the notion of equality of opportunity into the promotion structure of the Metropolitan Police, but the principle did not, however, become official policy as the Oaksey Committee, reporting in 1949, felt that the police service needed the best leaders it could get. When considering the proposition put to it by the Police Federation, that all chief constables be chosen from the ranks of the police, the Oaksey committee accepted that the introduction of outsiders into an occupation can be discouraging as it implies that it is "incapable of producing its own leaders". But, it felt that the policy of internal recruitment should be rejected "in the interests of the service" because "the police service needs, and deserves, the best leaders that can be obtained" (*Report of the Committee on Police Conditions of Service, Pt. 11*, 1949: para. 232). The committee did, however, suggest that it hoped that a new police college would improve the qualities of leadership to be found amongst serving police officers. Hopefully, this would "reduce the frequency with which senior officers need be introduced from outside the service" (*idem*). But, even if the police colleges were completely successful, the Oaksey committee could still envisage "that the introduction of fresh blood in the senior posts would bring new ideas and a fresh outlook that would be of great benefit to the efficiency of the service" (*idem*). On this basis, it recommended that the regulation should remain in its present, relatively vague, form.

The Oaksey committee clearly sat on the fence over the issue and a contradictory situation developed in which official policy allowed the external recruitment of chief constables, but the informal practice by the end of the Second World War was for the Home Secretary to approve only the selection of career police officers. There existed a gap between policy and practice. The solution to the problem of finding senior police leaders lay not in legislation, but in providing a mechanism that would ensure that the (unofficial) policy was supported. That mechanism was to be a National Police College.

The National Police College at Ryton-on -Dunsmore

Sir Philip Game proposed the idea of a police college and the post-war Labour Government accepted it, as it was keen to break the link between the armed forces and the police and also to promote the civilian nature of police work. In wishing to emphasise the civilian character of the Metropolitan Police Herbert Morrison, the Home Secretary, thought that the changed conditions of the post-war world called for experience of administration in a large civil department rather than military experience and chose Sir Harold Scott, a civil servant, as the new Metropolitan Commissioner of Police. Out of interest he also chose a police officer, Sir

Percy Sillitoe, the former chief constable of Chesterfield, East Riding, Sheffield, Glasgow and Kent, as the head of MI5.[13]

Whilst the possibility of chief constables being appointed directly from outside the service with only a token of "other" experience was virtually eliminated, there was however, still nothing to stop outsiders being appointed directly as assistant chief constables and remaining at that post. In practice, none was appointed in this manner, and this anomaly was cleared up by a provision in the Police Regulations of 1964[14] which included assistant and deputy chief constables in the regulations governing the appointment of chief constables.

Part of the remit of the Post-War Reconstruction Committee, was to consider the establishment of a national police college. Game persuaded the Home Office, before he retired as commissioner, that the new college should be organised on a national basis and that its function should be to prepare the middle ranks for positions of command. Both Game and the Post-War Reconstruction Committee reaffirmed the recommendations of the earlier Dixon plan and priority was given to establishing a system whereby potential leaders could be identified and developed within the police.

The National Police College was opened at Ryton-on-Dunsmore in 1949 and was, from the outset, considerably different from the Metropolitan Police College. Entry was restricted to serving police officers and the courses were temporary in nature to allow for curriculum development. The main course lasted about six-months and was for officers who had passed the ordinary examination for inspector. Police officers who had already become inspectors were given a shorter, three-month course. A series of shorter courses were run for officers in the other ranks. In his autobiography, Mark described how he enrolled on the C course for superintendents, which lasted only three weeks. He did this to improve his chances of promotion, but felt that "it was wholly without value of any kind". The main advantage of taking it was that it provided him with the label he wanted, but its benefits were limited to teaching him one thing, "how to write an application for a job. Its staff then consisted mostly of people who were doing very little else !" (Mark, 1978: 63-64).

---

[13] Attlee was distrustful of MI5, who he suspected of engineering the Zinovief letter in 1924 (Wright, 1987: 33).

[14] Police (amendment) (No. 2) Regulations 1964 (S1/831/1964) 9 June 1964.

Mark's assessment of the college's value was probably a little unfair, as its curriculum strengthened during the 1950s. This development was based on the continuing need to identify outstanding police officers and give them a broad and thorough police education while they were still young enough to benefit from it, so that they would go on to fill the more senior positions quickly.

A proposal to make entry to the college open to all with five year's police experience was rejected by the majority of the Post-War Reconstruction Committee which thought that a person must demonstrate their ability in the lower ranks first. The need to provide equal opportunity of entry to the college was part of the basic philosophy behind the college's structure. The National Police College remained at Ryton-on-Dunsmore until 1960 when it moved to Bramshill House near Basingstoke. It became known as the Police Staff College in 1979.[15]

The Police Staff College at Bramshill

On moving to Bramshill, the higher police training programme was revised because of the erosion of public confidence in the police that had been caused, in part, by almost a decade of scandals involving chief constables. Following the recommendations of the Royal Commission on the Police of 1960 and the 1961 White Paper on training of the higher ranks in the police service, a number of important changes were made to the training of chief officers (*Police Training in England and Wales*, 1961). In the years following the revision, Bramshill provided four main courses: junior, intermediate and senior command courses lasting between three and six months to equip officers for promotion to their next level of rank. The fourth course taught at the college was the special course, which is discussed below. The junior command course equipped inspectors for promotion to chief inspector; the intermediate command course prepared chief inspectors and superintendents for promotion to superintendent or chief superintendent and the senior command course prepared superintendents for promotion to the ACPO ranks.[16] Each course marked a

---

[15] Hereinafter referred to as Bramshill.

[16] Initially intended as pre-promotion courses, they gradually became post-promotion developmental courses.

key point in the career development of police officers, and attendance at Bramshill, although voluntary, rapidly became a very important factor in the career development of most senior police officers. Entry onto the special and senior command courses was by extended interview, during which a rigorous, independent, assessment of the individual takes place (discussed later).

These long residential courses contrast with today's in-service programmes which require participants to spend only a relatively short period away from their forces. This is primarily due to a change in the educational base of the students and the demands of their forces following the financial restructuring during the 1980s. The students taking the courses in the 1960s were very different to those of today, especially in terms of education. Their overall base level of educational attainment was much lower than that of other contemporary public service managers. John Alderson, who attended the first senior command course in 1963 explained that he and his colleagues:

> ... had to become cultured, we had to read the classics. Fifty per cent of our time was spent on liberal studies, the sort of thing that a lot of chaps have when they come into the police today. Their education is so much better. We had a liberal studies tutor who would give us essays to do on Chaucer and the like.[17]

In addition to liberal education, students on the special course were also taught social etiquette:

> I think that there was very much an explicit aspect of social training in the 1960s. When I went on the special course we were actually told of social solecisms to avoid, such as how the lady paraded on the left arm to keep the right sword arm free. We soaked it up with a mixture of interest and irreverence.[18]

Initially, training in police matters was not mixed with educational development as the college was split into a professional side and a liberal studies side. Although, much to the confusion of the students, the courses were mixed together within the same programme. "When I went", said one

---

[17] Interview with John Alderson, April 17, 1997.
[18] Interview with CC2.

chief constable referring to the special course, "both areas were intermingled, so you took history one session and burglary the next and you had exams on all of them".[19] Subsequently, the two aspects of the curriculum became separated. Another considerable difference between the earliest and recent courses, has been a change in style from a focus upon leadership towards a growing emphasis upon management:

> When I was there ... the models they were teaching were really leadership models and comprised of a succession of military people telling us how they led people here and there. Actually, many were bullshitting windbags, but they spoke well and looked nice. It was all about command.[20]

Since Sir Kenneth Newman's period as commandant between 1977 and 1982, the blend of operational policing and academic activities was increased. Subsequent revisions, driven by a higher educational attainment of recruits and also by new managerialist philosophies introduced in the 1980s[21] have led to the college becoming more client (police force) oriented and, importantly, to an emphasis upon training for leadership rather than command. In 1993, the Police Staff College, along with all other Home Office funded police training establishments, came under the umbrella of National Police Training, an organisation which encompasses all of the police training establishments in England and Wales. Today, the curriculum is largely focused upon the needs of individual police officers in so far as they also relate to the needs of their force. The more traditional teaching methods have been replaced with in-service schemes that are based around project-based learning. Furthermore, many aspects of higher education that were previously taught by the Police College have now been out-sourced to syndicates of higher education establishments.

In addition to the advanced promotion schemes (formerly the special course), operational, management[22] and strategic (formerly the senior) command schemes are many short courses which last from between one or two days, to a few weeks and which train officers in a broad range of

[19] Interview with CC4.

[20] Interview with CC4.

[21] Motivated by HOC 114/1983.

[22] Operational command and Police management are composed of a series of one and two week long modules and are aimed at middle managers in police forces. They replace the junior and intermediate command courses, but are not linked to the promotion structure.

issues relating to police operations or management (National Police Training, 1997).

Advanced promotion: the Special Course and other schemes
During the 1960s three new schemes were introduced to provide the police with future commanders. The most important of the three was the special course. The other two were the Bramshill Scholarship and the Graduate Entry Scheme.

The special course was introduced in 1962 as a result of the 1961 White Paper on Police Training in England and Wales (*supra*), and specific recommendations made by the Police Training Council (*Report of the Police Training Council on Higher Police Training*, 1961). It was founded on the principle "that the senior officers of the police service should be drawn from the service itself" (*idem*: 3, para. 3).[23] The objectives of the special course were to attract high quality recruits into the police service by improving career prospects, and also to provide training for young officers who had the potential to reach high rank (Adler, *et al.*, 1994: 3). The course would give constables who had gained the highest marks in the qualifying examinations for promotion to sergeant, both a working knowledge of police duty and also a wider education to enable them to acquire a broader and more liberal outlook. "It is ... important", said the White Paper, "that, if the service is to produce enough leaders of the right calibre, that training of the right sort should be made available to those who have demonstrated that they are suitable for the higher ranks" (*Police Training in England and Wales,* 1961). Successful students on the special course were automatically promoted to sergeant and received accelerated promotion to inspector, but promotion thereafter was on their own merits. In 1992 the special course became the advanced promotion course.

The first special course was run in 1962 with 60 students and all the places were filled, but only three quarters of the 60 places on the second course were filled. The overall unattractiveness of police work as a career was illustrated by that fact that at a time when further and higher education was more widely available than ever before, the police were recruiting a relatively poorly educated section of the population. At the time, police

---

[23] Originally cited in *Police Post-War Committee, Higher Training for the Police Service in England and Wales*, Cmd. 707.

wages were very low and police forces were recruiting candidates from the same pool as the armed forces. Davies found that the proportion of grammar school educated recruits fell from 43 per cent in 1962 to 35 per cent in 1966 (1973: 334).

The special course and its successor, the advanced promotion course, have been in operation for over 35 years and many of the graduates of the first courses are now in the most senior ranks of the police service. An evaluation of the first ten special courses in 1979 illustrated the way that they were starting to influence recruitment into the senior ranks (Director of Extended Interviews, 1979). It found that none had yet been appointed as chief constable,[24] but a number were already in the ACPO ranks (1979: 2). The study showed that the special course graduates were achieving promotion more quickly than the rest of the service and would continue to do so. These predictions were confirmed 25 years later by the findings of a very interesting survey of all participants of the special courses (Adler *et al.*, 1984; 1985). Based upon data from 956 of the 1108 graduates of the special courses between 1962 and 1992, Adler *et al.* illustrated the impact of the scheme by demonstrating that it had produced at least 35 chief constables, 31 deputy chief constables and 60 assistant chief constables, or their equivalent ranks in the Metropolitan Police (1985). By projecting the findings of Adler *et al.*, namely that 29 per cent of the first ten courses had reached ACPO rank by 1992, to include further promotion, it is probable over a third of special course graduates could reach ACPO rank before they retire. Adler *et al.* concluded their survey by observing that most officers who received accelerated promotion through the special course achieve high rank. However, whilst some do so in a relatively short space of time, some do not (1994: 20). More importantly, the representation of special course graduates increases at every rank, but at the rank of chief constable they exceeded the others. At the time of writing almost two thirds (64 per cent) of serving chief constables had taken the special course (see chapter 9). The impact of the special course is illustrated earlier in Figure 5, which clearly shows that it is having a profound effect as a source of recruiting chief constables. In 1981, none of the special course graduates had yet to be appointed as chief constable; a decade later in 1991 sixty per cent of chief constables had taken the special course. Since 1991,

---

[24] In 1982 Brian Hayes became chief constable of Sussex and was the first of the special course graduates to be appointed at that rank.

the percentage has risen slightly and levelled off at about 64 per cent, just less than two thirds.

Between 1962 and 1992, when it became the advanced promotion course, the special course underwent a considerable development (see Adler, *et al.*, 1994: 3; Feltham and Linnane, 1987: 14). Its initial objectives, which were to attract high quality recruits to the police service by improving career prospects and to provide training for young officers who had the potential to reach high rank, subsequently became focused more upon the needs of the individual and upon developing their personal effectiveness.[25]

The Bramshill Scholarship scheme was introduced in 1966 to enable serving police officers with undeveloped intellectual capabilities who had fallen through the educational net to go to university. Whilst it was not actually a formal advanced promotion scheme, it was long considered to be an important vehicle for improving the education of serving police officers. During the early 1960s, 'education' was felt to be as important as 'training' following the complaint by the Royal Commission on the Police that the police service was failing to attract recruits of the right calibre for future promotion to the higher ranks. It found "no recent instance of a university graduate entering the service" and discovered that only three had joined between 1945 and 1960 (*Report of the Royal Commission on the Police,* 1962). By the end of 1983, 493 Bramshill Scholarships had been awarded, there were very few failures (0.6 per cent) and most graduates were back serving in their forces (Bartlett, 1985: 1363). But the success of the scheme in providing future commanding officers has been questioned by Russell and Waters (1985: 1108), who observed that Bramshill Scholars were significant absentees from the ACPO ranks. In 1984, two chief constables were ex-Bramshill Scholars. This criticism was, however, slightly premature given that the first scholars would only be starting to enter the ACPO ranks at the time of their research (Charman *et al.* forthcoming). Moreover, it is not entirely clear as to why a university

---

[25] The objectives of the advanced promotion course are a) to develop the personal and professional skills of the officers who, whilst having limited experience, have been identified as having potential for advancement in the service; b) to enable officers to progress rapidly to the rank of inspector; c) to ensure that officers are highly effective in the ranks of sergeant and inspector; d) to lay the foundation for possible future advancement in the higher ranks (Police Staff College, 1993).

education itself would necessarily prepare someone for high rank, other than it would, perhaps, make them a more rounded individual.

A graduate entry scheme was introduced in 1968, to attract suitable university graduates into the police. The scheme was introduced after the report of a Home Office working party into the recruitment of people with higher educational qualifications into the service found that the public relations image of the police service did not suggest an attractive career and not enough emphasis was given to the intellectual challenge of police work (Police Advisory Board, 1967).[26] The working party therefore prioritised the need to attract well qualified people into the police service. Consequently, a scheme to select annually 20 graduates by extended interview was proposed and accepted. A modified version of the scheme is still in operation today and is now known as the advanced promotion course for graduates. Although the broad structure remains the same as before, the curriculum has been much revised. Upon being selected onto the graduate entry scheme, recruits served for two years as a constable after which time they undertook the special course. Entry onto the scheme was like entry onto the advanced promotion course today, by extended interview.

There has been some controversy over the effectiveness of the scheme. Hill and Smithers (1991) have argued that the scheme was inefficient and that the progress of graduates was not much greater than that of standard entrants. Those completing the scheme currently spend twice as long on average at the rank of inspector than the Home Office guidance recommends (Parker-Jones 1993: 214). But Parker-Jones (1993: 198) challenged Hill and Smithers' assertions by putting forward the counter argument that a more detailed examination of the outcomes of the scheme shows evidence to the contrary. He showed that although many applicants onto the scheme are rejected, many of these individuals subsequently join the police through the standard entry procedure (Parker-Jones, 1993: 213). Therefore, the majority of graduates joining the police do so as the result of applying through the advanced promotion scheme for graduates, even though they do not join the scheme. Furthermore, he emphasised the need to compete on favourable terms with other organisations which seek quality graduates (Parker-Jones, 1993: 213).

[26] This report is sometimes known as the Taverne Report.

Education or training: the recent debates over the role of Bramshill

The various schemes and scholarships function to broaden the recruitment base of potential high flyers and to identify and accelerate the promotion of police officers who have the leadership potential. Therefore, the aims of the schemes remain much the same, but what has changed however, are the educational and social profiles of recruits who entered the police since the expansion of higher education during the 1960s and 1970s, especially since the Edmund Davies agreement increased police wages and made the occupation more attractive to the educated middle-classes. In this sense, the need for a generic, liberal studies based, education, described earlier by Alderson, became fairly redundant and the focus was shifted towards training and personal effectiveness. The acquisition of a degree does not carry the qualities that were attributed to it a decade or more ago (Parker-Jones, 1993: 215). However, senior police officers still believe that the police still "ought to fish in the university pool because it keeps the idea police career at the fore-front of peoples' minds at a fairly impressionable age".[27]

Since the late 1980s, there has been considerable debate over the role of Bramshill. In 1989 the Home Affairs Committee conducted an inquiry into higher police training and the role of the Police Staff College. The Committee's report was very critical of Bramshill and identified two major weaknesses. Firstly, there was uncertainty about the translation of the ideas and methods learnt at Bramshill into the improvement of policy within forces. Secondly, there were difficulties in relating training at the college to the career development of individual police officers as not all senior officers at the time had advanced without training at Bramshill. Three chief constables (seven per cent),[28] 11 deputies and 67 assistants, had not attended the senior command course and 33 of those who had attended between 1978 and 1985 had not gained ACPO rank (Fielding, 1990: 204). During the same year, the Audit Commission (Police Paper No. 4) fanned

---

[27] Interview with CC3.

[28] The percentage of serving chief constables who had attended the senior command course doubled from 22 (54 per cent) in 1976 to 40 (98 per cent) (Russell and Waters, 1985: 1108) in 1984, falling to 38 (93 per cent) in 1989 (Home Affairs Committee, 1989).

the flames by reporting that whilst the police receive three times as much training as private sector employees, they make inadequate use of it (Fielding, 1990: 200). Subsequently, Bramshill's educational role diminished whilst its training function developed. The main flagship courses were revised and a number of educational functions were outsourced to universities. Those on the strategic command course[29] can now, for example, continue their studies with the University of Cambridge in order to gain a diploma or Master's degree in applied criminology (National Police Training, 1997: 23).

The increased importance of the extended interview process

One of the most important of the Home Affairs Committee's (1989) recommendations was that successful attendance on the senior command course[30] was requisite to promotion to ACPO rank. Circular 98/1991 made this effective from January 1992. This new policy was very important for a number of reasons. It formally linked Bramshill, for the first time, to the police promotion structure and thus increased its role. It also greatly increased the importance of the extended interview process, because all individuals entering the ACPO ranks, for the first time, had to have passed through the extended interview process. Therefore any idiosyncrasies in the extended interview process will now reflect themselves in the candidates who can go on to apply for chief constableships (see later). Another implication of this latter development is that it further diminishes the role of the police authority in appointing the chief constable by transferring the main decisions about applicants to the extended interviewers and, indeed, to the HMICs.

The extended interview is a three day course, during which, candidates undergo a variety of tests and exercises that are designed to assess not only their managerial capabilities, but also their potential for benefiting from the opportunities offered by the strategic command course and their ability to carry responsibilities at a higher level (National Police Training, 1997: 23). Three assessors are present, two chief officers and an

---

[29] In 1995, the senior command course was restructured and became known as the strategic command course.

[30] Later known as the strategic command course.

independent member from outside the police. They work from a manual of guidance which is constantly being updated. Upon passing, candidates can enter the strategic command course and then be eligible for appointment to ACPO rank.[31] It is widely regarded as a cost-effective and fair procedure (Home Affairs Committee, 1989; ACPO, 1990), although concerns have been raised about the extremely low success rate of about 20 per cent. On the one hand, there were the frustrations of applicants who had been rejected and who often felt unfairly treated. The following, fairly prominent, chief constable described his struggle to be accepted for the extended interview.

> I was rejected twice for the senior command course. I think that the first year I was not ready, probably it was a just decision on what I gave to the assessors. The second year I was actually quite surprised. I had a fairly substantial barney with a chief constable who was sitting as chairman of the assessors about whether or not members of the public should be surveyed about their interests and aspirations about policing ... the fact that I thought that people should have a view was clearly beyond the pale ... If I wasn't successful on the third occasion I was out. I was successful.[32]

He went on to describe his suspicion of the integrity of the extended interview process:

> ... when I got down to Bramshill I was given a staggering piece of feedback and that was, although I passed well, the board thought that once I got to Bramshill I would stop working and just sit on my laurels. That is so fundamental a misreading of my personality and went against everything that has ever been said to me at appraisals.[33]

On the other hand, there is also concern about the discrepancy that exists between the chief officer's assessment of an individual and the decisions made at extended interview, as between three-quarters and four-fifths of interviewees fail to be accepted (Miles, 1992: 5). The debate here is therefore over whose opinion within the selection process counts the most at a particular time. Applicants have to be recommended by their chief

---

[31] Entry to the advanced promotion course is by a similar process.
[32] Interview with CC2 April 22, 1997.
[33] *idem.*

constable before their application is accepted, but, in his study of the extended interview, Miles (1992) asks how accurate chief officers are in predicting the final decision and indeed, how far they should be expected to be able to anticipate the outcome of the extended interview. He found that before the policy of giving candidates face-to-face feedback was introduced in 1989, there were few avenues along which chief officers could gain an understanding of what was required, either of themselves or of the candidates. Although many of these chief officers, but not all, had been through the process themselves, the format had since changed. Therefore, by including the chief officer in the feedback procedure, they could gain a greater understanding of the personnel qualities that were required and be able to make more accurate assessments of the applicants.

Miles concluded by arguing that the extended interview system was superior to other selection methods and that this fact was established by research and experience in many other organisations (Miles, 1992: 13). This view is one that was broadly accepted by the senior officers at ACPO rank who were interviewed by Savage and Charman (1997). However, the existing procedure was not without its critics. Savage and Charman found that some of their respondents[34] were also quite critical about the extended interviews. Whilst these views are not the majority opinion, they are nevertheless being discussed at a high level and merit inclusion here. First, was a view that extended interview tends to be not capable of dealing with the individuals who do not fit into a mould. "Because of this the system tends to reject the most talented people, because of their irregular thought patterns or whatever".[35] Therefore, it tends to admit only people who fit the current, police-oriented, preconception of what a senior officer should be like. Second, the extended interview itself tends to be seen as the success, and because of this it is arguable that the strategic command course should also be assessed. Third, an argument was made that the one thing that the extended interview does not test very well is leadership.[36] Fourth, the wording on some of the tests on the extended interview tends to be very male oriented and examples of this can be found in both the wording of the tests used and also the sets of knowledge which underlie them.

---

[34] Interviewed in 1996/7.

[35] Savage and Charman (1997), interview with M04.

[36] Savage and Charman (1997), interview with M032.

Conclusion

The debate over the higher police training role of the Police Staff College continues and will do so as long as the central /local contradiction remains in British policing, even if the division is largely conjectural in practice. On the one hand, the primary function of Bramshill is to supply the local, independent police forces of England and Wales with a supply of potential senior officers. On the other hand, upon reaching the short-list for appointments, these individuals are the product of a centrally determined process, within which, the major decisions regarding their appointability have already been made. Decisions, such as the assessment of competence, would have once been made by the local police authority as the prospective employer. Today, decisions on an individual's competence have already been assessed both along the lines of centrally determined criteria of competence that are based upon a central understanding of what makes a good police manager and also through the peer assessment of individual abilities. It therefore becomes arguable that the local police authorities' task of appointing a chief constable becomes reduced to decisions about the suitability of personality, rather than assessing competence. Although, this role should not be underestimated, as a suitable personality can make a considerable difference in a job where successful media performance is crucial to the public image of policing.

Another function of Bramshill is both to underpin the policy of recruiting chief police managers from within the police service and also to sustain the accompanying ideology. One of the points to be made in chapter 10 is that the appointment process has become so bureaucratically controlled that it is now almost inconceivable that we could ever have chief police officers who had not served their careers in the police. The propagation and maintenance of such an ideology is important in order to fend off threats to the existing structure.

So Bramshill is one of the final scenes in the power play for control over policing. Whilst central government, via the Home Office, improved the efficiency of the administration of policing by introducing the selective training of future police managers from within the police, it effectively consolidated its own hold over policing by setting, even mobilising, the agenda for that training process through the policy of internal recruitment.[37] In addition to its formal training role, the chosen medium for that process, Bramshill, plays a crucial role in selecting, socialising, and in an informal sense controlling, all future police managers. The main point here is that the reorganisation of higher police training since the 1960s has, like the Hendon Scheme before it, led to the development of a new style of officer class within the police (Reiner, 1990: 217). The figures show quite clearly that participants on the special /advanced promotion courses annually represent only 0.6 per cent of all recruits into the police[38] compared with almost two thirds (64 per cent) of chief constables. The chances of standard entrants achieving the highest positions in the police have much reduced over the past decade and a half. In this sense the debate over internal recruitment has almost come full circle.

[37] Although not the training process itself.

[38] Calculation based upon an annual average intake of about 35 onto the special /advanced promotion course and an annual intake of about 5,600 new police officers in England and Wales. See Adler, *et al.*, (1994: 20).

8 The Careers of Chief Constables Appointed Between 1836 and 1996

Introduction

The previous chapters in this book have sought to catalogue and explain the historical processes that have shaped the recruitment, selection and appointment of chief constables since the introduction of the new police in the early 1800s. The following two chapters will seek to establish the impact of those policies and processes upon the individuals involved. Of particular interest is the impact of the policy of internal recruitment and the subsequent initiatives to standardise the qualifications of chief constables. The timing of any changes in the data will demonstrate, amongst other things, the extent to which police authorities fell in line with the Home Office initiative on internal recruitment. The data will also explore the degree to which the very different traditions of urban and rural policing were manifested in the types of people who managed them.

Such analysis is important because there is a lacuna in the literature on the police where it relates to the appointment of chief constables. There exists amongst that literature no complete empirical account of their individual characteristics. Only Reiner (1991a) has looked in any detail at the origins of chief constables and his valuable social and occupational survey of those holding office in 1986 will be drawn upon later. Furthermore, without a systematic study of all chief constables, many of the debates in police history will remain unsettled. Previous accounts have tended to be based upon selections of individuals who were chosen for their eccentricities rather than their representativeness. Indeed many of the individual examples that have been illustrated in this book were chosen for this very purpose, so that they could illustrate the ranges of characteristics. Therefore, we can only assume that all chief constables are drawn from the police or that the county chiefs of old were military trained social acolytes of the local aristocracy. More importantly, when did the policies and processes outlined in the earlier chapters of this book actually take effect? So, whilst the outcome of this study may be largely predictable, it will be based upon empirical analysis rather than speculation, assumption or hearsay.

Another important reason for looking at these individuals in greater detail is because, outside the police literature, the chief constables are the one group missing amongst the many studies of different élite groups that have been carried out. Reiner has argued that this was because of their different social characteristics compared with those of the other élite groups, which have traditionally been considered in assessments of the structure of power (Reiner 1991b: 59). He believes that these sociological differences have diverted attention away from consideration of police chiefs in the context of élite studies. Moreover, these idiosyncratic characteristics have to be made sense of in terms of the peculiar function of the police in the social structure. Whilst Reiner is right in saying this, a broader historical analysis of the backgrounds of chief constables reveals a slightly more complex picture. It will be demonstrated that the idiosyncrasies only began to emerge during the 1940s and 1950s, when the externally recruited county chief constables, whose social characteristics were more aligned with those groups that were the focus of the élite studies, retired and were replaced by career police officers. The borough chief constables had, of course, always been idiosyncratic. So, any assessment of the chief constable within the structure of power has to take into consideration a changing social profile which reflects the shifting locus of control over policing from local to central government.

The following two chapters will explore the characteristics of the 1485 individuals who, between 1836 and 1996, held the 1835 known appointments of chief police officers in the provincial forces of England and Wales. Broken down by generic force type, 1053 people held the 1241 known borough appointments between 1836 and 1974,[1] 320 held the 443 county chief constableships during the same period and 112 held the 151 appointments to the 41 provincial forces formed by the local government reorganisations in 1974. The data is analysed in terms of these three generic types of police force.

The following chapter (chapter 9) will focus upon their social, occupational and educational backgrounds, this chapter looks at their

[1] No distinction has been made here between borough, city or county-borough forces because of the frequent reorganisations that took place over the years. Neither have combined forces (either county or borough) been separately examined.

police careers. Part one will look at the careers of chief constables prior to their appointment, it will explore a range of variables relating to their mode of entry into the police and it will look at their experience immediately prior to becoming a chief constable: at their occupations and rank and type of force served in. Part two will look at their careers at the level of chief constable, at their age when appointed, number of years served, number of forces served in and their reasons for leaving office. Part three will summarise the findings of the empirical study and marry them with actual examples in order to draw up a series of typologies that will facilitate our understanding of this élite group.

The Careers of Chief Constables Prior to Their Appointment

Occupational Origins. Table 11 and Figure 6 show that the tradition of externally appointing chief constables was most common in the county police forces and confirms the many previous assumptions to this effect (Hart, 1951; Steedman, 1974; Emsley, 1991; Reiner, 1991). Almost a third (30 per cent) of all county chief constables had served previously in the armed forces before their appointment. When their first appointments as chief constable are examined, this figure rises to over two fifths (42 per cent). By comparison, only a very small percentage of borough chief constables (5 per cent) were appointed directly from outside the police. All of the chief constables appointed since the 1974 amalgamations were appointed from within the police.

Table 11: The previous occupations of chief constables

	Borough		County		Post-1973		Total	
Armed Forces	48	5%	129	30%	0	0%	177	12%
Other	4	0%	11	3%	0	0%	15	1%
Police	881	95%	286	67%	151	100%	1318	87%
Total	933	100%	426	100%	151	100%	1510	100%

Missing cases 325

Whilst these raw figures crudely demonstrate the different recruitment patterns within the different types of police force, they do not display any changing trends. Figure 6 shows in greater detail how the occupational origins of chief constables changed over time.

Figure 6: The occupational origins of chief constables 1836 - 1996

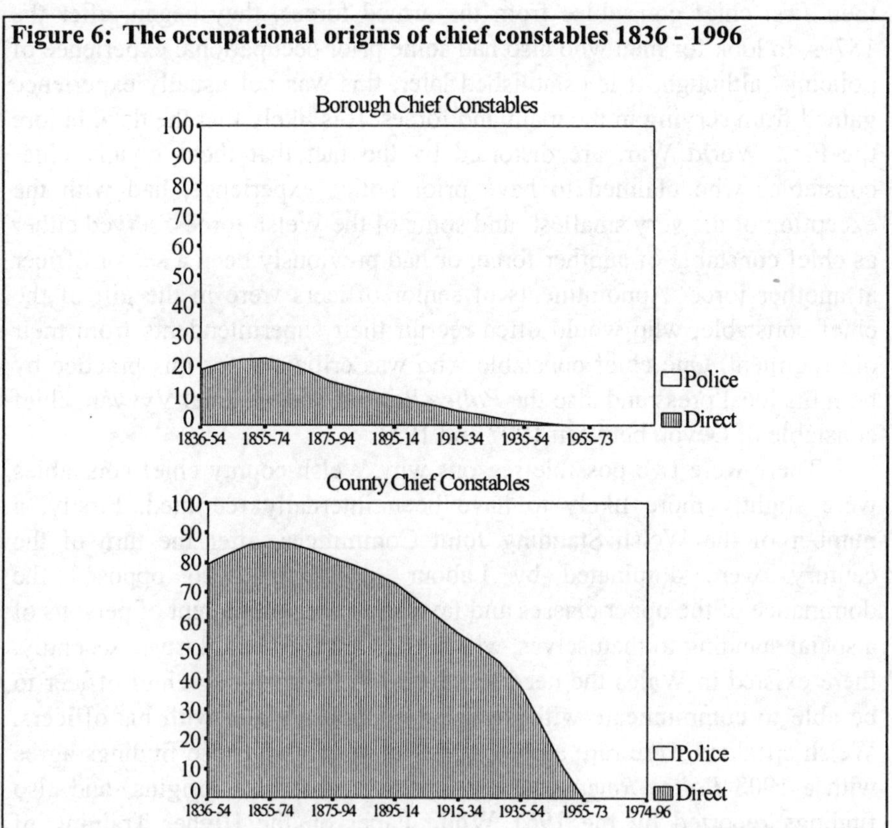

Figure 6 illustrates some quite dramatic differences in both the recruitment patterns for the different types of police forces and also in the origins of chief constables. The most significant observation is the large percentage of county chiefs who were externally recruited during the nineteenth century and their decline after the turn of the century, as the percentage of county chief officers with police careers gradually increased. An interesting point here is that only a very small percentage of externally recruited chief constables were drawn from other related occupations, such as the legal profession (Table 11). This suggests that the county police authorities placed a greater emphasis upon discipline and the maintenance of order, and also social background, rather than the detection and prosecution of crime.

It is clear from Figure 6 that whilst county police authorities drew their first chief constables from the armed forces, they began, after the 1870s, to look for men who also had some prior occupational experience of policing[2] although, it is established later, this was not usually experience gained from serving in the mainland forces. It is likely that the data, before the First World War, are distorted by the fact that those county chief constables who claimed to have prior police experience, had with the exception of the very smallest[3] and some of the Welsh forces, served either as chief constable of another force, or had previously been a senior officer at another force. Appointments of senior officers were in the gift of the chief constable, who would often recruit their superintendents from their old regiment. One chief constable who was criticised for this practice by both his local press and also the *Police Review*, was Colonel Vyvyan, chief constable of Devon between 1907 and 1931.

There were two possible reasons why Welsh county chief constables were slightly more likely to have been internally recruited. Firstly, a number of the Welsh Standing Joint Committees, after the turn of the century, were dominated by Labour councillors who opposed the dominance of the upper classes and favoured the appointment of persons of a social standing to themselves, whom they felt they could trust. Secondly, there existed in Wales the need to have a Welsh speaking chief officer to be able to communicate with the local community and with his officers. Welsh speakers were rare amongst the county class. These findings agree with a 1908 *Police Review* survey of chief constables' origins[4] and also findings reported by the 1961 White Paper on the Higher Training of Police Officers which indicated that most Welsh county chief constables were internally recruited. However, the fact that some Welsh chief constables were internally recruited stands in contrast to the other Welsh chief constables who were externally recruited members of the landed

---

[2] This experience is not to be confused with the placements (ch. 2) whereby aspirant chief constables voluntarily spent time in the office of a chief constable to gain experience.

[3] In particular Rutland, whose establishment was less than 20 before the turn of the century.

[4] Published in issues of the *Police Review* between August 7 and September 4, 1908.

gentry, for example, Lt-Col. Henry Gore Lindsay and his son Capt. Lionel A. Lindsay who, respectively, ran the Glamorganshire county force for 69 years (see chapters 5 and 9).

During the two decades before the turn of the century, many of the original chief constables retired and their replacements were drawn from military occupations. The county police authorities clearly wanted men with similar qualities to their predecessors: a number of these successors remained in office until the 1930s. As the policy of internal recruitment came into force, more and more county chief constables came to be drawn from police related occupations, the colonial police or the senior ranks. After the second world war their numbers fell away rapidly.

In contrast to county chief officers, most borough chief constables (95 per cent) came from UK police forces and only five per cent were appointed directly from the armed forces. Most of this externally recruited minority subsequently moved on to command the larger borough, and in some cases, county forces. The larger borough forces had very different policing agendas to the smaller forces due to their wealth, autonomy and, intensely urban character. The watch committees of these larger forces occasionally experimented by recruiting their chief officers from the legal or other professions. Whilst this trend did not develop, a few borough forces did attract criticisms for recruiting chief officers from the professions; for example, the watch committee at York sought a qualified lawyer, E.T. Lloyd. as their chief officer during the latter years of the nineteenth century (see chapter 4).

Mode of Entry into the Police

The individuals who would later become chief constables entered the police by a variety of routes. Table 12 shows the ways in which chief constables entered the police. Two thirds of all chief constables entered the police through the standard entry process, a quarter were direct entrants, and a small number had previously served in the senior ranks of the colonial police. The remainder were the product of the two accelerated promotion schemes illustrated earlier in chapter 7. These schemes were found to have had a profound effect upon the recruitment of chief constables.

Table 12: Mode of entry into the police

	Borough		County		Post-1973		Total	
Standard entrant	524	85%	87	29%	43	52%	654	66%
Hendon scheme	13	2%	28	9%	1	1%	42	4%
Special course	0	0%	0	0%	38	46%	38	4%
Colonial police	8	1%	9	3%	0	0%	17	2%
Direct entrant	73	12%	174	58%	0	0%	247	25%
Total	618	62%	298	30%	82	8%	998	100%

Missing Observations: 487

The borough and county chief constables entered the police in very different ways. Less than a third (29 per cent) of county chief constables, compared with more than four fifths (85 per cent) of borough chief constables, joined the police through standard entry procedures. The remainder were either recruited through the Hendon scheme (see chapter 7) or were directly recruited into the upper ranks from outside the police, usually as chief constable, although a hundred or so entered as assistant or deputy chief constable. By comparison, none of the post-1973 chief constables were direct entrants, nor were they drawn from the colonial police. It is notable that almost half (46 per cent) of this latter group were the product of the special course. This figure underestimates the true importance of the special /advanced promotion course as a source of future chief constables. It will be remembered from Figure 5 that the period, 1974-1996, includes a period during the late 1970s and early 1980s when the Hendon graduates had retired and the special course graduates had not yet reached a point in the rank structure where they could be considered for appointment as chief constable; these graduates began to be appointed in the early 1980s. Since the early 1990s, almost two thirds of chief constables have been graduates of the special course.

The changes over time in chief constables' mode of entry into the police is illustrated in Table 13.

Table 13: Mode of entry into the police over time[*]

	1[*]	2	3	4	5	6	7	1974-1996
Borough								
Standard entry	64%	62%	80%	88%	93%	91%	92%	N/A[**]
Hendon scheme	0%	0%	0%	0%	0%	7%	8%	N/A
Special course	0%	0%	0%	0%	0%	0%	0%	N/A
Colonial police	0%	0%	1%	2%	1%	1%	0%	N/A
Direct Entry	36%	39%	19%	9%	5%	1%	0%	N/A
County								
Standard entry	8%	8%	14%	26%	36%	39%	64%	52%
Hendon scheme	0%	0%	0%	0%	0%	23%	36%	1%
Special course	0%	0%	0%	0%	0%	0%	0%	46%
Colonial police	0%	0%	2%	2%	13%	8%	0%	0%
Direct Entry	92%	92%	84%	73%	52%	30%	0%	0%

[*] These data represent 20 year cohort groups of appointees.
1=1836-55, 2=1856-75, 3=1876-95, 4=1896-15, 5=1916-35, 6=1936-55, 7=1956-73
[**] N/A = Not Applicable

The percentage of externally appointed county chief constables decreased gradually until the inter-war years before falling sharply from thereon. Table 13 shows this group as increasingly being replaced by chief constables who had entered the police through normal entry procedures. After the Second World War, no county chief constables were recruited externally, all were career police officers. They were not, however, from the same pool of recruits as their subordinates or, for that matter, borough chief constables, because a comparatively large percentage did not enter the police by the standard entry procedure. Twenty per cent of those holding office in 1945, rising to forty per cent in 1965, were graduates of the Trenchard's Metropolitan Police College scheme (described earlier in chapter 7). Some of these individuals remained in office until the late 1970s.

In contrast to the large percentage of externally recruited county chief constables, only five per cent of borough chief constables were appointed from outside the police (Table 11), although twelve per cent had not entered the police by the standard entry process. Between the 1830s and 1870s, about a third of borough chief constables were externally recruited.

This group included the first chief officers who were appointed when the boroughs first set up their police forces under the Municipal Corporations Act 1835. Others were either the product of watch committees that were experimenting with different types of occupational background, or were ex-army personnel who sought appointment to borough forces with a view to gaining experience of command that would help them get appointed to a large borough or county force. By the turn of the century, the percentage of directly appointed borough chief officers had fallen from a third to one in ten. Although the trend was towards appointing police officers, some borough forces, such as Stockport and Leamington Spa, clearly favoured ex-army personnel. A further group were the product of early schemes that were designed to create an officer class in the police, for example, a small number of borough chief constables (approximately ten in total) had joined the police in the late 19th century as gentleman cadets in the Royal Irish Constabulary. Another thirteen, appointed after the 1940s, had entered the police through the Hendon scheme: both groups were appointed to the larger borough forces.

Police Careers Prior to Appointment

The differences in chief constables' career origins are further emphasised when their personal characteristics are compared. Table 14 shows the *ages at which chief constables joined the police*.

Table 14: Average age upon joining the police

	1*	2	3	4	5	6	7	1974-1996
Borough	23.3	22.9	24.1	22.0	22.0	21.5	20.7	N/A
County	37.0	35.3	34.4	33.7	29.5	25.6	20.7	N/A
All	26.3	27.4	26.4	24.9	24.1	23.1	20.1	20.6

*These data represent 20 year cohort groups of appointees.
1=1836-55, 2=1856-75, 3=1876-95, 4=1896-15, 5=1916-35, 6=1936-55, 7=1956-73

The externally recruited county chief constables were much older than the borough chief constables when they joined the police (a further analysis of their pre-police experiences is found in chapter 9), but as the practice of external recruitment decreased, then their average age upon entering the police understandably fell from about 40 in the mid-nineteenth century to between 20 and 21 years of age in the 1960s, which has remained the average age of entry for most police officers.[5] In stark contrast, borough chief constables entered the police whilst aged in their early 20s. They would then serve in the ranks for between 10 and 20 years, depending upon the size of their force, before becoming chief constable. Table 15 illustrates this trend by showing how the average *length of police service prior to appointment* increased over time for both groups of chief constables.

Table 15: Average length of service prior to appointment

	1*	2	3	4	5	6	7	1974-1996
Borough	10.9	12.8	13.1	15.2	18.9	21.7	27.4	N/A
County	6.3	5.2	7.3	9.9	15.3	20.6	26.1	N/A
All	9.8	11.0	11.9	14.1	18.1	21.3	26.9	28.6

*These data represent 20 year cohort groups of appointees.
1=1836-55, 2=1856-75, 3=1876-95, 4=1896-15, 5=1916-35, 6=1936-55, 7=1956-73

The average length of service prior to appointment increased for both borough and county chief constables, but the increase was far greater in the county forces. Other important trends to be identified from Table 15 are the marked increases in length of service after 1915 (which were mainly due to the post-Desborough changes) and also the fact that the lengths of service for both borough and county chief constables became more or less the same, as all chief constables came to be appointed from within the police. Length of service prior to appointment continued to increase after

[5] A detailed analysis of ages upon joining the police since 1976 reveals that there was a slight, but consistent, decrease: 1976 (20.7), 1981 (21), 1986 (20.5), 1991 (20.3), 1996 (19.8). This is largely due the overall decrease in chief constables who did national service.

Desborough because of the decrease in the number of smaller independent police forces. Today, chief constables tend to be appointed after about thirty years' police service.

Circulation between forces before appointment as chief constable. As the length of police service increased prior to appointment, then so did the *number of different forces served in*, although the two trends were not directly linked as circulation across forces became mandatory (see Table 16).

Table 16: Number of forces served in prior to appointment*

	Borough		County		Post-1973		Total	
One force	345	69%	84	68%	6	12%	435	64%
Two forces	119	24%	31	25%	20	39%	170	25%
Three forces	29	6%	7	6%	16	31%	52	8%
Four forces	4	1%	2	2%	7	14%	13	2%
Five forces	4	1%	0	0%	3	6%	7	1%
Six forces	1	0%	0	0%	0	0%	1	0%
All	502	100%	124	100%	52	100%	678	100%

* Direct entrants excluded.
Number of Missing Observations: 807

Most notable from Table 16, is the observation that over two thirds of borough and county chief constables had only served in one force. Those who did move force, tended to do so only once and only a relatively small percentage moved to another force more than once. It will be remembered from chapter 6 that this parochialism became a policy issue in the late 1950s and that from the early 1960s onwards, senior police officers were encouraged to serve in more than one force. Consequently virtually all of the post-1973 chief constables will have moved force at least once.[6] Table 17 illustrates any trends in the overall number of forces in which chief constables served.

[6] A small number of those in office immediately after 1973 were initially appointed as chief constable before the policy came into effect.

Table 17: Changes in number of forces served in before appointment

	1836-74		1875-14		1915-54		1955-73		1974-96
	Bo	Co	Bo	Co	Bo	Co	Bo	Co	
No change	76%	75%	60%	83%	76%	74%	69%	47%	12%
X1 change	19%	0%	28%	11%	19%	21%	29%	45%	39%
X2 change	3%	25%	11%	6%	3%	3%	0%	5%	31%
X3 change	1%	0%	0%	0%	1%	2%	2%	3%	14%
X4 change	1%	0%	0%	0%	1%	0%	0%	0%	6%
X5 change	0%	0%	0%	0%	0%	0%	0%	0%	0%
n=	91	8	206	18	153	61	52	38	51

Towards the end of the nineteenth century it had become fairly common practice for borough chief constables to be recruited from other forces (Table 17). Two fifths (40 per cent) of the borough chief constables who were appointed between 1875 and 1914 would have served in another force. After Desborough, it became more likely for county than borough chief constables to be drawn from another force, not surprisingly, because of the increasing agency of the policy of internal recruitment. Over half (53 per cent) of those appointed between 1955 and 1973 were recruited from another force. This compares with just under a third (31 per cent) of borough chief constables. These differences are the products of two events, the first was the Home Secretary's reluctance to approve the appointment of internal candidates after 1958 (see chapter 6). The second event was the impact of the amalgamations. Most of the borough chief constables appointed during this period, either retired when their forces were amalgamated, or finished their police careers as assistant or deputy chief constable in the new force. A few subsequently became chief constable, for example, W.J.H. Palfrey, who had been chief constable of the Accrington borough force until 1947 later became chief constable of the Lancashire force after serving as deputy chief constable during the interim period. Palfrey's case was, however, quite unique as there was little flow of personnel between the different types of forces. In order to illustrate this point more clearly, Table 18 shows the type of force that chief constables previously served in and the rank that they held.

Table 18: Previous rank and type of force served in

	Borough		County		Post-1973		Total	
*County forces**								
Ch. const[7]	2	0.2%	75	17.6%	33	24.4%	110	7.8%
Supt. +	45	5.3%	90	21.1%	86	63.7%	221	15.7%
Insp. -	21	2.5%	3	0.7%	0	0%	24	1.7%
Sub-total	*68*	*8%*	*168*	*39%*	*119*	*88%*	*380*	*27%*
Borough forces								
Ch. const	184	21.6%	46	10.8%	6	4.4%	236	16.7%
Supt +	204	24%	11	3%	3	2%	218	16%
Insp -	268	32%	3	0.7%	0	0%	271	19%
Sub-total	*656*	*77%*	*60*	*14%*	*9*	*7%*	*725*	*51%*
Metropolitan police	40	4.7%	30	7%	7	5.2%	77	5.5%
From elsewhere								
Colonial police	16	1.9%	28	6.6%	0	0%	44	3.1%
Direct entry	48	5.6%	138	32.4%	0	0%	186	13.2%
Old police	22	2.6%	2	0.5%	0	0%	24	1.7%
Sub-total	*86*	*10%*	*168*	*40%*	*0*	*0%*	*254*	*18%*
Total	850	100%	426	100%	135	100%	1411	100%

Number of Missing Observations: 425
* N.B. Previous ranks and forces in left column.

It is quite clear from Table 18 that, with only a few exceptions, the two policing traditions remained fairly independent of one another.[8] The county forces recruited from county forces and although the borough

[7] Also, the number of chief constables who came from Scottish forces was minimal. Only nine were identified as having left to take command of a Scottish force.

[8] The same could also be argued for the other mainland forces.

forces were less strict than the county forces, most of their chief constables came from other borough forces. Only 14 per cent (60) of all county chief constables had previously served in borough forces, most of this group (11 per cent, 46) having previously commanded a borough force. The remaining three per cent (14) of county chief constables were appointed to their post after having previously held positions in borough forces lower than that of chief constable. Two fifths (39 per cent, 168) of all county chief constables had prior experience of serving in a county force[9] and just over a sixth (18 per cent, 75) had been a county chief constable.[10] The remaining 93 had all served in the senior ranks of a county force.

The experience of the borough chief constables also reflected the independence of the two traditions, but their careers were quite different, particularly with regard to their circulation between forces. The widely perceived superiority of the county over the borough police[11] is reflected by the fact that only two borough chief constables had previously been county chief constables. Overall, only eight per cent (67) of borough chief constables came from county forces. Within the borough policing system, however, their path of ascendancy to chief constable bore some quite different characteristics to the paths of county chiefs. Most borough chief constables had experience of serving in the same type of force, usually the same force. Three-quarters (77 per cent, 656) of borough chief constables had previously served in a borough force, of which 22 per cent (184) had been a borough chief constable and 56 per cent (472) had either served in the senior ranks (24 per cent, 204) or lower ranks (32 per cent, 268) of a borough force.

Unlike the county chief constables who by comparison displayed a broader range of police and occupational experiences, just over a third (37 per cent) of the borough chief constables had previously served in a different police force. This means that almost two thirds (63 per cent) of all the borough chief constables with experience of serving in the ranks had served in the same borough force prior to their appointment, thus providing some substance to de Courcy Parry's allegation that borough chief

---

[9] The three county chief constables who were previously at the ranks of inspector were appointed to the smallest county forces such as Rutland.

[10] Some 40 or so of that number became chief constable of an amalgamated force of which their old force formed a major component.

[11] Perceived by the county police.

constables were appointed for reasons other than merit (see chapters 3 and 5).

An interesting observation made from Table 18, is the relatively low level of recruitment of provincial chief constables from the Metropolitan police (six per cent), which further emphasises the parochialism of the borough and county police authorities. This is slightly surprising given that the initial success of the Metropolitan Police was very important in the formation of the provincial police. Furthermore, quite a lot of the early watch committees consulted the Metropolitan police for advice about setting up a police force, but relatively few of the officers sent to advise, subsequently became the first chief constables (see chapter 2). Yet, the Metropolitan police was the singular most popular force that chief constables entered upon joining the police (Table 19).

Table 19: Chief constables whose first force was the Metropolitan police.[12]

	Borough		County		Post-1973		Total	
Metropolitan Police	73	8%	71	17%	34	30%	178	13%

Thirteen per cent of all chief constables first joined the Metropolitan police,[13] which means that although comparatively few chief constables had served in the Metropolitan police immediately prior to their appointment, it was the one police force, more than any other, which chief constables had experienced. This brings into perspective the observations made in chapter 2 about the impact of the Metropolitan police model upon the provincial police. This is worth bringing into further perspective. Eight per cent (73) of borough chief constables came into the police through the Metropolitan police whilst a much larger percentage (17 per cent) of county chief constables came through this route, with about half of this latter group entering via the Hendon scheme. Of far greater significance is the observation that almost a third (30 per cent) of the chief constables

[12] Tynemouth and Middlesborough were two such examples.

[13] Followed by the Manchester City Police, the Royal Irish Constabulary, Nottingham City police, Liverpool City police, the Scottish county and borough police (two per cent), Newcastle-upon-Tyne City police and the Indian Police each producing two per cent of all chief constables. A table is not given for these figures.

appointed since the 1974 amalgamations first joined the police through the Metropolitan police. In addition to providing an indication of the increased mobility of police officers today, this finding also suggests that knowledge of Metropolitan police practice will be circulated to the provincial forces, thus contributing to the alleviation of the long running mutual suspicion between the two types of force.

The above analysis of the careers of chief constables prior to their appointment demonstrates clearly the impact both of the policy of internal recruitment and also the advanced promotion schemes. It also shows how the occupational backgrounds of chief constables narrowed to include only police officers who had served their entire careers in the police.

Service whilst at the rank of Chief Constable

The convergence of police career paths, demonstrated above, shaped the chief constables' careers whilst at the rank of chief constable. This convergence can be illustrated by comparing the characteristics of the careers. A clear indication of this overall trend can be found from an examination of their *average age at appointment.*

Table 20: Average age on appointment as chief constable

	1*	2	3	4	5	6	7	1974-96
Borough	34.0	35.5	36.9	37.2	40.0	42.8	47.7	N/A
County	39.0	39.6	39.5	40.6	42.8	44.0	46.8	N/A
All	35.6	37.1	37.6	38.1	40.1	43.2	47.4	49.3

*These data represent 20 year cohort groups of appointees.
1=1836-55, 2=1856-75, 3=1876-95, 4=1896-15, 5=1916-35, 6=1936-55, 7=1956-73

As the length of time spent between joining the police and being appointed chief constable increased to just under 30 years (Table 15), so the average age of appointment as chief constable increased (Table 20). However, the picture is complicated by the presence of the direct entrants, and requires further explanation.

The average age of county chief constables upon appointment rose gradually from just less than 40 in the mid-nineteenth century, the age at which military officers might retire upon half pay after 21 years service, to about 50, approximately the average age of appointment today.[14] In contrast, the average age of borough chief constables increased from about 35 in the mid-nineteenth century to almost 50 in the 1960s when the borough forces disappeared. The significant observation here is that the average ages of both borough and county chief constables converged as internal recruitment increased and chief constables had full police careers. These trends also correspond with changes in the *ages at which they joined the police* (Table 14), *their length of time in service* (Table 21) and also their *ages upon leaving office* (Table 22). As the average age at appointment increased, the average length of time in office fell and so did the average upon leaving office.[15] However, another, contributing, factor to the decrease in the number of years served in office, was the overall increase in the number of different forces that chief constables commanded (see Table 21).

Table 21: Average number of years in office

	1*	2	3	4	5	6	7	1974-96
Borough	14.3	12.2	12.0	14.8	13.1	9.6	6.5	N/A
County	22.7	23.3	20.0	19.0	16.2	10.5	6.2	N/A
All	15.7	14.1	13.5	15.8	13.9	9.9	6.3	5.8

*These data represent 20 year cohort groups of appointees.
1=1836-55, 2=1856-75, 3=1876-95, 4=1896-15, 5=1916-35, 6=1936-55, 7=1956-73

14 Since 1976 the age upon appointment has fallen slightly from over 50 to marginally below: 1976 (52.5), 1981 (49.3), 1986 (49.2), 1991 (48.8), 1996 (49.2).

15 Since 1976 the age upon leaving office has, gradually, fallen by almost five years from 60.7 in 1976 to 56.5 in 1991. N.B. figures were not available for those still in office in 1996.

Table 22: Average age upon leaving office

	1*	2	3	4	5	6	7	1974-96
Borough	49.7	52.7	51.5	52.0	53.3	52.7	55.0	N/A
County	74.4	66.9	64.5	60.4	59.5	55.3	56.9	N/A
All	56.2	57.7	54.6	54.0	55.0	53.7	56.1	57.4

*These data represent 20 year cohort groups of appointees.
1=1836-55, 2=1856-75, 3=1876-95, 4=1896-15, 5=1916-35, 6=1936-55, 7=1956-73

Reasons for leaving office

One of the more striking observations from Table 22 are the rather dramatic differences in the ages at which the borough and county chief constable left their respective forces and, of course, their eventual convergence. Exploration of these differences illustrates both the different traditions of police and also the changes in the nature of the office(s) of chief constable since the last century. Table 23 summarises the reasons why chief constables left office.

Table 23: Reasons for leaving office

	Borough		County		Post-1973	
Chief constable of other force	230	26%	101	26%	18	17%
Serve in another force	52	6%	17	4%	8	8%
Become an HMIC	12	1%	21	6%	18	17%
Retired	420	47%	148	38%	57	55%
Died in office	98	11%	78	20%	1	1%
Dismissed /left under a cloud	54	6%	8	2%	1	1%
Other reasons	22	3%	12	3%	1	1%
Total	888		385		104	

The most frequent reasons for which chief constables left office were retirement, transfer to another command, and death. Another significant, although infrequent, reason for leaving office was dismissal from office.[16]

Retirement. As the internal recruitment policy and pensions legislation came into effect, the meaning of retirement changed over the years from being literally too old to do the job, towards becoming a reward sanctioned by the police authority, for dutiful service to the force. Eventually it became a legal right that police officers could claim after a set number of years' service, although for many years the regulation appears to have been ignored by a number of police authorities who found extenuating circumstances that would allow their chief constable to continue in office for a few more years.

During the Second World War, the Home Secretary used his powers under the war-time regulations to compel a number of, mostly borough, chief constables to retire on pension in the "interests of efficiency" (see chapters 3 and 6). This phrase held a variety of meanings, sometimes the chief constable was merely past the age of retirement, on other occasions the chief constable was failing to cope with the added burden of the war-time administration. Retirement through ill health was one option that would seem to have been given to individuals whom the Home Secretary, or in a number of cases, the watch committee, wanted to get rid of.

Displacement through amalgamation was a reality which many borough chief constables had to face over the years, particularly in the smaller borough forces. Most of the displaced chief constables took advantage of the generous incentives and retired from the police, a few took positions as assistant chief constables in the new forces. One quarter of borough chief constables who were appointed between 1845 and 1885 left office as a direct result of their post disappearing through amalgamation with another force. Most of these were the small borough forces forced to amalgamate by the 1888 Local Government Act. Attempts by the Desborough Committee to force the remainder of the non-county

[16] A smaller percentage of chief constables left to take up a range of police related jobs, for example in the War Department Constabulary, the UK Atomic Energy Authority Police, British Transport Police or police forces overseas. A similar percentage of chief constables subsequently became HM Inspectors of Constabulary, a post that has become increasingly significant in the process of appointing chief constables.

borough forces to amalgamate failed, as they did again in 1932. However, after the Second World War the Police Act 1946 forced all non county-borough forces (except Peterborough, it had a large population) to amalgamate with the county force. One quarter of all borough chief constables in 1946 lost their posts in the amalgamations of that year. Two decades later two thirds of the remaining borough chief constables lost their posts in the wake of the Police Act 1964 amalgamations and the remainder when the borough forces were abolished by the 1973 local government reorganisations (see Figure 1 in chapter 2).

The majority of displaced borough chief constables retired early from the police having taken the carrot of 15 years service to be added to their existing length of service. Those who declined the offer of early retirement, typically the younger chief constables, took reduced rank in the new combined force and a few of them rose through the ranks to take command of a new force once more.[17] A total of 117 (10 per cent of all) borough chief constables retired after their command disappeared. In contrast, the percentage of county chief constables who lost their post as a result of amalgamations was almost negligible, not surprisingly because fewer county chief constables were subject to their force being amalgamated and those who were forced to re-apply for their jobs in the post 1964 and 1973 reorganisations got preference over the borough chief constables (See Robert Mark's account in chapter 3).

Transfer to a new command. The second most frequent reason for leaving office was to take up another command. One of the main incentives for chief constables to move forces was to increase the size of their command. Some 85 per cent of changes of command in both borough and county forces were to a larger command. The rationale was simple, by increasing the size of their force chief constables could both increase their salary and get a job with greater social and occupational prestige. Only a very small percentage (4 per cent in the counties and 3 per cent in the boroughs) were moves to a smaller force. One of these was the case of Captain Herbert

---

[17] As in the case of W.J.H. Palfrey, who had been the chief constable of Accrington from 1940 until it was amalgamated into the Lancashire force following the Police Act 1946. Palfrey then became an assistant chief constable in the Lancashire force, which Accrington was amalgamated, and became chief constable in 1969.

Metcalf that was described in chapter 4. Table 24 gives a breakdown of the force sizes of changes in command.

Table 24: Force sizes and changes of command

	To a County Force		To a Borough Force	
Larger sized force	139	89%	160	85%
Same sized force	10	6%	22	12%
Smaller sized force	7	4%	6	3%
Total	156	99%	188	100%

N.B. Borough and County forces only

Over a quarter (29 per cent) of county and just under a quarter (23 per cent) of borough chief constables had previously been a chief constable in another force. When the distribution of the data is examined over time (Table 18 above) it is found that the movement of chief constables between forces was far greater in the boroughs than in the counties, particularly before the 1920s. But, after the 1920s the transfer of county chief constables increased whilst the transfer of borough chiefs decreased slightly.

Further evidence of the extent of transfer of chief constables is found when the number of appointments held per individual are examined. Although the overall percentage of transfers was small, a larger percentage of county chief constables held more than one appointment than did borough chief constables (Table 25). However, until the Second World War borough chief constables were more likely to have held more than one post than county chief constables. After the Second World War the trend reversed and the number of appointments held by county chief constables increased due to the post-Police Act 1964 amalgamations.

Although there was movement between forces within the borough and county systems, the evidence points towards very little movement of chief constables between the different types of forces. This complements the observation made earlier, that the movement of senior officers was restricted to forces of a similar type.

Table 25: Number of appointments held as chief constable

	Borough		County		Post-73		Total	
One appointment	1053	85%	320	72%	112	74%	1485	81%
Two appointments	152	12%	97	22%	21	14%	270	15%
Three appointments	35	3%	22	5%	15	10%	72	4%
Four appointments	1	0%	3	1%	3	2%	7	0%
Five appointments	1	0%						
Total	1242	100%	442	100%	151	100%	1834	100%

It is clear from Table 17 that any movement of chief constables that did take place was very one-sided. Over two thirds (43 out of 61) county chief constables who came from borough forces were ex-borough chief constables. By comparison 67 borough chief constables came from county forces, but only two had served previously as county chief constable. These were the ex-chief constable of Essex, Lt-Col Stockwell, who came out of retirement during the First World War to command the Colchester force whilst its chief was involved in the war effort and the chief constable of the East Riding of Yorkshire, Percy Sillitoe, who became the chief constable of Sheffield after falling out with his police authority in the East Riding of Yorkshire (see earlier chapters).

The main reason for the one-sided flow of transfers between chief constableships was that the county appointments were a greater prize than were the borough posts, the county posts carried greater social prestige and independence. Whilst there were no major differences in basic remuneration between the two types of force as chief constables' salaries were roughly apportioned to force size, the county chief constables did incur greater expenses despite larger personal allowances for transport and the provision of rent free accommodation. It was the latter which could be used as a tool by county police authorities to attract their desired type of candidate, for example, the county chief constable's house was often too large to be run on the salary alone and a person without private means could literally not afford to take on the job. On his appointment as chief constable of the East Riding of Yorkshire in 1925, Sillitoe described the attractions and drawbacks of being a county chief constable after commanding the small borough force at Chesterfield:

> it had what I considered to be two very big attractions. First the salary was £750 a year and secondly there was a very handsome house in the country that went with the appointment (Sillitoe, 1955: 52).

But:

> ... this post could have been most enjoyable if I had possessed a private income. But we needed three maids to run the handsome house that had so attracted me, and we had two children. Even in 1925 fifteen pounds a week did not stretch far enough to allow me to hunt as well (Sillitoe, 1955: 52).

The structure of police pensions was another reason for the lack of movement between forces before the First World War. Until the turn of the century, police pension funds were local and often excluded the chief constable. Where they did apply to the chief constable they were discretionary. So, not only did the Police Pension Act of 1890 improve general conditions of service, but it also gave the chief constable a little more independence from their police authorities, especially the watch committees, who could use the threat of withdrawal of the pension as a tool to ensure their compliance. It also gave chief constables, especially county chiefs, an incentive to retire early on an attractive pension.

The downside of the Pension Act was that it hindered the movement of individuals between forces because of the way it was framed. The pension regulations did not readily allow years of service, which determined eligibility to a pension, to be carried from one force to another. Pension funds tended to be separate and local, and whilst there were some local agreements between forces to allow transfers these were only at the discretion of the chief constable or police authority. In the early days of the pension schemes a police officer who had changed forces in mid-career would usually receive separate pensions from each of the forces served in.

The lack of common pension arrangements generally had a restraining effect on the movement of chief constables although a few distinct patterns can be observed. County chief constables with private means[18] who were unlikely to serve enough years to become eligible for a police pension moved readily between different forces. In contrast, movement between borough forces tended to take place either early in a career or much later, when the person involved had served enough years to become eligible for a pension. Table 17 shows that the overall movement of chief constables

---

[18] And who may have been receiving half-pay from their military service.

between borough forces was quite rare and that most borough chief constables tended to become chief officer of the force they had previously served in, which was often the only force that they had served in. The lack of mobility of chief constables and their reluctance to retire gave rise to much discontent within the police until the Second World War.

In the early part of the twentieth century, the practice developed for aspiring young men with a good education and a background in the colonial police to get the chief constableship of a small borough force and then use that experience to move to a larger force. Both Sillitoe and Athelstan Popkess, the chief constable of Nottingham City, were two of the more well known chief constables who took this route. A few small borough forces[19] became renowned for appointing their chief constables from outside the police with a view to gaining a larger command at a later date. Watch committees were willing to appoint these men because they were young, well educated, and would accept the low wages offered. They often had private means and were from a different social class to the main body of police officers under their command. The bulk of these appointments took place between 1900 and the 1939, and these candidates were an attractive proposition for the county standing joint committees who wanted a chief constable with a particular social background, but also with some police experience. However, the two traditions remained very independent of each other and each remained highly resistant to change because of the infrequent flow of personnel and their ideas and experiences of management between forces. Even if there did exist a flow of personnel between forces it is arguable that the potential for carrying over management ideas to the new force was limited, given that they had to adapt to an existing structure that was based upon previous local practice. The antithesis of this rigidity is found today where an exchange of ideas and experience between forces is actively promoted by a central training policy and Home Office encouragement of movement from one force to another to gain eligibility on the shortlist.

Death, whilst in office. The sharp decrease in the percentage of chief constables who died in office is most symptomatic of the change in the nature of the office of chief constable. Almost half of those appointed between 1906 and 1925 died in office, compared with less than 20 per cent

---

[19] Leamington and Oldham in particular.

of those appointed over the next two decades. However, by the 1950s only five per cent died in office and since then death while in office has become a very rare occurrence amongst chief constables. The decrease in the number who died in office was not simply the result of police pension age limits nor changes in mortality rates, rather it illustrated wider changes in both the nature of the office of chief constable and also the way in which it was perceived by its incumbents. The chief constableship ceased to be regarded as a social platform secure for life, to be held until retirement and became yet another, and often final, step in the police career for those who were able and determined to reach the top.

Whilst more borough chief constables were dismissed than county chiefs, a much smaller percentage died in office. However, the life of the borough chief officer was often hazardous by virtue of the fact that in addition to their police command they were often also in charge of the fire brigade as well,[20] which caused the death of at least one chief constable. Alexander Anderson, of the Tynemouth borough force, was killed in 1894 whilst demonstrating fire fighting equipment. In addition, their frequent involvement in policing also exposed them to danger. For example, Henry Solomon, chief constable of the Brighton Force in the 1840s, was murdered in his own office by a prisoner called Lawrence (see chapter 5; *Police Review* 1938: 488-489). They were killed whilst doing their job whereas the county chiefs tended to die either of old age or through misfortune. For example Capt. Fellowes of Hampshire, was killed in 1893 by a runaway horse and in 1936, Victor Bosanquet, of Monmouthshire, was killed when his car crashed. Coincidentally, one of his successors at Monmouthshire, Ronald Alderson, also died in a car crash twenty years later. Capt. J.A. Davidson, the chief constable of Kent, shot himself in 1942.

Dismissal. One of the more contentious reasons for leaving office was dismissal, however, it was very difficult to identify when a chief constable was dismissed, because they would only tend to be publicly dismissed if they had committed a considerable misdemeanour. More often than not chief constables who had fallen out of favour with their police authority would feel that their position was untenable and would resign: they left under a cloud. These 'engineered' removals ranged from, on the one hand,

[20] The fire brigade responsibilities of borough chief constables are not discussed here.

the face-saving resignation, whereby the chief constables in question were allowed to resign in order to keep their good name and, importantly, spare their police authority from any potential scandal and political backlash that might arise. On the other hand, these were situations which bore the hallmarks of a constructive dismissal. An example of the face saving resignation occurred in 1894, when Whitfield, then chief constable of York (see chapter 4), was found guilty by his watch committee of having "exceeding his duty" and lost a vote of confidence in him (Mins. York WC, 3/8/1894). Before he was dismissed he resigned on medical grounds and was awarded a pension. An example of the constructive dismissal occurred in 1909, when the Bedford watch committee requested the resignation of its chief constable, Arthur Danby (see chapter 9), for allegedly stealing a bicycle. The reality of the case was that Danby would appear to have fallen foul of local politics, he refused to resign and was dismissed (*Police Review*, 17/12/1909). Another example of the constructive dismissal, this time in a county force, was the departure of Sillitoe from the chief constableship of the East Riding of Yorkshire after he fell out with his police authority following his unsuccessful prosecution of a powerful member of the local gentry (Sillitoe, 1955: 54).

Consequently, although these situations are tantamount to dismissal, they appear in the records as normal retirements or resignations and are often mis-classified. However, thanks to the watchful eye of the reporters at the *Police Review*, who kept their readers attuned to the minutiae of watch committee proceedings, many cases where police authorities tried, both successfully and unsuccessfully, to get rid of their chief constables were reported and a representative number of cases were identified for this study. Dismissal from office was far more common in the borough forces than the county forces because of the tenuous position of the borough chief constable, and only a few county chief constables were ever forced out of office. Nine were dismissed, of which five resigned 'under a cloud', two were dismissed because they were too ill to continue, and two were dismissed because of misconduct. Both of the latter were, coincidentally, from Cardiganshire. In 1890 Maj. Bassett C. Lewis, described by his biographers as "a military martinet, an autocrat and a prominent County man", thought that his officers should suppress the tithe disturbances (*Police Review*, 1915: 190). Much to the annoyance of his Standing Joint Committee, he refused to obey their order to withdraw the police and allegedly became the first county chief constable to be dismissed for insubordination. The other Cardiganshire case was in 1956, when Chief Constable W. J. Jones was forced by the Cardiganshire Standing Joint Committee to resign after allegations of maladministration were made against him. Jones was later reinstated after appealing to the Home Secretary, only to retire shortly afterwards (*Police Review*, 1957: 347). A number of county chief constables were the subject of attempts to remove them but most, like Jones, survived upon appeal to the Home Secretary.[21]

It will be remembered from earlier chapters, that prior to the Police Act 1964, the constitutional position of the borough chief officer was not defined[22] in statute and was a position to which any powers were delegated by a police authority which had the power to hire and fire more or less at will: power which the watch committees did use from time to time, although with decreasing success. Before the Second World War, 50 (6 per cent) of borough chief constables were dismissed from office; 22 had been forced to resign, 18 were dismissed for misconduct, eight were dismissed for no identifiable reason and two were dismissed because it was felt that they could no longer do their job effectively.[23]

The independence of the borough chief constable grew with case law and incidental legislation. One important, but rarely quoted piece of legislation which decreased the watch committees' powers was the Police (Appeals) Act 1927, passed in the wake of the Bosanquet affair. The Act allowed borough and county chief constables who had been dismissed by their police authority to appeal to the Home Secretary and if the Home Secretary found them to have been dismissed unjustly then the police authority was forced to reinstate them.

The St Helens case in 1927 (*Police Review*, 1928: 398, 431), in which the Home Secretary overturned the Watch Committee's decision to reinstate the chief constable, and also *Fisher v Oldham* (1932), were both important cases that added to the borough chief constables' claim for independence. By the Second World War, the constitutional position of the borough chief officer was, in practice, virtually the same as that of the

---

[21] See for example the cases of Victor Bosanquet and Arthur Ellerington in chapter 3.

[22] Although the office was defined by the Home Secretary's post 1919 rules.

[23] 'left under a cloud' is a term used to describe the departure of a chief constable in circumstances that were not clear. They were either forced to resign or retire or resigned voluntarily under suspicious circumstances.

county chief constable, particularly after the war-time increase in the Home Secretary's effective power over policing. The increase in the independence of the chief constable is often referred to as the doctrine of constabulary independence (Jefferson and Grimshaw, 1984). Over the years a number of scandals led to successful and unsuccessful attempts by police authorities to get rid of their chief constables, but the most publicised dismissals of chief constables were in the late 1950s and early 1960s when a number of chief constables were dismissed for either misconduct, incompetence or fraud (see chapters 3 and 6).

The career trajectories of chief constables

It is clear from the above that the careers of chief constables varied between the type (borough and county) and size of the command. As the police gradually became more standardised after Desborough the career characteristics of the two types of chief constable converged, but that is where the similarity ends because borough and county policing traditions were independent of each other until the two systems were merged in 1974. This separation was reflected in the lack of cross-flow that took place between the two types of force. The careers of county chief constables were very distinct from those of borough chief constables and within each tradition a number of distinct career patterns can be observed which relate to the periods between the key changes in the police. Here is a summary of those careers.[24]

Before the Second World War, the majority of county chief constables were, 'county men', who were appointed whilst in their thirties or forties after a military career and stayed in office until their death. The chief constableship, to the 'county men', was considered to be more of a social position than a successful career move, and these men were the social equals rather than the subordinates of the police committee. Until the Second World War the majority of county chief constables were 'county men'. An example of a 'county man' was the Honourable, Colonel, Sir George Augustus Anson, KCB, CBE, MVO, DL. Anson was the second son of the Lord Lieutenant of Staffordshire, the Earl of Lichfield, and

---

[24] The following typologies denote career trajectories only and are not to be confused with Reiner's typologies of chief constables holding office in 1986.

educated at Harrow and the Royal Military Academy at Woolwich. Commissioned into the Royal Artillery in 1876 at the age of 21, he was promoted captain in 1885. In 1888, at the age of 31 and with no police experience, he was selected out of 68 candidates to be the new chief constable of Staffordshire. His seemingly uneventful chief constableship was punctuated by the First World War when he took leave from his force to rejoin the army as a Lt-Colonel in charge of a field artillery brigade.

Hon. Col. G. A. Anson
Police Review, 1893: 223

He retired as chief constable in 1929 and received the KCB in 1937. The presence of Anson and men of his ilk in the provincial police forces clogged up the promotions ladder causing considerable resentment amongst the ranks of their subordinates who were effectively barred from ever becoming chief constable. The highest position in the county forces that police officers could realistically aspire to was the rank of superintendent. Moreover, their longevity also meant that they remained chief constable for many years following the introduction of the policy of internal recruitment (see illustration).

A Familiar Traffic Jam[25]

[25] Source: *Police Review* (1951:838) reproduced from the 1930s.

After the turn of the century a few police authorities began to look for police experience in their chief constables and after the Desborough Committee's recommendations all were forced to demand it. The definition of police experience was, however, fairly broad and was not restricted to policing in mainland UK (see the discussion in chapter 6). In this environment a new type of chief constable began to appear instead of, but not replacing, the 'county men'. These chief constables are referred to here as 'spiralists' because of the way that they spiralled from smaller to larger commands. In many ways they were similar to the 'county men', particularly their backgrounds and military or colonial police training, but they saw the office of chief constable as a career in which they could further both their occupational and social ambitions. After serving a short period as an officer in the armed forces or the colonial police they would seek appointment as chief constable of a small county or borough force and use that experience to work their way up to command larger forces where the rewards were greater. Percy Sillitoe's career followed this 'spiral' pattern. It will be remembered from earlier chapters that after serving in the British South African and Rhodesian Police forces until aged in his mid-30s, Sillitoe returned to England to sit for the bar, he also applied for the chief constableships of small and medium sized borough forces. On his failure to become chief constable of the Hull City force, where his father-in-law was a magistrate, he applied for, and was appointed to, the small Chesterfield borough force in 1923. Sillitoe returned to the East Riding two years later on his appointment as the county's chief constable but after falling out with the local gentry (see earlier) he moved to command the larger Sheffield City Force. Each move was to a progressively larger force and from Sheffield he went on to Glasgow before commanding the large combined forces of Kent during the Second World War.

An alternative pattern taken by some 'spiralists' was to use their contacts to enter the senior ranks of a force under the wing of a friendly chief constable and work their way from there on. Like the 'county men' the 'spiralists' caused resentment and frustration amongst the career police officers because they tended to short circuit and therefore interfere with existing channels of promotion.

After the Second World War a quite considerable proportion of chief constables, mainly in the counties, were appointed after attending the Metropolitan Police College at Hendon. They received accelerated promotion through the ranks (chapter 7). Their admittance onto the Hendon scheme was due to their being regarded as suitable officer material. They tended to be fairly well educated and mainly from middle class backgrounds. They were 'officer class' material and provided police authorities with a suitable alternative candidate for the post of chief constable in a time when they were being forced to recruit internally (see discussion in chapters 6 and 7). The career of Col. Sir Eric T. E. St Johnston (described elsewhere), was typical of that 'officer class'.

As the 'county men', 'spiralists' and 'officer class' retired in the late 1960s and 1970s they were replaced by the 'timeservers' and the 'high flyers'. The 'timeservers' were men who had risen slowly, but steadily, through the ranks to spent their last few working years as chief constable, often being appointed on the premature retirement of their predecessor. They tended to be appointed because of the stability they could bring to their force and also because they only had a few years to serve before retirement. In contrast, the 'high flyers', or the "butterfly syndrome" as it has been referred to (*Police*, 1989: 3), are increasingly typical of many of today's chief constables. They tend to have risen quickly through the ranks with the assistance of the accelerated promotion provided by attendance on the special course. Before being appointed chief constable whilst aged in their mid to late 40s, most of their 25-30 year long police careers will have been spent in a variety of senior police positions that will have involved both local and national policing functions.[26]

The police careers of borough chief constables were markedly different, simply because of the many variations both in size and number of forces. Typically, there were variations of two basic types of career pattern. The first were reminiscent of the 'timeservers' described above and the second were the 'borough spiralists' who quickly rose through the ranks to become appointed as head of a small force, and who continually sought transfer to a larger borough command until they could get no further. They then stayed in office until their retirement. These men tended to have similar ambitions to their counterparts in the county forces, but lacked either the military or social background. Certain forces, for example

[26] Such as assistant HM inspector of constabulary.

Oldham, and Leamington Spa developed a reputation as a training ground for borough chief constables (chapter 6).

An interesting, if not eccentric, example of a frustrated 'borough spiralist' is found in the career of C.E. Butler, chief constable of Great-Grimsby between 1936 and 1962. After serving under his father, the chief constable of Barnsley, Butler became chief constable of the small Maidstone force at the age of 26. Five years later he became chief constable of the larger Great-Grimsby borough force. During the Second World War, Butler added to his responsibilities by commanding the massive regional auxiliary fire service. Despite his exceptional managerial skills and personal qualities he subsequently failed to get command of a larger force and turned his attentions to maximising the efficiency of his own force, where he remained until his retirement in 1962, aged about 70 years. He believed,[27] for reasons best known to himself, that the best police officers were either ex-professional footballers or Scotsmen, and he travelled around football clubs seeking to recruit professional footballers who were about to retire. Whenever possible, Butler combined his police work with his love for football and he created a crack football squad in his force which won the national police trophy a number of times in the early 1950s. It is said by his former police officers that he used his football squad as a tool by which he could effect revenge upon the county chief constables whose ranks he could not join because of his own 'inferior' social position.

In addition to the 'borough spiralists', there were the 'borough timeservers', chief constables who had spent most of their career in the ranks of the police and were appointed as chief officer, either, by virtue of their seniority (dead men's shoes) or as a reward for dutiful service to the watch committee. This practice tended to be common place before the First World War, but appeared to disappear between the wars as the Home Secretary became more actively involved in approving appointments. After the Second World War, the career trajectories of the majority of newly appointed borough chief constables were similar to the 'county timeservers' described above, particularly in the years leading up to the amalgamations of the 1960s.

---

[27] Based upon interviews with ex-police officers who had served under him at the beginning of their police careers.

Conclusion

The changes in the careers of borough and county chief constables, whilst very different, largely reflected the struggle between central and local government for overall control over policing. This chapter has demonstrated that the Home Office's enforced policy of internal recruitment (see chapter 6) led to career police officers being appointed as chief constable. This has always been assumed but never demonstrated. Furthermore, the Home Office's attempts to standardise the police would, on the one hand, appear to have been successful as it was found that many characteristics of the career patterns of provincial chief constables converged. On the other hand, it is found that the standardisation was probably only of appearance because it is clear from the above that the two provincial traditions of policing remained, almost vehemently, independent until the end of both systems in 1974. Whilst this chapter has described the changing police careers of chief constables, it has said little about who the chief constables were. Given that today, as in the past, chief constables enjoy a great deal of occupational independence and autonomy from formal accountability, an examination of who they are is important. This theme is taken up in the next chapter.

9 The Occupational and Social Origins of Chief Constables Appointed Between 1836 and 1996

Introduction

This chapter seeks to build up and explore a profile of the occupational and social origins of the chief constables holding office between 1836 and 1996 in order to identify any corresponding patterns of change. Of particular interest are any changes that occurred in the origins of the borough and county chief constables and any subsequent changes in those who were appointed to the amalgamated forces after 1973.

Because the data for this study were collected from published sources, they tended to be biased towards the chief constables' careers rather than their family backgrounds, as even the autobiographical accounts were a little short on this information. Therefore, in comparison to their police careers, comparatively little direct information was found about the social backgrounds of chief constables, and that which was obtained tends to relate more to the old borough and county chief constables rather than the more recent appointments. This was mainly the result of changes in the way that police news has been reported. Prior to the 1970s, for example, the police newspapers would describe the backgrounds of chief constables as part of their coverage of the appointment and would give basic information details of career or family background. This practice, in turn, contrasted with the coverage before the Second World War, when police journals would contain quite detailed biographies of chief officers. Sometimes the motives of the biographers were questionable, as it was often the case that an apparently respectful and detailed biography of a new chief constable, was in fact, a cynical exposition of their lack of policing experience. Regardless of motive, the information provided was, nevertheless, a valuable and accurate source.

In four parts, this chapter will first look at the occupational backgrounds of chief constables before they first joined the police and will include any military experience they may have had. The second part will look at their educational background, including any further or higher education and professional training. The third part will examine their family backgrounds and the fourth part explores their relative social status as chief constable.

The occupational backgrounds of chief constables before joining the police

Chief constables pursued a variety of occupations between leaving school and before joining the police.

Table 26: Occupation between leaving school and joining police

	Borough		County		Post-1973		Total	
Admin/Clerical	46	14.2%	4	1.7%	2	9.5%	52	8.9%
Tradesman	23	7.1%	2	0.8%	0	0%	25	4.3%
Land (farm work)	17	5.2%	4	1.7%	0	0%	21	3.6%
Police cadet /clerk	39	12%	11	4.6%	4	19%	54	9.2%
Student/trainee	24	7.4%	24	10.1%	3	14.3%	51	8.7%
Armed forces	154	47.4%	184	77.3%	11	52.4%	349	59.8%
Other	22	6.8%	9	3.8%	1	4.8%	32	5.5%
Total	325	55.7%	238	40.8%	21[1]	3.6%	584	100%

Number of Missing Observations: 901

Table 26 reveals not only a diverse range of pre-police experiences, but it also indicates the diverse occupational origins of the borough, county and post-1973 chief constables. Interestingly, the main pre-police occupation for each group of chief constables was military service, this is analysed later, followed to a much lesser extent by various other activities, of which

1 Little data was available on occupations between school and joining the police for those appointed after 1973. The data is slightly biased to those appointed before 1990.

the main was administrative or clerical work or being a trainee or student. When the distribution of these data is examined chronologically an overall decline can be observed in the percentage with military service backgrounds and an increasing percentage of those with administrative or other backgrounds.[2] However, whilst this overall trend certainly indicates changes in the nature of the role of the chief constable, from command oriented to more managerial and leadership styles, such a sweeping observation belies more complex developments. Not only do their chronologies differ, but there were qualitative differences as well.

The externally appointed county chief constables (see chapter 8) had mainly served in the military before being appointed directly to their posts. However, as they came to be internally recruited, especially after the Second World War, their prior occupations became more diverse. In particular, there was a marked increase in the percentage of county chief constables who had either been students or trainees, or had joined the police as a boy clerk, often working in the chief constable's office. After the Police Act 1964, these boy clerks became statutorily recognised as police cadets (Critchley, 1978: 322), although the term had been used colloquially for many years previously and officially in the Metropolitan police, and elsewhere, since the early 1950s.[3] A very small percentage of county chief constables had previously been in administrative or clerical work. In contrast, the borough chief constables had more diverse occupational backgrounds. Towards the latter part of the 19th century, they began to have pre-police administrative or clerical backgrounds, which reflected broader societal changes in employment practices. If they did not possess administrative backgrounds, then they, likely-as-not, had served as boy clerks in the police. Around the turn of the century, about ten per cent of all borough chief constables had served as either boy clerks or police cadets, compared with approximately two fifths by the early 1960s. Also, in contrast to the county chief constables, a substantial minority had been in craft and shop type work or manual work, typically farm labouring.

---

[2] N.B. these interpretations are based upon a relatively small number of cases.

3 They wore police uniforms with cadet flashes.

The Military Experiences of Chief Constables

The most common denominator in the occupational profiles of chief constables was their military experience and an analysis of this experience is very important to this study because the practice of police authorities to recruit military officers as their chief constables was an important driving force behind the subsequent policy of internal recruitment. It will be established here that a chief constable's military status, was as, if not more, significant than their military achievements; especially before the First World War.[4] Not only was it an important indicator of their skill to command, but it was also an important indicator of their social background. Research by Razzell into the social origins of army officers between 1758 and 1962, illustrated that the aristocracy and landed upper classes maintained their position within the commissioned ranks of the British army throughout the nineteenth century and even into the twentieth. Furthermore, whilst the presence of the aristocracy and the landed upper classes in the army declined following the First World War, they were replaced by the middle classes. Importantly, he concluded that "the sun has yet to set upon the English Gentleman" (Razzell, 1963: 259).

Table 26 illustrates that over three quarters (77 per cent) of county chief constables and almost half (47 per cent) of borough chief officers had military service between leaving school and joining the police, which compares with just over half of the chief constables appointed since 1973, most of whom did national service before joining the police. This figure is lower than Reiner's finding that 90 per cent of the chief constables holding office in 1986 had military experience prior to joining the police. This discrepancy can be explained by the fact that Reiner's chief constables were increasingly of the generation that left secondary school to join the army for either war or national service, depending upon their age. However, many of their post-73 predecessors tended to have missed military service because they were too young in the First World War. Similarly, many of their successors were of a later generation who were not required to do national service. When the nature of the chief constables' military service is explored in greater detail it is found that there existed some substantive differences in the nature of that service.

---

4 After the First World War the exclusive class base of the armed forces changed as soldiers from a broader class base achieved field rank.

Table 27 shows quite clearly that the percentage of borough chief constables with military service before joining the police decreased slightly, but nevertheless remained fairly constant throughout the three periods studied.

Table 27: Extent of military service

	Pre-1920	1920-39	1940-1973	Post-73
Borough Forces				
Military service	51.1%	43.2%	41%	N/A
No service	48.9%	56.8%	59%	N/A
County Forces				
Military service	92.2%	73.7%	31.9%	N/A
No service	7.8%	26.3%	68.1%	N/A
Post-1973				
Military service				52.4%
No service				47.6%

Of greater interest here, is the decrease in the percentage of county chief constables with pre-police military experience who were appointed after 1920; it fell by about a fifth, from 92 per cent to three quarters (74 per cent). A further, more dramatic increase, took place after 1940 when the percentage of military experienced county chiefs fell by another third to just under a third (32 per cent). This we can attribute directly to the impact of the internal recruitment policy. And it is important to note at this point that the military service of these post-war county chief constables, where applicable, was like that of the borough chiefs, short service undertaken before joining the police. It was not the career length service that characterised their predecessor as the examination of the respective lengths of service in Table 28 demonstrates.

Furthermore, the true impact of the policy of internal recruitment was, to some extent, hidden by the widespread conscription that took place during the First and Second World Wars, and afterwards with national service. It is found that the borough chief constables spent much less time in the armed forces than did county chief constables. Before 1920, the latter appear to have had full military careers before entering the police.

Table 28: Average length of military service (in years)[*]

	1[*]	2	3	4	5	6	7	1974-1996
Borough	8	7	14.1	9.7	5.4	4.9	3.9	N/A[**]
County	17.5	20.9	17.5	18.6	13.3	9.4	4.1	N/A
All	12.5	17.8	16.4	14.7	8.6	6.4	3.9	3.5

[*]These data represent 20 year cohort groups of appointees.
1=1836-55, 2=1856-75, 3=1876-95, 4=1896-15, 5=1916-35, 6=1936-55, 7=1956-73
[**]N/A = Not Applicable

However, as the internal recruitment policy slowly became effective, the county chief constables' average length of military service decreased quite rapidly to equal that of the borough chiefs. These changes explain the fairly rapid decrease in the ages at which the county chief constables joined the police (see chapter 8). They also suggest some fairly substantive differences in the nature of military service, which are confirmed by an analysis of the respective ranks held by the different types of chief constable.

An examination of the military ranks held by the chief constables with pre-police military experience (Table 29) shows that the greater majority of the county chief constables (89 per cent), compared with less than half of borough chiefs (48 per cent), were commissioned officers.[5] Furthermore, they tended to hold more junior commissioned positions. Just over half (52 per cent) of the borough chief constables held non-commissioned positions.

[5] Rank equivalents were observed between the different branches of the armed forces, for example, Captain RN is the equivalent to a Lt-Col. in the army.

Table 29: Highest military rank held

	Borough		County		Post-73	
General officer[6]	2	0.7%	13	4%	1	2.4%
Field rank[7]	64	21.1%	145	44.9%	1	2.4%
Junior commissioned[8]	80	26.3%	128	39.6%	13	31%
Non-commissioned[9]	158	52%	37	11.5%	27	64.3%
All	304	100%	323	100%	42	100%

No military service: 535
Missing cases: 631

Table 30: Changes in military rank

Borough Forces	Pre-Desborough	1920-1939	1940-1973	
General officer	1.5%	0%	0%	
Field rank	27.1%	13.5%	20.3%	
Junior commission	37.6%	19.8%	17.7%	
Non-commission	33.8%	66.7%	62%	
Counties Forces	Pre-Desborough	1920-1939	1940-1973	Post73*
General officer	5%	2%	3.6%	2.3%
Field rank	49.1%	58%	33%	2.3%
Junior commission	41%	36%	39.3%	34.9%
Non-commission	5%	4%	24.1%	60.5%

*N.B. the Post-1973 data represent all provincial police. Neither borough nor county forces existed.

When the various ranks held by chief constables are examined over time (Table 30), it can be seen that before 1920, ninety five per cent of the county chief constables with military experience, which was nearly all of

6 Includes the various grades of general officer and Royal Navy equivalents.

7 Includes the commissioned ranks of Major, Lt-Colonel and Royal Navy equivalents.

8 Includes the commissioned ranks of Lieutenant, Captain and Royal Navy and Air Force equivalents.

9 Included the non-commissioned ranks of Private, Corporal, Sergeant and Royal Navy and Air Force equivalents.

them, served at the rank of captain or above;[10] half had served at the rank of major or above. The previous ranks of the county chief constables appointed during the inter-war years remained more or less the same, although they held a slightly higher rank.

A significant change following the Second World War was the increasing diversity in the county chief constables' military service. On the one hand, it was the case that no more external appointments had been made after the outbreak of war, but a number of chief constables had attained field rank during both wars, either before they joined the police or whilst on secondment. On the other hand, there was an increase in the percentage of county chief constables who had been conscripted, typically during the First World War. During and after the Second World War, almost a quarter (24 per cent) of county chief constables had served in the non-commissioned ranks. This contrasts with four or five per cent previously (Table 30), but also contrasts quite sharply in the opposite direction with the three fifths of the chief constables appointed after 1973 who were in the non-commissioned ranks, typically resulting from their spell of national service. By comparison, the borough chief constables with military service, which was about half, held much lower ranks, although over two thirds of those in office before 1920 had previously held the rank of lieutenant or above. During the inter-war years this percentage reduced to a third, at which it remained thereafter.

Although the above analysis was based upon rank equivalents, the majority of chief constables' military experiences were in the army, rather than the navy or air force. Table 31 shows the branch of the forces served in by chief constables. There were few differences between the branch of the forces in which borough and county chief constables served, as nearly all with military service had served in the army. Only a small percentage served in the Royal Navy and RAF (after the First World War), although a large percentage of chief constables with military service who were appointed after 1973 had served in the RAF, mostly during national service. Within the respective services, only a few small differences in the service of borough and county chief constables could be identified. The county chief constables were more likely to have served in the Queen's, King's or Prince of Wales's divisions, the Indian Army or the Militia whereas the borough chief constables with military experience were more

[10] Captain is the lowest title of rank that can be used upon retirement from the army.

likely to have served in the Royal Artillery, Guards, Royal Armoured Corps or the Scottish Regiments. All of these regiments are non-specialist regiments.[11]

Table 31: Branch of armed forces served in

	Borough		County		Post-73		Total	
RAF	12	1.7%	21	5.2%	10	11.6%	43	3.6%
Royal Navy	24	3.4%	35	8.6%	11	12.8%	70	5.8%
Army	268	37.6%	267	65.8%	21	24.4%	556	46.2%
No military service	408	57.3%	83	20.4%	44	51.2%	535	44.4%
Total	712	100%	406	100%	86	100%	1204	100%

Number of Missing Observations: 631

This detailed examination of military experience is important, not only because it reveals much about the social backgrounds of chief constables, but because it also reveals much about the nature of police management cultures, past and present. It goes a long way to explaining why, for example, there is still a tendency for police managers to refer to their officers as "troops" and to their personal assistants as " staff officers" or in some cases even "batmen". It also explains why non-police officers are referred to as civilians rather than non-sworn staff; the British police have always been a uniformed civil police. Furthermore, it also explains why chief constables, and others, refer to their post as a command, and it also explains why for many years the inspections by the HM Inspectors of Constabulary were organised along the lines of a military drill parade. There were considerable changes during the 1990s which went a long way towards eradicating these military attitudes, but some still linger, partly due to the pervasive nature of police culture, but partly because of the continued ambiguity of the police role, which still requires officers to act as a disciplined unit in cases of public disorder.

---

[11] By way of contrast, the Metropolitan Commissioners tended, until the 1930s, to be drawn from specialist regiments such as the Royal Engineers.

Perhaps the most telling outcome of this analysis of military experience is that the military careers of the county chief constables were, until the policy of internal recruitment, one of the main criteria upon which their suitability for the post of chief constables was judged by the appointing police authority, but not as an indicator of their basic ability to command large groups of people, rather, the Sovereign's commission indicated to police authorities a particular social status. The analysis of the data suggests that a candidate's military status was as, if not more, important than their achievements, abilities or competence in command.

The educational backgrounds of chief constables

The chief constables' educational backgrounds were important indicators of the social world(s) from which they came (Stanworth, 1984: 251). Two important issues are examined here. The first is the difference, if any, between the educational backgrounds of the men who became borough and county chief constables; and the second is the difference, if any, between the men who became chief constables and the ordinary rank and file of the police. The (secondary) educational backgrounds of chief constables are shown in Table 32.

Table 32: Secondary education[12]

	Borough		County		Post-73		Total	
State secondary	27	14.7%	5	3.6%	12	26.1%	44	11.9%
Grammar	47	25.5%	12	8.6%	30	65.2%	89	24.1%
Non-state (public)	87	47.2%	113	80.7%	4	8.7%	204	55.2%
Other	23	12.5%	10	7.1%	0	0%	33	8.9%
Total	184	49.7%	140	37.8%	46	12.4%	370	100%

Number of Missing Observations: 1115

[12] N.B. The full predictive value of this data may be a little limited by the relatively small amount of data but it illustrates the main categories of education.

The educational profiles of borough and county chief constables were quite different from each other. The available data indicate that the county chief constables were far more likely than the borough chief constables to have attended a private, non-state, school.[13] The borough chief constables, on the other hand, were more likely to have attended a state or grammar school. Further analysis of the type of non-state school, for almost half of borough and over four fifths of county chief constables attended one, clearly reveals that they were far more likely to have been educated at Clarendon list schools than were the borough chief constables. A quarter of all borough chief constables (26 per cent),[14] compared with almost three quarters (72 per cent) of county chief constables had attended Clarendon list schools. About seven per cent of county chief constables had a religious or military style secondary education and thirteen per cent of borough chief constables had education linked to trades.[15]

Table 33: Changes in secondary education over time

		Pre-1920	1920-1939	1940-1973	Post-73
State secondary	Borough	12.7%	13.2%	20.5%	N/A
	County	4.5%	0%	5.1%	26.1%*
Grammar	Borough	14.7%	26.3%	50%	N/A
	County	1.5%	5.7%	23.1%	65.2%
Clarendon list (public)	Borough	31.4%	28.9%	9.1%	N/A
	County	78.8%	71.4%	61.5%	2.2%
Other non-state (public)	Borough	23.5%	28.9%	11.4%	N/A
	County	7.6%	8.6%	10.3%	6.5%
Other	Borough	17.6%	2.6%	9.1%	N/A
	County	7.6%	14.3%	0%	0%

*N.B. the Post-1973 data represent all provincial police. Neither borough nor county forces existed.

[13] Non-state, known colloquially in the UK as public school.

[14] This data is possibly probably biased towards the chief constables of the larger borough forces.

[15] A small number also had religious or military based education.

There were some interesting changes over time in the educational profiles of the chief constables (Table 33). Other than a modest increase in the percentage of grammar school educated borough chief constables, from less than a sixth (15 per cent) to just over a quarter (26 per cent), there were few changes in the educational profiles of either the borough or county chief constables before the Second World War. The main changes in educational profile took place after the Second World War as the percentage of non-state school educated county chief constables started to decrease whilst the percentage of those educated at a grammar school increased (Table 33). The percentage of grammar school educated county chief constables increased from six per cent to almost a quarter (23 per cent) and the borough chief constables from a quarter (23 per cent) to a half (48 per cent). The most notable difference, however, can be observed amongst the chief constables appointed after 1973. Almost two thirds (65 per cent) were educated at a state grammar school and just over a quarter (26 per cent) at state secondary schools. A further nine per cent attended non-state schools. When the chief constables holding office during 1986 are identified (Table 34), a fairly good fit is found with Reiner's (1991: 59) findings. Studying the chief constables holding office in September 1986 he found that just over three quarters (77.5 per cent) went to grammar school, a sixth (17.5 per cent) to state schools and five per cent to non-state schools. The differences (10 per cent) are due to this project covering all of the chief constables who held office in 1986 compared to just those in office in September. It is also possible that there may have been some confusion as to the definition of a grammar school as some non-state schools are also called grammar schools.

Table 34: Comparing secondary education (1976, 1986 and 1996)

	1976	1986	1996
State secondary	20%	27.8%	13.3%
Grammar	35%	66.7%	73.3%
Non-state (public)	55%	5.6%	13.3%

It is interesting to compare the 1986 chiefs' educational origins with those of the chief constables holding office a decade later in 1996. There appears to have been a slight increase in grammar school education, but interestingly, non-state school background as well.

Broadly speaking, the educational backgrounds of the chief constables appointed after 1973 were more like those of the old borough, than the county, chief constables. This observation suggests that whilst the policing careers of the borough and county chief constables became similar, as the policy of internal recruitment became effective, their educational, and social, backgrounds did not. In fact, it will be remembered from chapters 7 and 8, that it was not until the mid-to late 1970s that most of the old county chief constables, who had been appointed to run the new amalgamated forces, retired. Many of this group were graduates of the Hendon scheme and had backgrounds quite different to those of the standard entrants. Evidence of this can be found by comparing the educational profiles of chief constables holding office in 1976 (Table 34) with those of their successors; over half (55 per cent) had non-state school backgrounds, compared with six per cent a decade later.

So, the general theme running through the educational profiles of all types of chief constables was the decline of those with non-state education and their replacement with grammar school graduates. But even these profiles were quite, even considerably, different to the educational profiles of the officers under their command. Evidence from the Desborough report in 1919, the report of the Royal Commission on the Police in 1960 and more recently Reiner's survey of the lower police ranks (1978; 1982), showed that the educational backgrounds of most police officers were very basic, having taken place in state elementary or secondary schools.

Further or higher education

Whilst the majority of chief constables had only a secondary education, a small percentage did have experience of some form of further or higher education. An analysis of chief constables' education beyond secondary school is important because it provides further indicators about their backgrounds. For example, attendance at a university before the expansion of higher education in the 1960s was largely the preserve of a privileged minority. University experience was also important for developing extra-occupational social networks. The further and higher educational backgrounds of chief constables are shown in Table 35.

Table 35: Further or higher education

	Borough		County		Post-73		Total	
Oxbridge	10	2.2%	26	17.6%	3	4.5%	39	5.8%
Other UK. Univ.	25	5.5%	20	13.5%	47	70.1%	92	13.7%
Further ed. college	22	4.8%	2	1.4%	6	9%	30	4.5%
No known furth ed'n	401	87.6%	100	67.6%	11	16.4%	512	76.1%
Total	458	100%	148	100%	67	100%	673	100%

Number of Missing Observations: 812

Table 36: Changes in further or higher education

		Pre-1920	1920-1939	1940-1973	Post73*
University	Borough	4.3%	10.7%	18%	N/A
	County	14.1%	40%	55.6%	74.6%
F.ed. college	Borough	1.6%	12%	10.3%	N/A
	County	0%	4%	2.2%	9%
None known	Borough	94.1%	77.3%	71.8%	N/A
	County	85.9%	56%	42.2%	16.4%

*N.B. the Post-1973 data represent all provincial police. Neither borough nor county forces existed.

There were some interesting differences in the further or higher education of chief constables; the county chiefs (32 per cent) were far more likely than the borough chief constables (12 per cent) to have had such education. Almost a third (31 per cent) of the county chief constables attended a university, 18 per cent at an Oxbridge college and 14 per cent at another university. By comparison, only a small percentage (8 per cent) of borough chief constables attended university; five per cent attended a college of further education. These figures contrast sharply with the chief constables appointed since 1973, of whom three quarters had attended a university and nine per cent a college of further education. As a general rule of thumb the percentage of chief constables with some sort of further or higher education predictably increased as further and higher education became more freely available. Initially, a university education was a symbol of a privileged background, and one which was enjoyed by many of the old county chief constables and some of the chief constables of the larger borough forces. After the expansion of education in the 1960s and 1970s it came to symbolise meritocratic achievement.

Although the percentage of borough chief constables who attended a university[16] rose from about four per cent, before 1920, to 11 per cent during the inter-war years and then to 18 per cent after the Second World War, the percentage of borough chief constables with further or higher education was much less than in the counties. It was, however, the case and this can be seen in Table 36, that borough chief constables were more likely to have undergone some sort of further education than the county chief constables.

Before 1920, 14 per cent of county chief constables, had attended university: mostly at an Oxbridge college. As the century progressed, the percentage of university educated chief constables rose to two fifths (40 per cent) during the inter-war years and then to over a half (56 per cent) after the second World War.[17] During this period, the 1960 Royal Commission on the Police commented that it found "no recent instance of a university graduate entering the service" and discovered that only three had joined between 1945 and 1960 (see chapter 7). Approximately two thirds of this group had entered the police through the Hendon scheme after university.[18] An example of such an entrant was Col. Sir Eric T.E. St Johnston, mentioned in earlier chapters, who had studied at Cambridge before becoming an administrator in the Metropolitan police, from where he entered the police through the Hendon scheme.

By 1986, over two thirds (70 per cent) of chief constables had undergone some form of further or higher education. Over half (57 per cent) had been to a university and the rest to a further education institution.[19] A decade later, over nine tenths (93 per cent) had attended a university at some time during their lives. These are important developments, because a cursory look at the data reveals that the increases

---

[16] Not necessarily to undertake degree studies, for example to take one of the number of certificates in criminology and other subjects that were provided by adult and continuing education departments of a number of universities. Leeds was one such university.

[17] Based upon a small number of cases.

[18] A further four per cent had been externally recruited before 1939.

[19] Based upon a small number of cases.

in university attendance merely continued a long term trend. However, further examination reveals that the chief constables appointed from the mid-1970s onwards did not have the more privileged backgrounds of their predecessors; the county chief constables, as the earlier analysis of their secondary education revealed. These chief constables, as Reiner has observed, were meritocrats (1991a: 60).

As the percentage of chief constables attending a university increased then so did their possession of academic qualifications. Table 37 gives a breakdown of the academic qualifications held by chief constables.

Table 37: Academic qualifications

	Borough		County		Post-73		Total	
Degree	24	5.2%	40	22.3%	44	54.3%	108	14.9%
Law degree	*20*	*83%*	*25*	*63%*	*23*	*52%*	*68*	*63%**
Cert/diploma	10	2.2%	3	1.7%	7	8.6%	20	2.8%
No quals	429	92.7%	136	76%	30	37%	595	82.3%
Total	463	100%	179	100%	81	100%	723	100%

Number of Missing Observations: 762

* N.B. Law degrees are expressed as percentage of all degrees.

An interesting observation to be made from Table 37 is that it does not tally with Table 35. These discrepancies reflect different modes of study, because attendance at a university should not be mistaken with attainment of a degree. A number of universities, such as Leeds, have in the past provided a range of certificate courses in criminology and related studies, they have also provided a range of non-assessed adult and continuing education courses. Conversely, the attainment of a degree does not necessarily mean that a person has attended a university or college. The University of London, for example, provides an external LLB degree programme, which students can take through correspondence courses.

Of particular interest in Table 37, are the relatively large number of chief constables who possessed law degrees, with which there is an obvious occupational link. Of those with degrees, over four fifths of the borough chief constables, almost two thirds of the county chiefs and just over half of those appointed since 1973, had law degrees. Further analysis of this latter group reveals some interesting changes within its composition. Eighteen per cent of the chief constables holding office in 1976 had degrees (Table 38). They were typically ex-county chief constables whose backgrounds were quite different to those of their successors (see earlier) and who retired during the following years. Their replacements had very different backgrounds, they were Reiner's meritocrats, a group of chief constables, who were, possibly for the first and last time in the history of the police, drawn from individuals who had entered the police through the standard entry procedure and had risen through the ranks without the aid of an advanced promotion scheme. So, although the number with degrees had only increased by four per cent in the decade following 1976,[20] these degrees tended to have been obtained in-service, rather than before; many through the Bramshill scholarship scheme. Accordingly, a much higher percentage, over three quarters, were law degrees.[21]

Table 38: University degrees

	1976	1986	1996
Cert/Diploma	10%	10%	0%
Degree	18%	22%	68%
Law degree	*43%*	*78%*	*43%*[*]
No known qualifications	72%	68%	32%

* Law degree as a percentage of all degrees

[20] 22 per cent of chief constables in office in 1986 held degrees. This accords with Reiner's (1991) finding that 25 per cent of the chief constables in office in September of that year held degrees, the small difference in percentage arises from the differences in sampling. Interestingly, the figure would appear not to have changed since the late 1970s, as Halsey, Heath and Ridge (1980) found that 25 per cent of chief constables held degrees.

[21] Interviewees explained that although participants on the Bramshill scholar scheme could choose their course of study, it was felt that the degrees were relevant to the job, particularly as, at the time, all prosecutions were still conducted in the name of the chief constable. Whether or not they were appropriate to the job is highly debatable.

An interesting contrast is found between the chief constables in office in 1986 and those holding office in 1996. The overall percentage with degrees had trebled to over two thirds (68 per cent), but interestingly, only two fifths (43 per cent) of those degrees were law degrees, indicating that more had obtained their degrees prior to joining the police. Further light is shed upon this group by an interesting recent study by Charman *et al.*, (forthcoming), of 41 members of the ACPO ranks serving in 1996. They found that over seven tenths (71 per cent) had degrees (30 per cent had law degrees), which roughly equates with the statistic in Table 38. All of these degrees were obtained at "old" universities: two fifths (43 per cent) were funded through the Bramshill scholar scheme and two fifths (20 per cent) were graduate entrants to the police. Almost a quarter of those with degrees also held higher degrees. Three of these higher degrees were Ph.D.s and the remainder were taught courses. As this is the group from which all future chief constables will be appointed, it is reasonable to assume that it will be fairly representative.

These findings suggest that some interesting changes have taken place within the educational profiles of the chief constables appointed since 1986. Not only has the percentage of chief constables with degrees almost trebled, but the disproportionate number of law degrees found among the 1986 group has reduced to the percentage found amongst the 1976 chief constables. It will be remembered that unlike their predecessors, these are predominantly graduates of the special course.

To summarise briefly, the analysis of the educational profile of chief constables reveals some interesting features. The borough and county chief constables were clearly much better educated individuals than the broad mass of police officers. The fact that many borough chief officers, as well as the county chief constables, went to non-state schools indicates a slightly more diverse social class background than was previously anticipated. What is certain is that their educational attainment was far greater than that of the rank and file police officers. After the Second World War the percentage of those with a grammar school education increased and came to characterise the education of the chief constables who were appointed after 1973. Thus, meritocratic ability replaced privilege. This was also the case when further and higher education was examined. Although quite a few, mainly county chief constables, had attended university or obtained degrees this was, prior to the 1960s, largely indicative of a fairly privileged background. The post-1973 chief constables mostly gained their qualifications whilst in service, providing a further indication of their meritocratic achievement. An interesting development has been an increase in the numbers of police who entered the service with degrees after the expansion of the education system. Many of the most recent appointments were of such people, and this trend will continue. So, whereas the chief constables of the 1980s gained their formal education whilst in the police service, most of the recent appointments to chief constable and their successors will have gained their formal education prior to joining.

The family backgrounds of chief constables

This section will construct a picture of the chief constables' family backgrounds and the respective social positions they occupied. It will look first at their fathers' occupations and then their families.[22] Information was collected about the occupational backgrounds of the fathers of about of 230 borough and county chief constables. As stated above, comparatively little information was obtained on the fathers of the chief constables appointed since the mid-1970s. So, whilst these data do not always give an accurate indication of proportionality, they do, however, indicate the range of data and give an idea of the social processes which engendered class differences and also of their direction. Importantly, it will be argued later, the debate over social backgrounds becomes largely redundant as their period of service, training and professional socialisation increased.

The information on the fathers' occupations was more representative of the county than borough chief constables. It was the sort of information that was more likely to have been recorded in either the police force histories or in élite directories, simply because many of their fathers possessed characteristics that were of interest to readers. The data on the borough chief constables' fathers' occupations for many of the same reasons are biased towards those commanding the middle and large borough forces. Table 39 illustrates their different backgrounds. The data in Table 39 suggests that the county chief constables' fathers tended to

[22] Because social class has traditionally been based upon the father's status.

have either been in the armed forces,[23] the professions (including the clergy) or were businessmen. The borough chief constables' fathers, on the other hand, tended to have been police officers, or to a much lesser extent in the armed forces, professions or business.

After the First World War, the percentage of chief constables' fathers from the professions increased whilst the percentage of fathers in business and the armed forces fell.[24] This was not attributable to the policy of internal recruitment, but to broader changes that were taking place within the structure of society. Another noticeable, although relatively minor, development after the First World War was the increasing percentage of county chief constables' fathers who were senior police officers (at the rank of superintendent and above). These trends were also found in the available data for borough chief constables; although the percentage of borough chief constables' fathers in the police was considerably greater. As the borough chief constables came to be drawn from police families, the percentage with fathers who were businessmen, skilled/manual workers, or in the armed forces fell.

Table 39: Fathers' Occupations (Before 1974)[25]

	Borough		County	
Armed Forces	16	13%	32	31%
Professions (inc. Clergy)	19	15%	27	26%
Owner of large business	10	8%	27	26%
Senior police ranks(ch. insp+)	31	25%	13	12%
Lower police ranks (insp. -)	32	25%	2	2%
Owner of small business	12	9%	2	2%
Manual worker	6	5%	1	1%
Total	126	100%	104	100%
Missing cases	894		267	

N.B. Only Borough and County forces

[23] Where a military occupation was indicated it was usually retired. The majority of the fathers of county chief constables were members of the gentry (Steedman, 1984). Unfortunately the sources used in this study did not identify their social status.

[24] This trend is not shown in the table.

[25] The predictive value of this table is limited by the small number of cases that are represented. The tables does, however, indicate both the range of data and also some broad trends.

Drawing upon the above data, it is estimated that about 12 per cent of all county chief constables had fathers in the police. These figures compare with Reiner's findings that 15 per cent of the fathers of the chief constables in office in 1986 were police officers and also compares with the 14 per cent of police officer fathers he found in his sample of the Federated ranks a decade or so previously (Reiner, 1991a: 58; 1978: 150). Furthermore, a decade later, Savage and Charman found that 9.5 per cent of their 1996 sample of ACPO members had parents who were police officers (1997). A further 9.5 per cent had family members in the police. Given the differences in sample base and time frames one cannot make precise inferences from these figures, but, collectively, they suggest that a fairly stable figure of between 10 and 20 per cent of chief constables' fathers are police officers.[26] It is possible that this figure will eventually fall due to changing police recruitment patterns, especially following the various drives to increase the recruitment of ethnic minorities and women into the police.

A number of chief constables' fathers were themselves chief constables. Whilst these dynasties were relatively small in number and were the exception to the rule, they are interesting because of the nature of their pervasiveness and overall impact upon the policing of an area. It will be remembered from chapter 5, that there were some quite lengthy father and son dynasties, of which the more lengthy tenures were the Phillips from Carmarthenshire (1875-1940), the Lindsays from Glamorganshire (1868-1937), the Knights at Beverley borough (1870-1912), the Derhams at Blackpool (1887-1911 and 1920-1935), and the Eddys at Barnstaple (1905-1921).

Family members in the police were not merely restricted to fathers and sons, there were a number of examples of brothers who each held office of chief constables, such as the Danbys and the Wardes.[27] There

[26] Private correspondence. In this circumstance parents' occupation is clearly influential.

[27] Arthur Danby was chief constable of Louth 1901-1906 before becoming chief constable of Bedford, from where he was asked to resign in 1906. His two brothers were also chief constables, J.W.A. Danby was chief constable of Hyde from 1899 until his death in 1932 and Thos. Danby was chief constable of Congleton between 1912 and 1915 before becoming chief constable of Peterborough (Liberty and Soke) until 1944. Another example of brother chief constables were the Wardes: A. B. Warde was chief constable of Hampshire (1894-1929) and his brother was chief constable of Kent (1895-1921).

were also families in which a combination of different relatives were chief constable, for example, Sir William Nott-Bower's brother, Arthur, succeeded him as the chief constable of Leeds and his son, Sir John Nott-Bower, later became the Commissioner of the Metropolitan Police. There were also examples of inter-marriage between chief constables' children, such as the Williamsons. John Williamson was chief constable of Northampton (1924-1955) and his son Frank became the chief constable of Carlisle (1961-1963) and later Cumberland (1963-1967). John Williamson's other son married the daughter of William J. Hutchinson the chief constable of Worcester City (1928-1931), Huddersfield (1931-1933) and Brighton (1933-1956).[28]

The available information, occupation, education, titles and family information, indicate quite clearly that the county chief constables came from far more privileged family backgrounds than did the borough chief constables (see the later discussion on entries in élite directories). Initially, the majority of county chief constables came from the upper middle and even titled classes,[29] but during the inter-war years, they came to be drawn from the (professional) middle classes. In contrast to the county chief constables, most borough chief constables were from the lower middle and working classes with a sizeable proportion coming from police families. However, the range of size of the borough forces does confuse the issue slightly, as a number of the early borough chief constables were from middle and upper middle class backgrounds. These chief constables tended to be appointed to the largest borough forces which were as large as some of the large county forces, and therefore carried similar prestige. Although, generally speaking, the borough chief constables themselves were from quite different backgrounds to the men under their command. Others used the borough forces to gain experience of police command before moving to a county force. By and large, the greater majority of borough chief constables, especially after the inter-war years, tended to be from the lower middle or the working classes. This observation is supported by the preceding analysis of the chief constables' educational backgrounds.

Reiner's social profile of the chief constables holding office in 1986 revealed that most came from the manual classes and a minority from the non-manual classes (1991a: 57): typically social classes 3a and 3b on the

---

[28] From correspondence with David Hutchinson, William Hutchinson's son.
[29] Approximately 27 were from the titled classes.

Registrar General's scale. These chief constables were an upwardly mobile group, and they came from upwardly mobile families. Not only did a relatively large percentage of their fathers achieve upward social mobility during their lives, but he found that their children were even more socially mobile (1991a: 57). It is therefore interesting, when this profile is put into the context of the backgrounds of the preceding borough and county chief constables, that the social profile of Reiner's chief constables is more similar to that of the old borough than the county chief constables.

The little information that is available about the post-Reiner cohort of chief constables suggests that they have more socially diverse origins than their predecessors. But, the relevance of their origins declines in light of the fact that they have been through such a lengthy and centrally controlled socialisation process; most have degrees, over two thirds have been on the special course and all have attended the senior command course. Whilst social background was important with Reiner's chief constables because it was clearly an important reference point and motivating factor (1991a: 100), it is arguable that social background is far less relevant to the chief constables of today because of the relatively long process of selection, training and professional socialisation. They are meritocrats, but they are sponsored meritocrats, in so far as they were identified fairly early on as potential high flyers and in that sense were sponsored (Turner, 1960: 855). So their progress up the police ranks was a combination of sponsorship and meritocratic achievement. In this sense they contrasted with Reiner's chief constables who were mainly contest meritocrats (Reiner, 1991a).

The social status of the office of chief constable

This section will look at the social status of the chief constable by virtue of attaining that office. As the police have, over the past 160 years, increasingly become aligned with central government and the policing function has become more of a central rather than local issue, the relative social status of the office of chief constable has increased. It is also the case that there are now fewer chief constables than there were previously before the 1960s, and the forces that they command are considerably larger than those of their predecessors (chapter 3). Therefore, they are accorded the same status as other public service managers. In order to explore the social status of the chief constable, their inclusion in directories of élites will be examined as will their receiving civil honours and their involvement in a range of local and national organisations.

Directories of Elites

Directories are essentially social constructs of élites by self-created élites and a broader analysis of those included suggests that there exists some confusion between personal achievement and membership within an élite group. However, the inclusion of chief constables in directories of élites provides an admittedly crude, but nevertheless valuable, indicator of their social status in relation to other contemporary élite groups in society over time. Such an analysis will illustrate both the differences in the social background of borough and county chief constables (see earlier) and also changes in the status of the office of chief constable over time. *Who's Who* has been the most prominent of the directories of élites that have been published since the mid-19th century and has included over 230 chief constables since it was first published in 1849. The only other contemporary directory of élites to include chief constables was *Kelly's Handbook of the Official and Titled Classes* (*Kelly's Handbook*). Generally speaking, those who had entries in *Kelly's Handbook*[30] also tended to have entries in *Who's Who.* A number of other directories contained biographical details of notables, for example *Men of Our Time*, the predecessor of *Who's Who*, and *The Dictionary of National Biography*, but no chief constables were included in the former and only one in the latter.[31] The precise reasons why certain individuals are included in, and others are excluded from, directories of élites have never been made entirely clear, but in the case of *Who's Who,* individuals are invited to submit their biography if the selection board believes that it would be of "general and enduring public interest".[32] Such "interest" could be the product of either

[30] *Who's Who* has taken prominence as the leading directory of élites.
[31] Michael Whitty, the first chief constable of Liverpool (1836 - 1844).
[32] Correspondence with the publishers of *Who's Who*, A & C Black (Publishers) Ltd., October 2 1997. The publishers quite rightly point out that some candidates for inclusion do refuse on security grounds, but it is assumed here that most chief constables, because of the public nature of their position, will submit their biography, when invited to do so, on the

their ascribed social status or their contribution to public service. Solely being a chief constable has never qualified an individual for inclusion in *Who's Who*:

> Chiefs of the larger forces will be invited automatically, on appointment; others will be considered by our Selection Board, taking into account various individual attributes such as honours and awards (e.g. CBE), involvement in professional bodies or public commissions, publications or academic work.[33]

Given that the available data indicate that modern chief constables are unlikely to possess an ascribed social status that would warrant enough public interest for their inclusion, it is fair to assume here that their inclusion will be solely based upon their public service as a chief constable. Similarly, it is fair to assume that in the past, especially when policing was primarily a local issue and before the amalgamations increased the size of police forces, that service as a chief constable would be equally unlikely to have warranted enough public interest to justify inclusion. On the basis of this assumption, we can conclude that the past chief constables were considered for inclusion mainly upon their social merits or, in rare circumstances, their personal achievements. Table 40 shows the extent to which chief constables were included in directories of élites.

Table 40: Entry in a directory of élites by force type

	Borough		County		Post-73		Total	
Entry	64	6.1%	118	36.9%	53	47.3%	235	15.8%
None known	989	93.9%	202	63.1%	59	52.7%	1250	84.2%
Total	1053	70.9%	320	21.5%	112	7.5%	1485	100%

N.B. Where an entry appeared in both *Kelly's Handbook* and *Who's Who* the latter entry was recorded.

basis that the information they supply will probably be available through other published sources.

[33] *Idem.*

A broad sweep of the data illustrates quite clearly that the county chief constables were far more likely (37 per cent) to be included in an élite directory than were the borough chiefs (6 per cent). Bearing in mind the changes mentioned earlier in the inclusion policy of *Who's Who*, namely that chief constables with a certain stature may now be included, where as in the past they would not, it is prudent to take cross sections at ten year intervals in order to document the changes (see Table 41).

Table 41 illustrates a number of interesting trends. The first is that the number of chief constables with entries increased considerably towards the end of the nineteenth century. This was partly due to the increased popularity of *Who's Who* and *Kelly's Handbook* as signifiers of status in an increasingly status conscious Victorian society. But it was also due to the increase in the personal social status of the county chief constables who were appointed during the 1880s, 1890s and 1900s to replace the original chief constables. By 1906, 82 per cent (see Table 41) of county chief constables in office that year had an entry in a directory of élites, compared with 6 per cent of borough chiefs.

Table 41: Entry in a directory of élites: ten year intervals*

	Borough		County		Total		n=
1996	N/A		N/A		16	39%	41
1986	N/A		N/A		20	48.8%	41
1976	N/A		N/A		25	64.1%	39
1966	11	16.4%**	28	58.3%	39	33.9%	115
1956	14	19.7%	24	49%	38	31.7%	120
1946	13	13.7%	24	44.4%	37	24.8%	149
1936	7	5.9%	25	44.6%	32	18.4%	174
1926	5	4.1%	37	66.1%	42	23.7%	177
1916	11	8.7%	41	77.4%	52	28.9%	180
1906	8	6.4%	45	81.8%	53	29.4%	180
1896	7	5.6%	28	50.9%	35	19.3%	181
1886	3	1.9%	16	29.1%	19	8.8%	215
1876	0	0.0%	8	14.5%	8	3.7%	217

* N.B. Data is shown from 1876 onwards

** Percentages are of the total number of each type of chief constable

By 1916, the percentage had fallen to just over three quarters (77 per cent) and to two thirds (66 per cent) by 1926. As the old upper middle class, externally recruited, county chief constables were replaced by middle class colonial types from 1920 onwards (see earlier chapters), their entries in *Who's Who* fell to just less than half (45 per cent). What is interesting over the following decades is that the county chief constables continued to be recruited from the middle and lower middle classes, an increasing percentage being Hendon recruits, and yet the percentage with entries in élite directories increased again to almost two thirds (64 per cent) in 1976. Similarly, the percentage of borough chief constables with entries increased, to a fifth in 1956, falling to a sixth (16 per cent) in 1966. However, the increases in the case of the borough chiefs might be a little misleading because at this time the overall number of borough forces decreased quite considerably. Generally speaking, there were a number of reasons for these increases. Firstly, many of the chief constables who served during the war years performed a number of functions, often nationally based, for which they gained recognition. Some, such as St Johnston (see earlier chapters), were seconded into the armed forces where they performed important tasks. Others, such as Sillitoe (also see earlier chapters), who in 1943 when the threat of invasion was imminent, took control of the combined Kent county force, which included all of the 10 borough forces within its area. Secondly, after the Second World War, there developed more national forums for chief constables to participate in, for example, ACPO. This was also a period when the policing agenda became a national issue and a number of chief constables either sat upon or participated in Royal Commissions, Parliamentary Committees and so on.

One group which is particularly interesting are the large percentage holding office between 1976 and 1986, who had entries in *Who's Who*. This period, it will be remembered, was a time during which the last of the Hendon recruits were replaced by chief constables who had entered the police through the normal entry procedures and had risen through the ranks by their own merits. Many of these chief constables achieved a national profile as chief constable. What is even more interesting is that the percentage of this group with entries increased slightly between 1986 and 1990[34], but then started to decrease as they were replaced by the special

[34] 1986, 49%; 1987, 46%; 1988, 50%, 1989, 50%, 1990, 56%, 1991, 53%; 1992, 51%; 1993, 48%, 1994, 48%, 1995, 42%.

course graduates. About two fifths of today's chief constables appear in *Who's Who*. The main reason as to why the chief constables in office in 1996 had fewer entries than did their predecessors is that they are relatively recent appointments and have yet to attain the national public profile that many of their predecessors did. This observation substantiates the earlier claim that inclusion is now related to the office rather than the person.

Civil Honours

Another indicator of the growing status of chief constables is the increasing percentage of chief constables who are honoured for their police service through the regular honours lists which developed towards the end of the nineteenth century. There are a number of different ways in which such honours can be awarded, the Queen's Police Medal, knighthoods, and other honours awarded via the civil honours list.

In 1911 a special police honour, the King's Police Medal (KPM)[35], was created for this purpose. Nott-Bower described it as 'the policeman's VC' (Nott-Bower, 1926: 235), but his description slightly exaggerated its importance, mostly probably because he was one of its first recipients. The medal was certainly awarded to officers from all ranks who had distinguished themselves through bravery, but it was not a reward 'for valour' as Nott-Bower suggested, rather it was for meritorious service. It was, as it is now, mainly given to senior officers for their police service, and recipients are announced amongst the civil honours lists. Nearly all chief constables will probably receive the Queen's Police Medal during their careers, approximately ninety per cent of those in office at any one time will have received it.

A majority of chief constables will also, during the course of their career, probably be honoured with one of the levels of the Order of the British Empire for their public service (OBE, MBE or CBE). It is an order that tends to be reserved for higher civil servants, military officers and others in the public sector (Scott, 1982: 156), although those chief constables whose service has brought them within the orbit of the Royal Family have occasionally been awarded from another order.

---

[35] Later to be the Queen's Police Medal (QPM).

From the late nineteenth century onwards, a small number of chief constables have possessed titles, all, bar one, Lord Knights, were either Baronets or Knights. About five per cent of all chief constables have possessed the title "Sir" at some point during their careers: three per cent of borough chief constables, 13 per cent of county chief constables and 10 per cent of those appointed after 1973. Table 42 shows the annual percentage of chief constables with titles taken at 20 year intervals since 1856. It illustrates that until the later part of the nineteenth century very few chief constables were titled, but from the latter part of the century the percentage increased, especially in the county forces. The titled borough chief constables tended to be small in number and were typically those in command of the very large borough forces. It is the titled county chief constables who are the more interesting group.

Table 42: Chief Constables with titles*

	Borough		n= forces	County		n= forces	Post -1973		n= forces
1996*	N/A			N/A			1	2%	41
1986	N/A			N/A			7	17%	41
1976	N/A			N/A			13	33%	39
1956	5	7%	71	10	20%	49	0	0%	0
1936	4	3%	118	12	22%	54	0	0%	0
1916	5	4%	127	11	21%	53	0	0%	0
1896	2	2%	126	7	14%	52	0	0%	0
1876	0	0%	162	2	4%	55	0	0%	0
1856**	1	1%	139	0	0%	36	0	0%	0

* Annual cross sections at 10 year intervals.
** Annual cross sections at 20 year intervals.

During the latter part of the nineteenth century the percentage of titled chief constables increased from zero to about a fifth. This percentage remained fairly constant until after the 1974 amalgamations, when there was an increase; for example, a third of the chief constables holding office in 1976 received a knighthood, followed by a slow decrease. A decade later, in 1986, 17 per cent of those in office that year received a knighthood. This percentage decreased during the following decade as only two per cent of the chief constables in office in 1996 had been knighted, which is perhaps to be expected as most have not been in office for any great length of time. In time, it is estimated that about a fifth of the chief constables in office in 1996 will receive a knighthood during the course of their careers.

There are two interesting observations to be made from these trends, the first being that these titles were initially related to the chief constables' ascribed social positions: many were baronets who either inherited their title, or, in a few cases were rewarded by the monarch for their personal service. Interestingly, whilst the percentage of titled chief constables remained more or less the same for much of this century, the characteristics of those with titles have changed, as did the characteristics of the men who received them. All are now knights and none baronets. It must be remembered that this was a protracted period during which general attitudes towards the police in general changed, it was the period of the so-called "golden age of policing" (Reiner, 1992: ch. 2), which reached its zenith in the early 1950s. So, the individual social status of chief constables decreased, as the policy of internal recruitment became effective, but their broader social status as chief constable increased, and chief constables came to be rewarded for their contribution to police work. The greater majority of knighthoods have been of the order of the British Empire. This trend has continued, even since the early 1970s, after which there has been a sharp decline in the general public standing of the police. The only titled ex-chief constable who is not a knight is Lord Knights who, as Sir Philip Knights, was elevated to the House of Lords in 1990; which is evidence of the continued increase in the social status of the chief police officer (Reiner, 1991b: 62).

The second observation is that the number of national police roles that chief constables could perform either whilst in office or immediately upon their retirement increased after the Second World War. The two most prominent of these roles are the Presidency of ACPO (since 1947) and becoming one of Her Majesty's Inspectors of Constabulary. So, whilst it is true to say that there was an increase in the general social status of the chief constable during this century, it was also the case that holding the Presidency of ACPO and or becoming an inspector of constabulary increased one's chances of receiving a knighthood, in fact the former more so than the latter. Table 43 illustrates that three fifths (60 per cent) of ACPO presidents were knighted, compared with just under a quarter (24 per cent) of HMICs.

Table 43: ACPO presidents and HMICs with titles

	HMIC		ACPO		Both		None		Total	
Titled	8	24%	22	60%	3	38%	46	3%	79	5%
No title	26	77%	15	41%	5	63%	1360	97%	1406	95%
Total	34	101%	37	101%	8	101%	1406	100%	1485	100%

These honours are "ritualised affirmations of the values which underpin British Society and constitute its moral order" (Scott, 1982: 157). They not only serve to wed their recipients, the public service élites, to the values of public service and merit, but, importantly, they also provide a series of incentives for aspirants to maintain those values.

Conclusion

This chapter has illustrated the changes that have taken place in both the social backgrounds of chief constables and also the social status of the office of chief constable. They largely correspond to the changes identified in chapter 8. The main trend to emerge was that during the nineteenth century the office of chief constable, especially in the counties, became the preserve of members of the county ruling élite: the upper classes. Initially, they sought persons of similar social standing to themselves but who possessed proven skills in military command. These individuals stayed in office for some time and when appointing their replacements, the county police authorities appeared to rank social position over proven ability to command. Indeed, it was not unknown for the chief constable to be connected either socially or by family to members of the police authority. Upon appointment, the county chief constables effectively became members of the local power élites and even if they were not often personally in agreement with the views of the local élite, they were rarely in open disagreement.

The early borough chief constables were very different in both stature and social position to the county chief constable, but like the county chiefs, they were appointed because they were trusted by the police authority to enforce their particular understanding of the local order. Whilst there were some quite well-known examples of dissension, such as Nott-Bower and the Liverpool Watch committee (Brogden, 1982), these were fairly rare events. Borough chief constables were, because of either their willingness, or their perceived obligation to carry out the wishes of the police authority, effectively part of the local municipal ruling élite. Furthermore, it is clear in the cases of both the borough and county chief constables, that they were servants of local government and were initially appointed for reasons that were more related to their ideological or proven personal loyalty towards the local power élite than their abilities as professional police managers.

The policy of internal recruitment, which expressed the wishes of the central bureaucracy, and therefore central government, to increase central control over the police, can be seen to have impacted upon the positions of both borough and county chief constables within local government. As the relationship between the police and central government strengthened, and their local government origins became distant memories, they became more self-contained. Especially, with the introduction of common training for senior officers and also with the formation of the Association of Chief Police Officers in the late 1940s, which brought together the separate borough and county chief constables' associations and created a forum for both the expression of a collective opinion and later, the formation of police policy.

The findings in this chapter illustrate the ways in which the social origins of chief constables gradually converged as the idea of a professional police with internally recruited chief officers became reality; this complements the observations made in chapter 8. In short, the social origins of chief constables ceased to be similar to those of their employers, especially in the counties, and became more akin to those of the police they commanded, which, in turn, were representative of the people they policed. In becoming more representative of the people they policed, they of course became less socially or ideologically aligned with their police authorities. However, as the above analysis illustrated, they never became entirely representative of the body of officers they commanded except, perhaps, for a short period during the late 1970s and 1980s. This was because modern chief constables tend to have been marked out as potential high flyers from very early on in their careers, and the very long and involved professional socialisation within such a strong occupational culture, that modern chief constables experience(d) prior to appointment will arguably mitigate the effects of social background. Thus giving strength to the argument forwarded above that one of the main effects of the professionalisation of police management was to remove any local allegiances that existed and create new links between the profession and central government.

One of the most interesting outcomes of this analysis relates to the changes in the chief constables appointed since the amalgamations of 1973. Initially, it was thought that this group was a convergence of the borough and county traditions and that its characteristics would remain fairly static. However, the above findings unfolded a more complex and interesting story, which would provide the basis for further research. The chief constables of the newly amalgamated forces tended, with exceptions, to be the ex-county chief constables, many of whom had entered the police through the Hendon scheme. In sum, they had quite different backgrounds to the rest of the police. As these chief constables retired during the next few years following the amalgamations, they were replaced by a new group of chief constables. For the forthcoming decade, until the special course graduates started to be appointed, most of these chief constables had, for the first time since the formation of the police, entered the police and had risen through the ranks without the help of an accelerated promotion scheme or being appointed directly to the post. During this period chief constables had literally tended to carve out their own careers and former chief constable, John Alderson, has stated that because "there was no route and it was like going through a wood and picking your own way through instinct and intuition".[36] Alderson read for the bar, took up a years long fellowship in Australia and then attended courses at the police college, including the first senior command course. It is significant that this period of non-accelerated chief constables also produced some of the more controversial chief constables in Alderson himself, James Anderton

---

[36] Interview with John Alderson April 17, 1997.

and Kenneth Oxford.[37] Furthermore, it is unlikely that such outspoken chief constables will emerge in the future because of firstly the manner by which the current and future chief constables are identified at such an early stage in their careers, and secondly the processes of secondary selection, notably by extended interview, that they have to pass through before appointment.

---

[37] John Alderson was formerly the chief constable of Devon and Cornwall, Sir James Anderton was formerly the chief constable of the Greater Manchester Police and Sir Kenneth Oxford was formerly the chief constable of Merseyside. Each of the three was controversial in quite different ways.

10 The Ideology of Internal Recruitment and the Governance of Police Management

Introduction

The preceding chapters in this book have examined the historical processes by which chief constables became professional managers. More specifically, they have charted the changes in selection and appointment policies from the external, towards the internal recruitment of police managers to illustrate how two very different traditions of policing, upon which today's police are built, were brought together to form a unitary model of provincial police. In doing so they also identified some important changes within the governance of police management. This concluding chapter will summarise briefly, the main themes which emerged in the preceding chapters, before discussing the findings within the context of the main contemporary debates over the governance of police management.

A brief summary of the preceding chapters

The formation of the new police in the 1830s did not create a uniform system of policing in England and Wales. Rather, it introduced three main types of police force, the Metropolitan, borough and county police. By placing control over the police in local hands, the initial police legislation laid the basis for the development of three separate traditions of police in England and Wales, even though the Metropolitan police model influenced the construction of the provincial police. Furthermore, as the local police role grew in Victorian society, the three traditions developed independently of each other, with the result that by the early twentieth century the police were indeed a collection of Victorian bric 'a brac (Critchley, 1978: 176). The implications of this diversity were threefold.

Firstly, the many police forces were falling behind the societal demands being placed upon them: they were not only archaic in structure and practice, but also very ineffective. Secondly, the sheer number of, often quite small, independent forces were a bureaucratic nightmare for the Home Office, who had annually to inspect them and then administer grants to their police authorities in partial support of the policing costs for their areas. Thirdly, the many different and very local policing policies and local interpretations of law caused legal problems for the (uniform) policing of a country that not only shared the same legal system, but was also becoming increasingly united by new communications technologies. At the centre was the chief police officer, whose primary allegiance was to local government and therefore tended not to place central demands, suggestions or proposals as highly as those of their employers.[1]

This diversity generated a bureaucratic need on the part of the Home Office for a more standardised and therefore more efficient and effective police, and the policy of recruiting chief constables from within the ranks of serving police officers laid foundations for achieving that goal. It would be wrong, however, simply to make the reductionist assumption that central government simply wished to gain control over the police, the circumstances were much more complex and the policy brought together a number of contemporary issues. It was certainly the case that the bureaucratic need by the Home Office to reduce diversity in the police organisations was a prime motivating factor, and all the better for the Home Office and central government, if this weakened the link between the chief officer of police and local government. Even better if professional police, rather than military or municipal, based ideas would form the basis of policing policies. This was certainly one of the intended outcomes. Importantly, the policy of internal recruitment, which had been politicised by the *Police Review* campaign, also gained considerable support from within the police ranks as it applied the increasingly popular principle of promotion by merit to the police, with the result that officers could enter the police in the lower ranks and rise to the top by their own merits, thus contributing to the improvement of police morale, which was in a state of crisis at the end of the First World War.

Ordinarily, with so much obvious support, the introduction of such a policy would simply be a matter of tabling a bill in Parliament and then

---

[1] Unless they were in dispute with their authority, when the opposite might happen.

seeking its support. The problem with this particular policy was that the MPs who represented the many independent police forces posed a formidable opposition. So, the policy was implemented by means of quasi-legislation, through rules that could be made by the Home Secretary under various police acts and best practice issued by Home Office circulars. However, although introduced officially in the Home Secretary's (1920) rules, the policy of internal recruitment was not fully implemented until two decades later, due to considerable resistance by local police authorities to what they saw as the usurping of their traditional autonomy and power. In fact, it was not until the 1970s and early 1980s, that all chief constables had entered the police through the standard entry procedure and had risen through the ranks by their own merits, as for many years previously, graduates of the Hendon scheme had dominated the most senior policing positions in England and Wales. In fact, this group of chief constables were fairly short-lived, as their successors were predominantly graduates of the special course and were either marked out for accelerated promotion upon entry or soon after they joined the police. So, although the idea of an "officer class" within the police is an anathema to prevailing meritocratic police ideologies, it is nevertheless the case that we have a *de facto* officer class within the police.[2]

Internal recruitment and the governance of police management

The main impact of the policy of internal recruitment was to reconfigure the social structure of police management so that chief constables ceased to be part of the local ruling élite and became a self-contained élite group in their own right with special links to central government. In doing so, the policy of internal recruitment effectively realigned the mechanisms which effect control both over police management and also over the police in general. The policy of internal recruitment has not merely changed chief constables from being amateurs into professionals, but more importantly, it has led to the creation of a very special, self-selecting and internally accountable, professional élite with direct links to central government.

[2] Not in the sense of commissioned officers as in the armed services, but rather in the sense that there exists within the police a cohort of police officers who are, from an early stage in their police careers, destined for the more senior ranks.

This shift in control over the police, towards the chief constable and the Home Office, has taken place largely at the expense of the police authority, whose effective powers have been considerably weakened from what they once were. A position that has been further weakened by the fact that police authorities have subsequently tended to under-utilise their remaining powers. Underlying this change in the office of chief constable has been a powerplay between local and central government over control of the police. During the first one hundred and sixty years of the new police, not only has the meaning of policing changed, but so has its orientation. Once an instrument of local government, the police became firmly aligned with the central bureaucracy and thus with central government policy. So, a consequence of these developments was a *de facto*, but not a *de jure* national police force (Reiner, 1991a).

More recent events have, however, taken this trend a step further. During the early 1990s, attempts to reduce the overall number of police forces in the UK and therefore place control of policing in fewer hands were set out in the White Paper (1993), but were not implemented. However, the recent introduction of national policing bodies such as the National Crime Squad and to a lesser extent, the National Criminal Intelligence Service, through the Police Act 1997, has meant that, in effect, we now have emerging a *de jure* national police force. Moreover, this position has been further strengthened by the increased corporacy, and restructuring, of ACPO, which dissaggregated its policy making and representative functions so that it can formulate a single police view upon issues relating to policing policy. Central to this change has been the adoption of the principle of "presumption in favour of compliance", whereby individual members who depart from ACPO policy are expected to inform the ACPO president in writing, of their reasons for doing so (Savage and Charman, 1996: 15; Charman and Savage, 1998: 8). This policy has not only further structured the senior police hierarchy, but it has effectively reduced the number of players who participate in the construction of what has effectively become a national policing policy.

But, whilst historians might look on and argue that Peel's dream of a national police force has come true, we are also witnessing a broadening of the overall policing role to include, not only a range of private police agencies (Johnston, 1992), but also a general emphasis upon the local governance of crime which involves a range of local partnerships

(Crawford, 1997). This increasing plurality of policing during this post-structuralist period causes us to start to think about the appropriateness of current appointment policies and to ask whether the policy or ideology of internal recruitment may have run its course and that in the coming years we will have to rethink our policy on the recruitment of chief police officers. Indeed, the message coming from both the Sheehy (1993) proposals and also more generally from the ethos of new police management (Leishman *et al.*, 1996) is not only a demand for a new type of police manager who will direct a range of local police services rather than merely manage them. Most of these services will be funded, as at present, by local and central government, but it is anticipated that others could be provided by various local private concerns under the purview of the police. Consequently, this new role of chief officer would appear to prescribe a reversal of the ideology of internal recruitment in favour of professionally trained executives with proven experience of public, even large private, sector organisations.

Any discussion over the future recruitment of senior police officers is locked within the current paradigm of police management, of which the ideology of internal recruitment is an integral component. It naturalises the assumption that chief police officers must have previously been police officers, and in this sense it effectively creates a degree of false consciousness by precluding any competing theories from the debate. But, what exactly are those competing theories? The central ethos of new public management[3] was to cross-pollinate successful business ideas into the economically unsuccessful public sector in order to make them more economic, effective and efficient. Its actual impact upon the public sector has been varied. On the one hand it can be seen to have made some quite dramatic changes upon the funding structures of public sector organisations, whilst on the other hand, its impacts have been more limited in other areas of the same public sector organisations, particularly in terms of occupational cultures where it has often had little more impact than creating, what Hans Magnus Enzenberger has described as, “a luxuriant language running rampant upon barren soil” (Kane, 1993: 93).

---

[3] I am using the term new public management here, both in the past tense and also rather loosely, because there are many signs in the late 1990s that it has lost its initial impetus and therefore power as an influential management tool. See the debates in *Local Government Studies* (1996), *Theory, Culture and Society* (1996-7), also see Crawford (1997).

The longer term legacy of new public management for the police has been to stimulate debate about the structure of a future police service and to reconfigure existing debate so as to seek efficiency and effectiveness in terms of more measurable goals, such as the clear-up rate, rather than, for example, the slightly more esoteric goal of public tranquillity, that was previously accepted as a major goal of the police. Furthermore, this debate has called into question existing practices of executive recruitment. In some public sector organisations, for example the National Health Service, the traditional link between the professions and the management of the organisation was severed long ago. The police became the focus of this audit culture much later, during the late 1980s and early 1990s.[4] During this period, the Audit Commission recommended that the police adopt a proactive intelligence-led crime management approach to be carried out through basic command units (BCU) (Audit Commission, 1993; 1996).[5] In this model operational responsibilities end with the BCU commander, at the rank of superintendent, leaving the ACPO ranks to be primarily and formally concerned with force management.[6] Also during this period, the Sheehy inquiry recommended a number of sweeping changes to the upper management structure, such as fixed-term contracts for the ACPO ranks and the abolition of the rank of deputy chief constable. At the time of Sheehy (1993) and also the White Paper (1993) there was public discussion in the media of the possibility of appointing business managers with proven track records to manage police forces. This followed an earlier discussion of the possibilities of appointing military commanders who had been made surplus to requirements by the decline of the Cold War (Leishman and Savage, 1993). Like many of the proposals put forward at that time, this idea fell before reaching the first hurdle[7], but the important

[4] Whilst initiatives were started as early as 1983 (HO Circular 114/1983) to increase control over the overall police budget the issue really came to a head in the late 1980s and early 1990s.

[5] At the time of writing the Audit Commission had completed 15 papers on the police. The Audit Commission commented in 1995 that the police were "among the Commission's most enthusiastic partners", Charman and Savage, (1998: 12) argue that this may be because the Audit Commission may have been pursuing an ACPO shaped agenda.

[6] Although in principle this was the position previously.

[7] The impact of other proposals was limited, such as the abolition of deputy chief constables which was to some extent negated by the creation of the assistant chief constable designate, who is effectively the deputy chief constable. Of the original proposals, the fixed term contract is perhaps the main one to be still in force.

issue here was that it was discussed at all. Yet it is already the case that some positions of assistant chief constable have been filled by specialist non-police personnel and a number of lay inspectors of constabulary have been appointed from non-police occupations. It is estimated that at the time of writing there are between 60 and 100 ACPO equivalents, typically either personnel and training or finance officers, although there is no set pattern, serving in the 43 police forces in England and Wales. This compares with 230 at ACPO level. In addition, the police authority, which appoints the chief constable, has itself been restructured by the Police and Magistrates' Courts Act 1994 so that not only is it half its previous size but five of its members are now appointed from a Home Office approved shortlist. The resizing and inclusion of such people will further fragment the composition of the police authorities and, arguably, questions their capacity to represent local interests (Loveday, 1991), although not necessarily their effectiveness (Jones and Newburn, 1997).

What is certain, as is likely to be the case in the future, is that if police forces become fewer in number and therefore larger, they will gain even greater self control over the management of their resources. A new breed of chief constable, the executive director, will be required to replace the bureaucrats so eloquently described by Reiner (1991). The main difference between the two being that the function of bureaucrats is to execute pre-formulated policy, even if in practice they may have had a hand in developing it, whereas the executive director formulates strategic policy for their area. Indeed, the flattening of the police hierarchy during the early to mid 1990s, signified an important development in the role of chief constable. Whereas chief constables were previously conceived in the literature as chief executives of a large public service organisation, their current role is increasingly becoming more akin to that of a director of local police services. This means, as stated earlier, that increasingly, there is no practical need for chief constables to possess operational experience as their prime domain will be the quasi-political world of resource management. It therefore follows that the existing police service related criteria for their selection will become redundant, and there will be no need for them to have social backgrounds that are representative of local communities, particularly as the nature of the police authorities has also changed (Jones and Newburn, 1997). Instead, professional resource managers will be required who can head a management team, be equally at ease with the power brokers in central government and also, in the words of Manning (1977), "manage the public appearance of law enforcement". So, why hang onto a notion that is so clearly outdated and why not recruit proven public sector managers as future chief constables? There are certainly some compelling reasons to recruit externally, but their logic derives from the philosophy of new public management and largely ignores the peculiar status of the police within British society.

Within the present structure and ethos of police management there are five main areas of concern over the external recruitment of chief constables. The first and possibly the most serious concern, is for constabulary independence in operational decision making from direct political interference. Currently, chief constables are in a position whereby they are responsible for all aspects of police work, including police operations. In this sense they are indeed the chief constable of their force in so far as they can perform all of the functions of a constable. Furthermore, they are often called upon in their capacity as a chief constable to conduct investigations of other police forces. Arguably, the externally appointed chief constable would have no grounding in police work and would therefore would have some difficulty in making decisions upon operational matters and would not be able to perform investigations as effectively. Not only would they be reliant upon others for crucial information, but they would also be vulnerable to pressures from a number of sides. Moreover, if the overall outcome of the decision was less than was politically desirable then they would probably find themselves more vulnerable to dismissal. This has certainly been the case within the prison service during recent years.[8] Of course, the recent restructuring of existing police forces into basic command units, combined with the growth in regional and national police squads has effectively meant that, on a day to day basis, the rank of superintendent is currently the highest operational rank. The current arrangements cover all eventualities.

Were chief officers to be externally appointed, then a decision would therefore have to be made here as to the demarcation of labour between operational and administrative functions. Existing experience of the relationship between the police and lay bodies, for example in the relationship between the chief constable and their police authority, would suggest that a major stumbling block in trying to implement such a

[8] For example, in the case of Derek Lewis.

division would be that the police, those who have sworn the oath of constable, would claim the right to make decisions upon matters relating to policing operations. Such a claim would be supported by the decisions in a number of recent cases which place the responsibility for decisions on matters concerning police operations firmly in the hands of the chief constable, see for example the decisions in, *R v Chief Constable of the Devon and Cornwall Constabulary, ex parte CEGB*, *R v Secretary of State for the Home Department, ex parte Northumbria Police Authority*, *R v Chief Constable of Sussex, ex parte International Trader's Ferry Ltd.*

The second area of concern is the effect that external recruitment might have upon existing structures of accountability, especially at an informal level. The classic line of argument over the accountability of chief constables is that the mechanisms to which they were once accountable have now become ineffective and that they are no longer formally accountable for their actions. Particularly since the decline of their accountability to the police authority, to whom they are no longer obedient or subordinate. They are now subject to a form of accountability which requires them to give, rather than take account (Marshall, 1965, 1979; Reiner, 1995).[9] The problem with this line of argument is that it does not recognise the informal structures of accountability that still exist and the probability that they would not be as effective if chief constables were to be externally recruited. Additionally, there has been a tendency to underplay the importance of account giving, especially within the context of the chief constable's role of managing the appearance of law enforcement. Chief constables have to give account of their actions to their police authority, but they are also frequently called to give account for those actions to the people they police through the various media outlets. The chief constable's good, local, reputation is necessary, not only to foster a positive relationship between the local police and their public, but also to foster a good working relationship between the chief constable and their subordinates. Furthermore, whilst the chief constables now have an account-giving relationship with their police authority, it is also the case that they have developed more of an obedient or subordinate relationship with the Home Office (see Reiner 1991a; 1991b). Not only do the Home

[9] At the time of writing there are some embryonic indications of the development of a more contractual form of accountability that Reiner (1995a) thought would evolve from the changes introduced by the PMCA etc. (see chapter 3).

Office hold the purse strings, but let us not forget that they also control the selection and appointment of chief constables as well as defining many aspects of the police role through the issue of circulars. They also have increasingly subordinate relationships with the HM Inspectors of Constabulary and also to their peers within the ACPO ranks. In the case of the latter, they are not only responsible to their immediate management team, but also to ACPO itself through various committees, courses and conferences.[10] Externally appointed chief constables would not experience the same level of informal accountability to these bodies.

The third area of concern is the impact that the external recruitment of chief constables would have upon the overall morale of a police force.[11] Whilst good police morale is an extremely intangible concept, it is nevertheless important to the running of an organisation like the police. Although externally appointed chief constables may be more experienced managers and micro-politicians, there would certainly be a backlash within what is still a fairly tight police culture. Police occupational culture is fairly contradictory in so far as it is frequently cynical towards police management and furthermore, the chief constable's police experiences will not automatically produce confidence in his /her management. Yet, there is a symbolic importance in the fact that the chief constable entered the police by the same route as the rank and file police officers, even if their subsequent career paths differed. This backlash could lead to considerable resentment and considerable resistance within the police, and an example of such resistance was experienced in 1993, when the unpopularity of the Sheehy proposals led to the biggest mass rally held at any point since the introduction of the new police in the 1830s (Morgan and Newburn, 1997: 6). It will be remembered that one of the arguments in support of the policy of internal recruitment was that it freed up the promotion structure to provide the opportunity, if only in theory rather than in practice, for an individual to rise from the bottom to the top of the police organisation upon their own merits. Whilst the ideology of internal recruitment may be in the slow process of being reversed, it is still an essential component of

---

[10] It is of course the case that in some circumstances these so-called informal accountabilities are undesirable in that they can engender corruptive relationships between the various parties. In such cases they should be avoided.

[11] Theoretically, managers could be externally appointed at any point in the management hierarchy. The debate here relates mainly to the appointment of chief constables from outside the police.

police culture. In any organisation, the success of managerial policies depend upon the confidence that the managed have in the managers and an essential part of the common police psyche is the confidence that senior officers have experience of operational police-work and understand the pressures of 'the job'. So, although it is more of a symbolic act than a practical necessity, the operational experience of chief officers tends to be closely scrutinised by police officers at all levels.

The fourth area of concern is that externally appointed chief officers may be simply unable to manage complexities of the police organisation because of their lack of practical policing experience. Without such experience, it is arguable as to whether these external appointees may fully appreciate the public service ethos upon which policing is based. The police organisation is quite typical in so far as it is a hierarchical organisation, but it is quite atypical in so far as those who are at the bottom of the hierarchy possess the broadest discretion in their interpretation of both the law and also of managerial rules. It will be remembered from earlier chapters that the governance of the police was, next to dealing with crime, the most important function of the police organisation. So, the effective governance of the police largely depends upon both the confidence that the managed have in their managers, but also that the rules that they are expected to follow are implementable and not too ambitious. This latter view has been supported by a number of research findings, such as those by Smith and Gray (1985), Bottomley *et al.*, (1991), Dixon *et al.*, (1989). These findings showed quite clearly, that although rules and formal structures may attempt to change police practice, they can be actively resisted, mis-interpreted or circumnavigated, if they are not internalised into working practice by the officers charged with their enactment. In this way, the organisation and practice of policing cannot be likened to a free-market business model. This is a point that has been raised many times before in the debate over performance indicators. The management ethos of the public sector is fundamentally different to the business world which revolves around the input/output model and public service is by nature a complex business of managing physical acts, public perceptions and political considerations.[12]

---

[12] Ironically, if could be argued that many large businesses also perform these functions, and that the public sector has reformed around a very narrow, US based, free-market model of business.

The fifth concern relates to the closed nature of the police and the perceived possibilities for corruption that can arise from prior commercial relations. External appointees would be subjected to considerable scrutiny from within the police, because like most 'closed' occupations, the police are naturally suspicious of outsiders. These problems could manifest themselves in two ways. Firstly, the position may be open to commercial gain, and there have, for example, been a number of allegations against business people involved in the management of the Health Service who secured lucrative contracts to service or provide buildings within that area. Secondly, under the intense scrutiny that was mentioned earlier, activities that are perceived to be legitimate business activities may subsequently conflict with the police disciplinary code. There are many instances of minor charges being brought against chief constables, under the police disciplinary code, for using police vehicles when they should not have done or for irregularities in their expenses. All of the appointees' actions prior to appointment would be also placed under scrutiny.

So, there are some compelling arguments for retaining the policy of internal recruitment, the main argument being because it resolves many of the contradictions which arise from the peculiar position of the police in UK society. But, whilst for the time being this situation may remain, it is clearly the case that the civilianisation programme that has taken place within the police during the past two decades or so, has led to the external recruitment of specialists at all levels within the police, including senior management. With this in mind it is therefore interesting that the experience of a similar type of external recruitment (of non-medical personnel) policy has resulted in most senior managerial posts being occupied by people from the health service, but with administrative rather than medical backgrounds.

Concluding remarks

This social history of the chief constable has demonstrated that debates in the history of the police do have the habit of repeating themselves and that many contemporary debates find a resonance in the past. This study has also shown that the current policing arrangements are similar, in a number of ways, to those originally intended by Robert Peel 160 years ago, but not realised within his lifetime. We now have both a *de facto* and effectively a *de jure* national police force that is run by an élite of professional police managers, the chief constables, who are drawn from the body that they manage.

The significance of this study for the debate over the governance of police management is that it has illustrated that the policy of internal recruitment has not only solved what was perceived as the problem of senior command, which vexed policing policy makers before, during and after the Second World War, but it also ensures that chief constables not only have a degree of common training and, police defined, competence. More importantly, those same arrangements, which include a lengthy period of socialisation and training, combined with the various hurdles that high flyers have to climb over, mean that it is unlikely that a maverick or rogue chief constable would be appointed today. Appointees are not only identified as potential police managers very early on in their careers, but during their thirty years of service prior to appointment, they are carefully vetted for their continued suitability for office. Of course, policies of internal recruitment and symmetry of social and professional origin do not ensure a symmetry of action (decision making) and neither do they completely design out dissent. But the lengthy, and supervised, professional socialisation does, however, negate the effect of social origin and ensures that all senior police managers possess a similar *weltanschauung,*[13] speak a common occupational language and share broad assumptions about policing. In sum, it ensures that standard methods of reasoning are applied in decision making by reducing the extent to which decision-makers apply private standards instead of public ones. It also makes it easier for the powers-that-be to predict how decision makers will act, what kinds of instructions they will produce and what kind of responses they will give (Schneider, 1992: 81). But safety also has its

[13] World Outlook or Philosophy of Life.

price, because it is highly unlikely that the same system of checks would also facilitate the appointment of a visionary.

As for the future, there are a number of trends that are currently taking place which are causing concern, and therefore require further research. For example, one of the by-products of the continuing empowerment of the chief constable is their increasing role as a (police) policy making élite. The main worry here is that the continued strengthening of ACPO will not only provide the intended single police voice on the policy making table, but that the chief constables, along with ACPO colleagues and other criminal justice élites, plus key civil servants, could effectively create a policy making circle that not only defines and effects policing policy, but will effectively bypass both the conventional bureaucratic or, where applicable, democratic processes. These concerns will increase proportionally with the development of national police organisations. Whilst these concerns are unlikely to develop into a problem during the foreseeable future with the current cohort of liberal chief constables, it is nevertheless the case that little constitutional protection would be provided were the general political complexion to change dramatically.

In addition to concerns over this policy making circle are some very important developments within the policing model. Not only are the police becoming more plural, but policing is also broadening to cover a wide range of activities. Firstly, there has been an increase in the number of formal police organisations, the most notable of which has been the introduction of the National Criminal Intelligence Service and the National Crime Squad, but also included here is the expanded role of the national security agencies to include some domestic policing issues, especially those relating to drugs. Secondly, there has been a rapid expansion of private policing organisations (Johnston, 1992, Jones and Newburn, 1998) and also an expansion of policing activities being performed within other public sector organisations, such as the Department of Social Security and local councils. Thirdly, there has also been an explosion in the technologies of surveillance which make it an easier, cheaper and more effective strategy as policing can take place some distance from the site being policed. These are the challenges that the future holds.

To finish, a commonly heard phrase during the early 1990s was "could the chief executive from ICI or some other large corporation become a chief constable", as indeed they had done in other areas of public sector management. As we face the millennium, it is apparent that the nature of the professional police manager has changed so substantively during recent years, that we might be more likely to ask: "could a chief constable become a chief executive of ICI?".

Appendix

TABLE A1 The annual number of independent provincial police forces in England and Wales with chief officers (excl. Met., City of London and River Tyne and Wear Police)

Year	Co	Boro	Total	Year	Co	Boro	Total	Year	Co	Boro	Total
1835	0	23	23	1868	57	159	216	1901	57	126	183
1836	0	115	115	1869	57	161	218	1902	57	126	183
1837	0	119	119	1870	57	164	221	1903	57	126	183
1838	0	122	122	1871	57	164	221	1904	57	126	183
1839	6	127	133	1872	57	164	221	1905	57	126	183
1840	17	128	145	1873	57	164	221	1906	57	126	183
1841	20	129	149	1874	57	164	221	1907	57	126	183
1842	20	130	150	1875	57	164	221	1908	57	127	184
1843	21	130	151	1876	57	165	222	1909	57	127	184
1844	22	132	154	1877	57	162	219	1910	57	127	184
1845	23	132	155	1878	57	162	219	1911	57	127	184
1846	23	134	157	1879	57	161	218	1912	57	127	184
1847	23	135	158	1880	57	161	218	1913	57	128	185
1848	24	142	166	1881	57	160	217	1914	57	128	185
1849	24	143	167	1882	57	161	218	1915	57	128	185
1850	24	144	168	1883	57	160	217	1916	57	128	185
1851	26	145	171	1884	57	159	216	1917	57	128	185
1852	26	146	172	1885	57	159	216	1918	57	128	185
1853	26	146	172	1886	57	159	216	1919	57	128	185
1854	26	145	171	1887	57	164	221	1920	57	120	177
1855	27	145	172	1888	57	163	220	1921	57	127	184
1856	33	160	193	1889	57	123	180	1922	57	123	180
1857	57	162	219	1890	57	123	180	1923	57	122	179
1858	57	161	218	1891	57	123	180	1924	57	122	179
1859	57	159	216	1892	57	123	180	1925	57	122	179
1860	57	159	216	1893	57	123	180	1926	57	121	178
1861	57	159	216	1894	57	123	180	1927	57	121	178
1862	57	159	216	1895	57	123	180	1928	57	121	178
1863	57	160	217	1896	57	124	181	1929	57	120	177
1864	57	162	219	1897	57	124	181	1930	57	120	177
1865	57	159	216	1898	57	125	182	1931	57	120	177
1866	57	159	216	1899	57	126	183	1932	57	120	177
1867	57	159	216	1900	57	126	183	1933	57	120	177

Year	Co	Boro	Total	Year	Co	Boro	Total
1934	57	120	177	1956	50	71	121
1935	57	120	177	1957	50	71	121
1936	57	120	177	1958	49	71	120
1937	57	120	177	1959	49	71	120
1938	57	120	177	1960	49	71	120
1939	57	120	177	1961	49	71	120
1940	57	119	176	1962	49	71	120
1941	57	119	176	1963	49	71	120
1942	57	119	176	1964	49	71	120
1943	56	109	165	1965	47	69	116
1944	56	107	163	1966	48	63	111
1945	56	106	162	1967	43	43	86
1946	56	106	162	1968	39	23	62
1947	56	72	128	1969	39	5	44
1948	54	72	126	1970	39	5	44
1949	54	71	125	1971	39	5	44
1950	52	71	123	1972	39	5	44
1951	51	71	122	1973	39	5	44
1952	51	71	122	1974	41	0	41
1953	51	71	122				
1954	51	71	122				
1955	51	71	122	1974 - 1996 no change			

TABLE A2 The annual number of all independent provincial police forces in England and Wales N.B Includes forces with no chief officers (excl. Met., City of London and River Tyne and Wear Police)

Year	Co	Boro	Total	Year	Co	Boro	Total
1835	0	30	30	1865	57	164	221
1836	0	137	137	1866	57	164	221
1837	0	141	141	1867	57	164	221
1838	0	144	144	1868	57	164	221
1839	6	148	154	1869	57	164	221
1840	17	150	167	1870	57	167	224
1841	20	150	170	1871	57	167	224
1842	20	151	171	1872	57	167	224
1843	21	151	172	1873	57	167	224
1844	22	153	175	1874	57	167	224
1845	23	153	176	1875	57	167	224
1846	23	154	177	1876	57	168	225
1847	23	155	178	1877	57	165	222
1848	24	163	187	1878	57	165	222
1849	24	164	188	1879	57	164	221
1850	24	163	187	1880	57	164	221
1851	26	164	190	1881	57	163	220
1852	26	164	190	1882	57	164	221
1853	26	164	190	1883	57	163	220
1854	26	164	190	1884	57	162	219
1855	27	162	189	1885	57	162	219
1856	33	177	210	1886	57	162	219
1857	57	176	233	1887	57	167	224
1858	57	172	229	1888	57	165	222
1859	57	168	225	1889	57	124	181
1860	57	165	222	1890	57	124	181
1861	57	165	222	1891	57	124	181
1862	57	165	222				
1863	57	166	223				
1864	57	167	224				

From 1891 onwards the figures are the same as those in table A1 above

Bibliography

ACPO (1990) *Providing the future Chief Officers of Police*, (report of a working party chaired by C. Smith) London: Association of Chief Police Officers.

Adler, S., Lowden, S. and Snell, J. (1995) "Fast Track", *Policing*, vol. 11, no. 1, pp. 14-24.

Adler, S., Lowden, S. and Snell, J. (1994) *Fast Tracking in the Police Service*, Bramshill: The Police Staff College.

Allen, Lord (1982) "Reflections of a Bureaucrat", *The Home Office: Perspectives on Policy and Administration*, London: Royal Institute of Public Administration, pp. 23-33.

Audit Commission (1989) *Police Paper Number Four*, London: HMSO.

Audit Commission (1993) *Helping with Enquiries: tackling crime effectively*, London: Audit Commission.

Audit Commission (1996) *Tackling Crime Effectively Volume 2*, London: Audit Commission.

Barnes, J. (1984) *Flaubert's Parrot*, London: Picador.

Bartlett, R. (1985) "The Bramshill Scholarship Scheme", *Police Review*, July 5, p. 1363.

Bottomley, A.K., Coleman, C., Dixon, D., Gill, M.L., and Wall, D.S. (1991) *The Impact of P.A.C.E.: policing in a northern force*, Hull: Centre for Criminology and Criminal Justice.

Bourdieu, P. (1987) "The Force of Law: Towards a Sociology of the Juridical Field", *Hastings Law Journal*, vol. 38, pp. 805-852.

Boyle, A. (1962) *Trenchard*, London: Collins.

Bridgeman, I. and Emsley, C. (1989) *A Guide to the Archives of the Police Forces of England and Wales*, Milton Keynes: Police History Society.

Brogden, M. (1982) *The Police: autonomy and consent*, London, Academic Press.

Buckle, H. (unpublished) *Power and Authority in the East Riding of Yorkshire from 1888 to 1940*, Humberside College of Further Education, PhD thesis.

Cale, M. (1996) *Law and Society: an introduction to sources for criminal and legal history from 1800*, London: Public Record Office Publications.

Charman, S., and Savage, S. (1998) "Singing From the Same Hymn Sheet: The professionalisation of the Association of Chief Police Officers", *International Journal of Police Science and Management*, vol. 1, pp. 6-16.

Charman, S., Savage, S. and Cope, S. (1996) "Police Governance, the Association of Chief Police Officers and Constitutional Change", *Public Policy and Administration*, vol. 11, no. 2, pp. 92-106.

Charman, S., Savage, S. and S. Cope, (Forthcoming) "Getting to the Top: selection and training for senior managers in the police service", early draft.

Clay, E.W. (ed) (1974) *The Leeds Police 1836-1974*, Leeds: Leeds City Police.

Colquhoun, P. (1796) *Treatise on the Police in the Metropolis explaining the various Crimes and Misdemeanours which are at present felt as a pressure upon the Community, and suggesting Remedies for their Prevention, by a Magistrate,* Second Edition, London: H. Fry.

Cowley, R. (1996) "Police under scrutiny: the Inspectors of Constabulary 1856-1990", *Journal of the Police History Society*, vol. 11, pp. 25-30.

Crawford, A. (1997) *The Local Governance of Crime*, Oxford: Oxford University Press.

Critchley, T.A. (1978) *A History of the Police in England and Wales*, Constable, London.

Davies, G.P. (1973) *The Police Service in England and Wales between 1918 and 1964, with particular reference to problems of personnel, recruitment and command*, PhD thesis, London: London School of Economics.

Davies, N. (1997) "Second Front: it's a square cop", *Guardian*, January 29, p. T2.

De Lint, W. (1997) "The Constable Generalist as Exemplary Citizen, networker and problem-solver: some implications", *Policing and Society*, vol. 6, pp. 247-264.

Director of Extended Interviews (1979), *Report on the Special Course*, (unpublished).

Dixon, D., Bottomley, A.K., Coleman, C., Gill, M.L., and Wall, D.S. (1989) "Reality and Rules in the Construction and Regulation of Police Suspicion", *International Journal of the Sociology of Law*, vol. 17, pp. 185-206.

Emsley, C. (1983) *Policing and its Context 1750-1870*, London: Macmillan.

Emsley, C. (1996) *The English Police: A political and social history*, Second edition, London: Longman.

Emsley, C. and Clapson. M. (1994) "Recruiting the English policeman c. 1840-1940", *Policing and Society*, vol. 4, pp. 269-286.

Evans, J. (1988) "The Newcastle upon Tyne City Police 1836-1969", *Journal of the Police History Society*, vol. 3, pp. 74-80.

Feltham, R. and Linnane, J. (1987) *Police Extended Interviews: a long term follow up of successful candidates*, Home Office CSSB.

Fielding, J. (1768) *Extracts from such of the penal laws, as particularly relate to the peace and good order of this Metropolis* (new edition), London.

Fielding, N. (1990) "Training the Boss: higher police training in Britain", *The Howard Journal of Criminal Justice*, vol. 29, pp 199-205.

Foxcroft, Rev R. (1960) "Brotherhood of Man", *Listener*, 24 April.

Gale, M. (1996) *Law and Society: An Introduction to Sources for Criminal and Legal History from 1800*, Kew: PRO Publications.

Ganz, G. (1987) *Quasi-Legislation: recent developments in secondary legislation*, London: Sweet and Maxwell.

Gash, N. (1961) *Mr Secretary Peel: the life of Sir Robert Peel to 1830*, London: Longmans.

Giddens, A. (1990) *The consequences of modernity*, London: Polity Press.

Graef, R. (1989) *Talking Blues: the police in their own words*, London: Collins Harvill.

Hallett, H.A. (1974) *The Police Forces of England and Wales*, London: International Police Association.

Halsey, A., Heath, A. and Ridge, J. (1980) *Origins and Destinations: Family, Class and Education in Modern Britain*, Oxford: Oxford University Press.

Hart, J. (1951) *The British Police*, London: Allen and Unwin.

Hart, J. (1955) "Reform of the borough police, 1835-1856", *English Historical Review*, July, pp. 411-427.

Hart, J. (1963) "Some Reflections on the report of the Royal Commission on the Police", *Public Law,* pp. 283-298.

Hart, J. (1978) "Commentary on the IUP papers", in Cornish, W., (ed) (1978) *Crime and the Law*, Dublin: Irish University Press.

Hennock, E.P. (1968) "The Social Composition of Borough Councils in Two Large Cities, 1835 - 1914" in Dyos, H.J. (ed) (1968) *The Study of Urban History: proceedings of an international round-table conference of the Urban History Group,* New York : St. Martin's Press, pp. 315-336.

Humphrey, C., Chatterton, M. and Watson, A. (1996) *Debating the history and status of the financial management reforms in the police service of England and Wales*, Chartered Institute of Management Accountants (CIMA).

Jefferson,T. and Grimshaw. R. (1984) *Controlling the Constable*, London: Frederick Muller.

Johnston, L. (1992) *The Rebirth of Private Policing*, London: Routledge.

Jones, T. and Newburn, T. (1998) *Private Security and Public Policing*, Oxford: Clarendon Press.

Jones, T. and Newburn, T. (1997) *Policing after the Act: police governance after the Police and Magistrates' Courts Act 1994*, London: Policy Studies Institute.

Jones, T. and Newburn, T. (1995) "Local Government and Policing: Arresting the Decline of Local Influence", *Local Government Studies*, vol. 21, pp. 448-460.

Kane, P. (1993) *Tinsel Show: pop, politics and Scotland*, Edinburgh: Polygon.

Keith-Lucas, B. (1962) "Poplarism", *Public Law*, vol. 52, p. 85.

Knight, S. (1983) "A helping handshake", *Police Review*, 1983, p. 2017.

Knight, S. (1984) *The Brotherhood*, London: Granada.

Leishman, F. and Savage, S. (1993) "Officers or managers: direct entry into British police management", *International Journal of Public Sector Management*, vol. 6, no. 5, pp. 4-11.

Leishman, F., Savage, S. and Loveday, B. (1996) *Core Issues in Policing*, London: Longman.

Loveday, B. (1995) "Contemporary Challenges to Police Management in England and Wales: Developing Strategies for Effective Service Delivery," *Policing and Society*, vol. 5, pp. 281-303.

Loveday, B. (1991) "The New Police Authorities in the Metropolitan Counties," *Policing and Society*, vol. 1, pp. 193-212.

Lustgarten, L. (1986) *The Governance of the Police*, London: Sweet and Maxwell, 1986.

McNee, Sir D. (1983) *McNee's Law*, London: Collins.

Manning, P.K. (1979) "The Social Control of Police Work", in Holdaway, S. (ed) *The British Police*, London: Edward Arnold.

Manning, P.K. (1977) *Police Work: The social organisation of policing*, Cambridge, Mass: M.I.T. Press.

Mark, R. (1978) *In the Office of Constable*, London: Collins.

Marshall, G. (1965) *Police and Government*, London: Methuen.

Marshall, G. (1979) "Police Accountability Revisited", in Butler, D. and Halsey, Marshall, G. (1984) *Constitutional Conventions*, Oxford: Oxford University Press.

Miles, R. (1992) "Assessing Senior Command", *Policing*, vol. 8, pp. 4-14.

Morgan, J. (1987) *Conflict and Order: The police and labour disputes in England and Wales, 1900-1939*, Oxford: Clarendon Press.

Morgan, R. and Newburn, T. (1997) *The Future of Policing*, Oxford: Oxford University Press.

Morris, S. (1981) "British Chief Constables: the Americanisation of a role?", *Political Studies*, vol. 29, no. 3, pp. 352-364.

National Police Training (1997) *From potential to performance: the portfolio*, London: Central Office of Information.

Newman, Sir K. (1985) *The Principles of Policing and guidance for professional behaviour*, London: Metropolitan Police.

Nott-Bower, Sir J.W. (1926) *Fifty Years a Policeman*, London: Edward Arnold.

Osborne, D. and Gaebler, T. (1992) *Reinventing Government: how the entrepreneurial spirit is transforming the public sector*, New York: Addison-Wesley.

Parris, H. (1961) "The Home Office and the provincial police in England and Wales - 1856-1870", *Public Law*, pp. 230-255.

Pellew, J. (1982) *The Home Office 1848-1914: from clerks to bureaucrats*, London: Heinemann Educational.

Phillips, D. (1977) *Crime and Authority in Victorian England*, London: Croom Helm.

Police (1989) "The Butterfly Syndrome", *Police*, vol. 21, no. 11, pp. 3-6.

Police Staff College (1993) *Handbook to the Accelerated Promotion Course*, Bramshill: Police Staff College.

Prince, M. (1988) *God's Cop: the biography of James Anderton*, London: New English Library.

Provincial Grand Lodge (1893) *Installation of the R.W. Prov. Grand Master on Wednesday 27th Sept. 1893*, Leeds: Privately Published.

Radzinowicz, L. (1956) *A History of English Criminal Law and its Administration from 1750*, Vol. 3, London: Sweet and Maxwell.

Rawlings, P. (1995) "The Idea of Policing: a history", *Policing and Society*, vol. 5, no. 2, pp. 129-149.

Razzell, P.E. (1963) "Social Origins of Officers in the Indian and British Home Army: 1758-1962", *British Journal of Sociology*, vol. 14, pp. 248-260.

Reiner, R. (1978) *The Blue Coated Worker*, Cambridge: Cambridge University Press.

Reiner, R. (1982) "Who are the Police?", *Political Quarterly*, vol. 53, no. 2.

Reiner, R. (1991a) *Chief Constable: bobby or bureaucrat*, Oxford: Oxford University Press.

Reiner, R. (1991b) "Chief Constables in England and Wales: a social portrait of a criminal justice élite", in Reiner, R. and Cross, M. (eds) *Beyond Law and Order: criminal justice policy into the 1990s*, London: Macmillan, pp. 59-77.

Reiner, R. (1992) *The Politics of the Police*, Second edition, London: Harvester Wheatsheaf.

Reiner, R. (1995a) "Counting the Coppers: antinomies of accountability in policing", in Stenning, P. (ed) *Accountability for Criminal Justice: Selected Essays*, Toronto: University of Toronto Press, pp. 74-92.

Reiner, R. (1995b) "From Sacred to Profane: the Thirty Years' War of the British police", *Policing and Society*, vol. 5, no. 2, pp. 121-128.

Reith, C. (1943) *The British Police and the Democratic Ideal*, Oxford: Oxford University Press.

Richer, A.F. (1990) *Bedfordshire Police 1840-1990*, Bedford: Hooley and Associates.

Rumbelow, D. (1989) *I Spy Blue: Police and Crime in the City of London from Elizabeth I to Victoria*, London: Macmillan.

Russell, K., and Waters, J. (1985) "Portrait of a Chief", *Police Review*, 31 May, p. 1108.

St Johnston, E. (1978) *One Policeman's Story*, Chichester: Barry Rose.

Savage, S. and Charman, S. (1996) "In favour of compliance", *Policing Today*, vol. 2., no. 1, pp. 10-17.

Savage, S. and Charman, S. (1997) *ACPO: The views of the membership*, unpublished, University of Portsmouth.

Schneider, C.E. (1992) "Discretion and Rules: a lawyer's view", in Hawkins. K. (ed) *The Uses of Discretion*, Oxford: Clarendon Press, pp. 47-48.

Scott, H. (1970) *Scotland Yard*, London: Mayflower.

Scott, J. (1982) *The Upper Classes: property and privilege in Britain*, London: Macmillan Press.

Shearing, C. (1996) "Public and Private Policing", in Saulsbury, W., Mott, J. and Newburn, T. (eds) *Themes in Contemporary Policing*, London: Independent Committee of Inquiry into the role and responsibilities of the police, pp. 83-95.

Sheptycki, J.W. (1996) "Law Enforcement, Justice and Democracy in the Transnational Arena: Reflections on the War on Drugs," *International Journal of Sociology*, vol. 24, pp. 61-75.

Short, M. (1989) *Inside the Brotherhood: further secrets of the freemasons*, London: Grafton Books.

Sillitoe, P.J. (1955) *Cloak Without Dagger*, London: Cassell and Co.

Smiles, S. (1860) *Self-help; with illustration of character and conduct*, Revised Edition, London.

Smith, D.J. (1990) "The establishment and development of the Worcestershire County Constabulary 1839-1843", *Journal of the Police History Society*, vol. 5, pp. 3-23.

Smith, D.J. and Gray, J. (1985) *Police and People in London: The P.S.I. Report*, Aldershot: Gower.

Smith, G. (1973) *Bradford's Police*, Bradford: City of Bradford Police.

Smith, Sir H. (1910) *From Constable to Commissioner*, London: Edward Arnold, 1910.

Stalker, J. (1988) *Stalker*, London: Penguin Books.

Stallion, M.R. (1997) *British Police Force Histories: a Bibliography*, Essex: M.R. Stallion.

Stanworth, P. (1984) "Elites and Privilege", in Abrams, P. and Brown, R. (1984) *UK Society: work, urbanism and inequality*, London: Weidenfeld and Nicholson, pp. 247-293.

Steedman., C. (1984) *Policing The Victorian Community*, London: Routledge, Kegan and Paul.

Swift, R. (1988) *Police Reform in Early Victorian York*, 1835-1856, York: Borthwick Papers No. 73, p. 6.

Tobias, J.J. (1979) *Crime and Police in England 1700-1900*, Dublin: Gill and Macmillan.

Topping, I. (1997) "Police officers and membership of organisations", *New Law Journal*, vol. 147, p. 63.

Troup, Sir E. (1928) "Police Administration, Local and National", *Police Journal*, vol. 1, pp. 5-18.

Troup, Sir, E. (1926) *The Home Office: 2nd ed.*, London: Putnam Ltd.

Turner, R.H. (1960) "Sponsored and Contest Mobility and the School System", *American Sociological Review*, vol. 25, pp. 855-867.

Walker, C.P. (1990) "Police and Community in Northern Ireland", *Northern Ireland Law Quarterly*, vol. 41, no. 2, p. 105.

Wall, D.S. (1987) "Chief Constables: a changing élite", *Policing Britain*, R.I. Mawby (ed.), Plymouth Polytechnic.

Wall, D.S. (1989) *The Selection of Chief Constables 1835 - 1985*, York, unpublished M.Phil. dissertation, University of York.

Wall, D.S. (1993a) "The Open Secret", *Police Review*, 8 January, pp. 22-23.

Wall, D.S. (1993b) "The Outsiders", *Police Review*, 30 July, pp. 16-17.

Wall, D.S. (1994a) "Putting Freemasonry into Perspective: the centenary of the debate over freemasonry and police appointments", *Policing and Society*, vol. 3, no. 4. pp. 257-268.

Wall, D.S. (1994b) "The Ideology of Internal Recruitment: the selection of chief constables within the tripartite arrangement", *British Journal of Criminology*, vol. 34, no. 3, pp. 322-338.

Wall, D.S. (1997) "Policing the Virtual Community: the internet, cyber-crimes and the policing of cyberspace", in Francis, P., Davies, P. and Jupp, V. (1997) *Policing Futures*, London: Macmillan.

Wall, D.S. and Johnstone, J. (1997) "The Industrialisation of Legal Practice and the Rise of the New Electric Lawyer: the impact of information technology upon legal practice" *International Journal of the Sociology of Law*, vol. 25, pp. 95-116.

Webb, S. and B. (1906) *The Parish and the County*, London: Longmans.

Weinberger, B. (1986) "Police Perceptions of Labour in the Inter War Period: the case of the unemployed and of the miners on strike", in Snyder, F., and Hay, D. (1986) *Labour, Law and Crime in Historical Perspective*, London: Tavistock.

Whalen,, W.J. (1958) *Christianity and American Freemasonry*, Milwaukee: Bruce.

Whittaker, B. (1979) *The Police In Society*, London: Eyre Methuen.

Wilson, J. (1987) "Choosing the Chief Constable of Buckinghamshire, 1896", *Journal of the Police History Society*, vol. 2, pp. 39-44.

Wright, P. (1987) *Spycatcher*, Victoria: Heinemann.

Young, G.M. and Haydock, W.D. (eds) (1956) *English Historical Documents*, London: Eyre and Spottiswode.

Zangerl, (1971) "The Social Composition of the Magistracy", *Journal of British Studies*, vol. xi, p. 113.

Parliamentary Papers, Rules and Reports (listed chronologically)

Report of the Select Committee on the Police of the Metropolis, 1834, [600] XVI.

Royal Commission on County Rates, 1836: XXVII, (see Young and Haydock, 1956: 630).

Report of the Royal Commission on establishing an efficient constabulary force in the counties of England and Wales 1839, [169] XIX.1.

Home Secretary's Rules (1840) *Rules made by the Marquis of Normanby, one of Her Majesty's Principal Secretaries of State, pursuant to the 3rd Section of the 2 & 3 Vict., c.93, for establishing an Uniform System for the Government, Pay, clothing, accoutrements and necessities for constables appointed under the Act* - December 1 1840 (reprinted H.C. 1856 (75) L.639).

Select Committee on establishing a Uniform System of Policing in England and Wales 1852-3, H.C., first report (603) XXXVI.1 and second report (715) XXXVI.

Home Secretary's Rules (1857) *Rules made by the Right Hon. Sir George Grey, Bart, one of Her Majesty's Principal Secretaries of State, pursuant to the 3rd Section of the 2 & 3 Vict., c.93, for establishing an Uniform System for the Government, Pay, clothing, accoutrements and necessities for constables appointed under the Act* - February 2 1857. (H.C. 1857, Sess. 1, XIV. 157).

Departmental Committee on Metropolitan Police Personnel, 1868, cited in *Report on the Administration and Organisation of the Metropolitan Police Force*, 1886 [493] XXXIV.

Report of the Select Committee on Police Superannuation Funds, 1877, P.P. XV.

Returns of Police Established in Each Counties or Divisions of a County in England and Wales under the Acts of 3 Vict., c.93 and 3 & 4 Vict, (1877), c.88 P.P XXXII.

Committee on the State, Discipline and Organisation of the Metropolitan Police, 1879, cited in *Report on the Administration and Organisation of the Metropolitan Police Force*, 1886 [493] XXXIV.

Home Secretary's Rules (1886) *Rules made by H.C.E. Childers, one of Her Majesty's Principal Secretaries of State, pursuant to the 3rd Section of the 2*

& 3 Vict., c.93, for establishing an Uniform System for the Government, Pay, clothing, accoutrements and necessities for constables appointed under the Act. April 12 1886 (HO 158/3).

Report on the Administration and Organisation of the Metropolitan Police Force, 1886 [493] XXXIV.

Report from the Select Committee on the Police Forces (Weekly Rest Day) Bill, with the Proceedings of the Committee, Evidence, Appendix and Index; HC 1908 Cmd. 353, 354 ix. 679; HC 1909 Cmd. 132 viii. 339.

Report of the Committee on the Police Service of England, Wales and Scotland. Part 1; HC 1919 Cmd.253 xxvii. 708: Part II; HC 1920 Cmd.574 xxii. 539: Evidence; HC 1920 Cmd.974 xxvii. 573.

Home Secretary's Rules (1920) *The Police Regulations of the 20th August 1920 made by the Secretary of State under section 4 of the Police Act 1919* (Statutory Rules and Orders 1920, No. 1484) (HOC/HO 158/21).

Report of the Tribunal appointed under the Tribunals of Inquiry (Evidence) Act, 1921, in regard to the Interrogation of Miss Savidge by the Police, HC 1928, Cmd. 3147, xii. 87.

Report of the Royal Commission on Police Powers and Procedures (1928-1929), HC Cmd.3297 ix. 127.

Report of His Majesty's Inspectors of Constabulary, 1929, (1929-30), Cmd. 3600 xvii. 41.

Report from the Select Committee on Police Forces (Amalgamations) (1931-32), HC (106) v.123.

Report of the Commissioner of the Metropolis for 1932, (1932-33), Cmd. 4294. xv, 319.

Report of the Commissioner of the Metropolis for 1933, (1933-34), Cmd. 4562 xiv, 747.

Police Post-War Committee, Higher Training for the Police Service in England and Wales (1947), Cmd. 707.

Report of the Committee on Police Conditions of Service, Part 1; HC 1948-49 Cmd. xix. 251: Part II; HC 1948-49 Cmd 7831 xix. 379.

Police Training in England and Wales, 1961, Cmd. 1450.

Report of the Police Training Council on Higher Police Training, 1961, December 19.

Final Report of the Royal Commission on the Police, 1962, HC, Cmd. 1728, xx. 515.

Absorption of Ex-Colonial Police Officers into United Kingdom Police Forces, 1962, (POL50/1/42 also in HO 45/287/29)

Police Advisory Board (1967) *Working Party on the Recruitment of people with Higher Educational Qualifications into the Police Service: Report*, 1967. Sometimes referred to as the Taverne Report.

Report three of the Committee of Inquiry on the Police (1979), July, Cmnd 7633.

Home Affairs Committee (1989), *Higher Police Training and the Police Staff College*, Vol. 1: HMSO.

White Paper (1993), *Police Reform: A Police Service for the 21st Century, White Paper, The Government's Proposals for the Police Service of England and Wales*. Cm 2281, HMSO.

Chief Officer Appointments in the Police Service: Guidelines on Selection Procedures (1996), accompanies HOC 52/96, 2 December.

Home Affairs Committee (1997) *Freemasonry in the Police and the Judiciary*, Vol. 1, HC 192-I, 1996/7.

Index

—A—

—B—

—C—

—D—

—E—

—F—

—S—

—T—

—U—

—V—

—W—

—Y—

—Z—